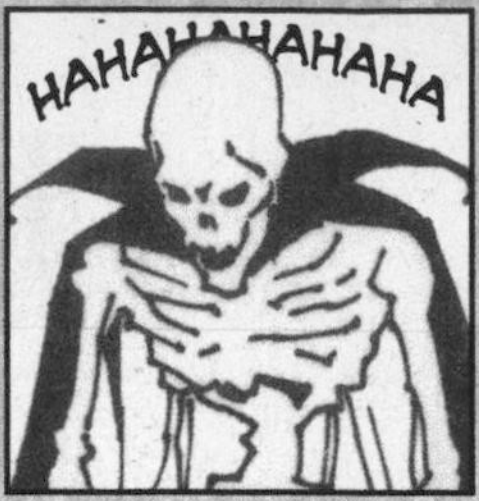
HAHAHAHAHAHA

I REALLY LOVED THE OLD TV SHOW ŌGON *BAT*. THE MAIN CHARACTER WAS A GOLD SKELETON WITH A CREEPY LAUGH, BUT HE WAS A GOOD GUY! AM I THE ONLY ONE WHO'D LIKE TO SEE A MODERN REMAKE USING CGI?
-TAKESHI OBATA

Tsugumi Ohba
Born in Tokyo.
Hobby: Collecting teacups.
Day and night, develops manga plots
while holding knees on a chair.

Takeshi Obata was born in 1969 in Niigata, Japan, and is the artist of the wildly popular SHONEN JUMP title **Hikaru no Go**, which won the 2003 Tezuka Shinsei "New Hope" award and the Shogakukan Manga award. Obata is also the artist of **Arabian Majin Bokentan Lamp Lamp**, **Ayatsuri Sakon**, and **Cyborg Jichan G.**

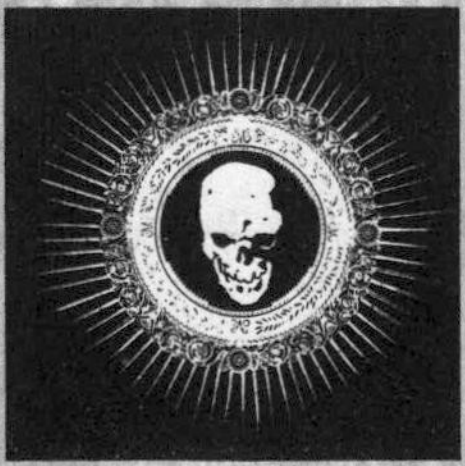

DEATH NOTE VOL 4
SHONEN JUMP ADVANCED Manga Edition

STORY BY TSUGUMI OHBA
ART BY TAKESHI OBATA

Translation & Adaptation/Alexis Kirsch
Touch-up Art & Lettering/Gia Cam Luc
Design/Sean Lee
Editor/Pancha Diaz

Published by VIZ Media, LLC
P.O. Box 77010
San Francisco, CA 94107

14
First printing, March 2006
Fourteenth printing, April 2011

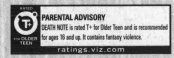

VIZ
MEDIA
www.viz.com

THE WORLD'S MOST
CUTTING-EDGE MANGA
SHONEN
JUMP
ADVANCED
www.shonenjump.com

SHONEN JUMP ADVANCED MANGA

DEATH NOTE

デスノート

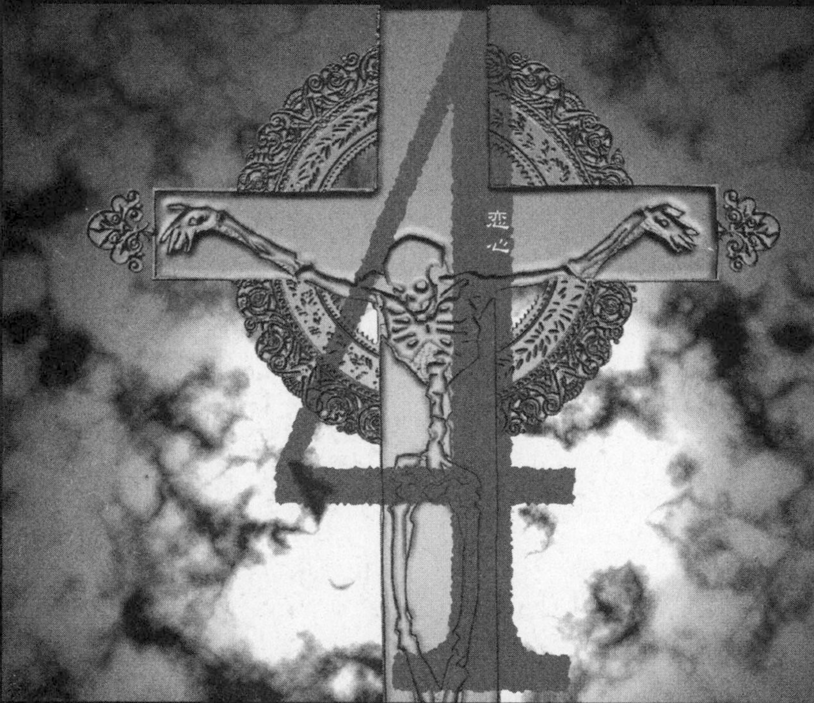
恋心

Vol. 4

Love

Story by Tsugumi Ohba

Art by Takeshi Obata

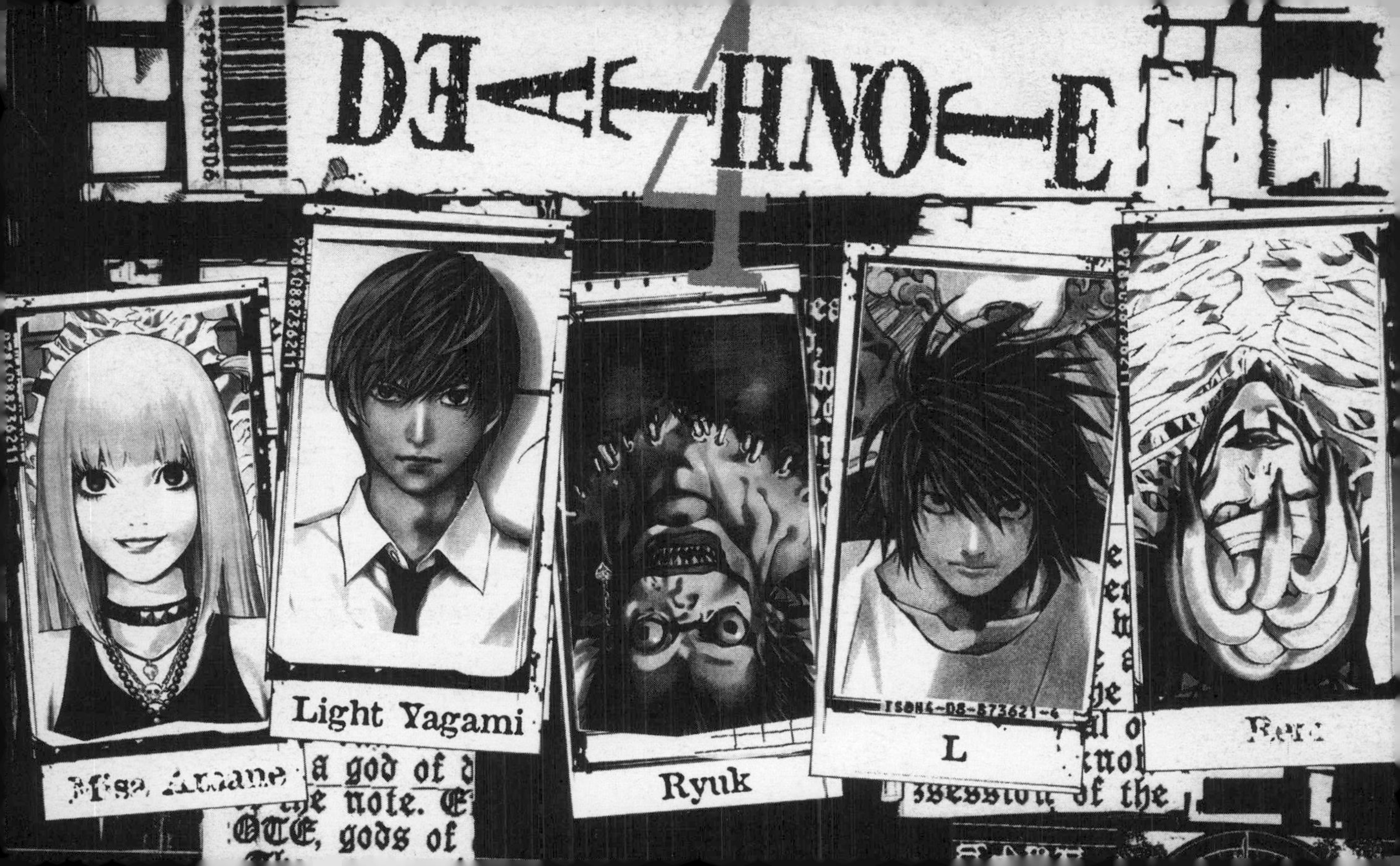

DEATH NOTE
4
Light Yagami
Ryuk
L

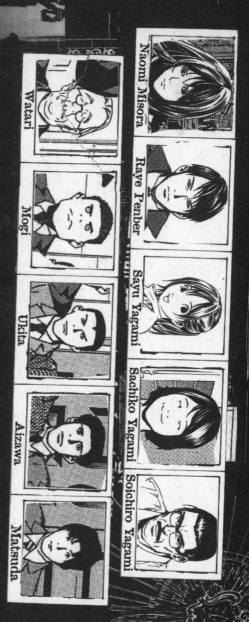

Naomi Misora

Raye Penber

Sayu Yagami

Sachiko Yagami

Soichiro Yagami

Watari

Mogi

Ukita

Aizawa

Matsuda

"THE HUMAN WHOSE NAME IS WRITTEN IN THIS NOTE SHALL DIE"... LIGHT YAGAMI, A STRAIGHT-A HIGH SCHOOL HONOR STUDENT, PICKS UP THE "DEATH NOTE" DROPPED INTO THE HUMAN WORLD BY THE SHINIGAMI RYUK. HALF DISBELIEVING, LIGHT USES THE NOTEBOOK, ONLY TO SEE THE PEOPLE WHOSE NAMES HE HAS WRITTEN DROP DEAD! INITIALLY HORRIFIED BY THE NOTEBOOK'S POWERS, LIGHT EVENTUALLY DECIDES TO USE THE DEATH NOTE TO PURGE THE WORLD OF VIOLENT CRIMINALS AND CREATE AN IDEAL SOCIETY. MEANWHILE, AS CRIMINALS WORLDWIDE START DYING MYSTERIOUSLY, THE ENIGMATIC L, A SECRETIVE GENIUS WHO SPECIALIZES IN SOLVING UNSOLVED CASES, ENTERS THE PICTURE. HE USES A TV BROADCAST TO ANNOUNCE HE WILL CATCH WHOEVER IS RESPONSIBLE, SETTING OFF AN ALMIGHTY BATTLE OF THE WITS BETWEEN LIGHT AND HIMSELF...

LIGHT BEGINS KILLING OFF ALL WHO STAND IN HIS WAY, INCLUDING A TEAM OF FBI AGENTS. HOWEVER, THROUGH HIS POWERS OF DEDUCTION, L BEGINS TO SUSPECT LIGHT AND PLANTS HIDDEN CAMERAS AND MICROPHONES THROUGHOUT THE YAGAMI HOME. LIGHT IMMEDIATELY DETECTS THIS, AND THEIR BATTLE AS SEEN THROUGH THE SMALL LENSES BEGINS TO UNFOLD. AFTER LIGHT SUCCEEDS IN NOT REVEALING ANYTHING INCRIMINATING, L DECIDES TO ENROLL AT THE SAME UNIVERSITY IN ORDER TO KEEP TRACK OF LIGHT'S ACTIVITIES. HE THEN ANNOUNCES TO LIGHT THAT HE IS L AND TRIES TO FURTHER SHAKE HIM. SOON AFTER, A VIDEOTAPE CONTAINING "KIRA'S MESSAGE" ARRIVES AT A TV STATION AND THE PEOPLE MENTIONED ON IT DIE ONE BY ONE. IN ORDER TO STOP THIS TRAGEDY, LIGHT'S FATHER, WHO HAD BEEN IN THE HOSPITAL, CRASHES INTO THE TV STATION AND RECOVERS THE TAPES. THEN THE BOMBSHELL IS REVEALED—THE PERSON BEHIND THIS PLOT WASN'T LIGHT, BUT A "SECOND KIRA"!!

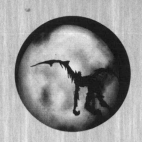

DEATH NOTE
Vol. 4

CONTENTS

chapter 26 Reversal

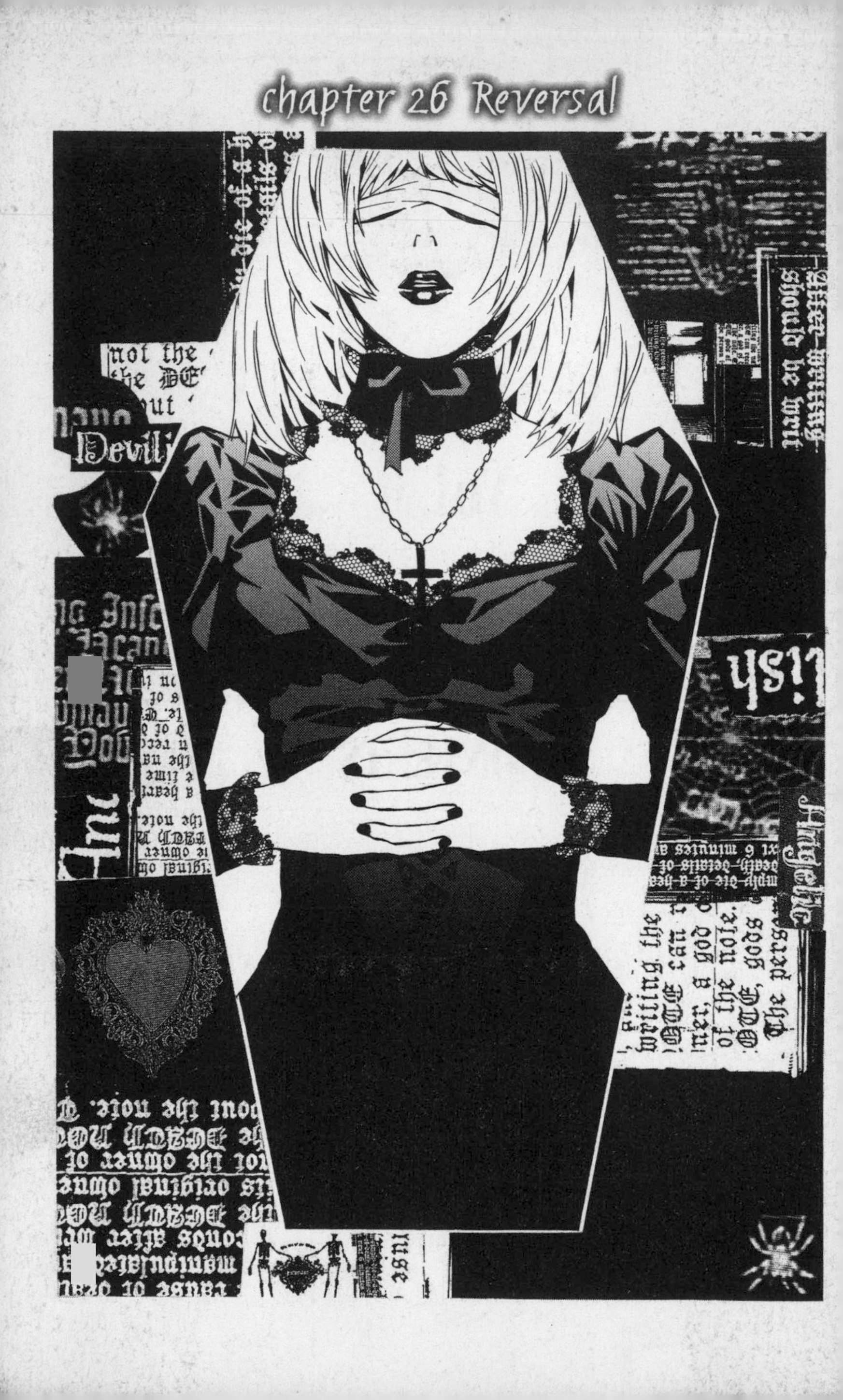
not the
Devil

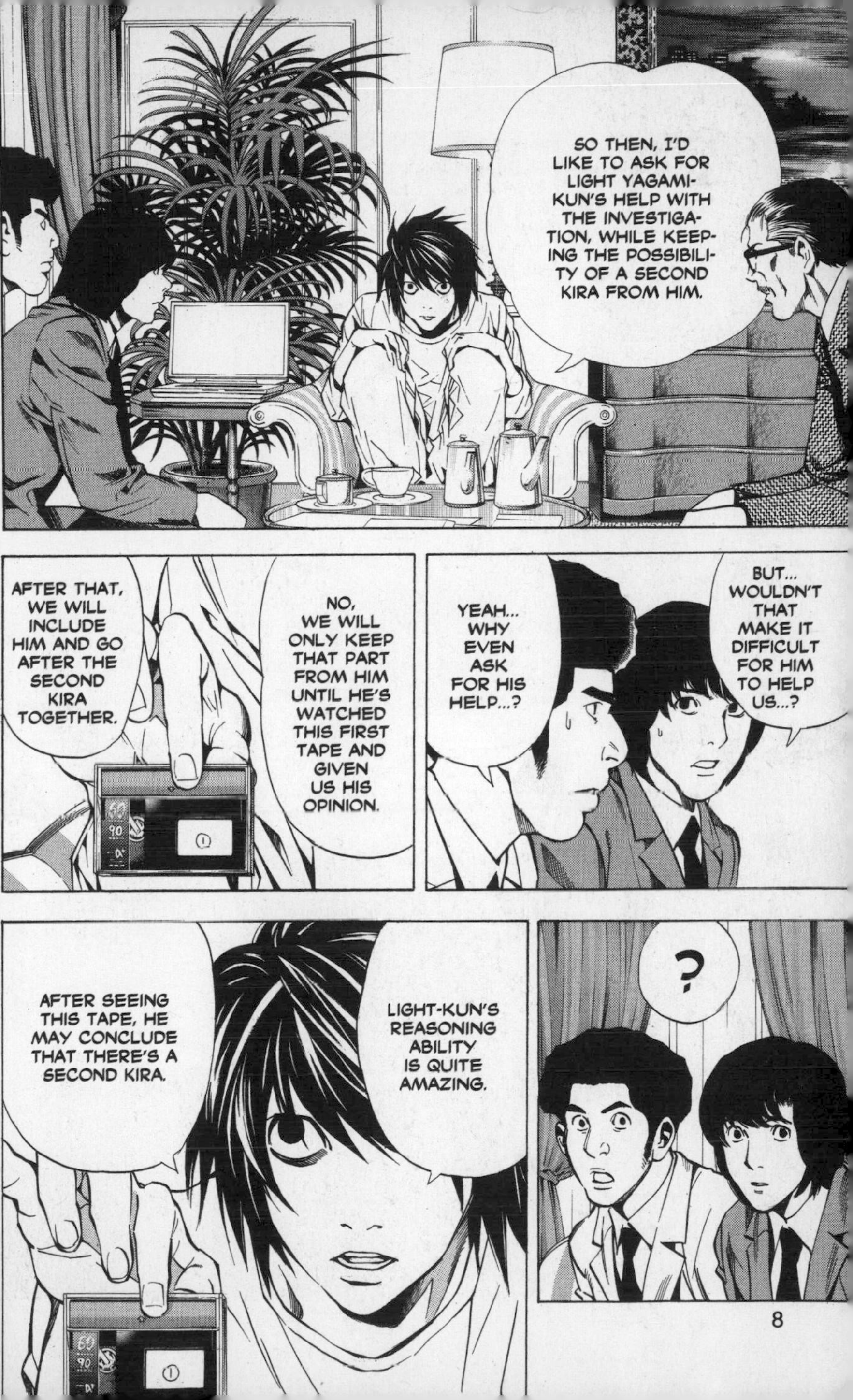
SO THEN, I'D LIKE TO ASK FOR LIGHT YAGAMI-KUN'S HELP WITH THE INVESTIGATION, WHILE KEEPING THE POSSIBILITY OF A SECOND KIRA FROM HIM.
BUT... WOULDN'T THAT MAKE IT DIFFICULT FOR HIM TO HELP US...?
YEAH... WHY EVEN ASK FOR HIS HELP...?
NO, WE WILL ONLY KEEP THAT PART FROM HIM UNTIL HE'S WATCHED THIS FIRST TAPE AND GIVEN US HIS OPINION.
AFTER THAT, WE WILL INCLUDE HIM AND GO AFTER THE SECOND KIRA TOGETHER.
?
LIGHT-KUN'S REASONING ABILITY IS QUITE AMAZING.
AFTER SEEING THIS TAPE, HE MAY CONCLUDE THAT THERE'S A SECOND KIRA.

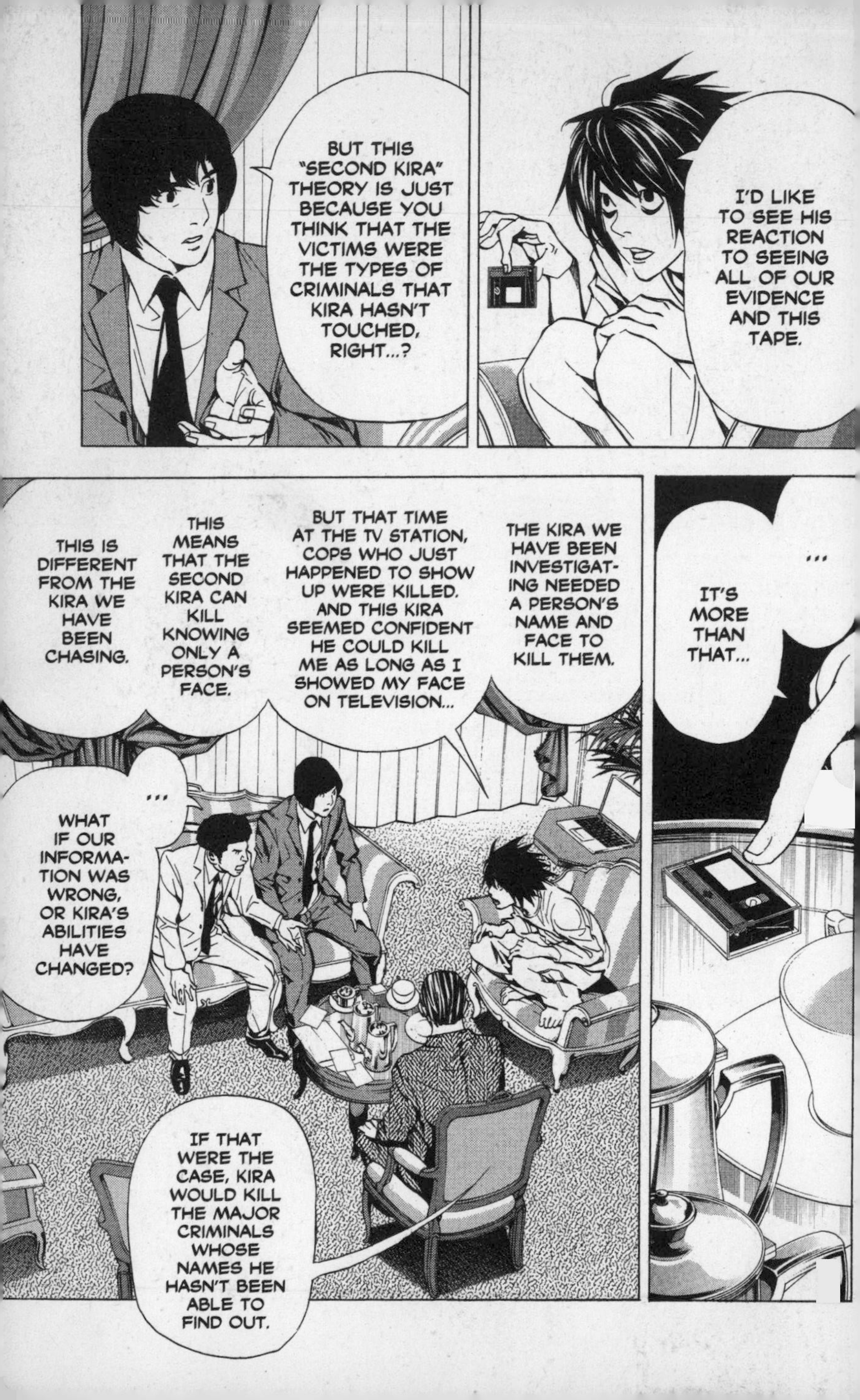
I'D LIKE TO SEE HIS REACTION TO SEEING ALL OF OUR EVIDENCE AND THIS TAPE.
BUT THIS "SECOND KIRA" THEORY IS JUST BECAUSE YOU THINK THAT THE VICTIMS WERE THE TYPES OF CRIMINALS THAT KIRA HASN'T TOUCHED, RIGHT...?
...
IT'S MORE THAN THAT...
THE KIRA WE HAVE BEEN INVESTIGAT-ING NEEDED A PERSON'S NAME AND FACE TO KILL THEM.
BUT THAT TIME AT THE TV STATION, COPS WHO JUST HAPPENED TO SHOW UP WERE KILLED. AND THIS KIRA SEEMED CONFIDENT HE COULD KILL ME AS LONG AS I SHOWED MY FACE ON TELEVISION...
THIS MEANS THAT THE SECOND KIRA CAN KILL KNOWING ONLY A PERSON'S FACE.
THIS IS DIFFERENT FROM THE KIRA WE HAVE BEEN CHASING.
...
WHAT IF OUR INFORMA-TION WAS WRONG, OR KIRA'S ABILITIES HAVE CHANGED?
IF THAT WERE THE CASE, KIRA WOULD KILL THE MAJOR CRIMINALS WHOSE NAMES HE HASN'T BEEN ABLE TO FIND OUT.

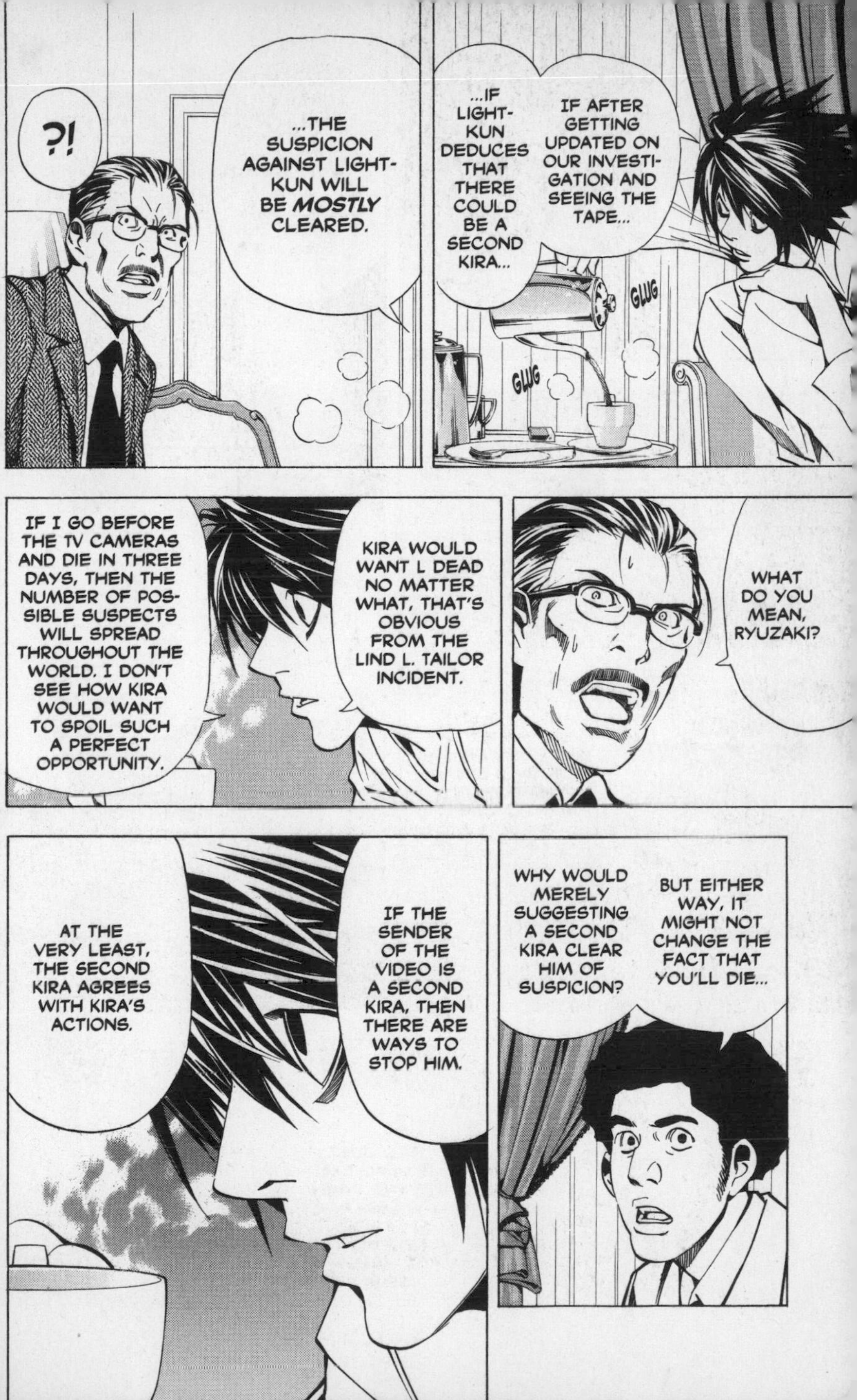
IF AFTER GETTING UPDATED ON OUR INVESTIGATION AND SEEING THE TAPE...
...IF LIGHT-KUN DEDUCES THAT THERE COULD BE A SECOND KIRA...
GLUG
GLUG
...THE SUSPICION AGAINST LIGHT-KUN WILL BE *MOSTLY* CLEARED.
?!
WHAT DO YOU MEAN, RYUZAKI?
KIRA WOULD WANT L DEAD NO MATTER WHAT, THAT'S OBVIOUS FROM THE LIND L. TAILOR INCIDENT.
IF I GO BEFORE THE TV CAMERAS AND DIE IN THREE DAYS, THEN THE NUMBER OF POSSIBLE SUSPECTS WILL SPREAD THROUGHOUT THE WORLD. I DON'T SEE HOW KIRA WOULD WANT TO SPOIL SUCH A PERFECT OPPORTUNITY.
BUT EITHER WAY, IT MIGHT NOT CHANGE THE FACT THAT YOU'LL DIE...
WHY WOULD MERELY SUGGESTING A SECOND KIRA CLEAR HIM OF SUSPICION?
IF THE SENDER OF THE VIDEO IS A SECOND KIRA, THEN THERE ARE WAYS TO STOP HIM.
AT THE VERY LEAST, THE SECOND KIRA AGREES WITH KIRA'S ACTIONS.

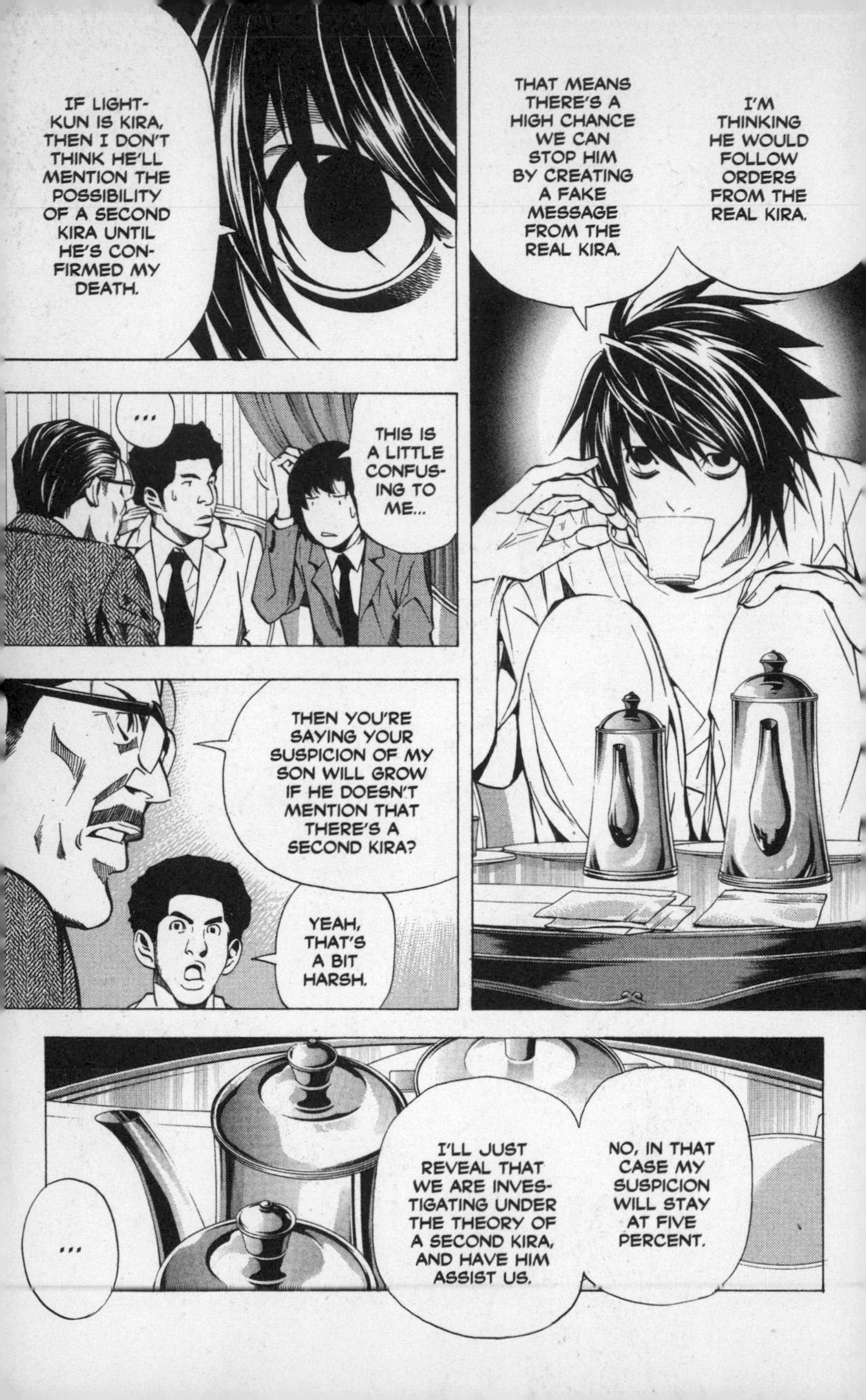
I'M THINKING HE WOULD FOLLOW ORDERS FROM THE REAL KIRA.
THAT MEANS THERE'S A HIGH CHANCE WE CAN STOP HIM BY CREATING A FAKE MESSAGE FROM THE REAL KIRA.
IF LIGHT-KUN IS KIRA, THEN I DON'T THINK HE'LL MENTION THE POSSIBILITY OF A SECOND KIRA UNTIL HE'S CONFIRMED MY DEATH.
THIS IS A LITTLE CONFUSING TO ME...
...
THEN YOU'RE SAYING YOUR SUSPICION OF MY SON WILL GROW IF HE DOESN'T MENTION THAT THERE'S A SECOND KIRA?
YEAH, THAT'S A BIT HARSH.
NO, IN THAT CASE MY SUSPICION WILL STAY AT FIVE PERCENT.
I'LL JUST REVEAL THAT WE ARE INVESTIGATING UNDER THE THEORY OF A SECOND KIRA, AND HAVE HIM ASSIST US.
...

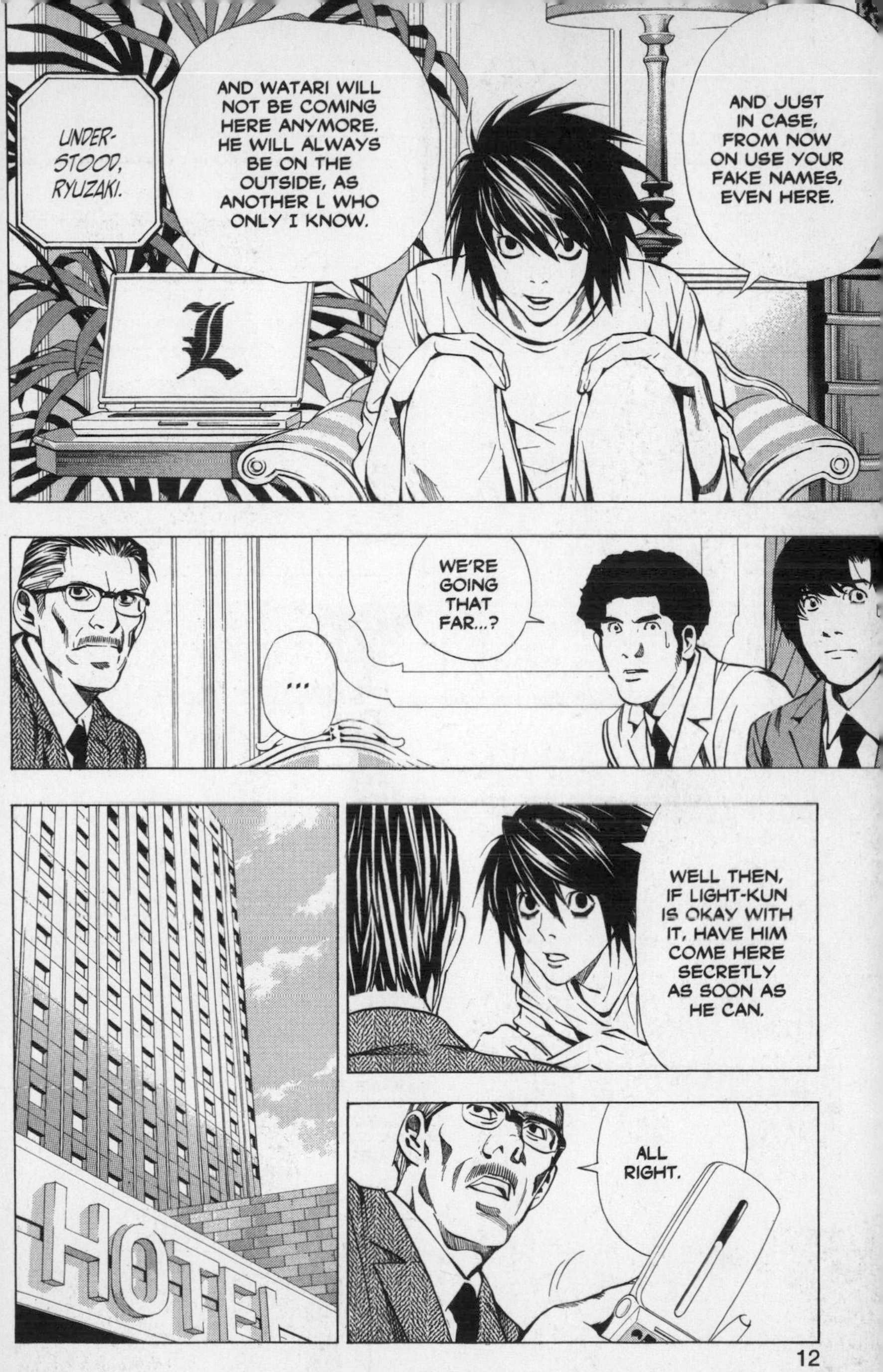
AND JUST IN CASE, FROM NOW ON USE YOUR FAKE NAMES, EVEN HERE.
AND WATARI WILL NOT BE COMING HERE ANYMORE. HE WILL ALWAYS BE ON THE OUTSIDE, AS ANOTHER L WHO ONLY I KNOW.
UNDER-STOOD, RYUZAKI.
L
WE'RE GOING THAT FAR...?
...
WELL THEN, IF LIGHT-KUN IS OKAY WITH IT, HAVE HIM COME HERE SECRETLY AS SOON AS HE CAN.
ALL RIGHT.
HOTEL

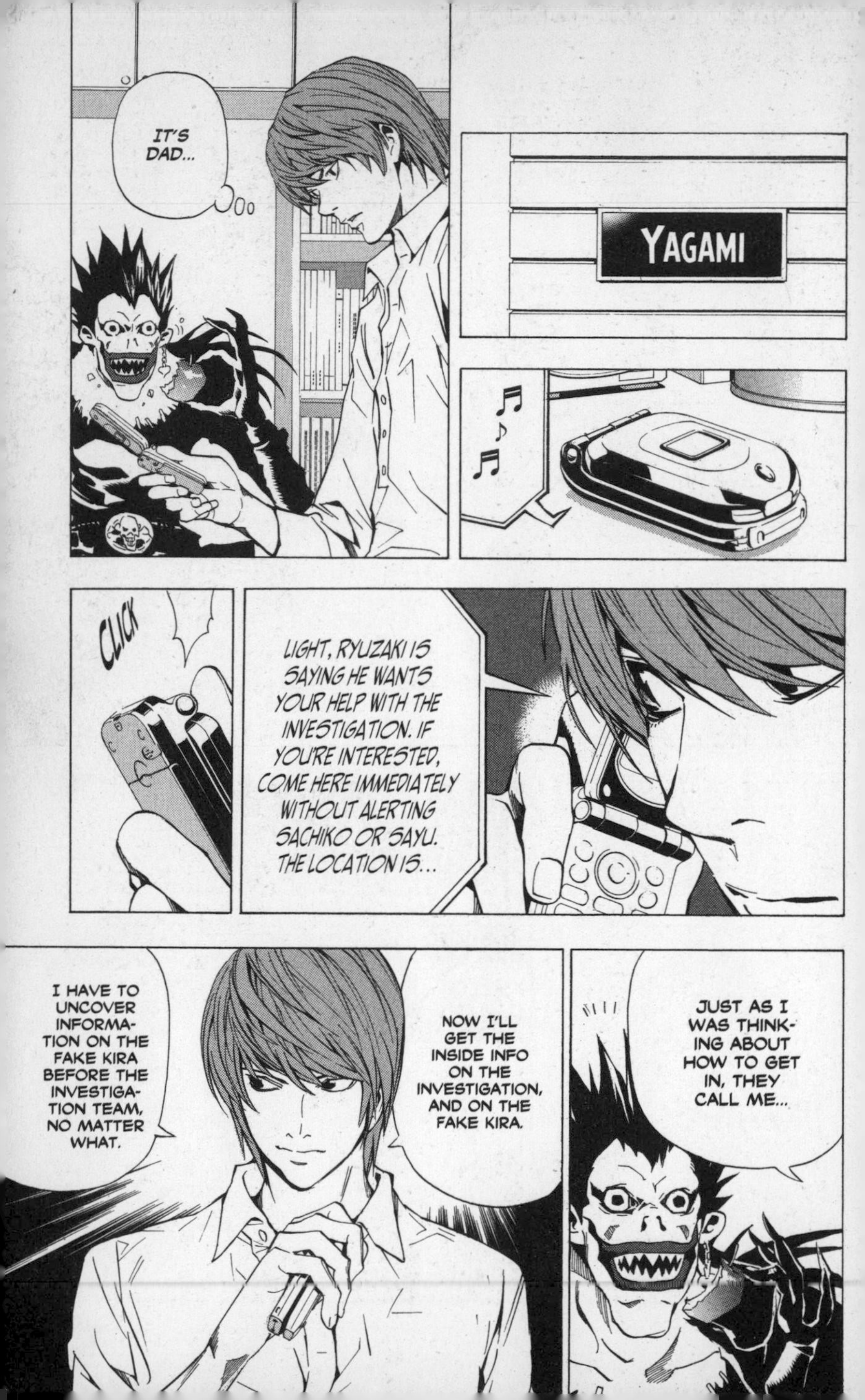
YAGAMI
IT'S DAD...
LIGHT, RYUZAKI IS SAYING HE WANTS YOUR HELP WITH THE INVESTIGATION. IF YOU'RE INTERESTED, COME HERE IMMEDIATELY WITHOUT ALERTING SACHIKO OR SAYU. THE LOCATION IS...
CLICK
JUST AS I WAS THINKING ABOUT HOW TO GET IN, THEY CALL ME...
NOW I'LL GET THE INSIDE INFO ON THE INVESTIGATION, AND ON THE FAKE KIRA.
I HAVE TO UNCOVER INFORMATION ON THE FAKE KIRA BEFORE THE INVESTIGATION TEAM, NO MATTER WHAT.

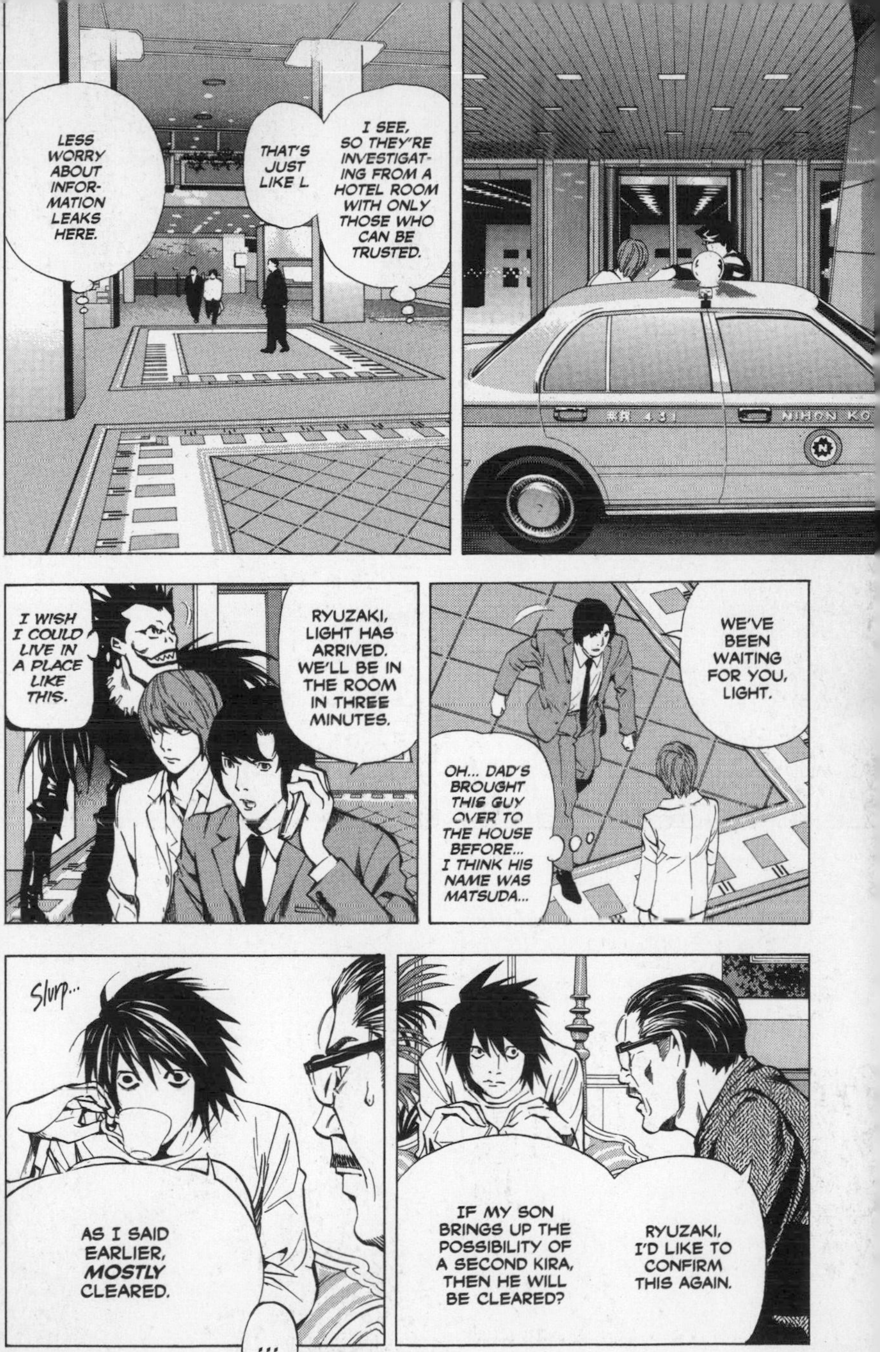
I SEE, SO THEY'RE INVESTIGATING FROM A HOTEL ROOM WITH ONLY THOSE WHO CAN BE TRUSTED.
THAT'S JUST LIKE L.
LESS WORRY ABOUT INFORMATION LEAKS HERE.
WE'VE BEEN WAITING FOR YOU, LIGHT.
OH... DAD'S BROUGHT THIS GUY OVER TO THE HOUSE BEFORE... I THINK HIS NAME WAS MATSUDA...
RYUZAKI, LIGHT HAS ARRIVED. WE'LL BE IN THE ROOM IN THREE MINUTES.
I WISH I COULD LIVE IN A PLACE LIKE THIS.
RYUZAKI, I'D LIKE TO CONFIRM THIS AGAIN.
IF MY SON BRINGS UP THE POSSIBILITY OF A SECOND KIRA, THEN HE WILL BE CLEARED?
Slurp...
AS I SAID EARLIER, *MOSTLY* CLEARED.
...

READ THIS WAY

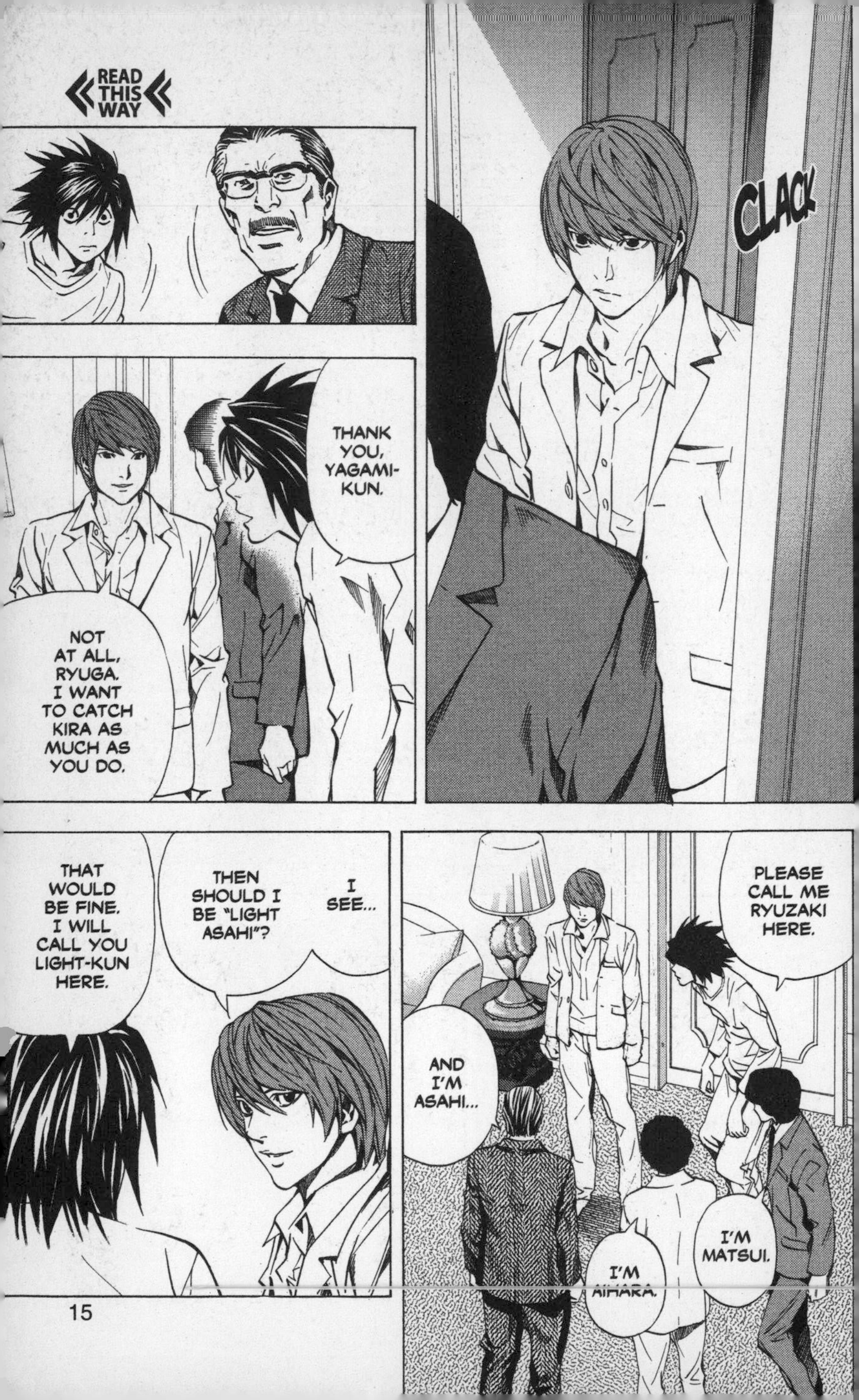
CLACK
THANK YOU, YAGAMI-KUN.
NOT AT ALL, RYUGA. I WANT TO CATCH KIRA AS MUCH AS YOU DO.
PLEASE CALL ME RYUZAKI HERE.
AND I'M ASAHI...
I'M MATSUI.
I'M AIHARA.
I SEE...
THEN SHOULD I BE "LIGHT ASAHI"?
THAT WOULD BE FINE. I WILL CALL YOU LIGHT-KUN HERE.

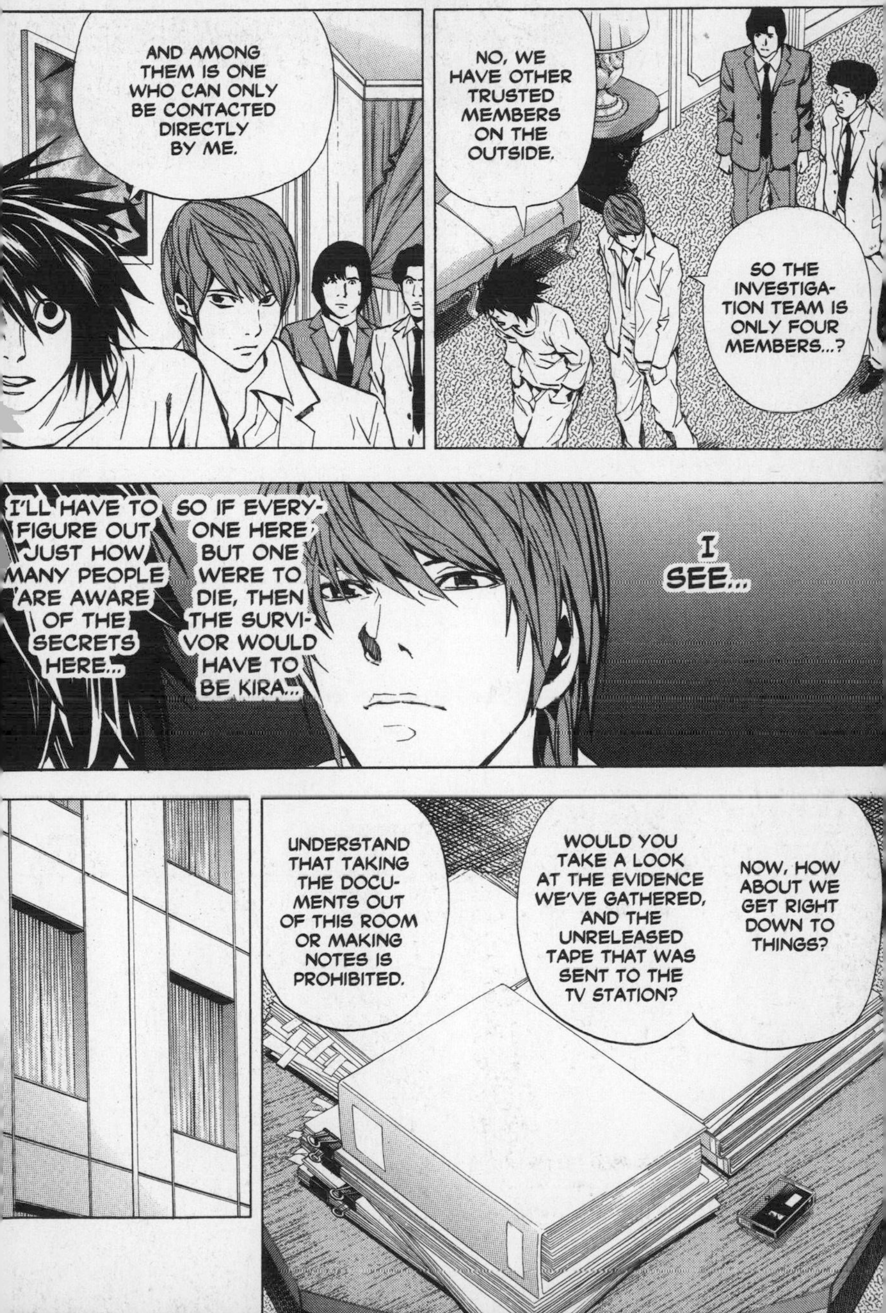
SO THE INVESTIGA-TION TEAM IS ONLY FOUR MEMBERS...?
NO, WE HAVE OTHER TRUSTED MEMBERS ON THE OUTSIDE.
AND AMONG THEM IS ONE WHO CAN ONLY BE CONTACTED DIRECTLY BY ME.
I SEE...
SO IF EVERY-ONE HERE BUT ONE WERE TO DIE, THEN THE SURVI-VOR WOULD HAVE TO BE KIRA...
I'LL HAVE TO FIGURE OUT JUST HOW MANY PEOPLE ARE AWARE OF THE SECRETS HERE...
NOW, HOW ABOUT WE GET RIGHT DOWN TO THINGS?
WOULD YOU TAKE A LOOK AT THE EVIDENCE WE'VE GATHERED, AND THE UNRELEASED TAPE THAT WAS SENT TO THE TV STATION?
UNDERSTAND THAT TAKING THE DOCU-MENTS OUT OF THIS ROOM OR MAKING NOTES IS PROHIBITED.

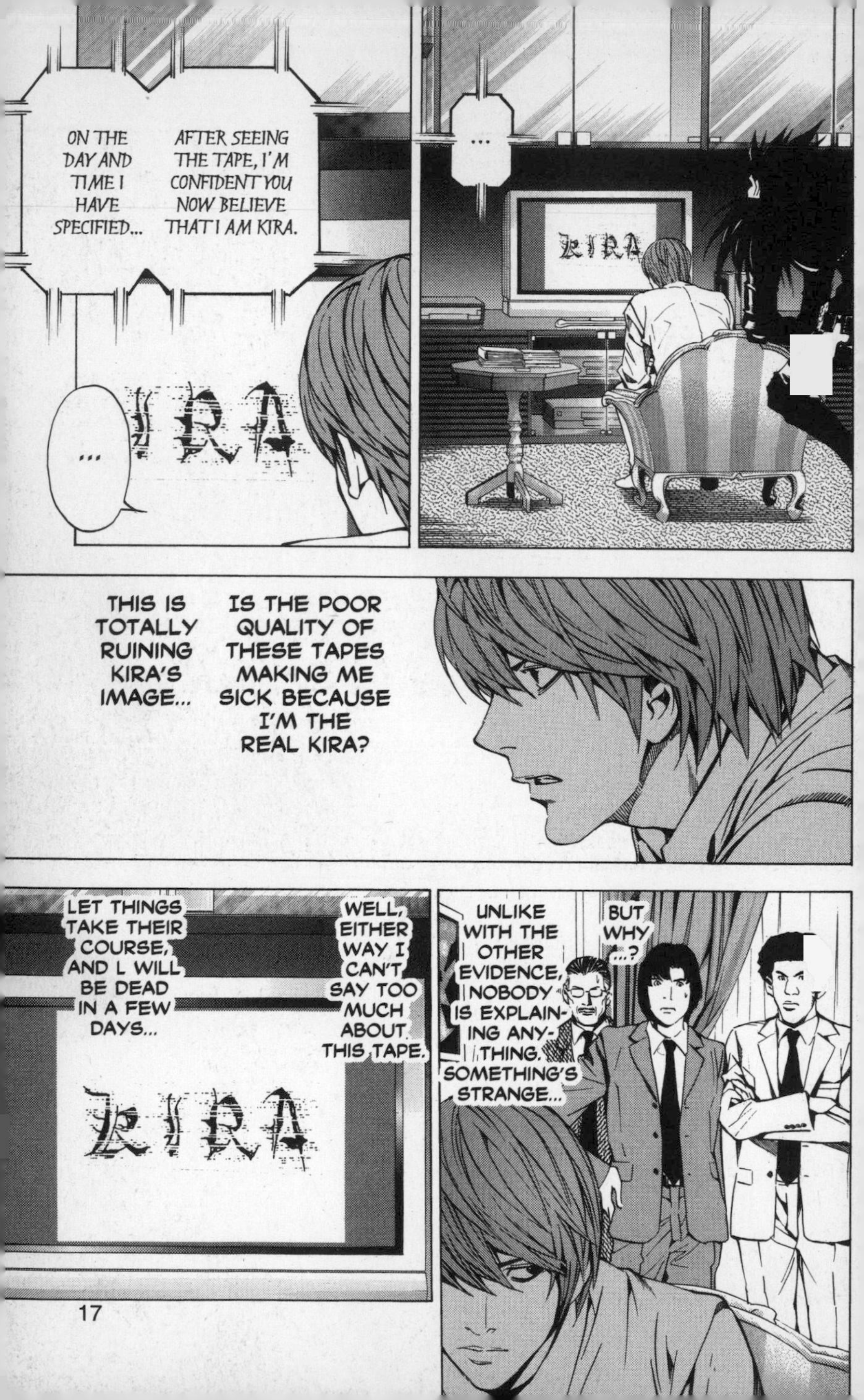
...
AFTER SEEING THE TAPE, I'M CONFIDENT YOU NOW BELIEVE THAT I AM KIRA.
ON THE DAY AND TIME I HAVE SPECIFIED...
...
IS THE POOR QUALITY OF THESE TAPES MAKING ME SICK BECAUSE I'M THE REAL KIRA?
THIS IS TOTALLY RUINING KIRA'S IMAGE...
BUT WHY ...?
UNLIKE WITH THE OTHER EVIDENCE, NOBODY IS EXPLAINING ANYTHING. SOMETHING'S STRANGE...
WELL, EITHER WAY I CAN'T SAY TOO MUCH ABOUT THIS TAPE.
LET THINGS TAKE THEIR COURSE, AND L WILL BE DEAD IN A FEW DAYS...

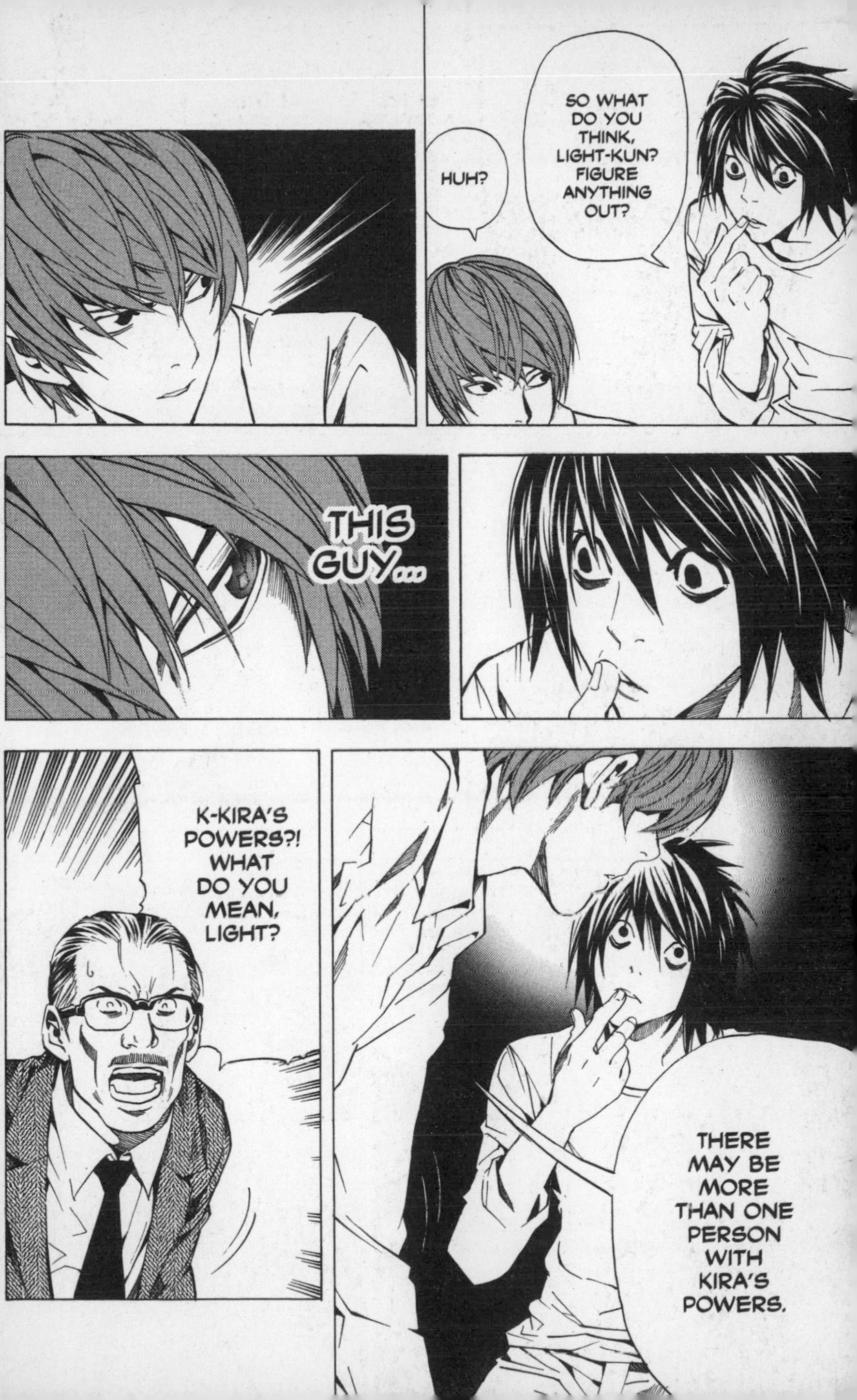
SO WHAT DO YOU THINK, LIGHT-KUN? FIGURE ANYTHING OUT?
HUH?
THIS GUY...
THERE MAY BE MORE THAN ONE PERSON WITH KIRA'S POWERS.
K-KIRA'S POWERS?! WHAT DO YOU MEAN, LIGHT?

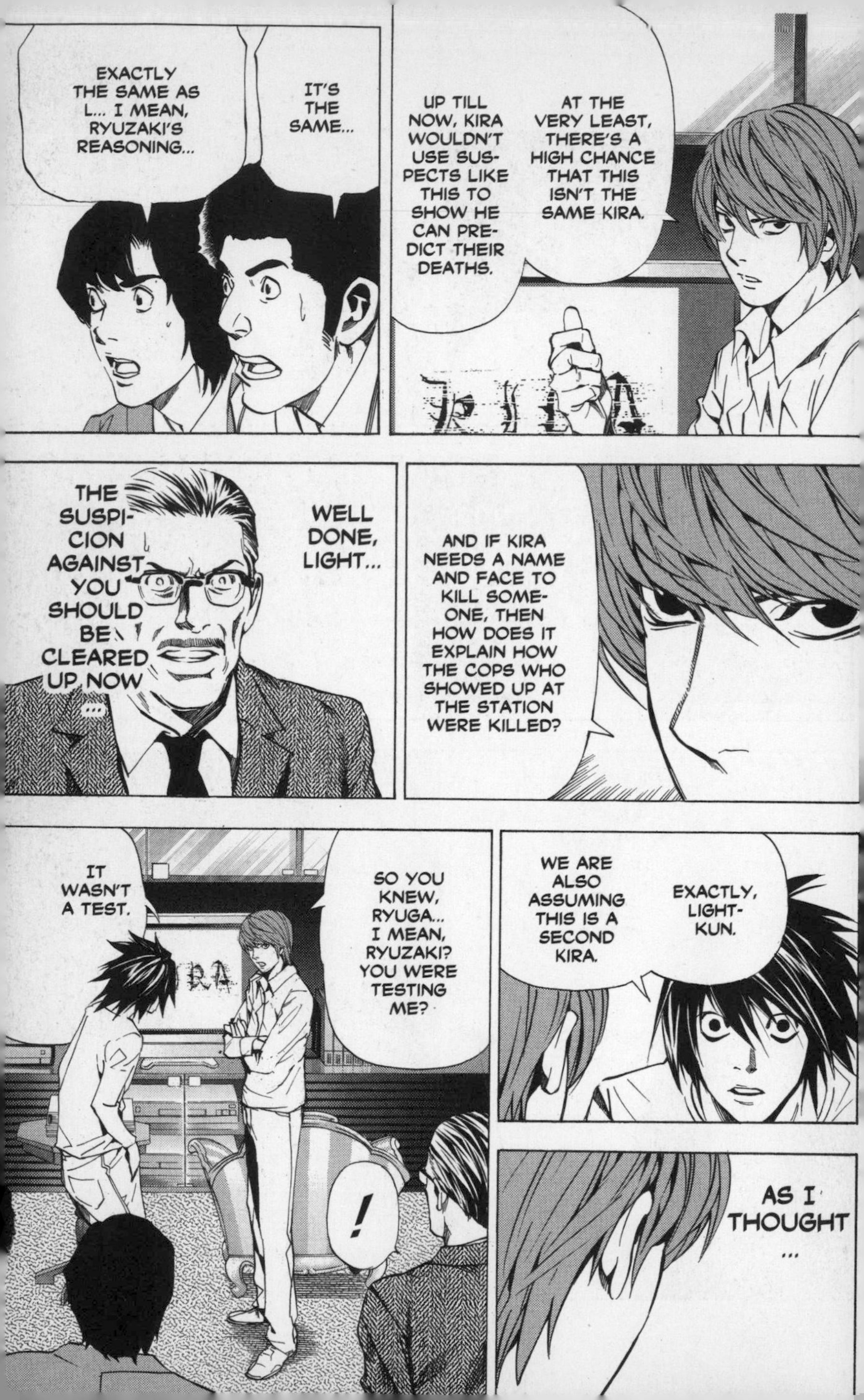
AT THE VERY LEAST, THERE'S A HIGH CHANCE THAT THIS ISN'T THE SAME KIRA.
UP TILL NOW, KIRA WOULDN'T USE SUSPECTS LIKE THIS TO SHOW HE CAN PREDICT THEIR DEATHS.
IT'S THE SAME...
EXACTLY THE SAME AS L... I MEAN, RYUZAKI'S REASONING...
AND IF KIRA NEEDS A NAME AND FACE TO KILL SOMEONE, THEN HOW DOES IT EXPLAIN HOW THE COPS WHO SHOWED UP AT THE STATION WERE KILLED?
WELL DONE, LIGHT...
THE SUSPICION AGAINST YOU SHOULD BE CLEARED UP NOW...
EXACTLY, LIGHT-KUN.
WE ARE ALSO ASSUMING THIS IS A SECOND KIRA.
AS I THOUGHT...
SO YOU KNEW, RYUGA... I MEAN, RYUZAKI? YOU WERE TESTING ME?
IT WASN'T A TEST.
!

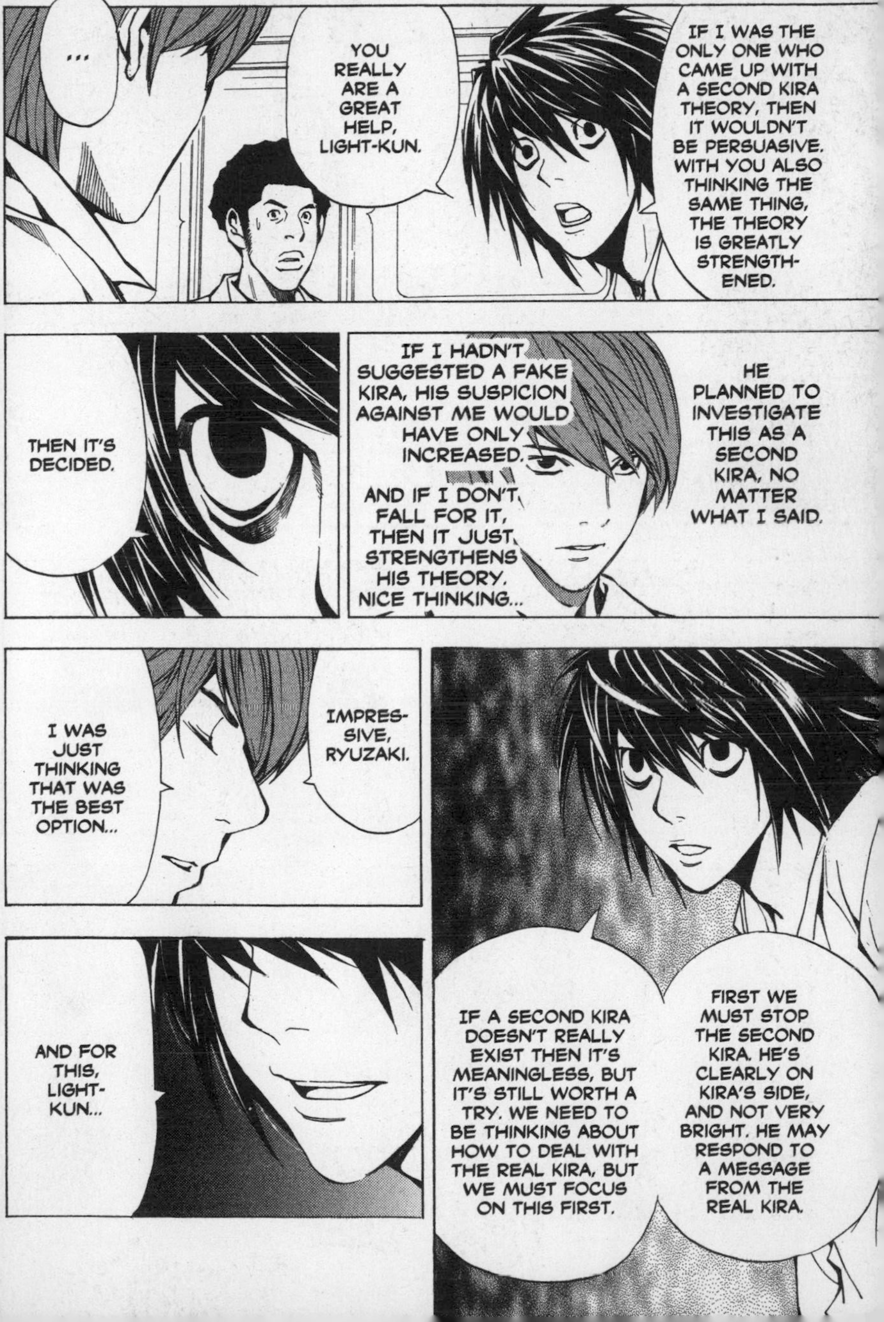
IF I WAS THE ONLY ONE WHO CAME UP WITH A SECOND KIRA THEORY, THEN IT WOULDN'T BE PERSUASIVE. WITH YOU ALSO THINKING THE SAME THING, THE THEORY IS GREATLY STRENGTH-ENED.
YOU REALLY ARE A GREAT HELP, LIGHT-KUN.
...
HE PLANNED TO INVESTIGATE THIS AS A SECOND KIRA, NO MATTER WHAT I SAID.
IF I HADN'T SUGGESTED A FAKE KIRA, HIS SUSPICION AGAINST ME WOULD HAVE ONLY INCREASED.
AND IF I DON'T FALL FOR IT, THEN IT JUST STRENGTHENS HIS THEORY. NICE THINKING...
THEN IT'S DECIDED.
FIRST WE MUST STOP THE SECOND KIRA. HE'S CLEARLY ON KIRA'S SIDE, AND NOT VERY BRIGHT. HE MAY RESPOND TO A MESSAGE FROM THE REAL KIRA.
IF A SECOND KIRA DOESN'T REALLY EXIST THEN IT'S MEANINGLESS, BUT IT'S STILL WORTH A TRY. WE NEED TO BE THINKING ABOUT HOW TO DEAL WITH THE REAL KIRA, BUT WE MUST FOCUS ON THIS FIRST.
IMPRES-SIVE, RYUZAKI.
I WAS JUST THINKING THAT WAS THE BEST OPTION...
AND FOR THIS, LIGHT-KUN...

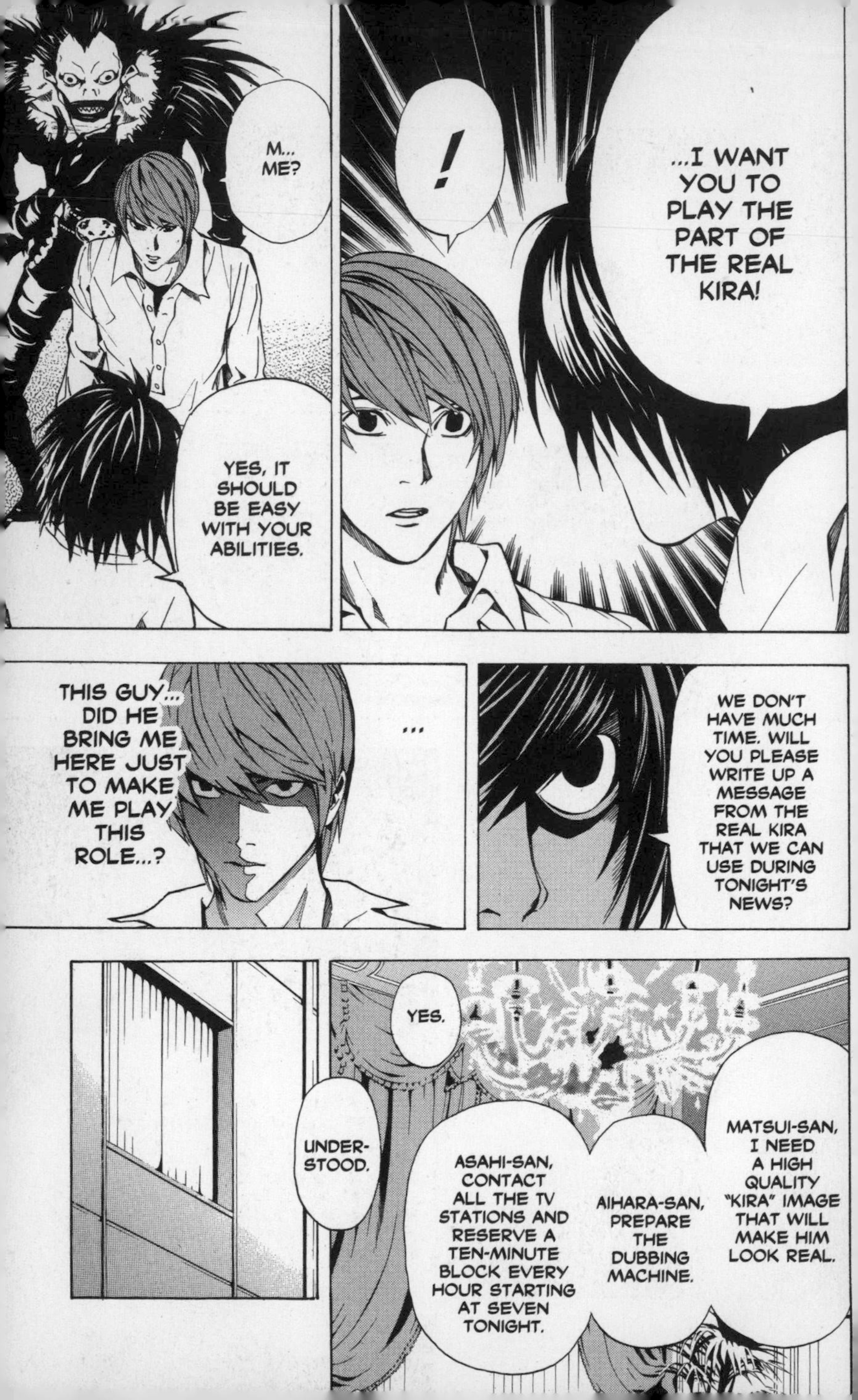
...I WANT YOU TO PLAY THE PART OF THE REAL KIRA!
!
M... ME?
YES, IT SHOULD BE EASY WITH YOUR ABILITIES.
WE DON'T HAVE MUCH TIME. WILL YOU PLEASE WRITE UP A MESSAGE FROM THE REAL KIRA THAT WE CAN USE DURING TONIGHT'S NEWS?
...
THIS GUY... DID HE BRING ME HERE JUST TO MAKE ME PLAY THIS ROLE...?
MATSUI-SAN, I NEED A HIGH QUALITY "KIRA" IMAGE THAT WILL MAKE HIM LOOK REAL.
AIHARA-SAN, PREPARE THE DUBBING MACHINE.
ASAHI-SAN, CONTACT ALL THE TV STATIONS AND RESERVE A TEN-MINUTE BLOCK EVERY HOUR STARTING AT SEVEN TONIGHT.
UNDER-STOOD.
YES.

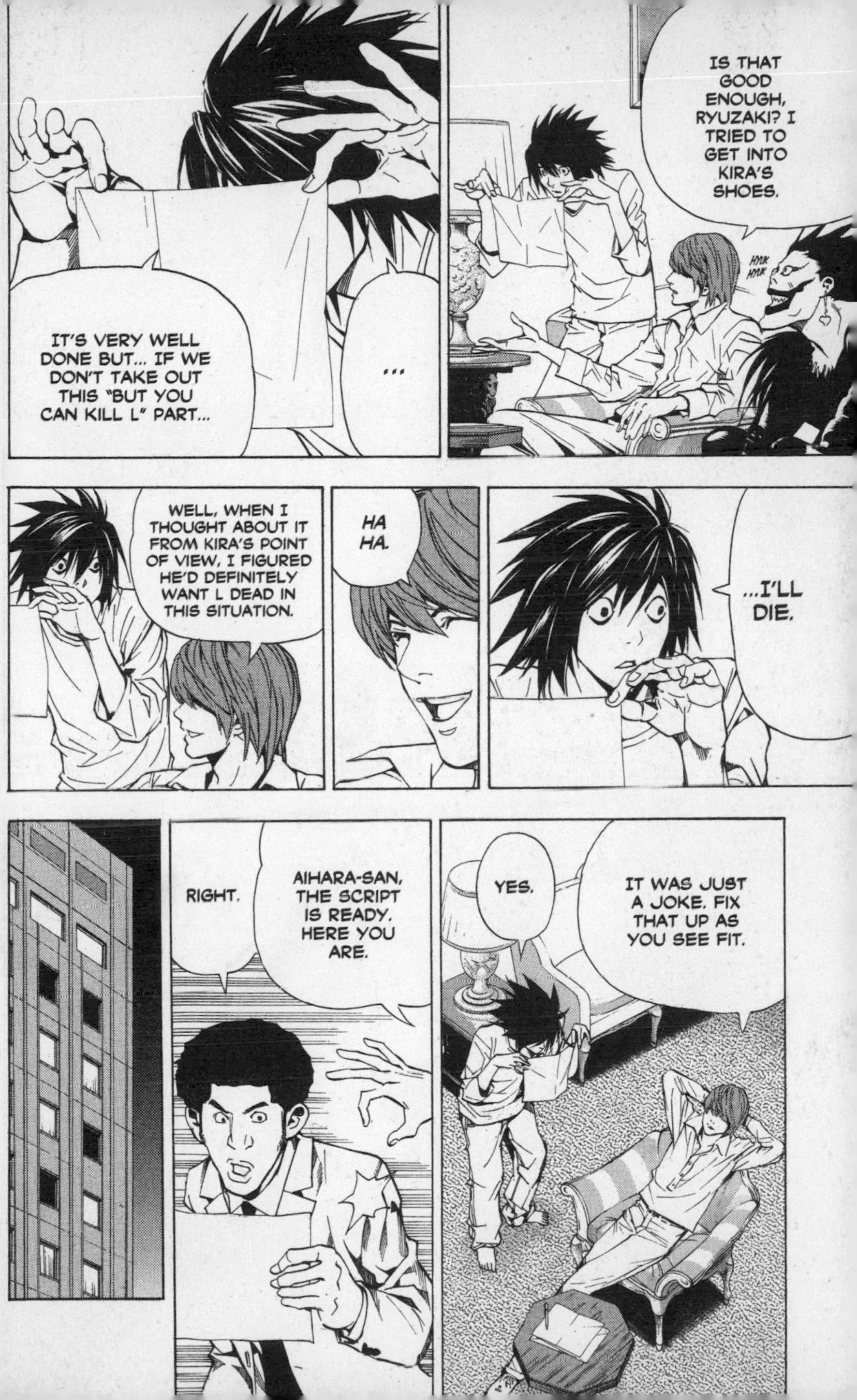
IS THAT GOOD ENOUGH, RYUZAKI? I TRIED TO GET INTO KIRA'S SHOES.
HYUK HYUK
...
IT'S VERY WELL DONE BUT... IF WE DON'T TAKE OUT THIS "BUT YOU CAN KILL L" PART...
...I'LL DIE.
HA HA.
WELL, WHEN I THOUGHT ABOUT IT FROM KIRA'S POINT OF VIEW, I FIGURED HE'D DEFINITELY WANT L DEAD IN THIS SITUATION.
IT WAS JUST A JOKE. FIX THAT UP AS YOU SEE FIT.
YES.
AIHARA-SAN, THE SCRIPT IS READY. HERE YOU ARE.
RIGHT.

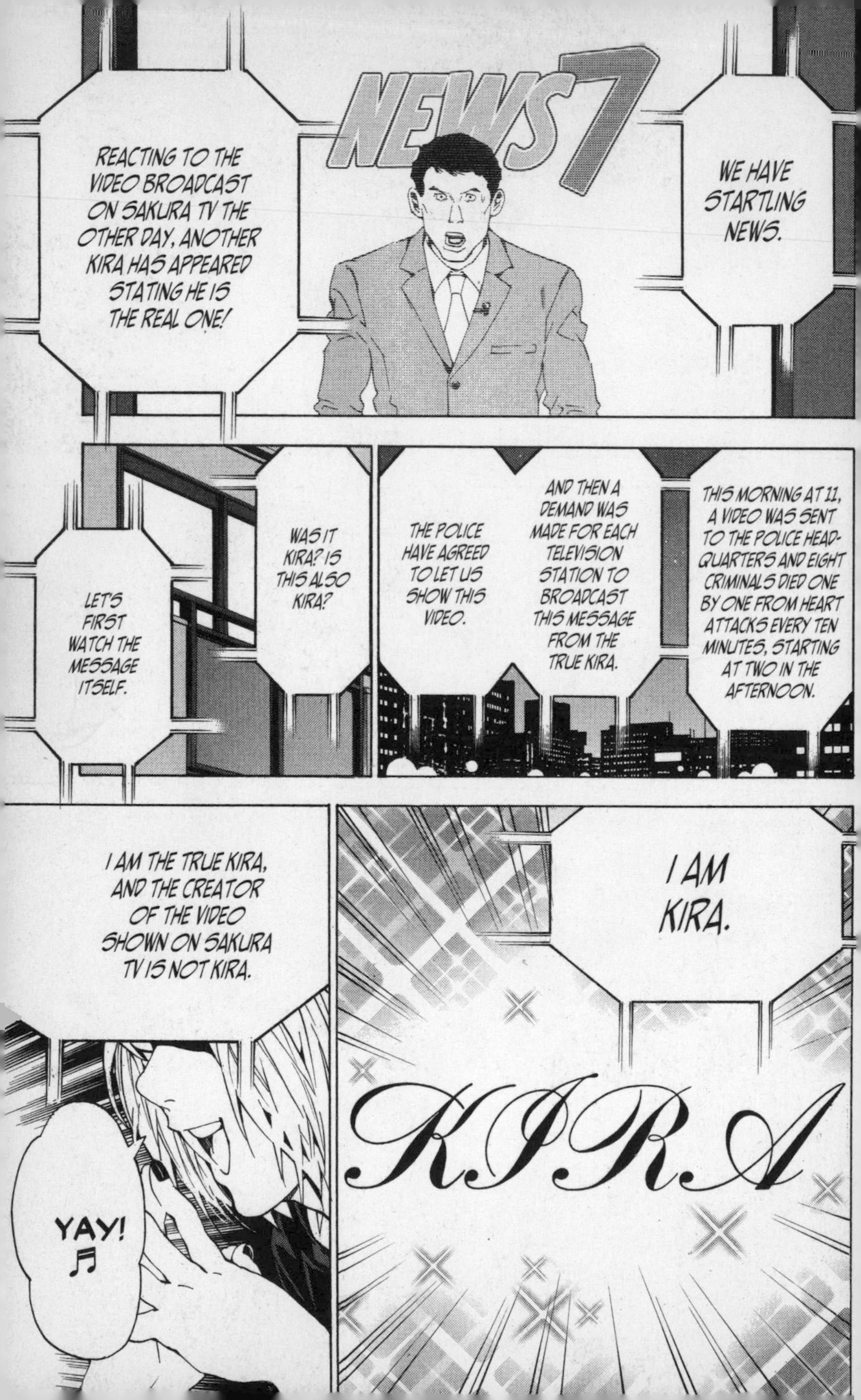
NEWS 7
WE HAVE STARTLING NEWS.
REACTING TO THE VIDEO BROADCAST ON SAKURA TV THE OTHER DAY, ANOTHER KIRA HAS APPEARED STATING HE IS THE REAL ONE!
THIS MORNING AT 11, A VIDEO WAS SENT TO THE POLICE HEAD-QUARTERS AND EIGHT CRIMINALS DIED ONE BY ONE FROM HEART ATTACKS EVERY TEN MINUTES, STARTING AT TWO IN THE AFTERNOON.
AND THEN A DEMAND WAS MADE FOR EACH TELEVISION STATION TO BROADCAST THIS MESSAGE FROM THE TRUE KIRA.
THE POLICE HAVE AGREED TO LET US SHOW THIS VIDEO.
WAS IT KIRA? IS THIS ALSO KIRA?
LET'S FIRST WATCH THE MESSAGE ITSELF.
I AM KIRA.
KIRA
I AM THE TRUE KIRA, AND THE CREATOR OF THE VIDEO SHOWN ON SAKURA TV IS NOT KIRA.
YAY! ♫

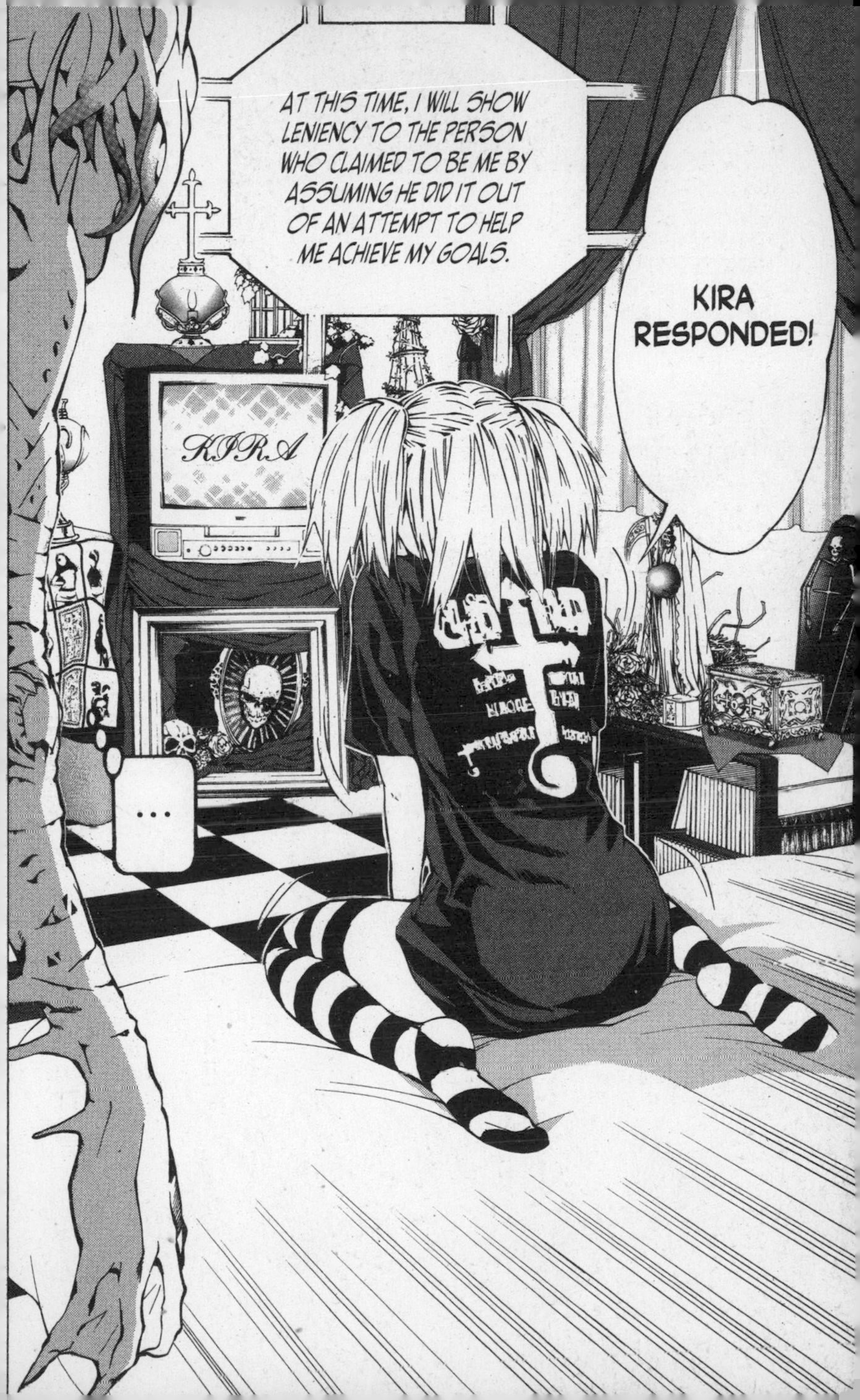
KIRA RESPONDED!
AT THIS TIME, I WILL SHOW LENIENCY TO THE PERSON WHO CLAIMED TO BE ME BY ASSUMING HE DID IT OUT OF AN ATTEMPT TO HELP ME ACHIEVE MY GOALS.
KIRA
...

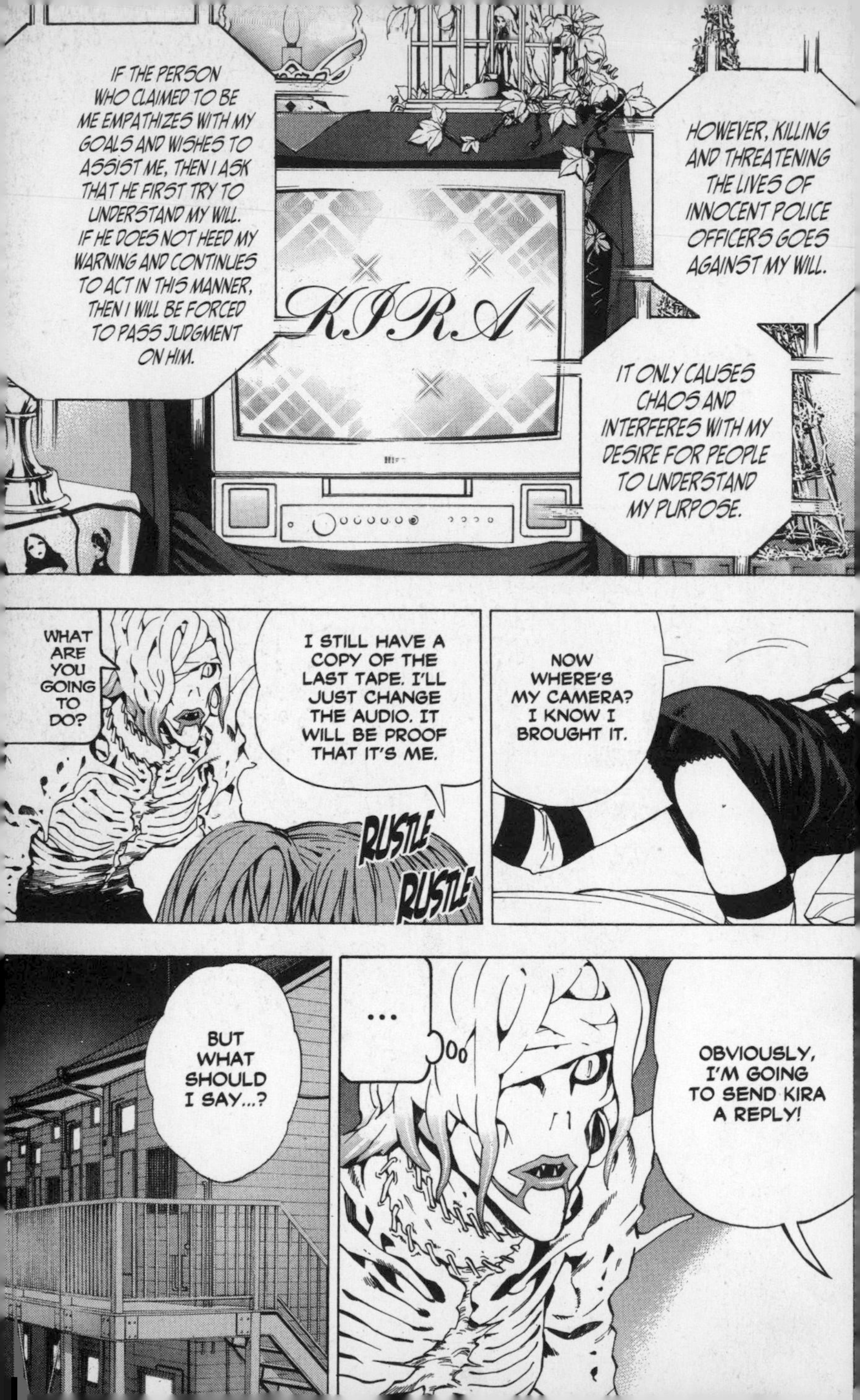
HOWEVER, KILLING AND THREATENING THE LIVES OF INNOCENT POLICE OFFICERS GOES AGAINST MY WILL.
IT ONLY CAUSES CHAOS AND INTERFERES WITH MY DESIRE FOR PEOPLE TO UNDERSTAND MY PURPOSE.
KIRA
IF THE PERSON WHO CLAIMED TO BE ME EMPATHIZES WITH MY GOALS AND WISHES TO ASSIST ME, THEN I ASK THAT HE FIRST TRY TO UNDERSTAND MY WILL. IF HE DOES NOT HEED MY WARNING AND CONTINUES TO ACT IN THIS MANNER, THEN I WILL BE FORCED TO PASS JUDGMENT ON HIM.
NOW WHERE'S MY CAMERA? I KNOW I BROUGHT IT.
I STILL HAVE A COPY OF THE LAST TAPE. I'LL JUST CHANGE THE AUDIO. IT WILL BE PROOF THAT IT'S ME.
RUSTLE RUSTLE
WHAT ARE YOU GOING TO DO?
OBVIOUSLY, I'M GOING TO SEND KIRA A REPLY!
...
BUT WHAT SHOULD I SAY...?

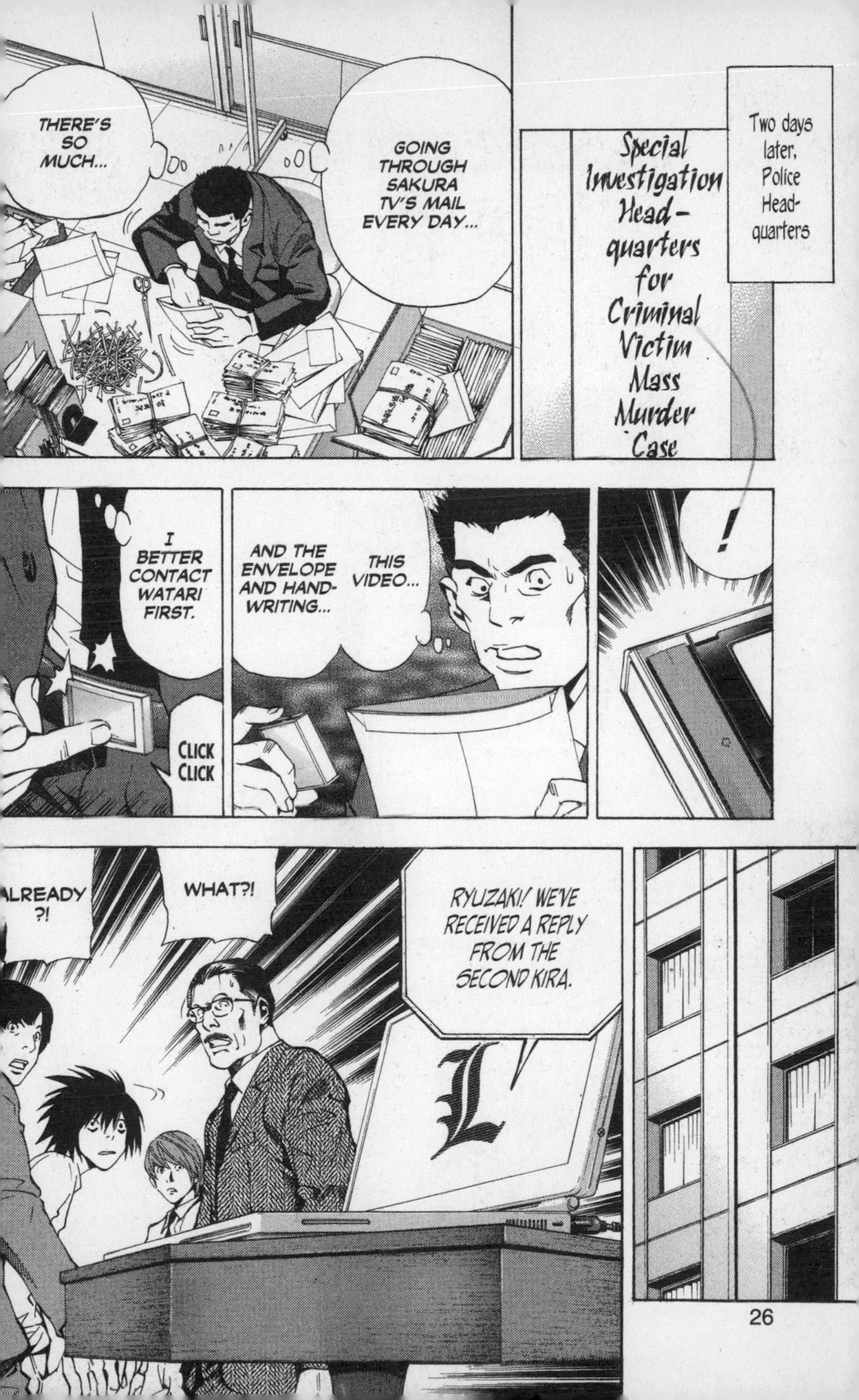

Two days later, Police Headquarters
Special Investigation Headquarters for Criminal Victim Mass Murder Case
GOING THROUGH SAKURA TV'S MAIL EVERY DAY...
THERE'S SO MUCH...
!
THIS VIDEO...
AND THE ENVELOPE AND HAND-WRITING...
I BETTER CONTACT WATARI FIRST.
CLICK CLICK
RYUZAKI! WE'VE RECEIVED A REPLY FROM THE SECOND KIRA.
L
WHAT?!
ALREADY ?!

READ THIS WAY

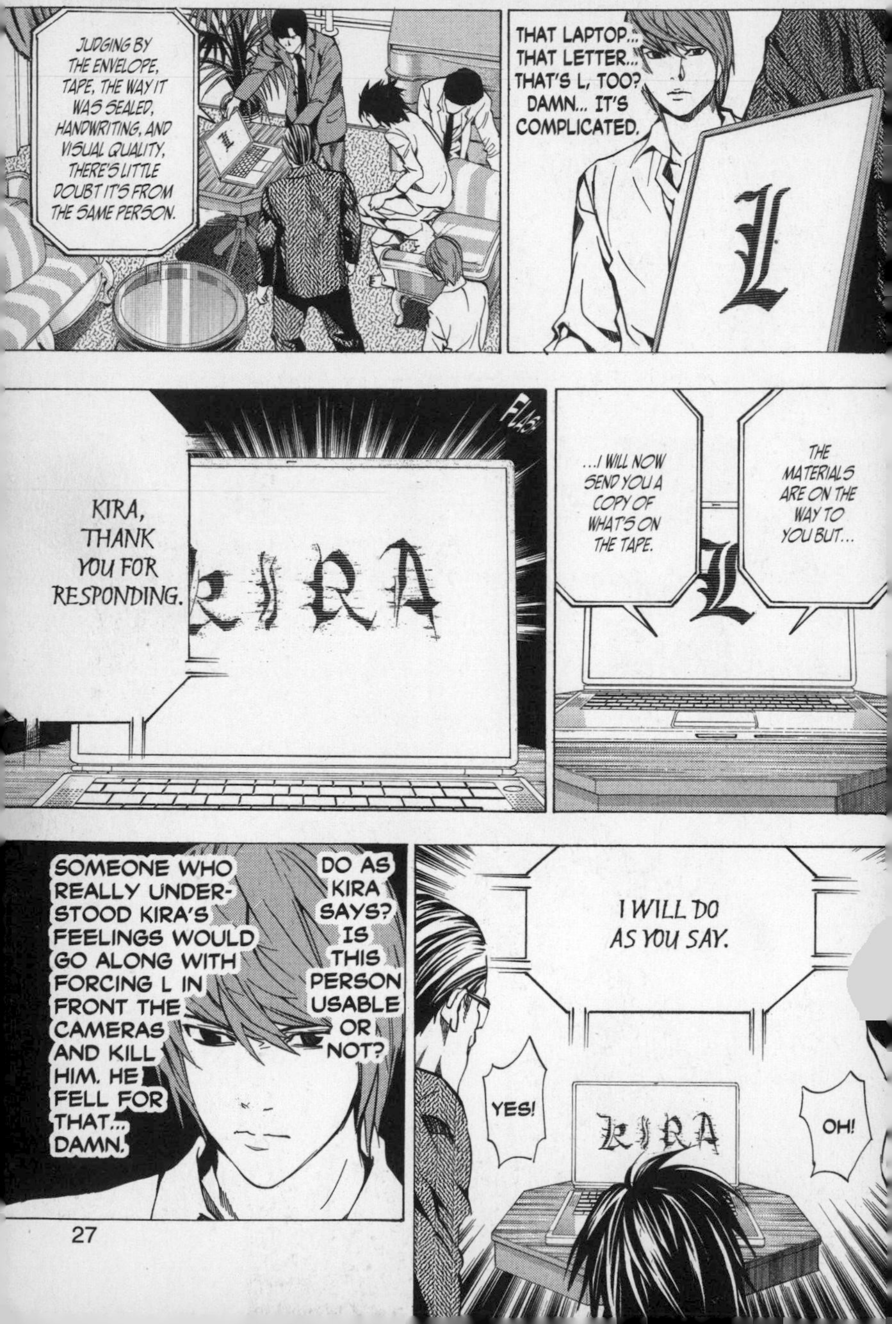
THAT LAPTOP... THAT LETTER... THAT'S L, TOO? DAMN... IT'S COMPLICATED.
L
JUDGING BY THE ENVELOPE, TAPE, THE WAY IT WAS SEALED, HANDWRITING, AND VISUAL QUALITY, THERE'S LITTLE DOUBT IT'S FROM THE SAME PERSON.
THE MATERIALS ARE ON THE WAY TO YOU BUT...
...I WILL NOW SEND YOU A COPY OF WHAT'S ON THE TAPE.
L
FLAS
KIRA, THANK YOU FOR RESPONDING.
KIRA
I WILL DO AS YOU SAY.
OH!
YES!
KIRA
DO AS KIRA SAYS? IS THIS PERSON USABLE OR NOT?
SOMEONE WHO REALLY UNDER-STOOD KIRA'S FEELINGS WOULD GO ALONG WITH FORCING L IN FRONT THE CAMERAS AND KILL HIM. HE FELL FOR THAT... DAMN.

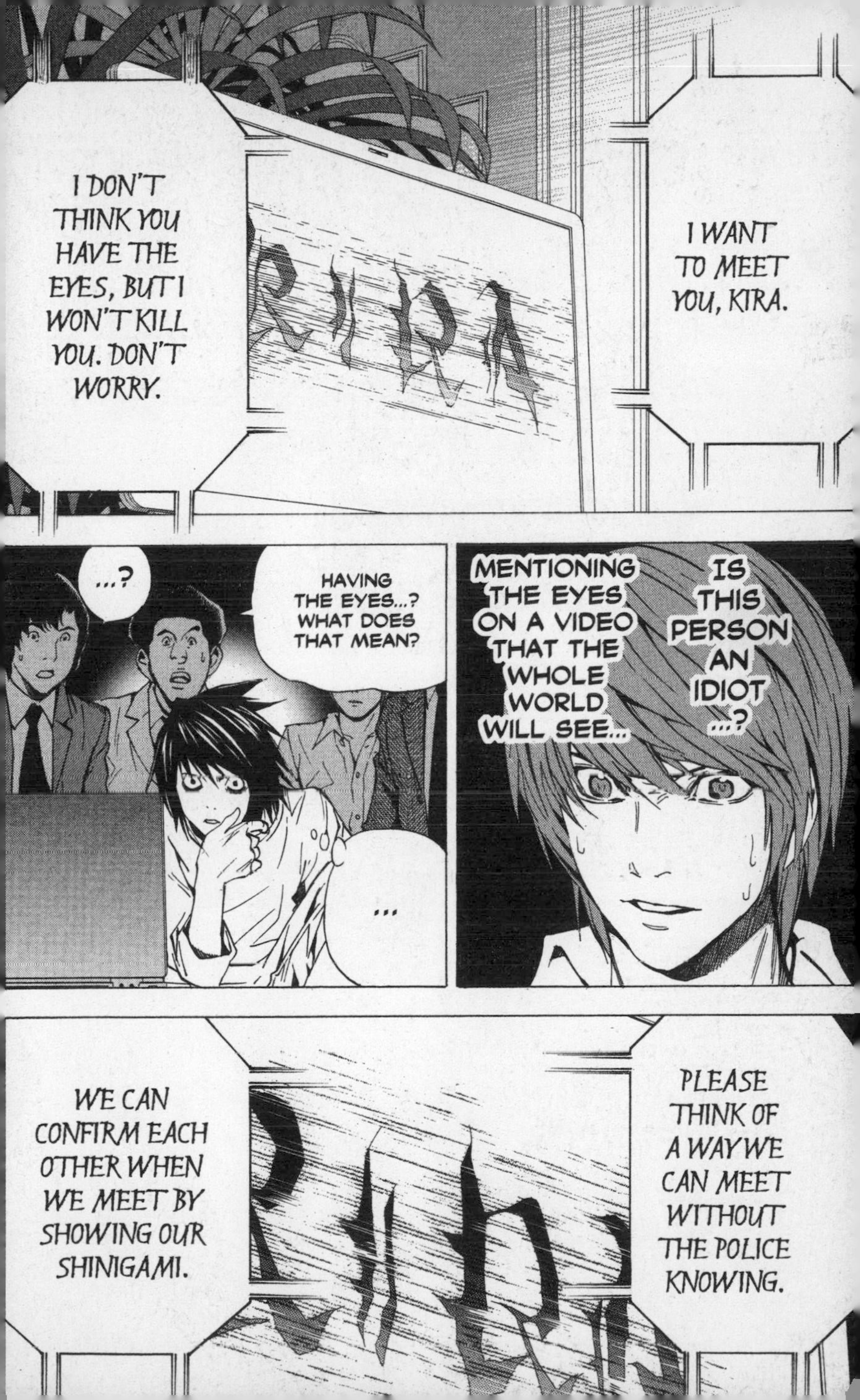
I WANT TO MEET YOU, KIRA.
KIRA
I DON'T THINK YOU HAVE THE EYES, BUT I WON'T KILL YOU. DON'T WORRY.
IS THIS PERSON AN IDIOT ...?
MENTIONING THE EYES ON A VIDEO THAT THE WHOLE WORLD WILL SEE...
HAVING THE EYES...? WHAT DOES THAT MEAN?
...?
...
PLEASE THINK OF A WAY WE CAN MEET WITHOUT THE POLICE KNOWING.
WE CAN CONFIRM EACH OTHER WHEN WE MEET BY SHOWING OUR SHINIGAMI.

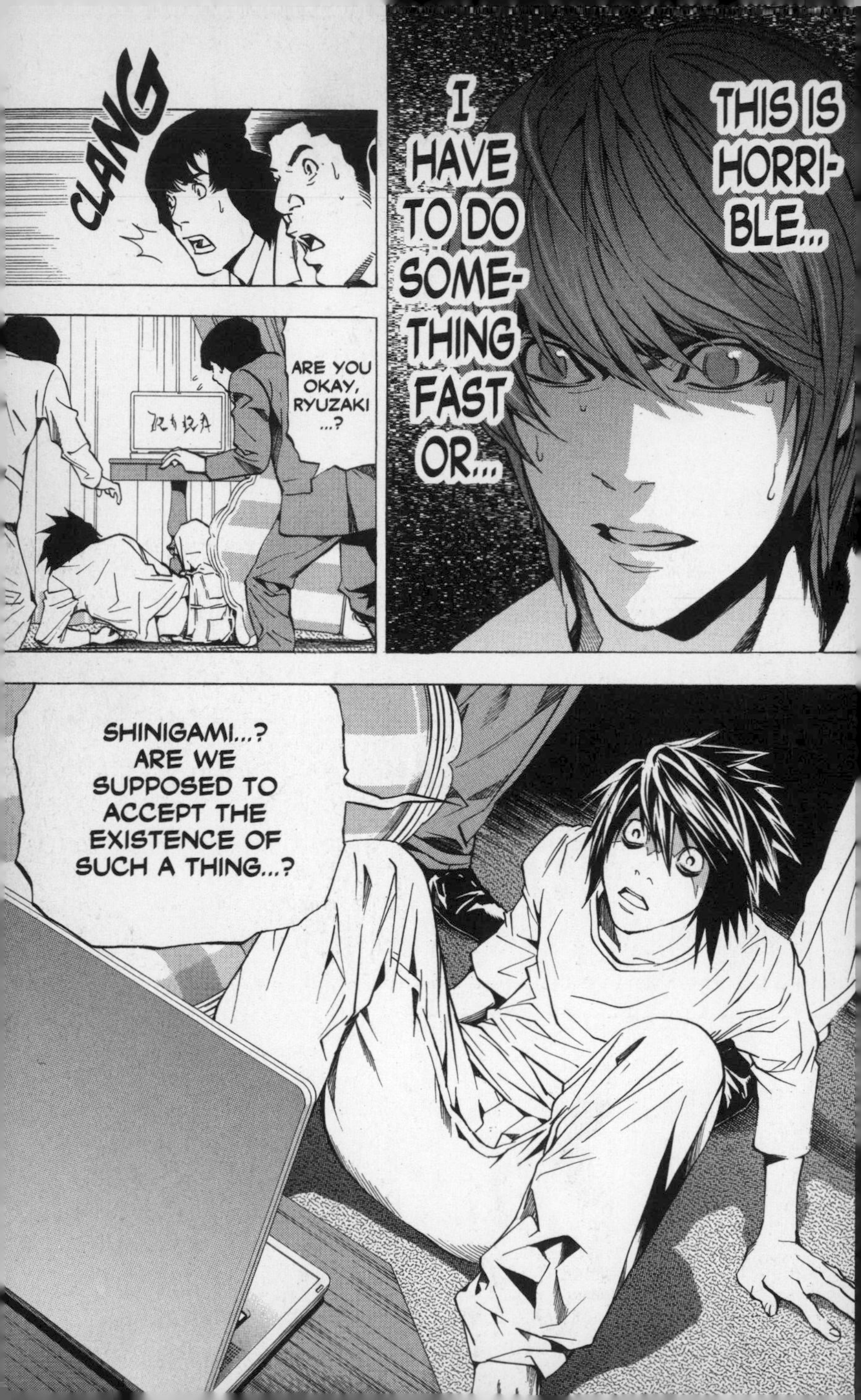
THIS IS HORRIBLE...
I HAVE TO DO SOMETHING FAST OR...
CLANG
ARE YOU OKAY, RYUZAKI ...?
SHINIGAMI...? ARE WE SUPPOSED TO ACCEPT THE EXISTENCE OF SUCH A THING...?

DEATH NOTE
How to use it

XVI

○ The god of death must at least own one DEATH NOTE.
that DEATH NOTE must never be lent to or written on
by a human.

死神は必ずデスノートを一冊は所有していなければならない。
その一冊は人間に譲渡できないし、人間に書き込ませる事も許されない。

○ Exchanging and writing on the DEATH NOTE
between the gods of death is no problem.

死神同士のデスノートの交換や他の死神のノートへの書き込みは、
なんら問題ない。

chapter 27 Love

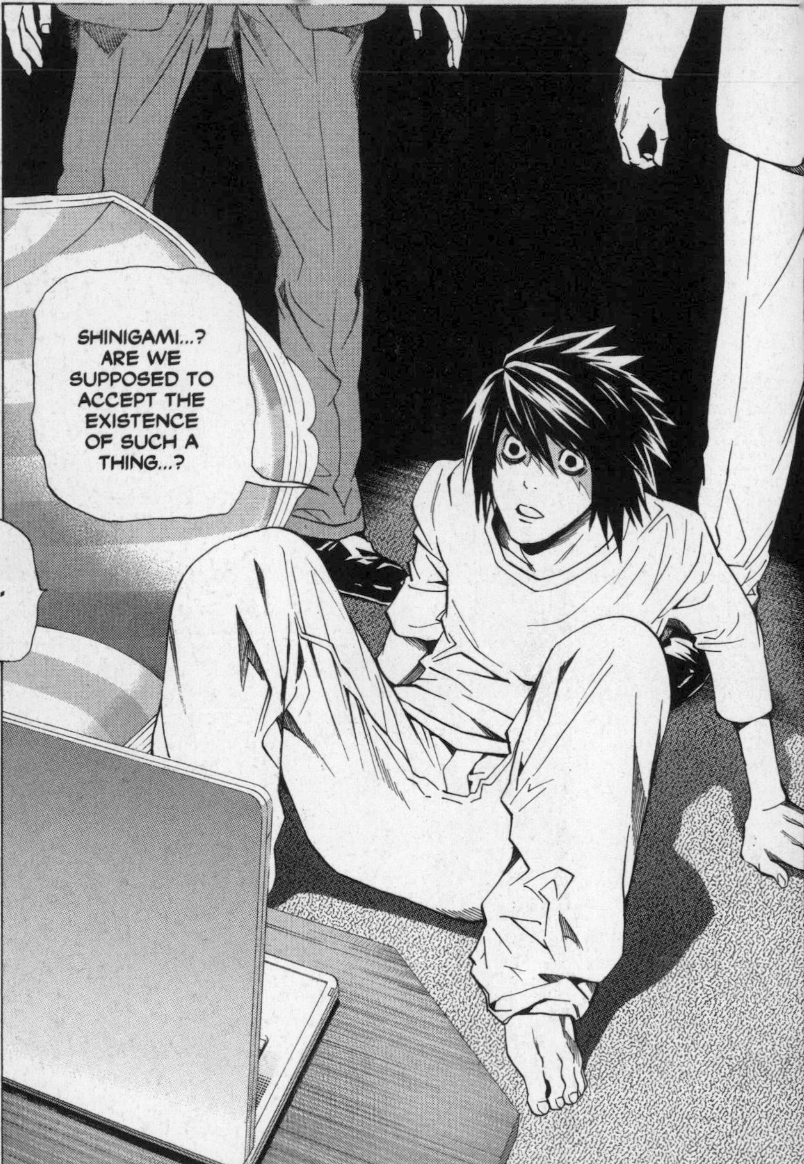
SHINIGAMI...? ARE WE SUPPOSED TO ACCEPT THE EXISTENCE OF SUCH A THING...?
...

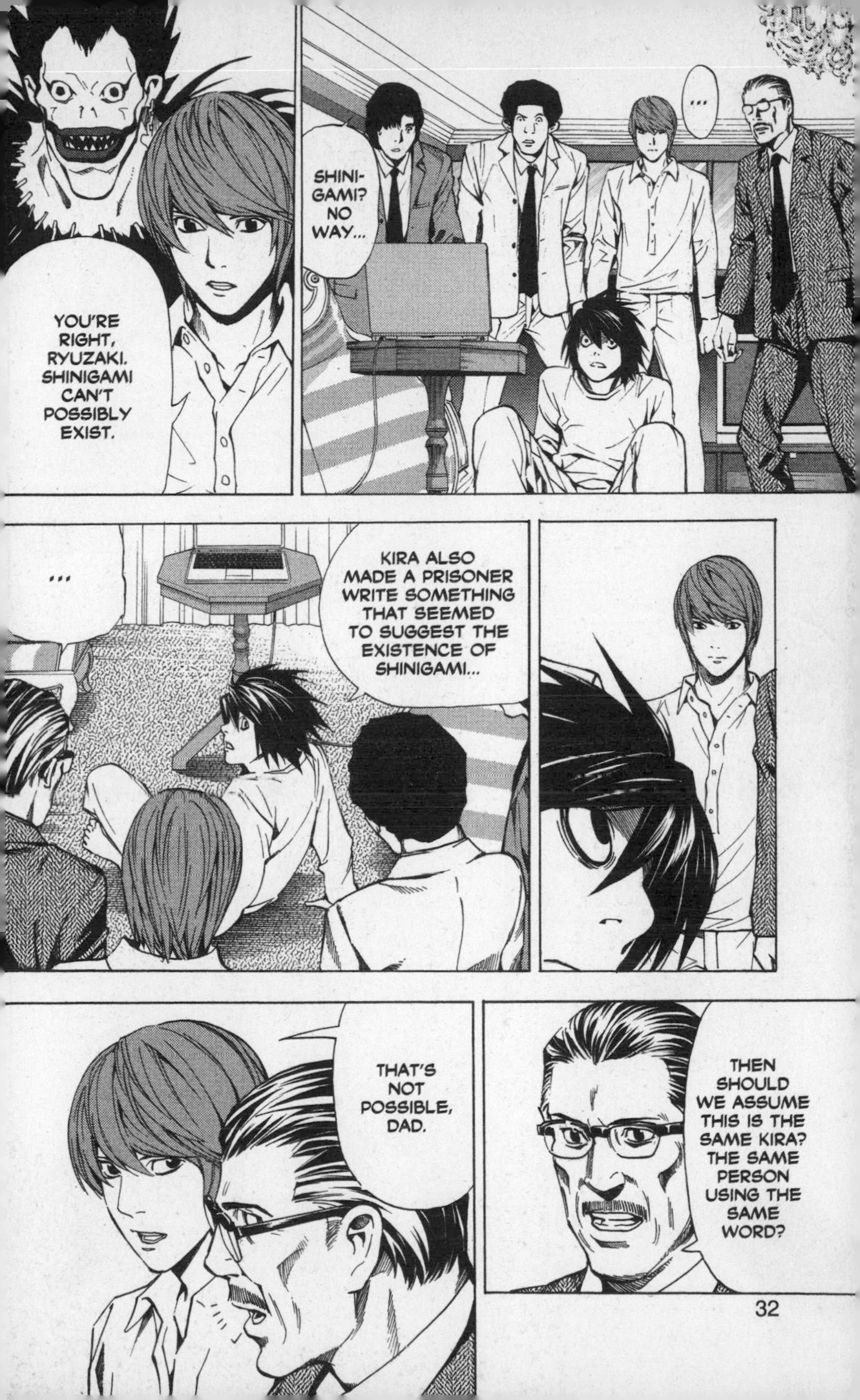
...
SHINIGAMI? NO WAY...
YOU'RE RIGHT, RYUZAKI. SHINIGAMI CAN'T POSSIBLY EXIST.
KIRA ALSO MADE A PRISONER WRITE SOMETHING THAT SEEMED TO SUGGEST THE EXISTENCE OF SHINIGAMI...
...
THEN SHOULD WE ASSUME THIS IS THE SAME KIRA? THE SAME PERSON USING THE SAME WORD?
THAT'S NOT POSSIBLE, DAD.

READ THIS WAY

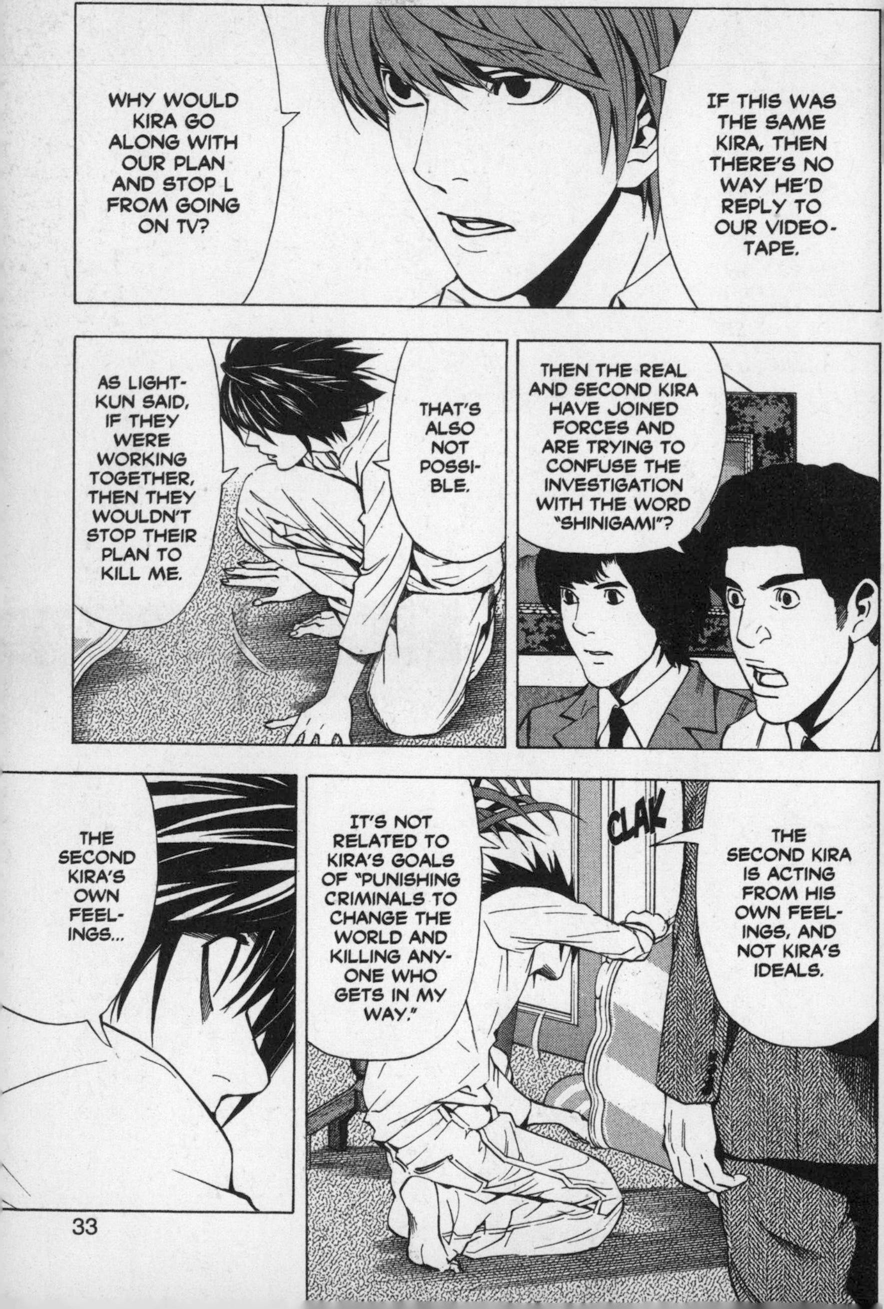
IF THIS WAS THE SAME KIRA, THEN THERE'S NO WAY HE'D REPLY TO OUR VIDEO-TAPE.
WHY WOULD KIRA GO ALONG WITH OUR PLAN AND STOP L FROM GOING ON TV?
THEN THE REAL AND SECOND KIRA HAVE JOINED FORCES AND ARE TRYING TO CONFUSE THE INVESTIGATION WITH THE WORD "SHINIGAMI"?
THAT'S ALSO NOT POSSI-BLE.
AS LIGHT-KUN SAID, IF THEY WERE WORKING TOGETHER, THEN THEY WOULDN'T STOP THEIR PLAN TO KILL ME.
THE SECOND KIRA IS ACTING FROM HIS OWN FEEL-INGS, AND NOT KIRA'S IDEALS.
CLAK
IT'S NOT RELATED TO KIRA'S GOALS OF "PUNISHING CRIMINALS TO CHANGE THE WORLD AND KILLING ANY-ONE WHO GETS IN MY WAY."
THE SECOND KIRA'S OWN FEEL-INGS...

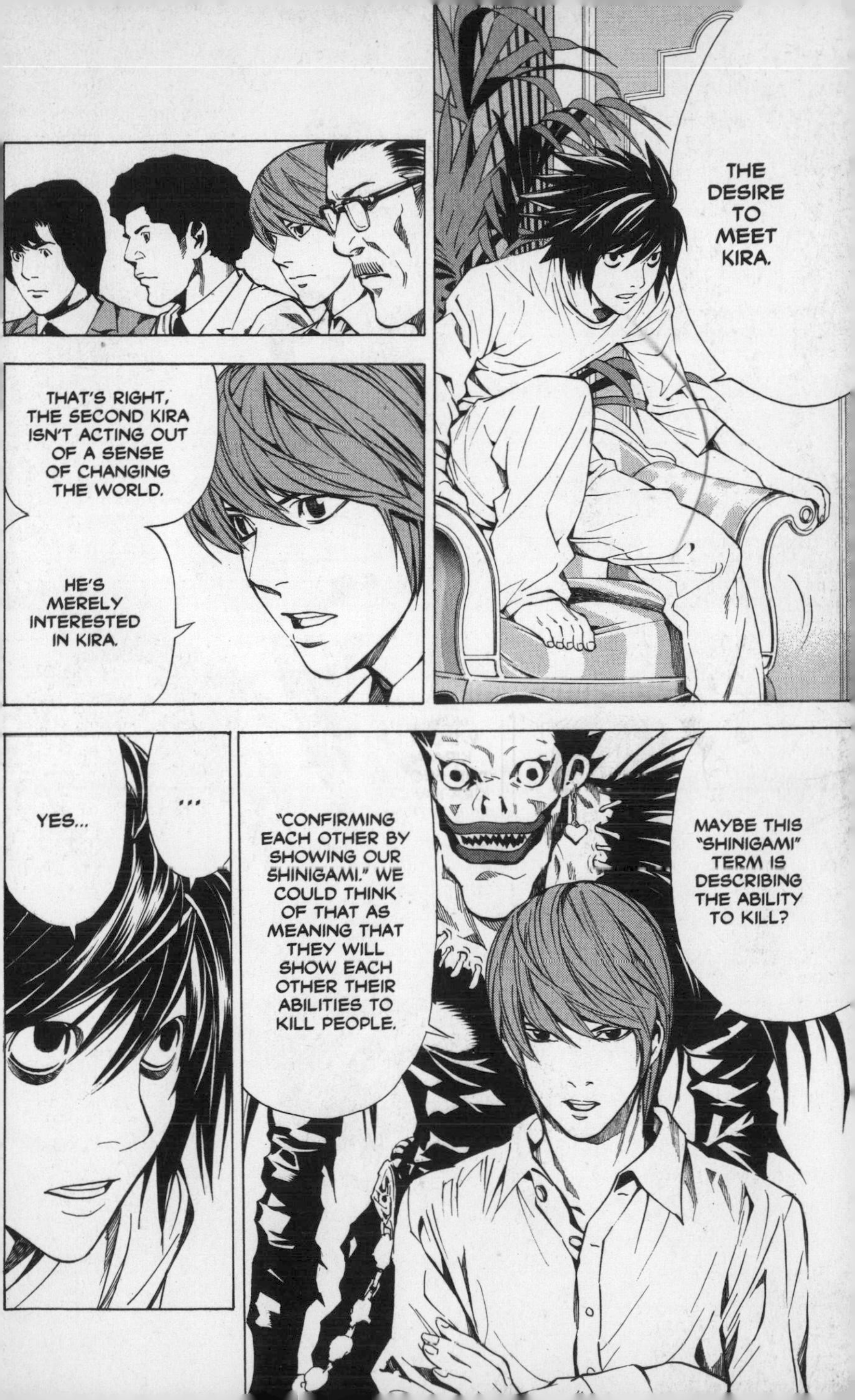
THE DESIRE TO MEET KIRA.
THAT'S RIGHT, THE SECOND KIRA ISN'T ACTING OUT OF A SENSE OF CHANGING THE WORLD.
HE'S MERELY INTERESTED IN KIRA.
MAYBE THIS "SHINIGAMI" TERM IS DESCRIBING THE ABILITY TO KILL?
"CONFIRMING EACH OTHER BY SHOWING OUR SHINIGAMI." WE COULD THINK OF THAT AS MEANING THAT THEY WILL SHOW EACH OTHER THEIR ABILITIES TO KILL PEOPLE.
...
YES...

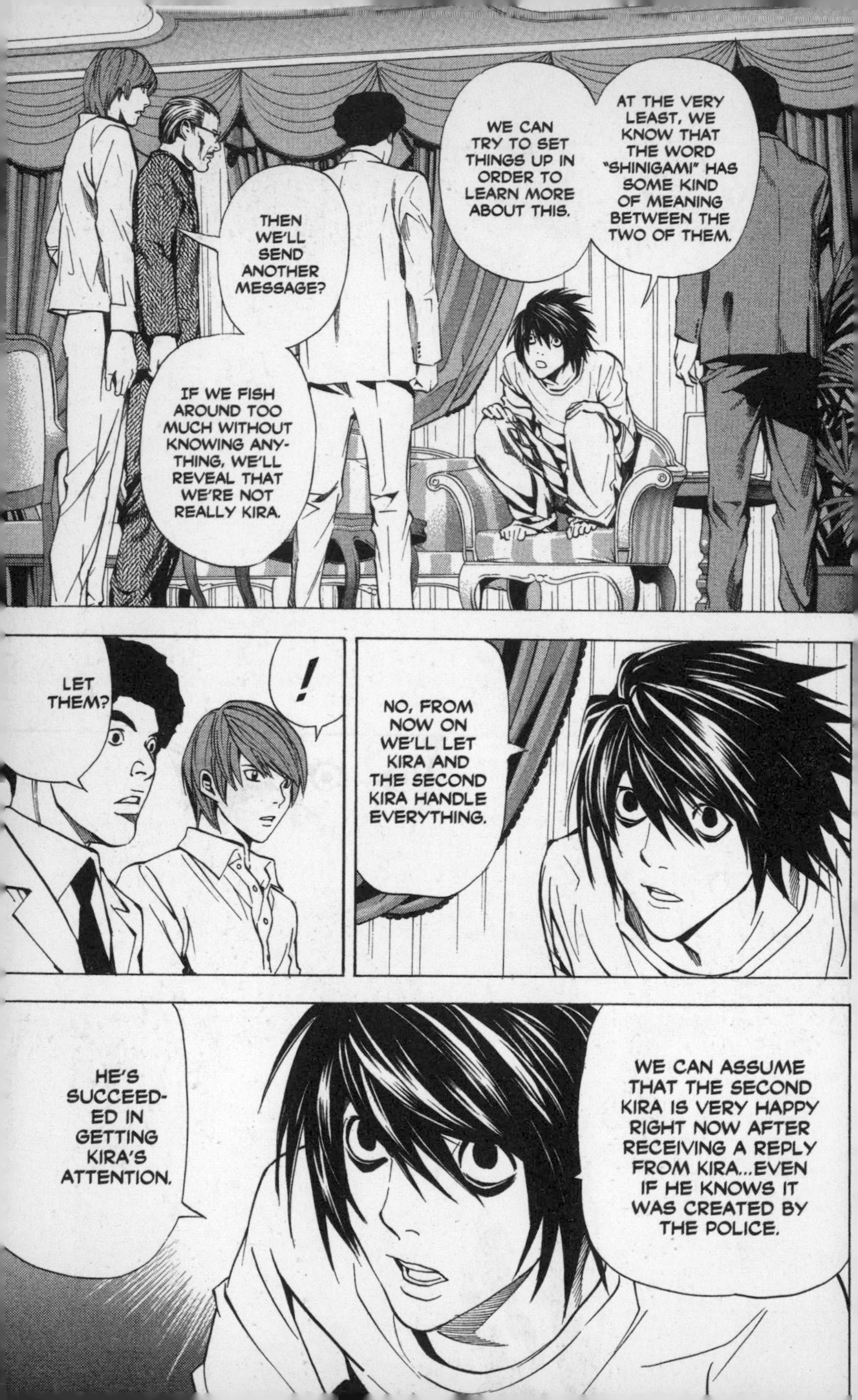
AT THE VERY LEAST, WE KNOW THAT THE WORD "SHINIGAMI" HAS SOME KIND OF MEANING BETWEEN THE TWO OF THEM.
WE CAN TRY TO SET THINGS UP IN ORDER TO LEARN MORE ABOUT THIS.
THEN WE'LL SEND ANOTHER MESSAGE?
IF WE FISH AROUND TOO MUCH WITHOUT KNOWING ANY-THING, WE'LL REVEAL THAT WE'RE NOT REALLY KIRA.
NO, FROM NOW ON WE'LL LET KIRA AND THE SECOND KIRA HANDLE EVERYTHING.
!
LET THEM?
WE CAN ASSUME THAT THE SECOND KIRA IS VERY HAPPY RIGHT NOW AFTER RECEIVING A REPLY FROM KIRA...EVEN IF HE KNOWS IT WAS CREATED BY THE POLICE.
HE'S SUCCEED-ED IN GETTING KIRA'S ATTENTION.

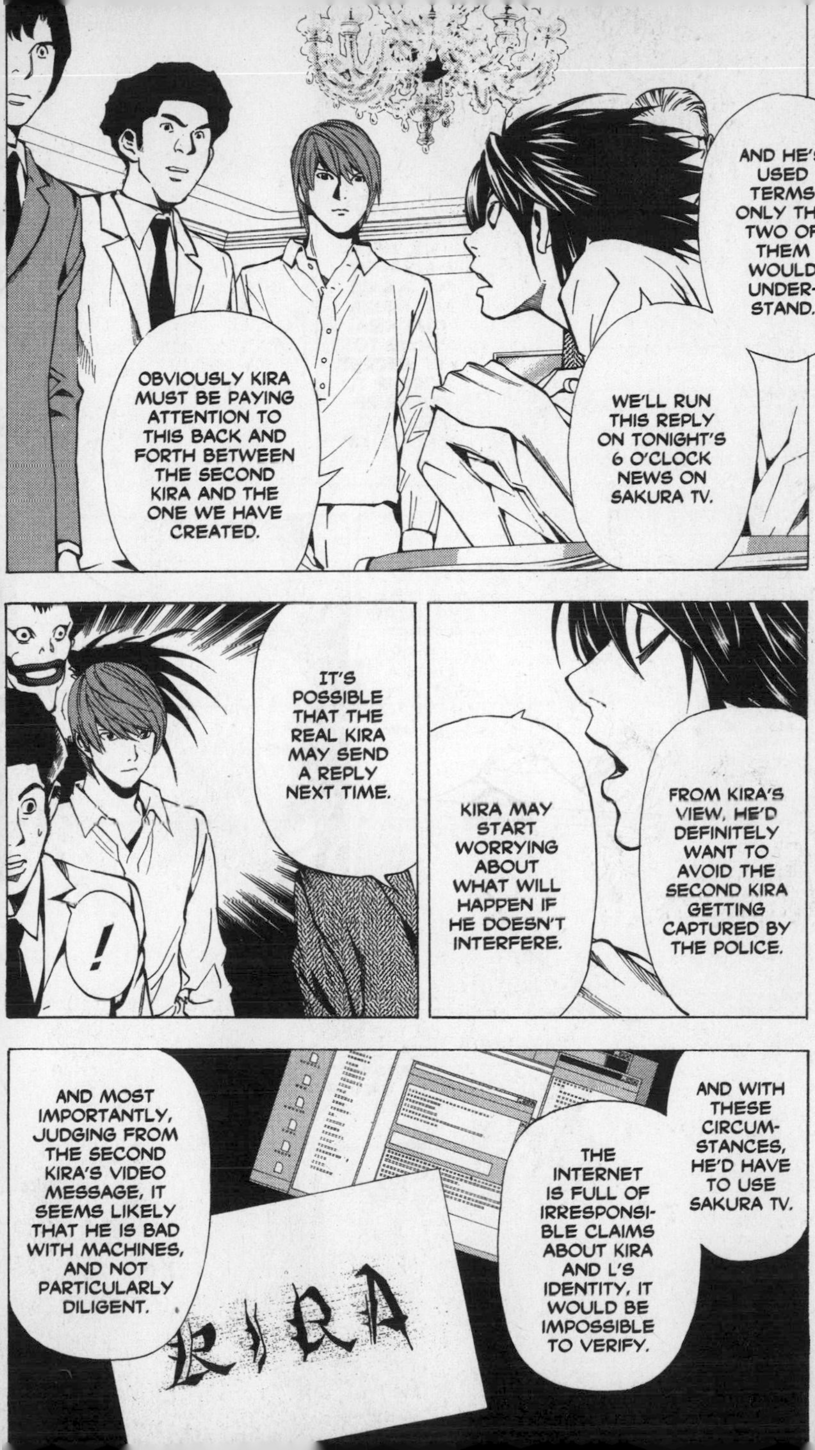
AND HE'S USED TERMS ONLY THE TWO OF THEM WOULD UNDERSTAND.
WE'LL RUN THIS REPLY ON TONIGHT'S 6 O'CLOCK NEWS ON SAKURA TV.
OBVIOUSLY KIRA MUST BE PAYING ATTENTION TO THIS BACK AND FORTH BETWEEN THE SECOND KIRA AND THE ONE WE HAVE CREATED.
FROM KIRA'S VIEW, HE'D DEFINITELY WANT TO AVOID THE SECOND KIRA GETTING CAPTURED BY THE POLICE.
KIRA MAY START WORRYING ABOUT WHAT WILL HAPPEN IF HE DOESN'T INTERFERE.
IT'S POSSIBLE THAT THE REAL KIRA MAY SEND A REPLY NEXT TIME.
!
AND WITH THESE CIRCUMSTANCES, HE'D HAVE TO USE SAKURA TV.
THE INTERNET IS FULL OF IRRESPONSIBLE CLAIMS ABOUT KIRA AND L'S IDENTITY, IT WOULD BE IMPOSSIBLE TO VERIFY.
AND MOST IMPORTANTLY, JUDGING FROM THE SECOND KIRA'S VIDEO MESSAGE, IT SEEMS LIKELY THAT HE IS BAD WITH MACHINES, AND NOT PARTICULARLY DILIGENT.
KIRA

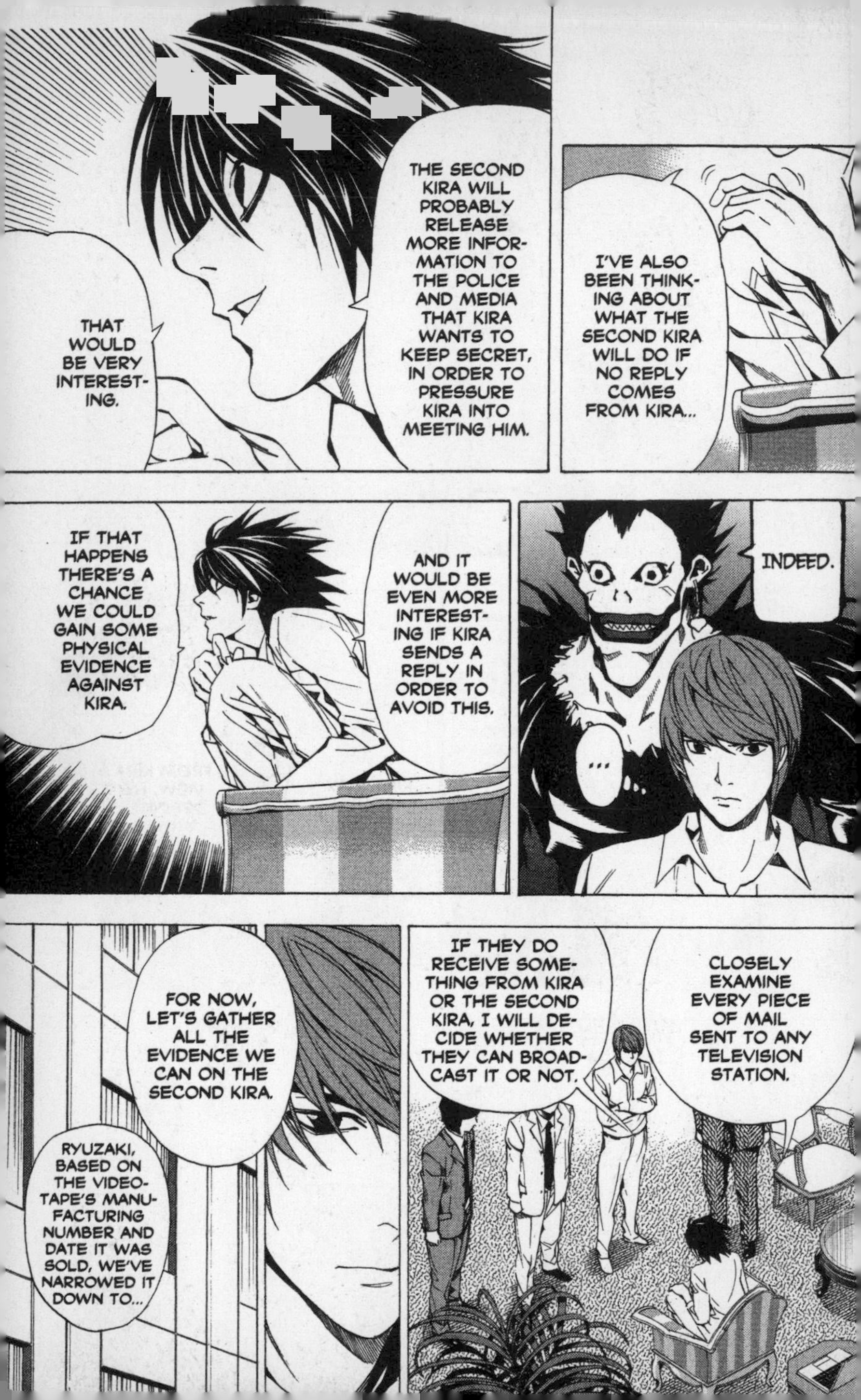
I'VE ALSO BEEN THINKING ABOUT WHAT THE SECOND KIRA WILL DO IF NO REPLY COMES FROM KIRA...
THE SECOND KIRA WILL PROBABLY RELEASE MORE INFORMATION TO THE POLICE AND MEDIA THAT KIRA WANTS TO KEEP SECRET, IN ORDER TO PRESSURE KIRA INTO MEETING HIM.
THAT WOULD BE VERY INTERESTING.
INDEED.
...
AND IT WOULD BE EVEN MORE INTERESTING IF KIRA SENDS A REPLY IN ORDER TO AVOID THIS.
IF THAT HAPPENS THERE'S A CHANCE WE COULD GAIN SOME PHYSICAL EVIDENCE AGAINST KIRA.
CLOSELY EXAMINE EVERY PIECE OF MAIL SENT TO ANY TELEVISION STATION.
IF THEY DO RECEIVE SOMETHING FROM KIRA OR THE SECOND KIRA, I WILL DECIDE WHETHER THEY CAN BROADCAST IT OR NOT.
FOR NOW, LET'S GATHER ALL THE EVIDENCE WE CAN ON THE SECOND KIRA.
RYUZAKI, BASED ON THE VIDEOTAPE'S MANUFACTURING NUMBER AND DATE IT WAS SOLD, WE'VE NARROWED IT DOWN TO...

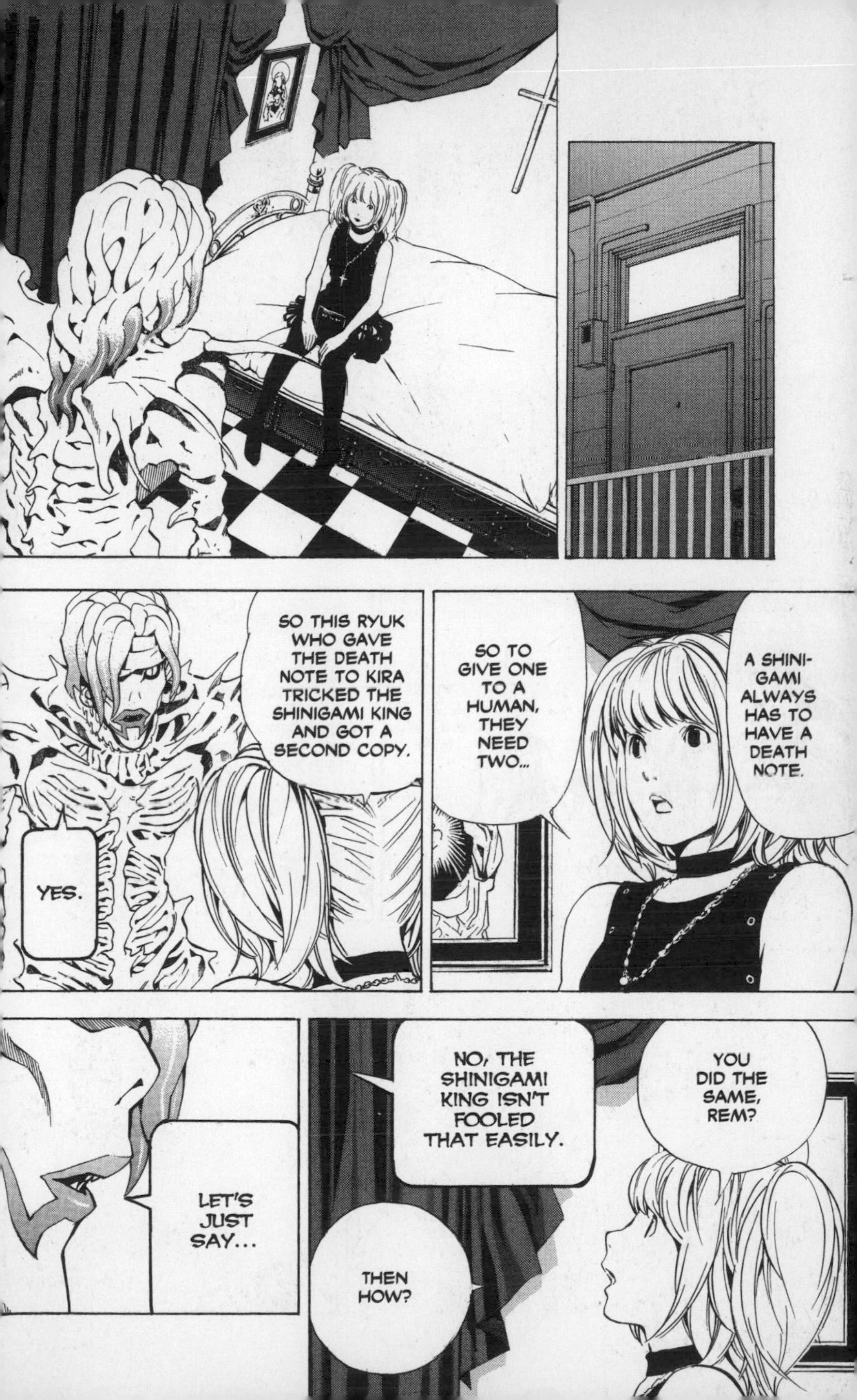
A SHINI-GAMI ALWAYS HAS TO HAVE A DEATH NOTE.
SO TO GIVE ONE TO A HUMAN, THEY NEED TWO...
SO THIS RYUK WHO GAVE THE DEATH NOTE TO KIRA TRICKED THE SHINIGAMI KING AND GOT A SECOND COPY.
YES.
YOU DID THE SAME, REM?
NO, THE SHINIGAMI KING ISN'T FOOLED THAT EASILY.
THEN HOW?
LET'S JUST SAY...

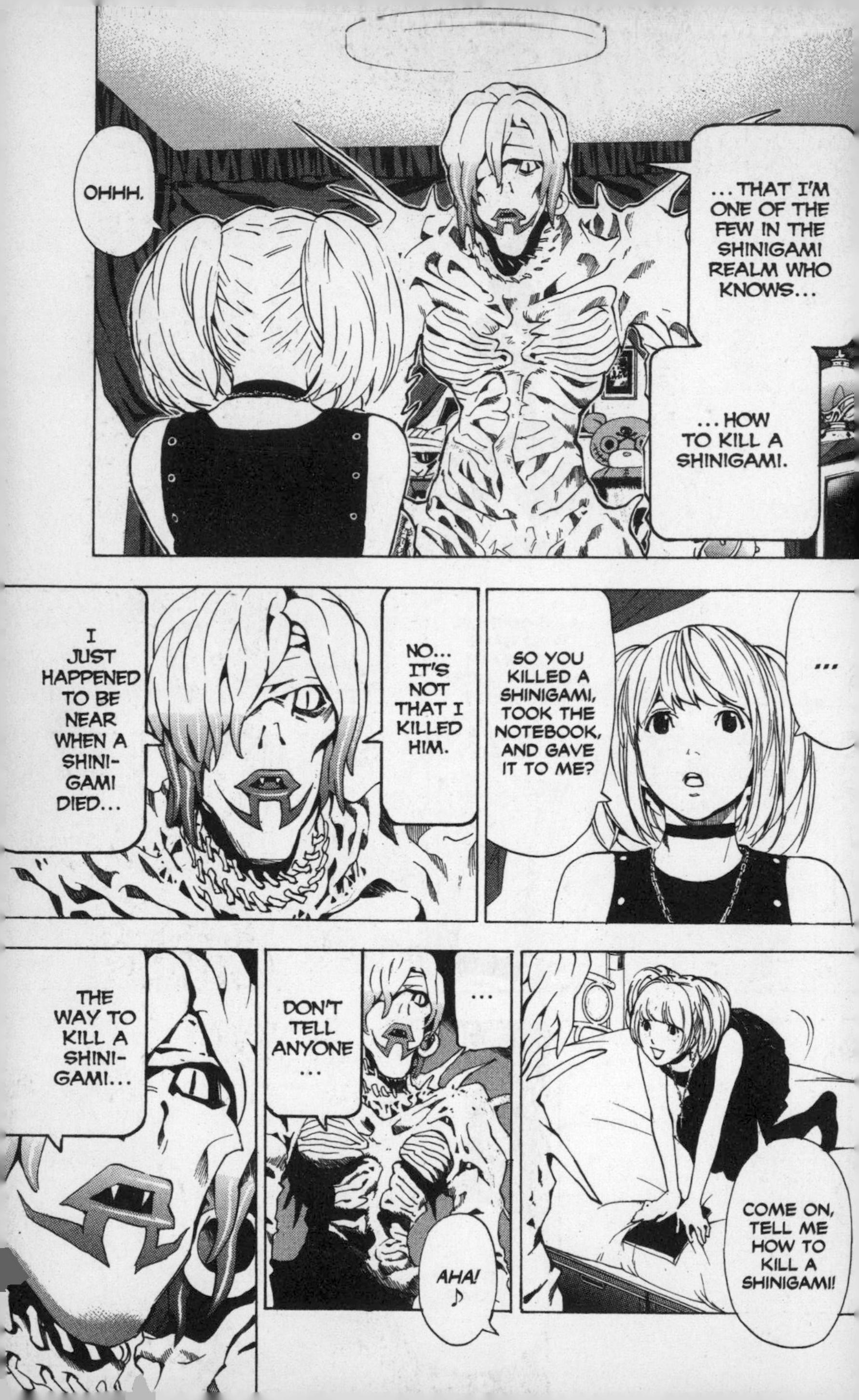
...THAT I'M ONE OF THE FEW IN THE SHINIGAMI REALM WHO KNOWS...
...HOW TO KILL A SHINIGAMI.
OHHH.
...
SO YOU KILLED A SHINIGAMI, TOOK THE NOTEBOOK, AND GAVE IT TO ME?
NO... IT'S NOT THAT I KILLED HIM.
I JUST HAPPENED TO BE NEAR WHEN A SHINI-GAMI DIED...
COME ON, TELL ME HOW TO KILL A SHINIGAMI!
...
DON'T TELL ANYONE ...
AHA! ♪
THE WAY TO KILL A SHINI-GAMI...

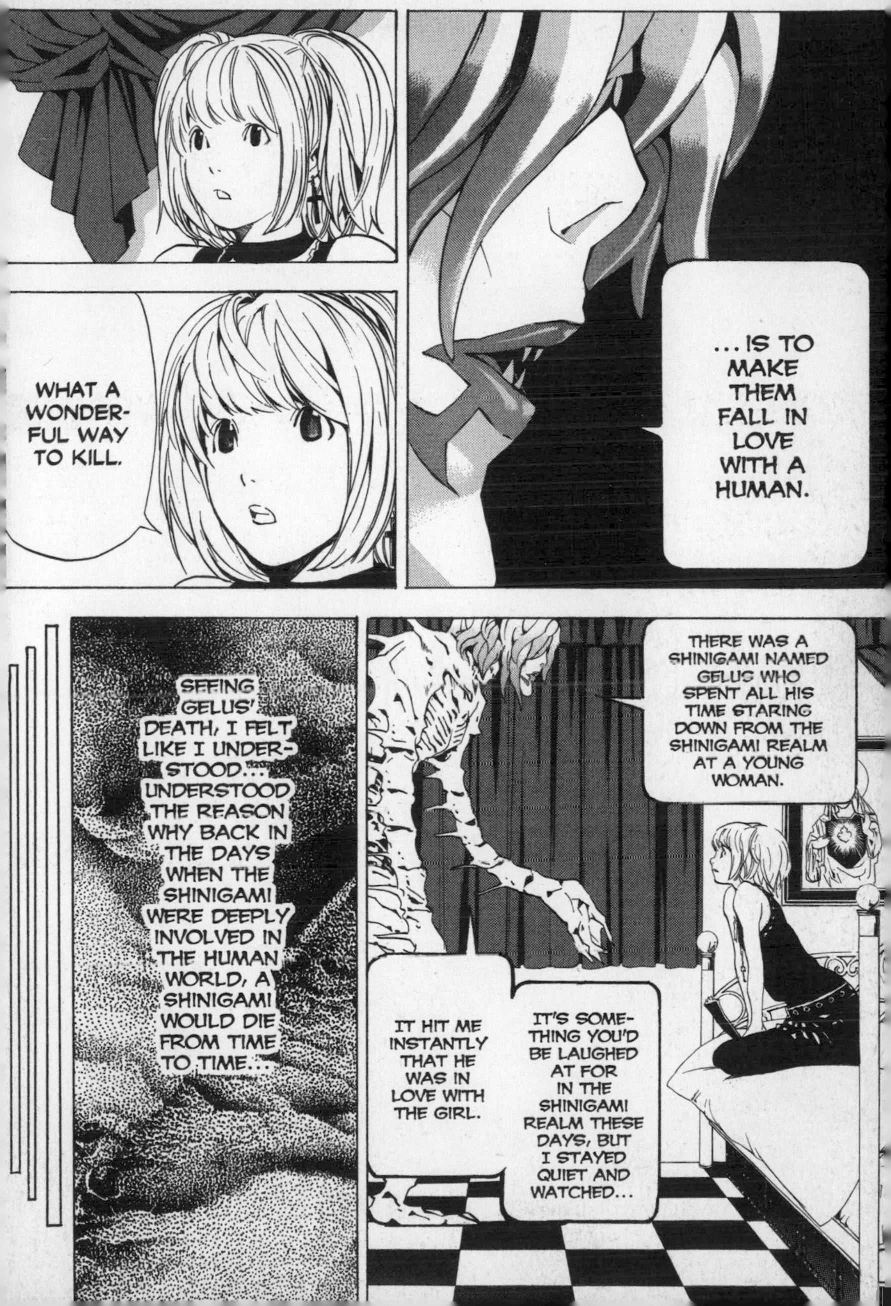
...IS TO MAKE THEM FALL IN LOVE WITH A HUMAN.
WHAT A WONDERFUL WAY TO KILL.
THERE WAS A SHINIGAMI NAMED GELUS WHO SPENT ALL HIS TIME STARING DOWN FROM THE SHINIGAMI REALM AT A YOUNG WOMAN.
IT'S SOMETHING YOU'D BE LAUGHED AT FOR IN THE SHINIGAMI REALM THESE DAYS, BUT I STAYED QUIET AND WATCHED...
IT HIT ME INSTANTLY THAT HE WAS IN LOVE WITH THE GIRL.
SEEING GELUS' DEATH, I FELT LIKE I UNDERSTOOD... UNDERSTOOD THE REASON WHY BACK IN THE DAYS WHEN THE SHINIGAMI WERE DEEPLY INVOLVED IN THE HUMAN WORLD, A SHINIGAMI WOULD DIE FROM TIME TO TIME...

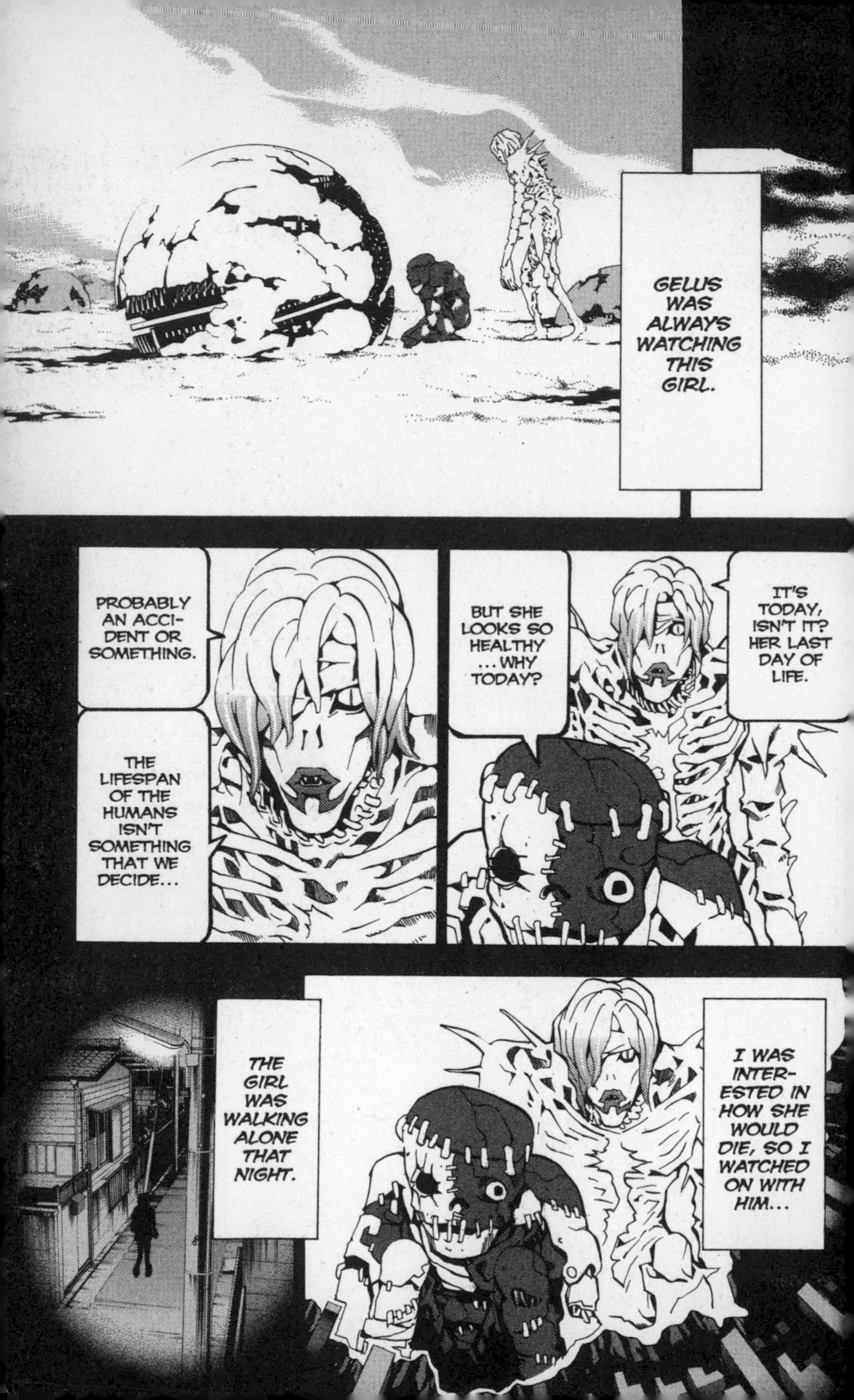
GELUS WAS ALWAYS WATCHING THIS GIRL.
IT'S TODAY, ISN'T IT? HER LAST DAY OF LIFE.
BUT SHE LOOKS SO HEALTHY ...WHY TODAY?
PROBABLY AN ACCI-DENT OR SOMETHING.
THE LIFESPAN OF THE HUMANS ISN'T SOMETHING THAT WE DECIDE...
I WAS INTER-ESTED IN HOW SHE WOULD DIE, SO I WATCHED ON WITH HIM...
THE GIRL WAS WALKING ALONE THAT NIGHT.

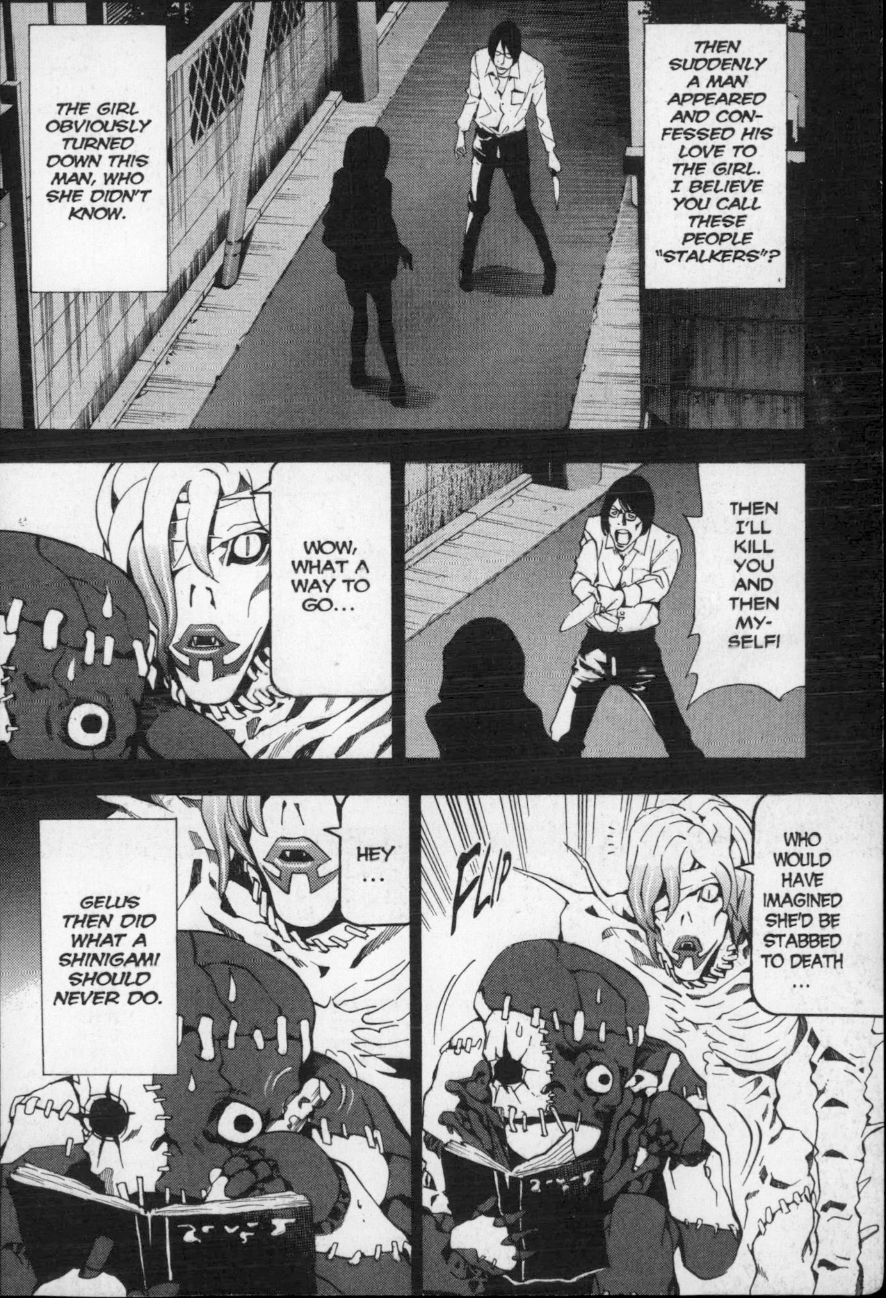
THEN SUDDENLY A MAN APPEARED AND CONFESSED HIS LOVE TO THE GIRL. I BELIEVE YOU CALL THESE PEOPLE "STALKERS"?
THE GIRL OBVIOUSLY TURNED DOWN THIS MAN, WHO SHE DIDN'T KNOW.
THEN I'LL KILL YOU AND THEN MYSELF!
WOW, WHAT A WAY TO GO...
WHO WOULD HAVE IMAGINED SHE'D BE STABBED TO DEATH...
FLIP
HEY...
GELUS THEN DID WHAT A SHINIGAMI SHOULD NEVER DO.

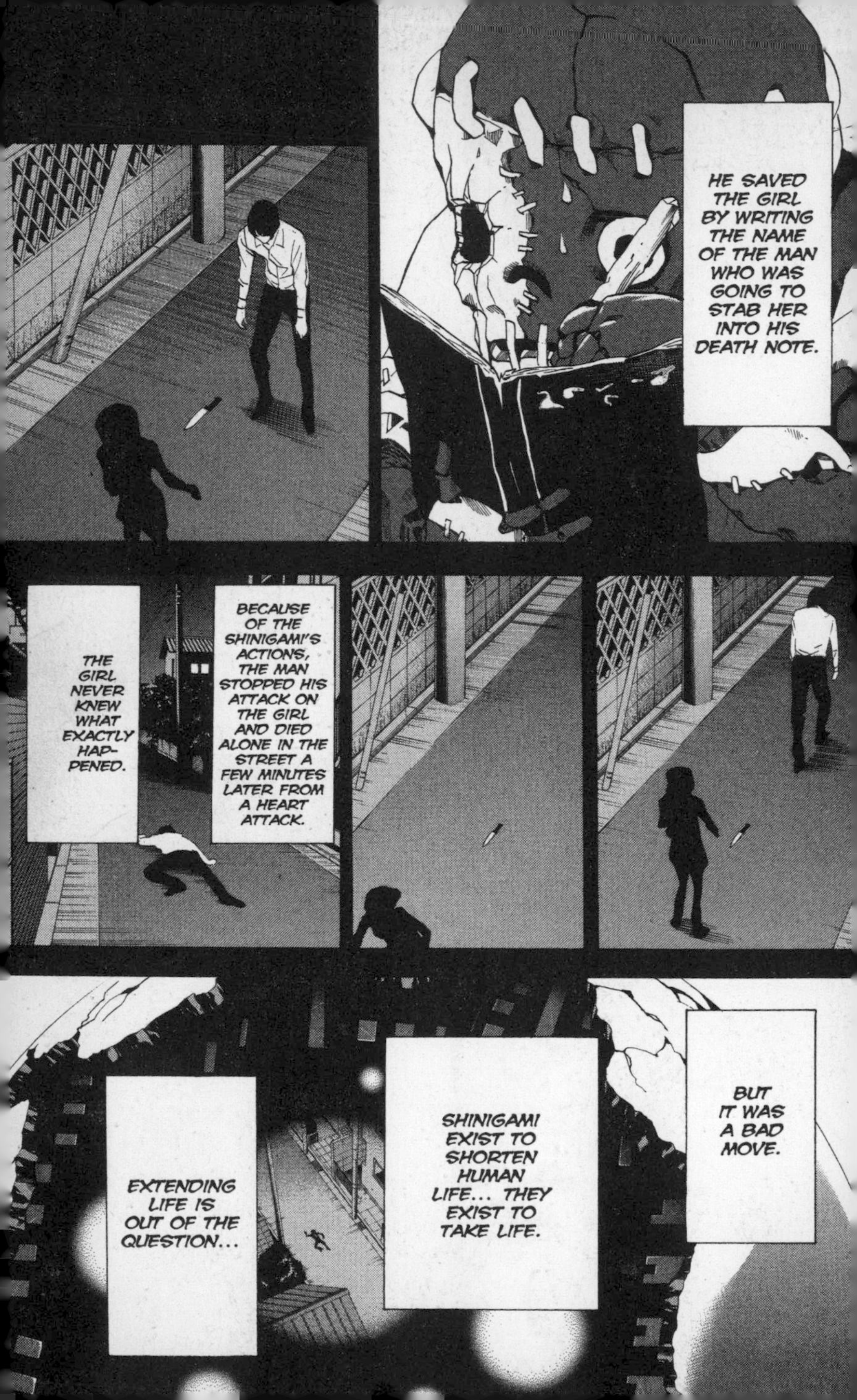
HE SAVED THE GIRL BY WRITING THE NAME OF THE MAN WHO WAS GOING TO STAB HER INTO HIS DEATH NOTE.
BECAUSE OF THE SHINIGAMI'S ACTIONS, THE MAN STOPPED HIS ATTACK ON THE GIRL AND DIED ALONE IN THE STREET A FEW MINUTES LATER FROM A HEART ATTACK.
THE GIRL NEVER KNEW WHAT EXACTLY HAP-PENED.
BUT IT WAS A BAD MOVE.
SHINIGAMI EXIST TO SHORTEN HUMAN LIFE... THEY EXIST TO TAKE LIFE.
EXTENDING LIFE IS OUT OF THE QUESTION...

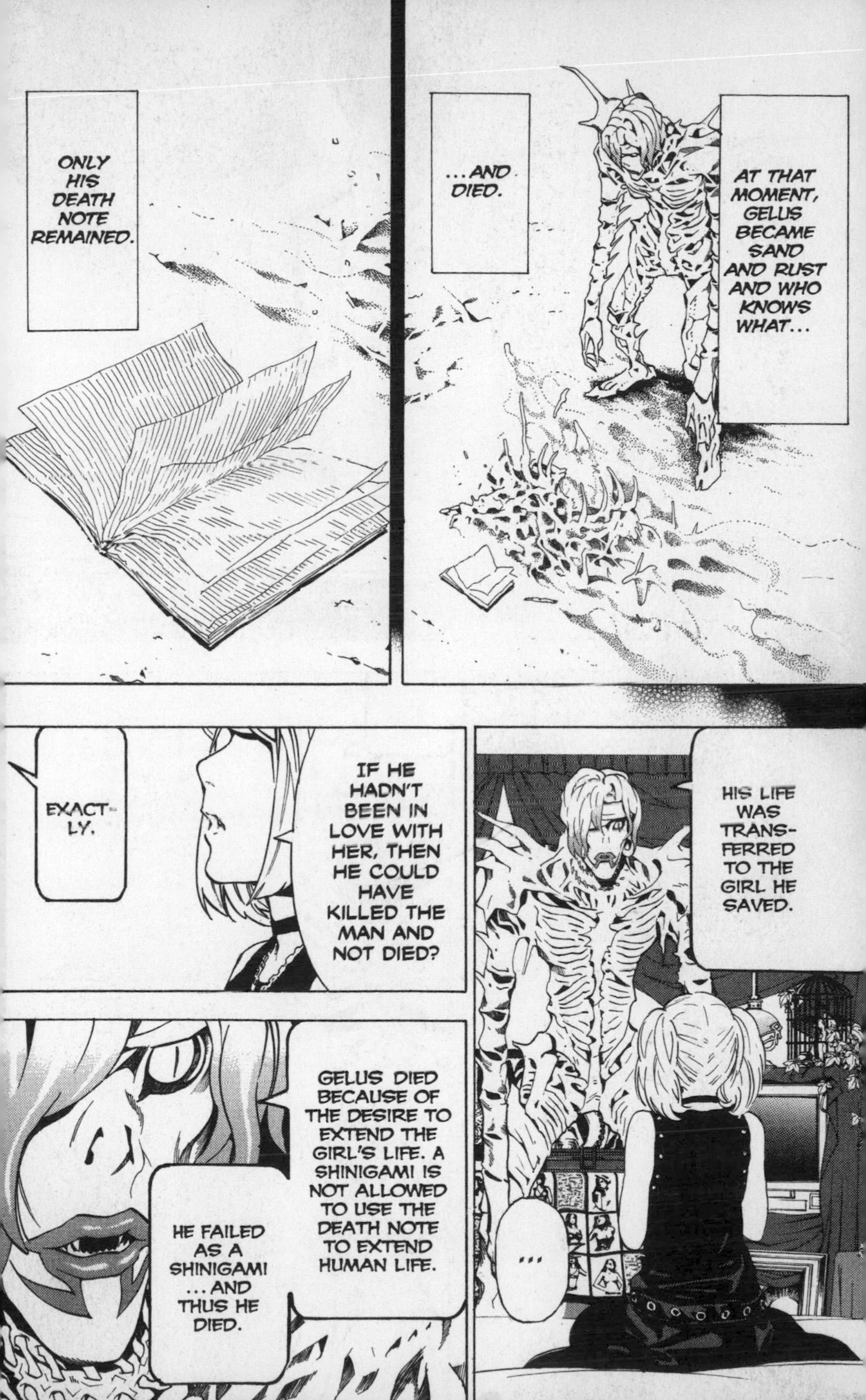
AT THAT MOMENT, GELUS BECAME SAND AND RUST AND WHO KNOWS WHAT...
...AND DIED.
ONLY HIS DEATH NOTE REMAINED.
HIS LIFE WAS TRANS-FERRED TO THE GIRL HE SAVED.
...
IF HE HADN'T BEEN IN LOVE WITH HER, THEN HE COULD HAVE KILLED THE MAN AND NOT DIED?
EXACT-LY.
GELUS DIED BECAUSE OF THE DESIRE TO EXTEND THE GIRL'S LIFE. A SHINIGAMI IS NOT ALLOWED TO USE THE DEATH NOTE TO EXTEND HUMAN LIFE.
HE FAILED AS A SHINIGAMI ...AND THUS HE DIED.

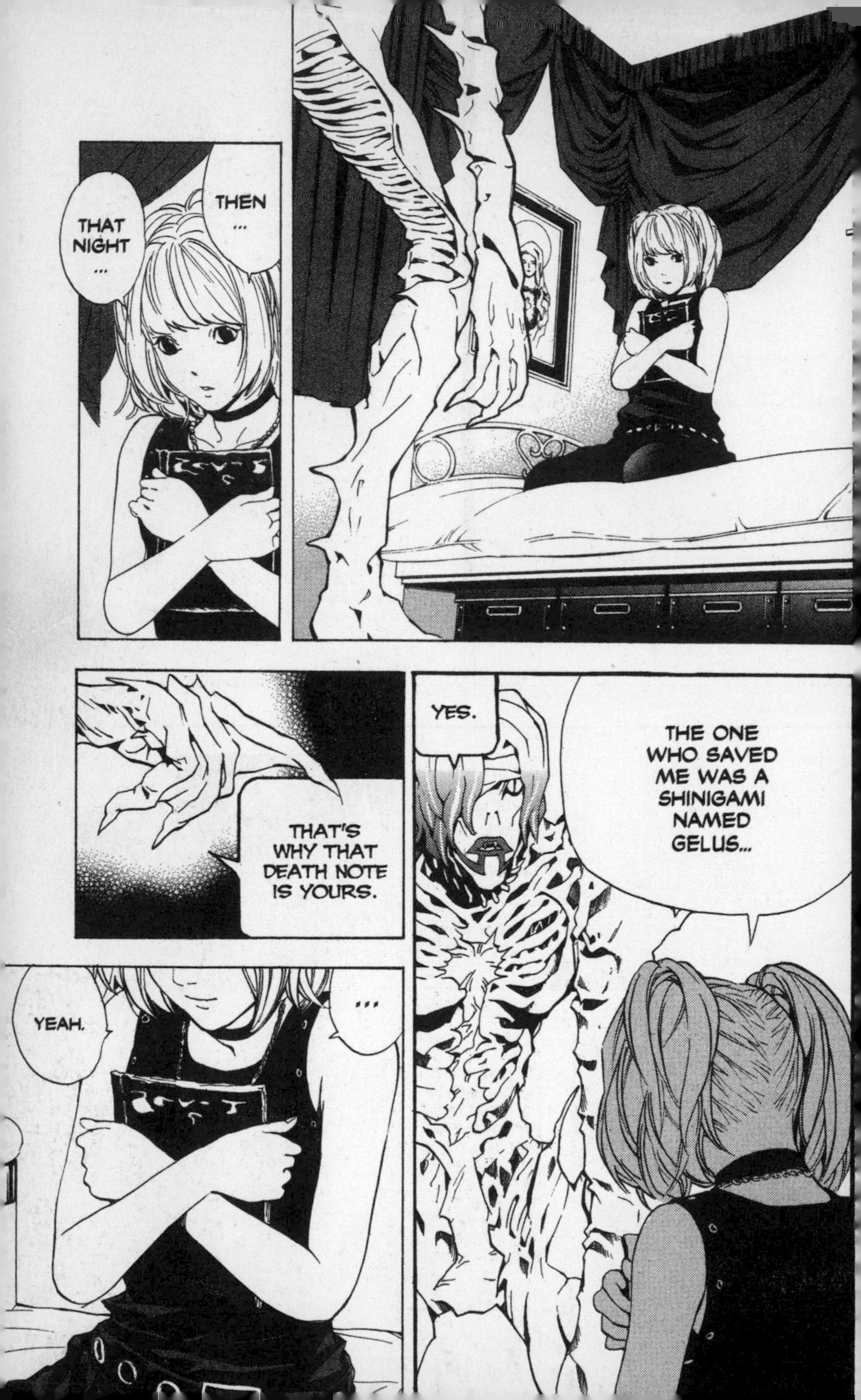
THEN ...
THAT NIGHT ...
THE ONE WHO SAVED ME WAS A SHINIGAMI NAMED GELUS...
YES.
THAT'S WHY THAT DEATH NOTE IS YOURS.
...
YEAH.

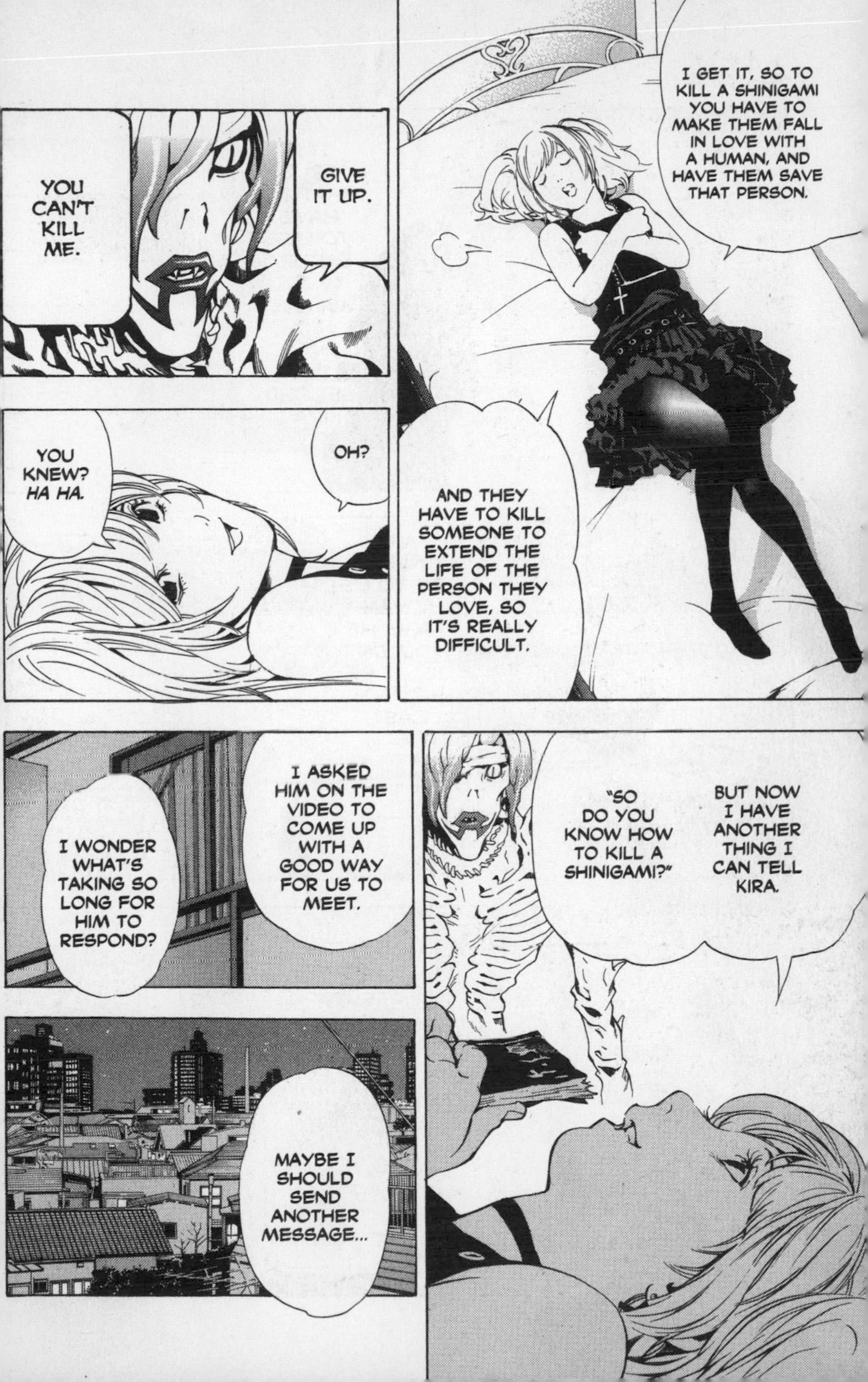
I GET IT, SO TO KILL A SHINIGAMI YOU HAVE TO MAKE THEM FALL IN LOVE WITH A HUMAN, AND HAVE THEM SAVE THAT PERSON.
AND THEY HAVE TO KILL SOMEONE TO EXTEND THE LIFE OF THE PERSON THEY LOVE, SO IT'S REALLY DIFFICULT.
GIVE IT UP.
YOU CAN'T KILL ME.
OH?
YOU KNEW? *HA HA.*
BUT NOW I HAVE ANOTHER THING I CAN TELL KIRA.
"SO DO YOU KNOW HOW TO KILL A SHINIGAMI?"
I ASKED HIM ON THE VIDEO TO COME UP WITH A GOOD WAY FOR US TO MEET.
I WONDER WHAT'S TAKING SO LONG FOR HIM TO RESPOND?
MAYBE I SHOULD SEND ANOTHER MESSAGE...

READ THIS WAY

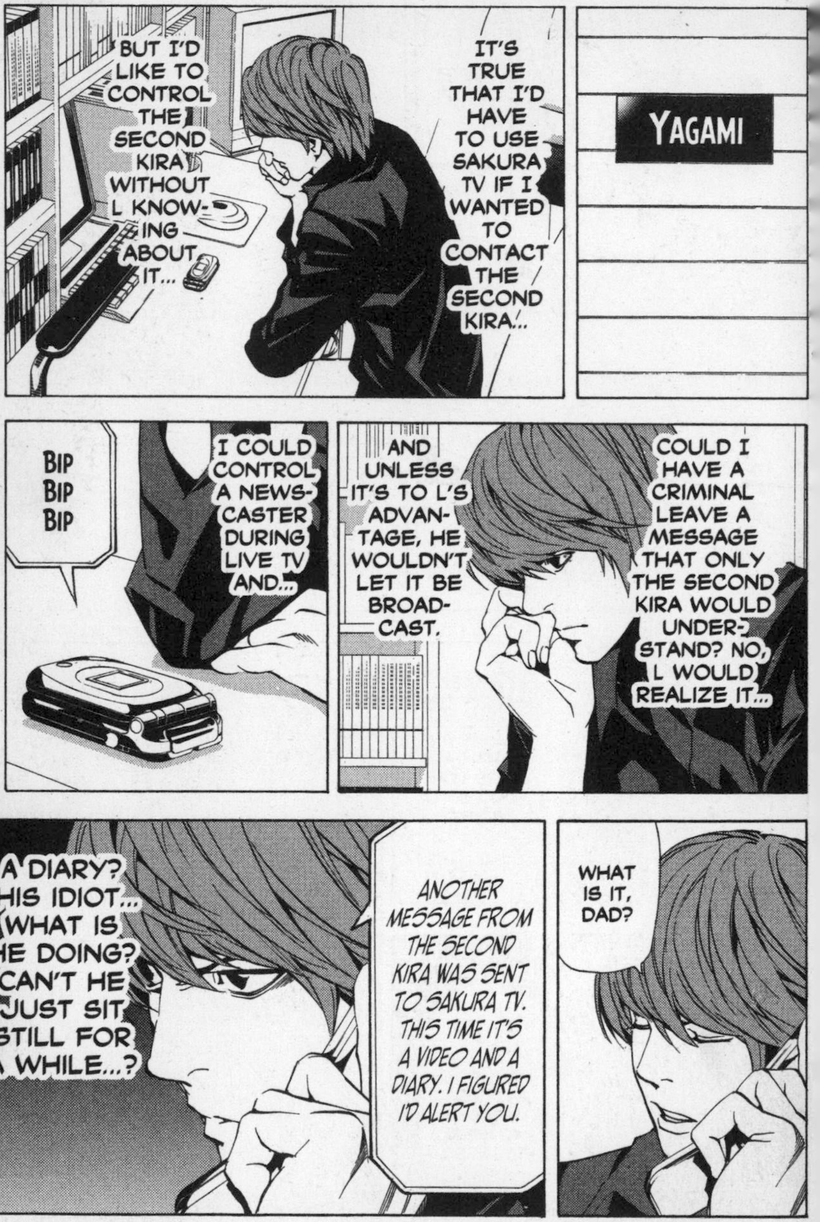
YAGAMI
IT'S TRUE THAT I'D HAVE TO USE SAKURA TV IF I WANTED TO CONTACT THE SECOND KIRA...
BUT I'D LIKE TO CONTROL THE SECOND KIRA WITHOUT L KNOWING ABOUT IT...
COULD I HAVE A CRIMINAL LEAVE A MESSAGE THAT ONLY THE SECOND KIRA WOULD UNDERSTAND? NO, L WOULD REALIZE IT...
AND UNLESS IT'S TO L'S ADVANTAGE, HE WOULDN'T LET IT BE BROADCAST.
I COULD CONTROL A NEWSCASTER DURING LIVE TV AND...
BIP BIP BIP
WHAT IS IT, DAD?
ANOTHER MESSAGE FROM THE SECOND KIRA WAS SENT TO SAKURA TV. THIS TIME IT'S A VIDEO AND A DIARY. I FIGURED I'D ALERT YOU.
A DIARY? THIS IDIOT... WHAT IS HE DOING? CAN'T HE JUST SIT STILL FOR A WHILE...?

May 2003

1st I said I wouldn't be participating in club activities during Golden Week but my friend called and invited me anyway.

4th I went to the Saitama Super Arena with a friend to see the Morning Musume concert.

5th It was the last day of vacation but I just sat around the house being lazy.

7th School has started but I just borrowed my friend's notes and skipped class.

10th My friend invited me to go drinking but I declined. Yokohama is too far.

13th The friend I promised to lend a CD to came by so I let her borrow it.

16th I forgot to do my report so I copied it off my friend.

19th I bought Jump for the first time in a while. The short story was really good.

22nd My friend and I showed off our notebooks in Aoyama.

23rd I ran into **HIM** in the cafeteria. He was eating pork curry rice.

24th I met a friend in Shibuya. We bought some clothes to wear this summer.

28th I heard they're coming out with something better than the PS2 called the PSX. WOW!

30th We confirmed our Shinigami at the Giants game at the Tokyo Dome.

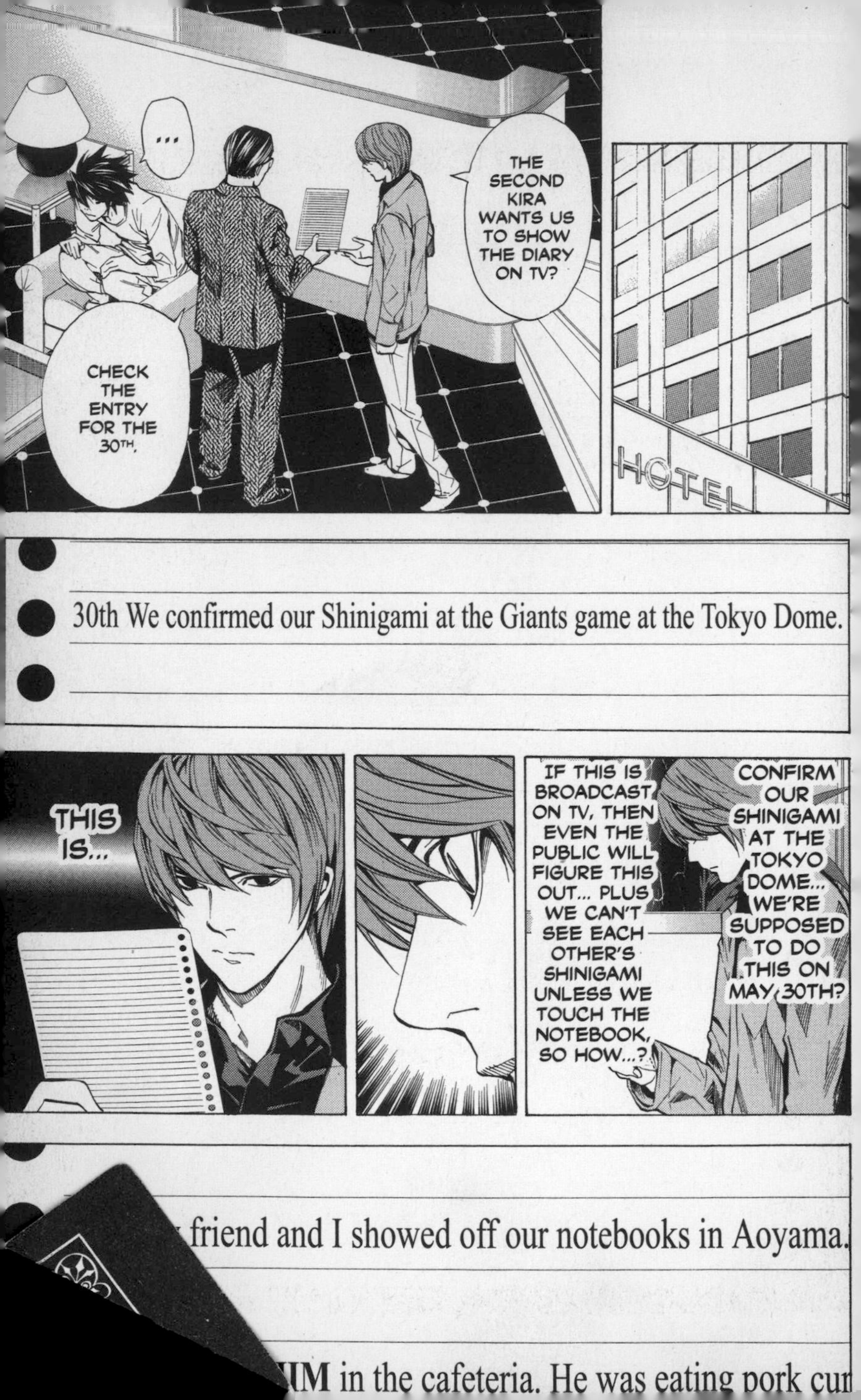
HOTEL
THE SECOND KIRA WANTS US TO SHOW THE DIARY ON TV?
...
CHECK THE ENTRY FOR THE 30TH.
30th We confirmed our Shinigami at the Giants game at the Tokyo Dome.
CONFIRM OUR SHINIGAMI AT THE TOKYO DOME... WE'RE SUPPOSED TO DO THIS ON MAY 30TH?
IF THIS IS BROADCAST ON TV, THEN EVEN THE PUBLIC WILL FIGURE THIS OUT... PLUS WE CAN'T SEE EACH OTHER'S SHINIGAMI UNLESS WE TOUCH THE NOTEBOOK, SO HOW...?
THIS IS...
friend and I showed off our notebooks in Aoyama.
IM in the cafeteria. He was eating pork cu

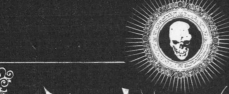

DEATH NOTE
How to use it
XVII

- If the god of death decides to use the DEATH NOTE to kill the assassin of an individual he favors, the individual's life will be extended, but the god of death will die.

死神は特定の人間に好意を持ち、その人間の寿命を延ばす為に
デスノートを使い、人間を殺すと死ぬ。

- the dead god of death will disappear, but the DEATH NOTE will remain. The ownership of this DEATH NOTE is usually carried over to the next god of death that touches it, but it is common sense that it is returned to the Great god of death.

死んだ死神は消えるが、デスノートは残る。
そのノートの所有権は、通常、次にノートに触れた死神に移るが、
死神大王に返上するのが常識とされている。

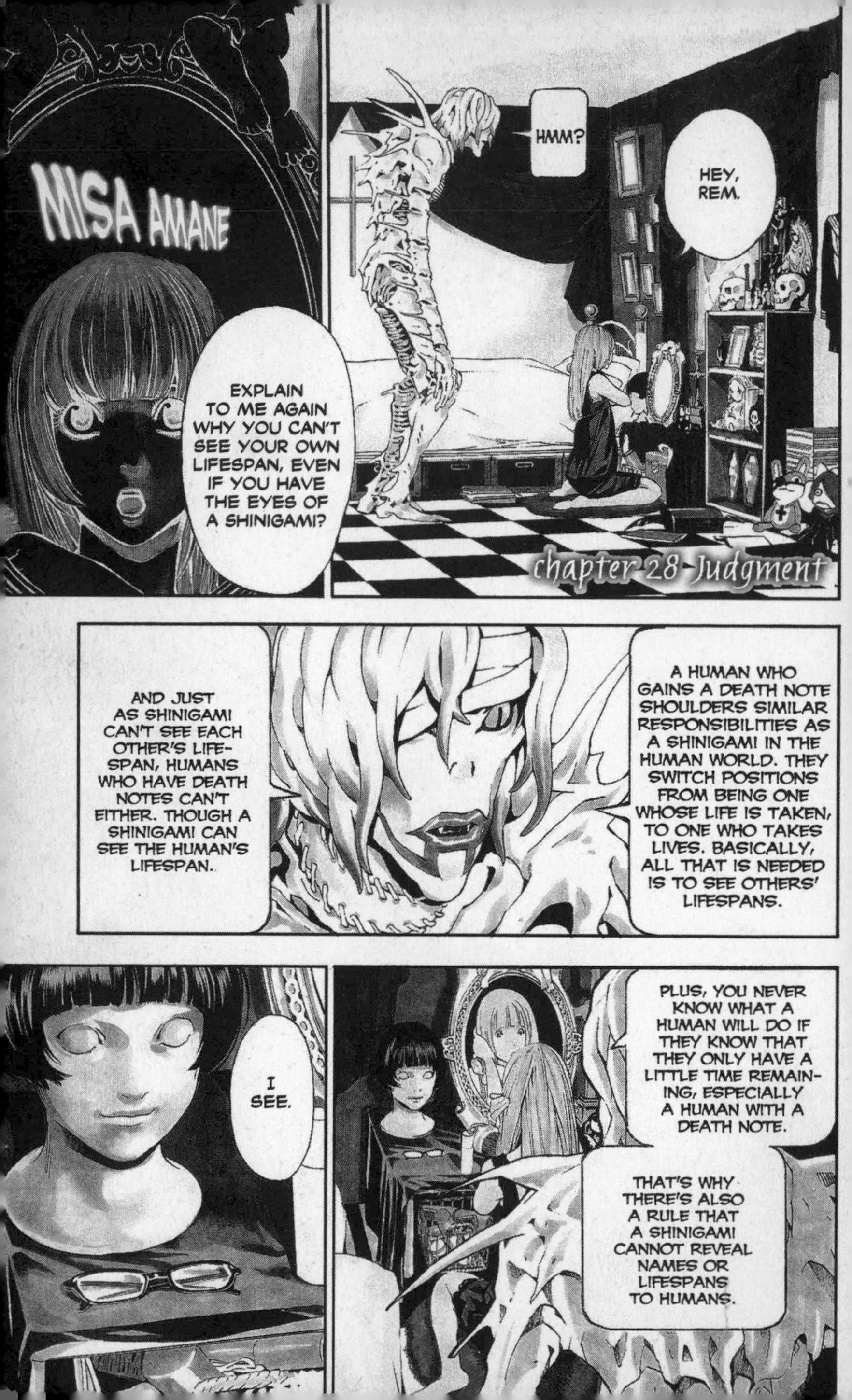
HEY, REM.
HMM?
chapter 28 Judgment
MISA AMANE
EXPLAIN TO ME AGAIN WHY YOU CAN'T SEE YOUR OWN LIFESPAN, EVEN IF YOU HAVE THE EYES OF A SHINIGAMI?
A HUMAN WHO GAINS A DEATH NOTE SHOULDERS SIMILAR RESPONSIBILITIES AS A SHINIGAMI IN THE HUMAN WORLD. THEY SWITCH POSITIONS FROM BEING ONE WHOSE LIFE IS TAKEN, TO ONE WHO TAKES LIVES. BASICALLY, ALL THAT IS NEEDED IS TO SEE OTHERS' LIFESPANS.
AND JUST AS SHINIGAMI CAN'T SEE EACH OTHER'S LIFE-SPAN, HUMANS WHO HAVE DEATH NOTES CAN'T EITHER. THOUGH A SHINIGAMI CAN SEE THE HUMAN'S LIFESPAN..
PLUS, YOU NEVER KNOW WHAT A HUMAN WILL DO IF THEY KNOW THAT THEY ONLY HAVE A LITTLE TIME REMAIN-ING, ESPECIALLY A HUMAN WITH A DEATH NOTE.
THAT'S WHY THERE'S ALSO A RULE THAT A SHINIGAMI CANNOT REVEAL NAMES OR LIFESPANS TO HUMANS.
I SEE.

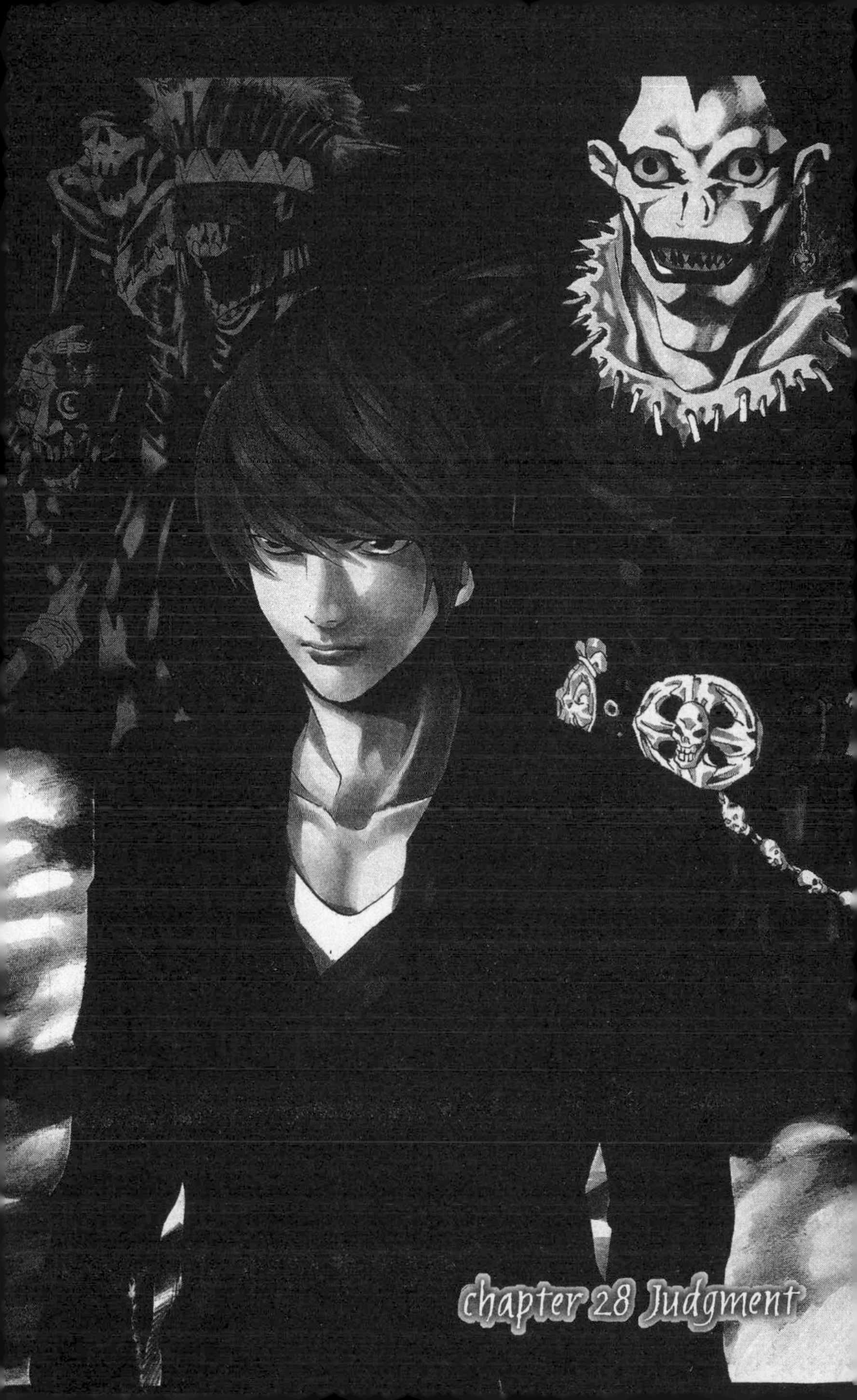
chapter 28 Judgment

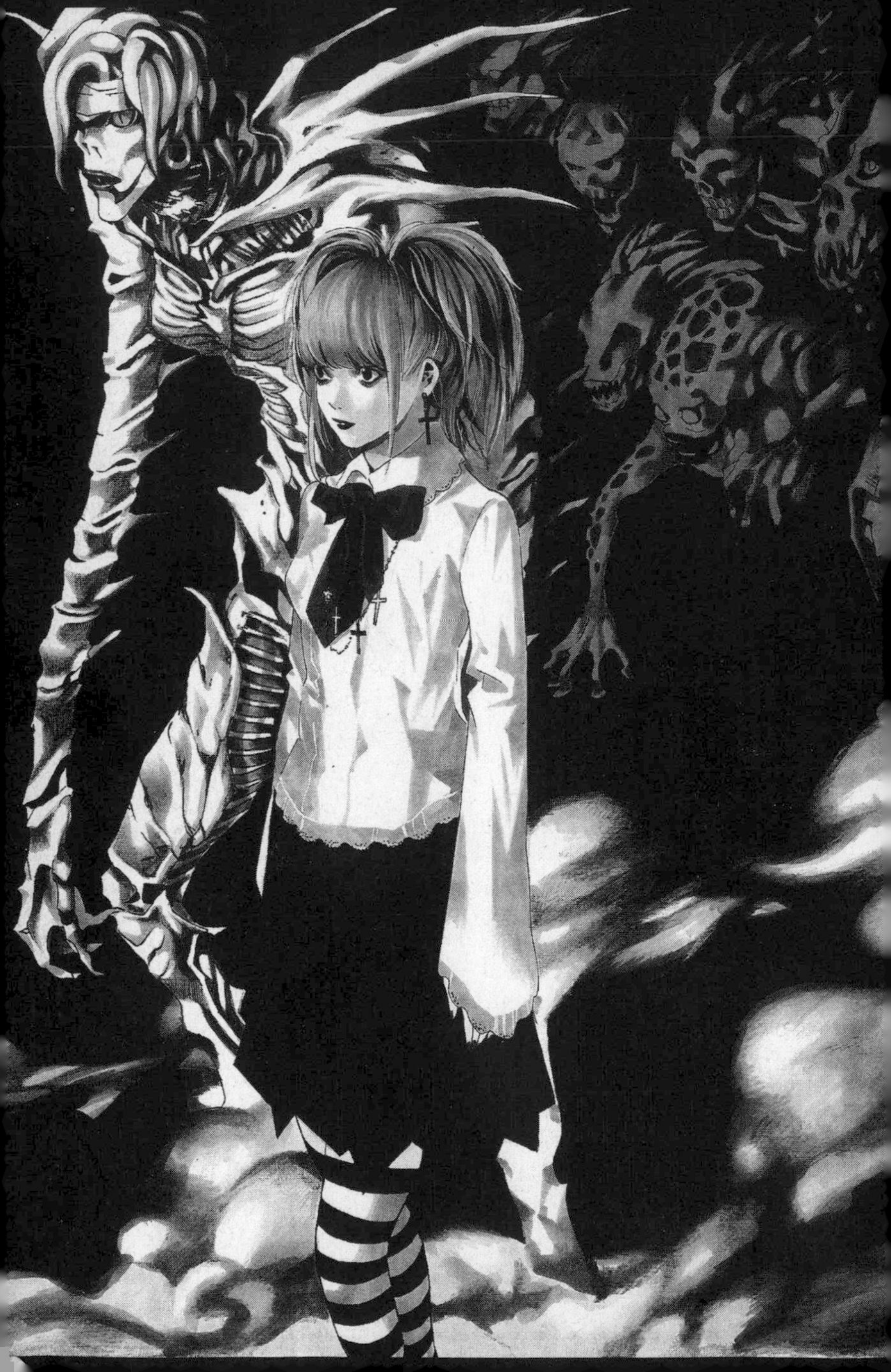

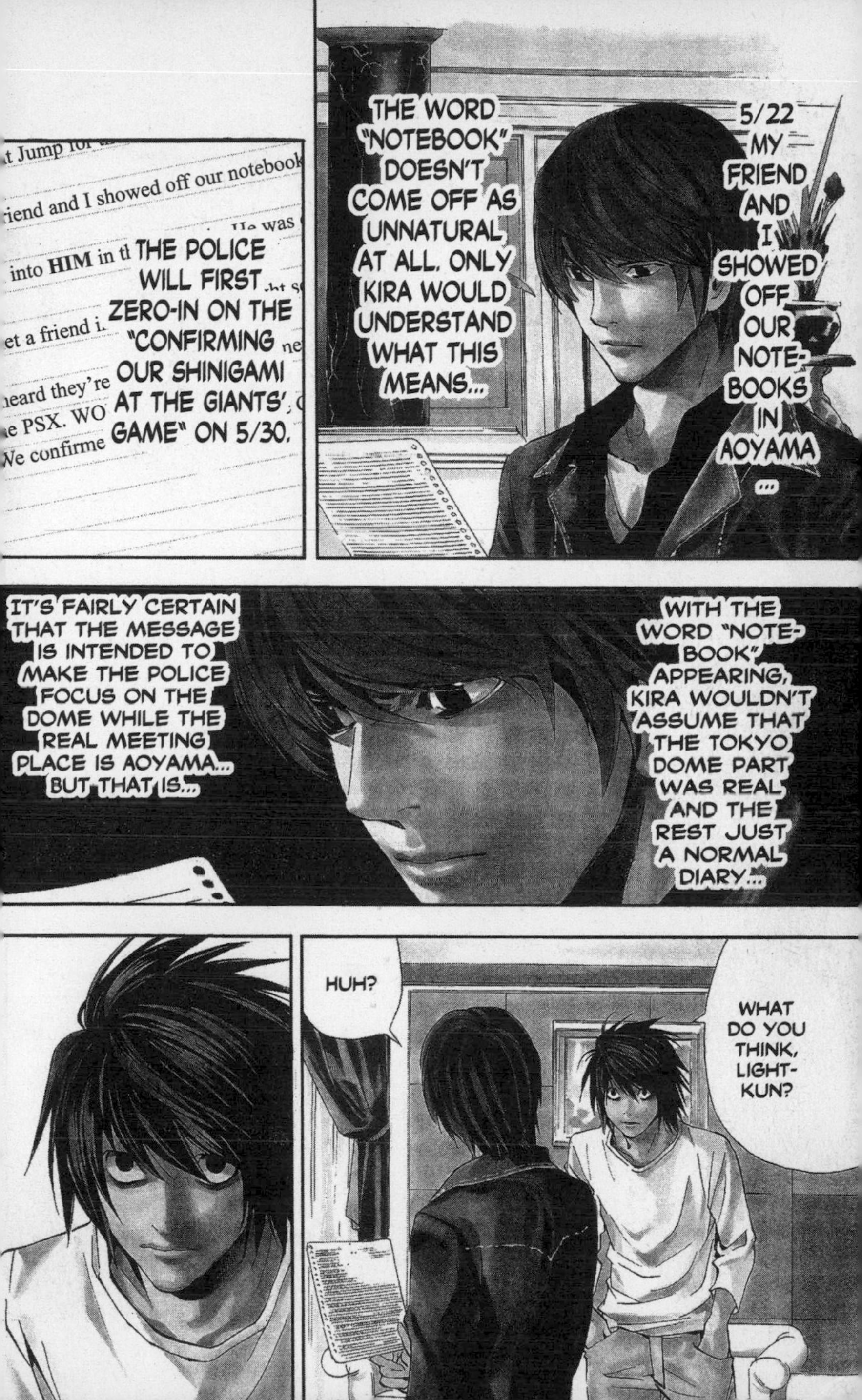
5/22 MY FRIEND AND I SHOWED OFF OUR NOTEBOOKS IN AOYAMA ...
THE WORD "NOTEBOOK" DOESN'T COME OFF AS UNNATURAL AT ALL. ONLY KIRA WOULD UNDERSTAND WHAT THIS MEANS...
riend and I showed off our notebook
into HIM in t
et a friend i
heard they're
e PSX. WO
We confirme
THE POLICE WILL FIRST ZERO-IN ON THE "CONFIRMING OUR SHINIGAMI AT THE GIANTS' GAME" ON 5/30.
WITH THE WORD "NOTEBOOK" APPEARING, KIRA WOULDN'T ASSUME THAT THE TOKYO DOME PART WAS REAL AND THE REST JUST A NORMAL DIARY...
IT'S FAIRLY CERTAIN THAT THE MESSAGE IS INTENDED TO MAKE THE POLICE FOCUS ON THE DOME WHILE THE REAL MEETING PLACE IS AOYAMA... BUT THAT IS...
WHAT DO YOU THINK, LIGHT-KUN?
HUH?

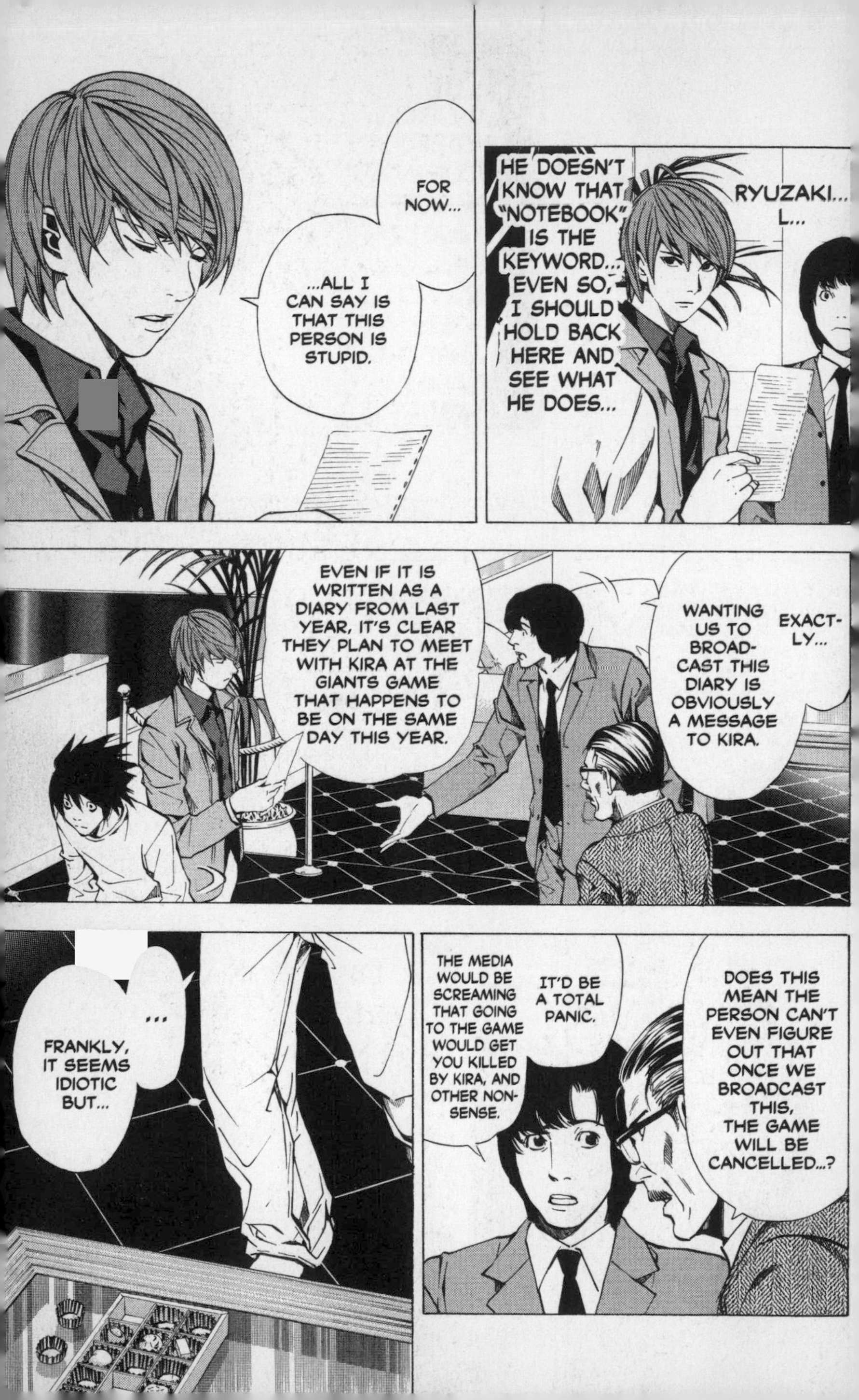
RYUZAKI... L...
HE DOESN'T KNOW THAT "NOTEBOOK" IS THE KEYWORD... EVEN SO, I SHOULD HOLD BACK HERE AND SEE WHAT HE DOES...
FOR NOW...
...ALL I CAN SAY IS THAT THIS PERSON IS STUPID.
EXACT-LY...
WANTING US TO BROAD-CAST THIS DIARY IS OBVIOUSLY A MESSAGE TO KIRA.
EVEN IF IT IS WRITTEN AS A DIARY FROM LAST YEAR, IT'S CLEAR THEY PLAN TO MEET WITH KIRA AT THE GIANTS GAME THAT HAPPENS TO BE ON THE SAME DAY THIS YEAR.
DOES THIS MEAN THE PERSON CAN'T EVEN FIGURE OUT THAT ONCE WE BROADCAST THIS, THE GAME WILL BE CANCELLED...?
IT'D BE A TOTAL PANIC.
THE MEDIA WOULD BE SCREAMING THAT GOING TO THE GAME WOULD GET YOU KILLED BY KIRA, AND OTHER NON-SENSE.
...
FRANKLY, IT SEEMS IDIOTIC BUT...

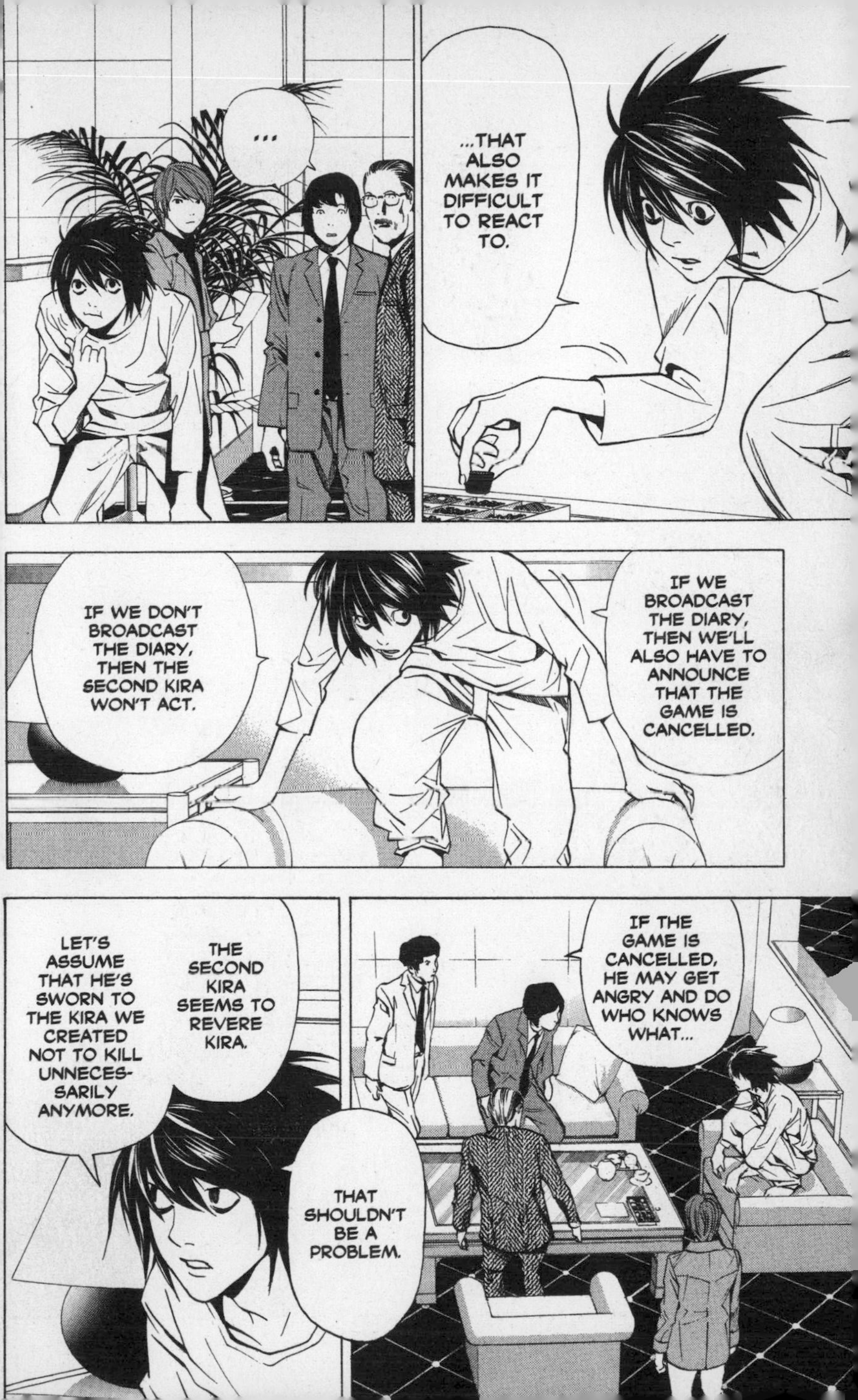
...THAT ALSO MAKES IT DIFFICULT TO REACT TO.
...
IF WE BROADCAST THE DIARY, THEN WE'LL ALSO HAVE TO ANNOUNCE THAT THE GAME IS CANCELLED.
IF WE DON'T BROADCAST THE DIARY, THEN THE SECOND KIRA WON'T ACT.
IF THE GAME IS CANCELLED, HE MAY GET ANGRY AND DO WHO KNOWS WHAT...
THE SECOND KIRA SEEMS TO REVERE KIRA.
LET'S ASSUME THAT HE'S SWORN TO THE KIRA WE CREATED NOT TO KILL UNNECES-SARILY ANYMORE.
THAT SHOULDN'T BE A PROBLEM.

READ THIS WAY

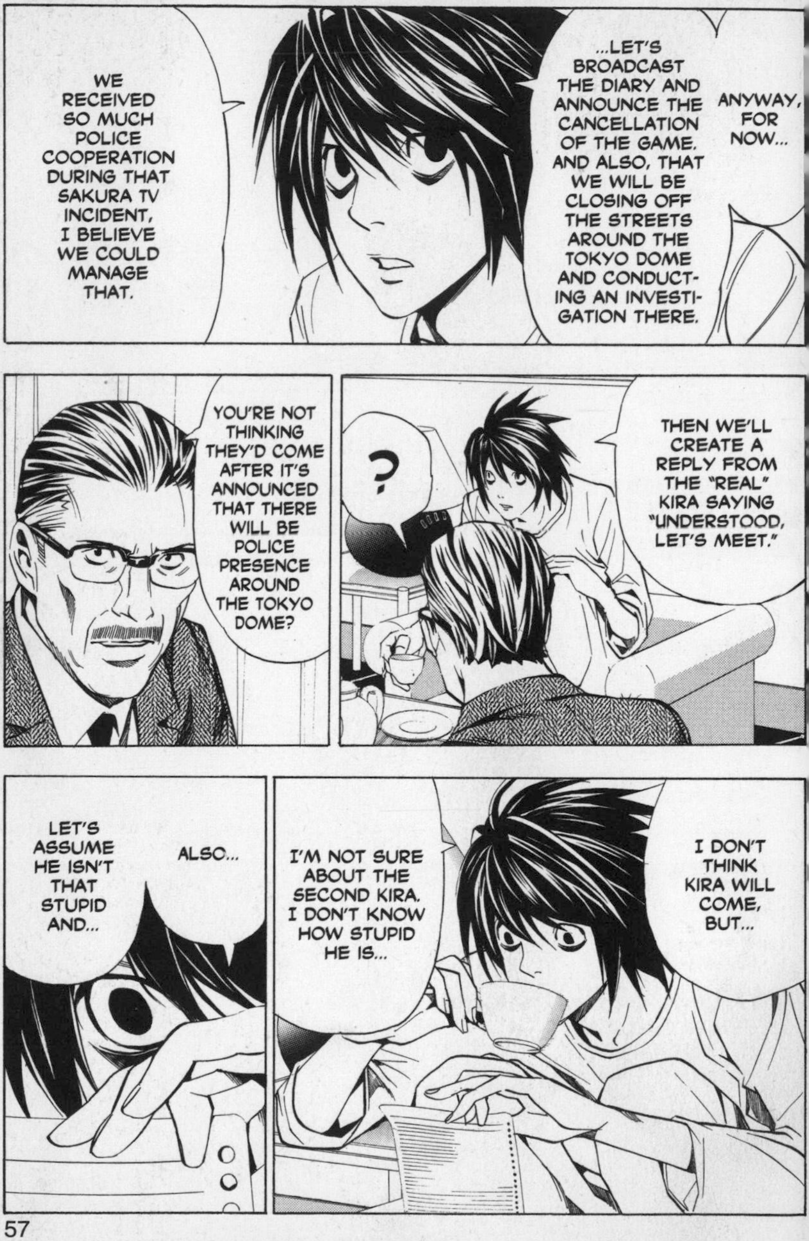
ANYWAY, FOR NOW...
...LET'S BROADCAST THE DIARY AND ANNOUNCE THE CANCELLATION OF THE GAME. AND ALSO, THAT WE WILL BE CLOSING OFF THE STREETS AROUND THE TOKYO DOME AND CONDUCTING AN INVESTIGATION THERE.
WE RECEIVED SO MUCH POLICE COOPERATION DURING THAT SAKURA TV INCIDENT, I BELIEVE WE COULD MANAGE THAT.
THEN WE'LL CREATE A REPLY FROM THE "REAL" KIRA SAYING "UNDERSTOOD, LET'S MEET."
?
YOU'RE NOT THINKING THEY'D COME AFTER IT'S ANNOUNCED THAT THERE WILL BE POLICE PRESENCE AROUND THE TOKYO DOME?
I DON'T THINK KIRA WILL COME, BUT...
I'M NOT SURE ABOUT THE SECOND KIRA. I DON'T KNOW HOW STUPID HE IS...
ALSO...
LET'S ASSUME HE ISN'T THAT STUPID AND...

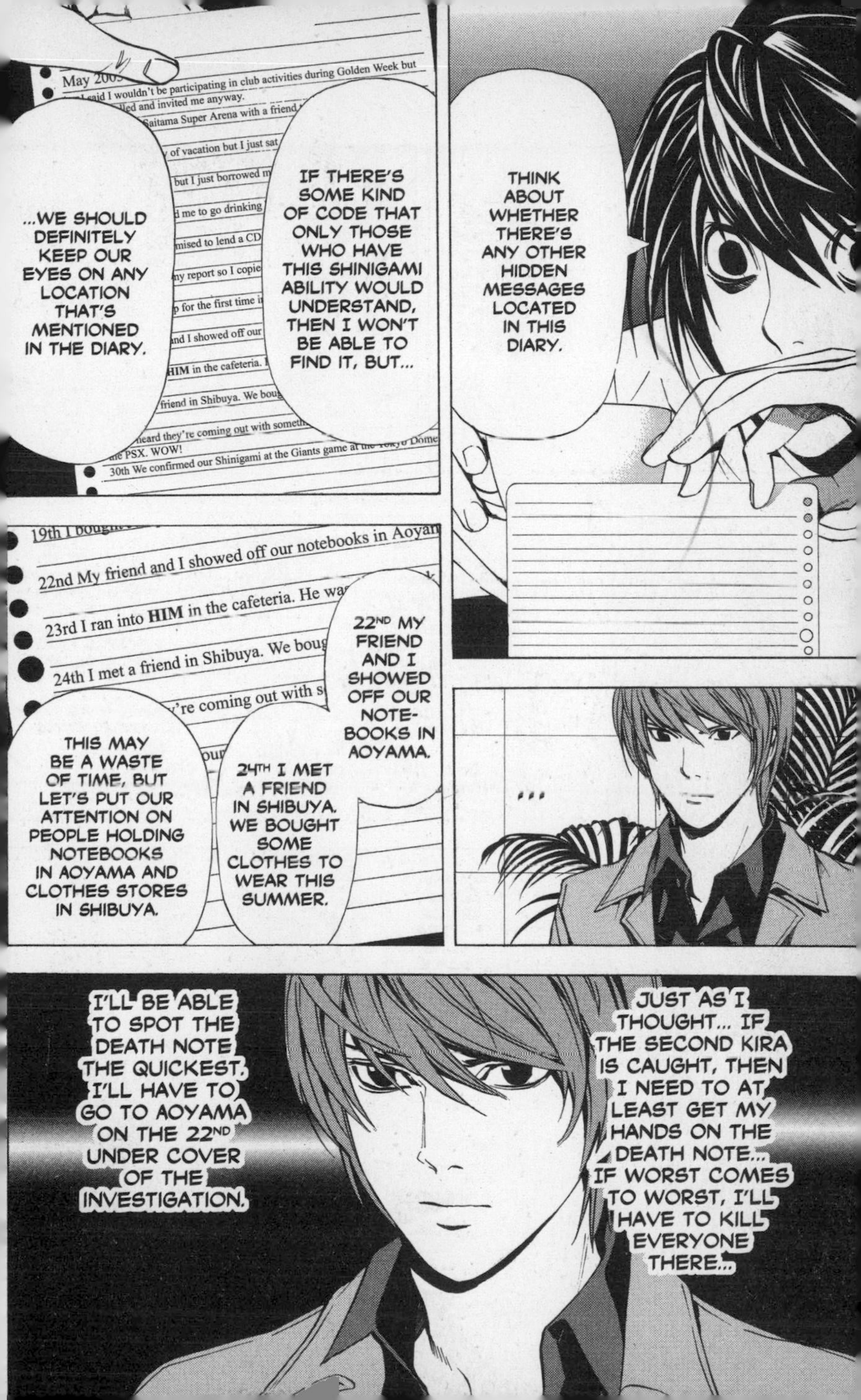

THINK ABOUT WHETHER THERE'S ANY OTHER HIDDEN MESSAGES LOCATED IN THIS DIARY.
IF THERE'S SOME KIND OF CODE THAT ONLY THOSE WHO HAVE THIS SHINIGAMI ABILITY WOULD UNDERSTAND, THEN I WON'T BE ABLE TO FIND IT, BUT...
...WE SHOULD DEFINITELY KEEP OUR EYES ON ANY LOCATION THAT'S MENTIONED IN THE DIARY.
I said I wouldn't be participating in club activities during Golden Week but
30th We confirmed our Shinigami at the Giants game at the Tokyo Dome
22nd My friend and I showed off our notebooks in Aoyama
23rd I ran into HIM in the cafeteria.
24th I met a friend in Shibuya.
22ND MY FRIEND AND I SHOWED OFF OUR NOTEBOOKS IN AOYAMA.
24TH I MET A FRIEND IN SHIBUYA. WE BOUGHT SOME CLOTHES TO WEAR THIS SUMMER.
THIS MAY BE A WASTE OF TIME, BUT LET'S PUT OUR ATTENTION ON PEOPLE HOLDING NOTEBOOKS IN AOYAMA AND CLOTHES STORES IN SHIBUYA.
...
JUST AS I THOUGHT... IF THE SECOND KIRA IS CAUGHT, THEN I NEED TO AT LEAST GET MY HANDS ON THE DEATH NOTE... IF WORST COMES TO WORST, I'LL HAVE TO KILL EVERYONE THERE...
I'LL BE ABLE TO SPOT THE DEATH NOTE THE QUICKEST. I'LL HAVE TO GO TO AOYAMA ON THE 22ND UNDER COVER OF THE INVESTIGATION.

READ THIS WAY

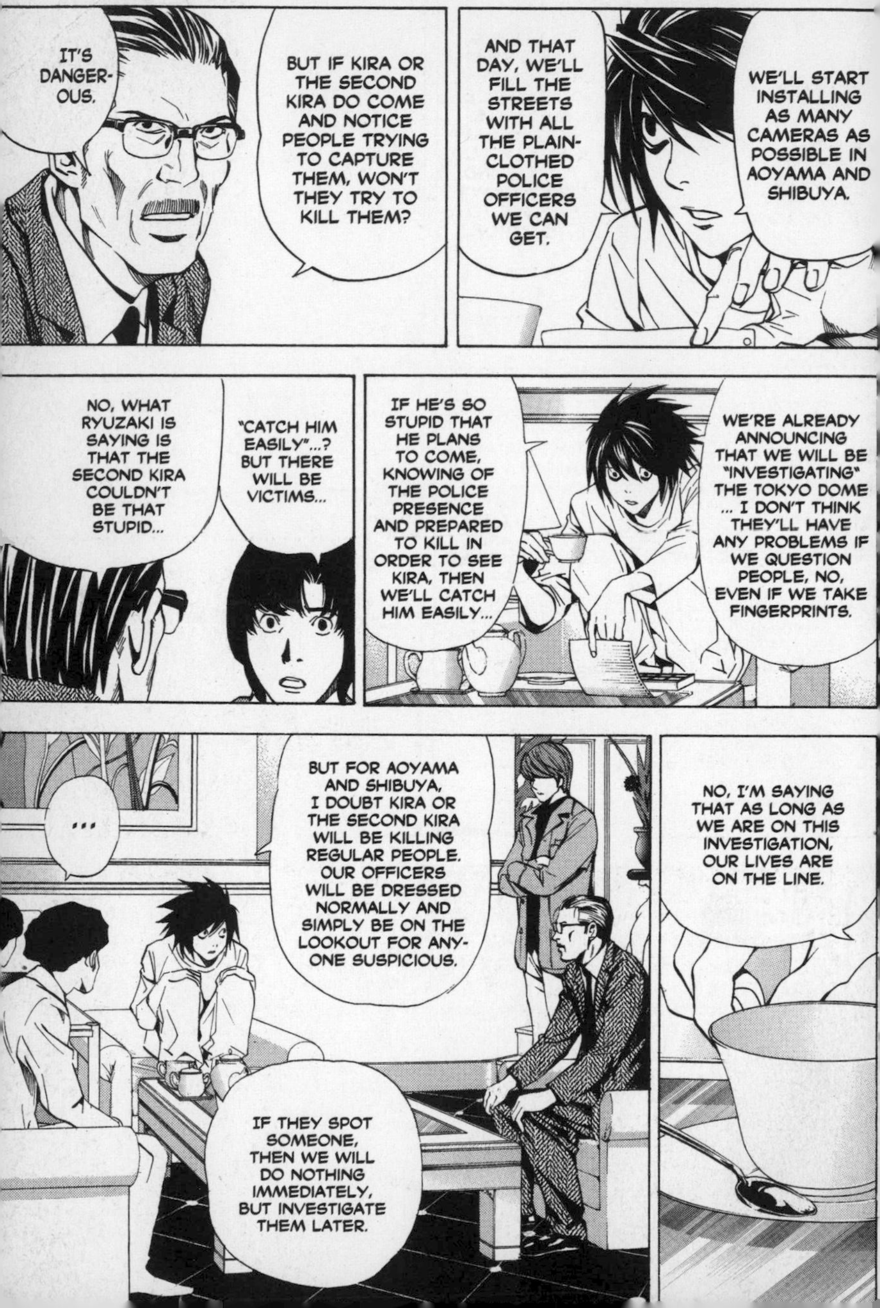
WE'LL START INSTALLING AS MANY CAMERAS AS POSSIBLE IN AOYAMA AND SHIBUYA.
AND THAT DAY, WE'LL FILL THE STREETS WITH ALL THE PLAIN-CLOTHED POLICE OFFICERS WE CAN GET.
BUT IF KIRA OR THE SECOND KIRA DO COME AND NOTICE PEOPLE TRYING TO CAPTURE THEM, WON'T THEY TRY TO KILL THEM?
IT'S DANGER-OUS.
WE'RE ALREADY ANNOUNCING THAT WE WILL BE "INVESTIGATING" THE TOKYO DOME ... I DON'T THINK THEY'LL HAVE ANY PROBLEMS IF WE QUESTION PEOPLE, NO, EVEN IF WE TAKE FINGERPRINTS.
IF HE'S SO STUPID THAT HE PLANS TO COME, KNOWING OF THE POLICE PRESENCE AND PREPARED TO KILL IN ORDER TO SEE KIRA, THEN WE'LL CATCH HIM EASILY...
"CATCH HIM EASILY"...? BUT THERE WILL BE VICTIMS...
NO, WHAT RYUZAKI IS SAYING IS THAT THE SECOND KIRA COULDN'T BE THAT STUPID...
NO, I'M SAYING THAT AS LONG AS WE ARE ON THIS INVESTIGATION, OUR LIVES ARE ON THE LINE.
BUT FOR AOYAMA AND SHIBUYA, I DOUBT KIRA OR THE SECOND KIRA WILL BE KILLING REGULAR PEOPLE. OUR OFFICERS WILL BE DRESSED NORMALLY AND SIMPLY BE ON THE LOOKOUT FOR ANY-ONE SUSPICIOUS.
...
IF THEY SPOT SOMEONE, THEN WE WILL DO NOTHING IMMEDIATELY, BUT INVESTIGATE THEM LATER.

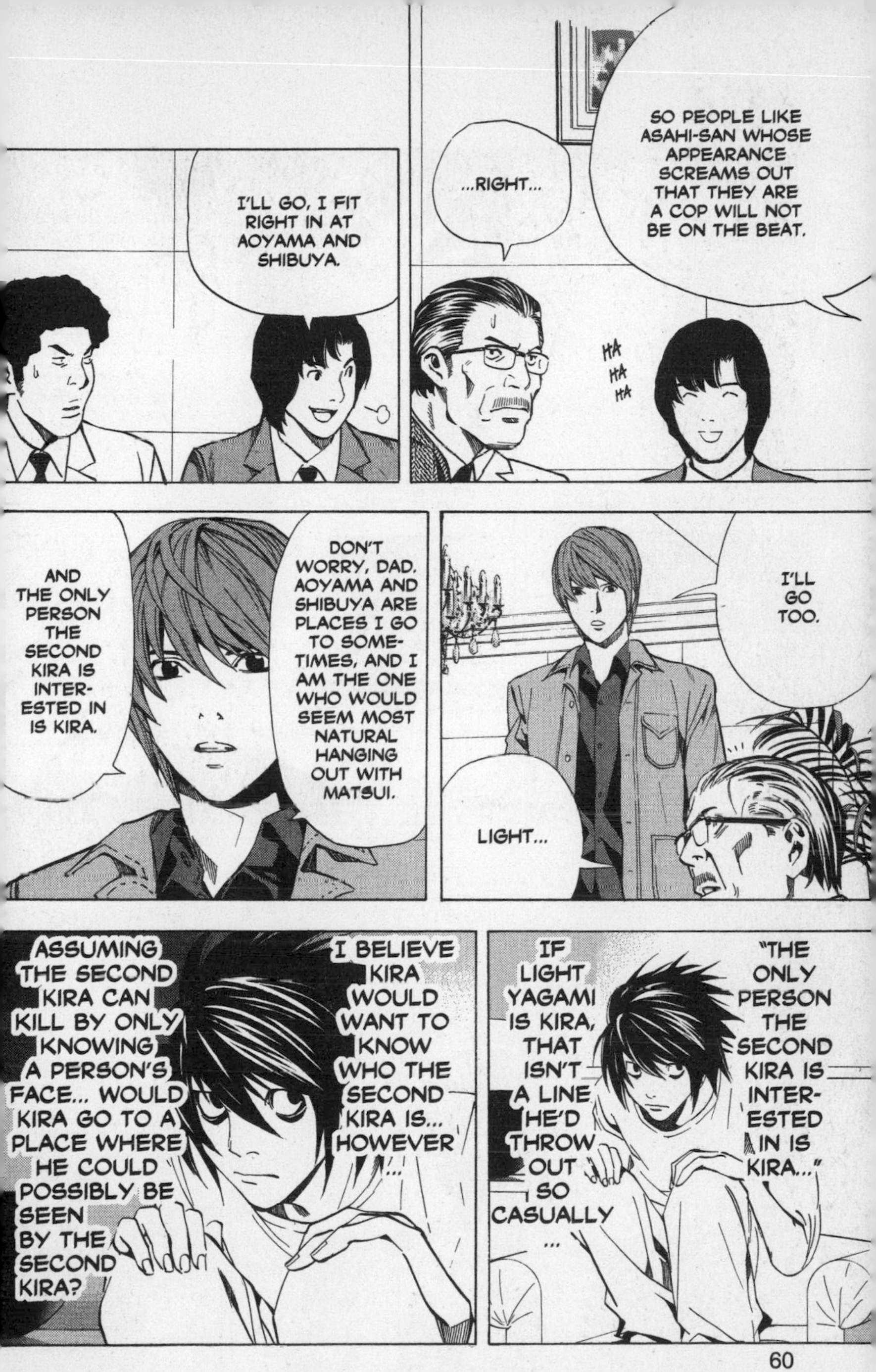
SO PEOPLE LIKE ASAHI-SAN WHOSE APPEARANCE SCREAMS OUT THAT THEY ARE A COP WILL NOT BE ON THE BEAT.
...RIGHT...
HA HA HA
I'LL GO, I FIT RIGHT IN AT AOYAMA AND SHIBUYA.
I'LL GO TOO.
LIGHT...
DON'T WORRY, DAD. AOYAMA AND SHIBUYA ARE PLACES I GO TO SOMETIMES, AND I AM THE ONE WHO WOULD SEEM MOST NATURAL HANGING OUT WITH MATSUI.
AND THE ONLY PERSON THE SECOND KIRA IS INTERESTED IN IS KIRA.
"THE ONLY PERSON THE SECOND KIRA IS INTERESTED IN IS KIRA..."
IF LIGHT YAGAMI IS KIRA, THAT ISN'T A LINE HE'D THROW OUT SO CASUALLY...
I BELIEVE KIRA WOULD WANT TO KNOW WHO THE SECOND KIRA IS... HOWEVER...
ASSUMING THE SECOND KIRA CAN KILL BY ONLY KNOWING A PERSON'S FACE... WOULD KIRA GO TO A PLACE WHERE HE COULD POSSIBLY BE SEEN BY THE SECOND KIRA?

READ THIS WAY

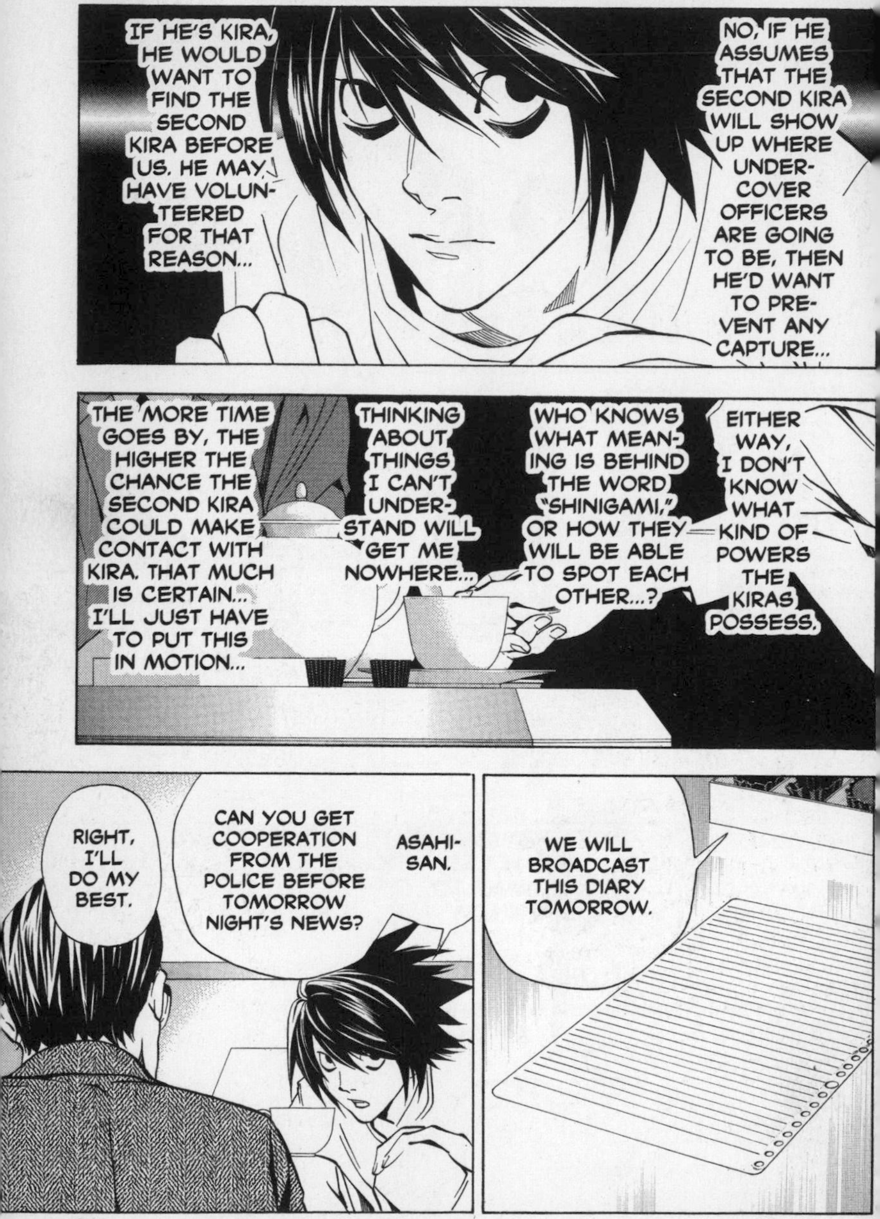
NO, IF HE ASSUMES THAT THE SECOND KIRA WILL SHOW UP WHERE UNDER-COVER OFFICERS ARE GOING TO BE, THEN HE'D WANT TO PRE-VENT ANY CAPTURE...
IF HE'S KIRA, HE WOULD WANT TO FIND THE SECOND KIRA BEFORE US. HE MAY HAVE VOLUN-TEERED FOR THAT REASON...
EITHER WAY, I DON'T KNOW WHAT KIND OF POWERS THE KIRAS POSSESS.
WHO KNOWS WHAT MEAN-ING IS BEHIND THE WORD "SHINIGAMI," OR HOW THEY WILL BE ABLE TO SPOT EACH OTHER...?
THINKING ABOUT THINGS I CAN'T UNDER-STAND WILL GET ME NOWHERE...
THE MORE TIME GOES BY, THE HIGHER THE CHANCE THE SECOND KIRA COULD MAKE CONTACT WITH KIRA. THAT MUCH IS CERTAIN... I'LL JUST HAVE TO PUT THIS IN MOTION...
WE WILL BROADCAST THIS DIARY TOMORROW.
ASAHI-SAN.
CAN YOU GET COOPERATION FROM THE POLICE BEFORE TOMORROW NIGHT'S NEWS?
RIGHT, I'LL DO MY BEST.

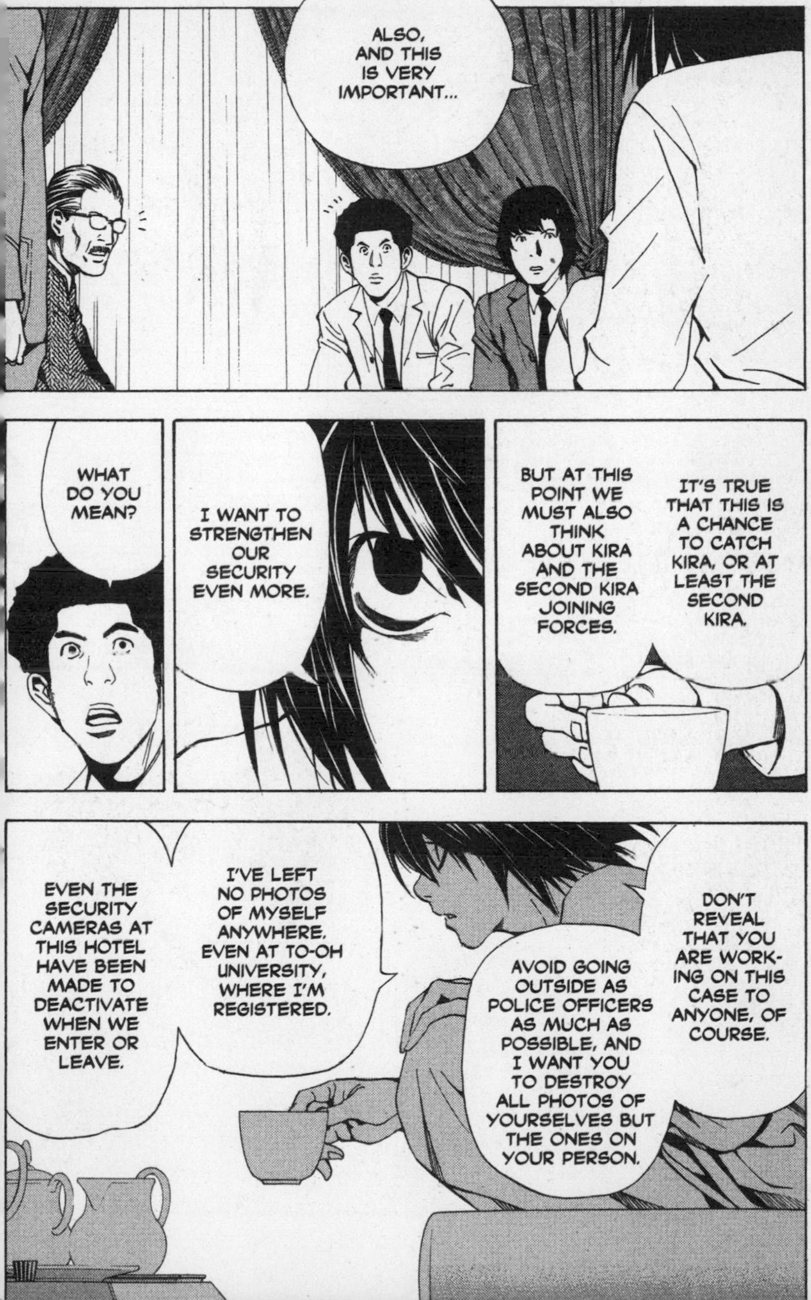
ALSO, AND THIS IS VERY IMPORTANT...
IT'S TRUE THAT THIS IS A CHANCE TO CATCH KIRA, OR AT LEAST THE SECOND KIRA.
BUT AT THIS POINT WE MUST ALSO THINK ABOUT KIRA AND THE SECOND KIRA JOINING FORCES.
I WANT TO STRENGTHEN OUR SECURITY EVEN MORE.
WHAT DO YOU MEAN?
DON'T REVEAL THAT YOU ARE WORKING ON THIS CASE TO ANYONE, OF COURSE.
AVOID GOING OUTSIDE AS POLICE OFFICERS AS MUCH AS POSSIBLE, AND I WANT YOU TO DESTROY ALL PHOTOS OF YOURSELVES BUT THE ONES ON YOUR PERSON.
I'VE LEFT NO PHOTOS OF MYSELF ANYWHERE. EVEN AT TO-OH UNIVERSITY, WHERE I'M REGISTERED.
EVEN THE SECURITY CAMERAS AT THIS HOTEL HAVE BEEN MADE TO DEACTIVATE WHEN WE ENTER OR LEAVE.

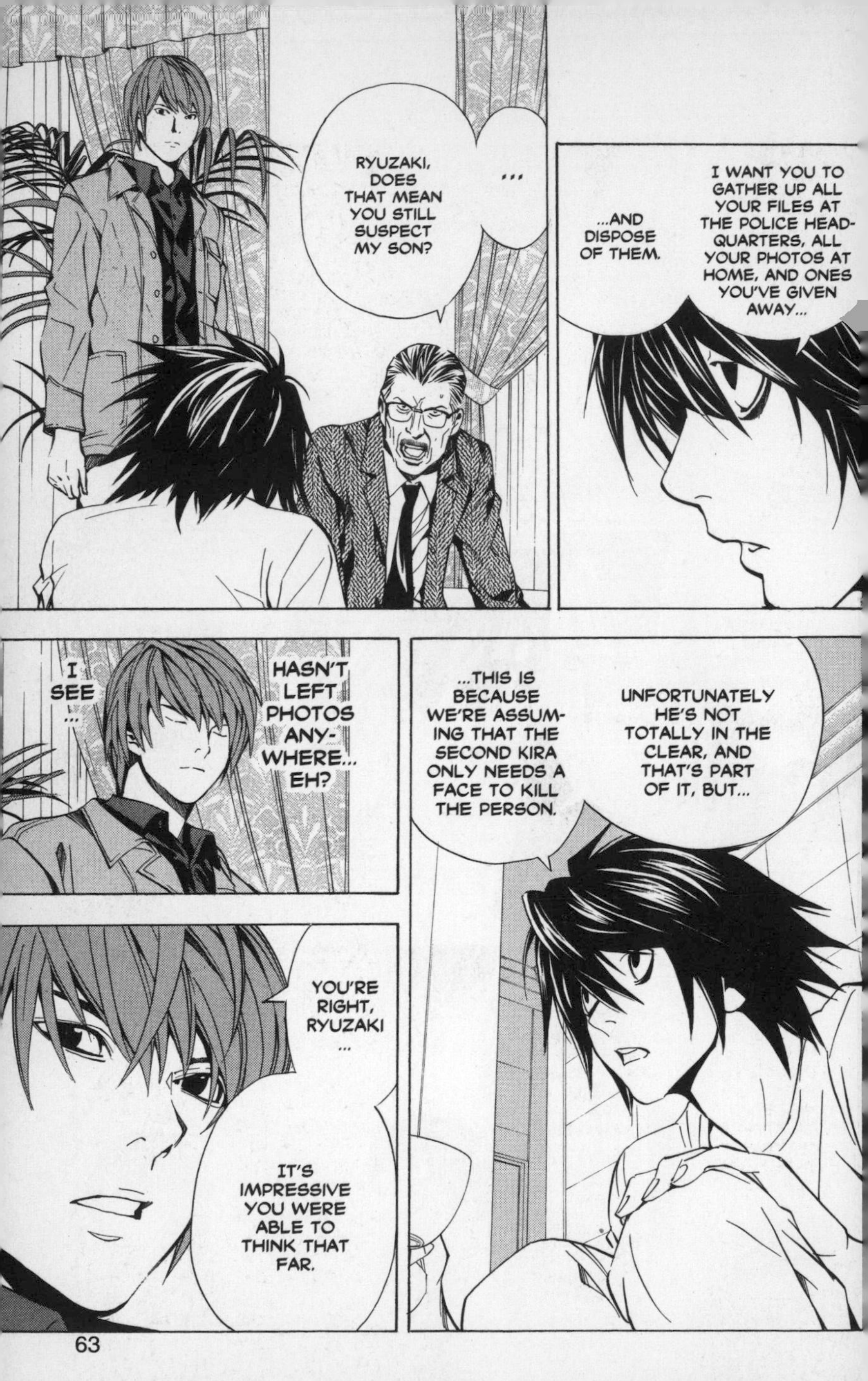
I WANT YOU TO GATHER UP ALL YOUR FILES AT THE POLICE HEAD-QUARTERS, ALL YOUR PHOTOS AT HOME, AND ONES YOU'VE GIVEN AWAY...
...AND DISPOSE OF THEM.
...
RYUZAKI, DOES THAT MEAN YOU STILL SUSPECT MY SON?
UNFORTUNATELY HE'S NOT TOTALLY IN THE CLEAR, AND THAT'S PART OF IT, BUT...
...THIS IS BECAUSE WE'RE ASSUM-ING THAT THE SECOND KIRA ONLY NEEDS A FACE TO KILL THE PERSON.
HASN'T LEFT PHOTOS ANY-WHERE... EH?
I SEE ...
YOU'RE RIGHT, RYUZAKI ...
IT'S IMPRESSIVE YOU WERE ABLE TO THINK THAT FAR.

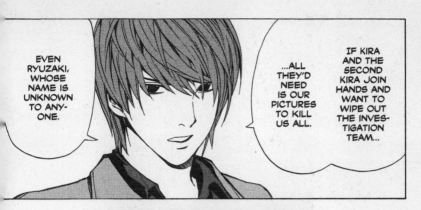

IF KIRA AND THE SECOND KIRA JOIN HANDS AND WANT TO WIPE OUT THE INVESTIGATION TEAM...

...ALL THEY'D NEED IS OUR PICTURES TO KILL US ALL.

EVEN RYUZAKI, WHOSE NAME IS UNKNOWN TO ANYONE.

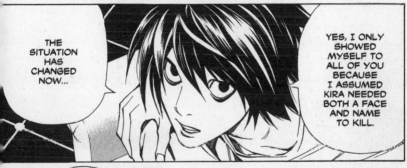

YES, I ONLY SHOWED MYSELF TO ALL OF YOU BECAUSE I ASSUMED KIRA NEEDED BOTH A FACE AND NAME TO KILL.

THE SITUATION HAS CHANGED NOW...

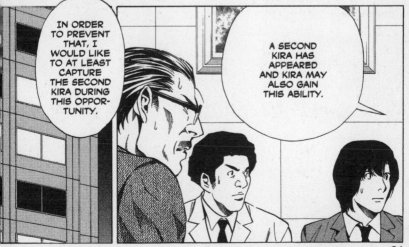

A SECOND KIRA HAS APPEARED AND KIRA MAY ALSO GAIN THIS ABILITY.

IN ORDER TO PREVENT THAT, I WOULD LIKE TO AT LEAST CAPTURE THE SECOND KIRA DURING THIS OPPORTUNITY.

READ THIS WAY

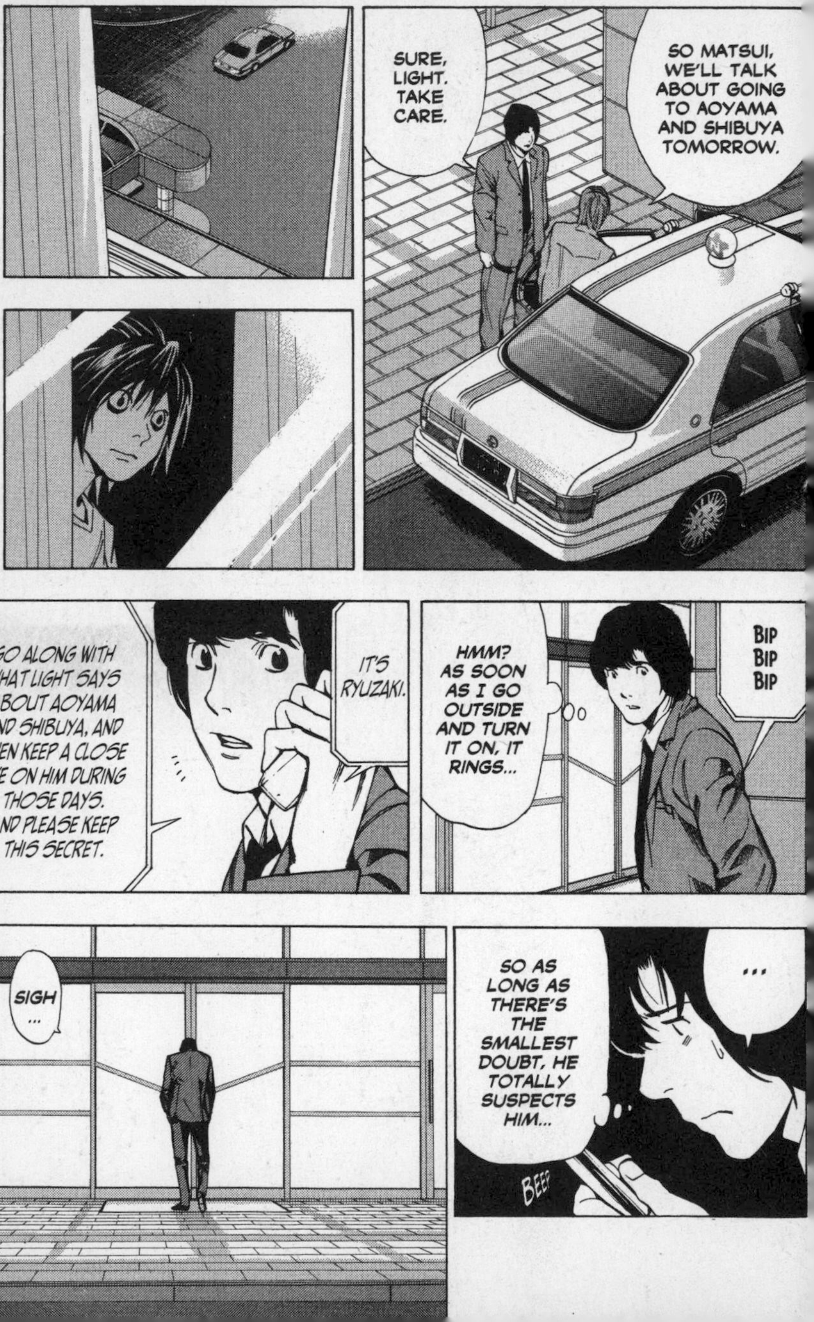
SO MATSUI, WE'LL TALK ABOUT GOING TO AOYAMA AND SHIBUYA TOMORROW.
SURE, LIGHT. TAKE CARE.
BIP BIP BIP
HMM? AS SOON AS I GO OUTSIDE AND TURN IT ON, IT RINGS...
IT'S RYUZAKI.
GO ALONG WITH WHAT LIGHT SAYS ABOUT AOYAMA AND SHIBUYA, AND THEN KEEP A CLOSE EYE ON HIM DURING THOSE DAYS. AND PLEASE KEEP THIS SECRET.
...
SO AS LONG AS THERE'S THE SMALLEST DOUBT, HE TOTALLY SUSPECTS HIM...
BEEP
SIGH ...

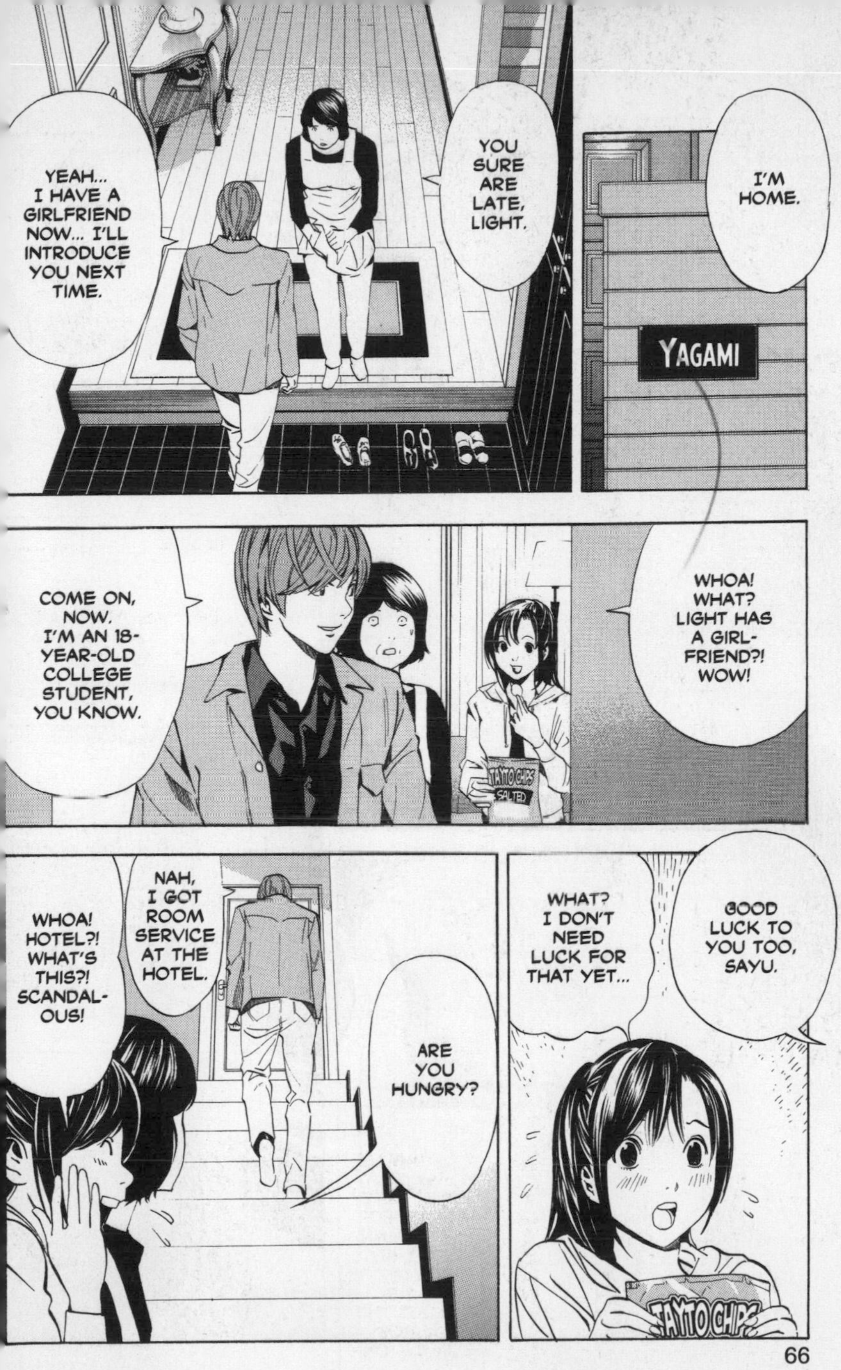
I'M HOME.
YAGAMI
YOU SURE ARE LATE, LIGHT.
YEAH... I HAVE A GIRLFRIEND NOW... I'LL INTRODUCE YOU NEXT TIME.
WHOA! WHAT? LIGHT HAS A GIRL-FRIEND?! WOW!
TAYTO CHIPS
SALTED
COME ON, NOW. I'M AN 18-YEAR-OLD COLLEGE STUDENT, YOU KNOW.
GOOD LUCK TO YOU TOO, SAYU.
WHAT? I DON'T NEED LUCK FOR THAT YET...
TAYTO CHIPS
ARE YOU HUNGRY?
NAH, I GOT ROOM SERVICE AT THE HOTEL.
WHOA! HOTEL?! WHAT'S THIS?! SCANDAL-OUS!

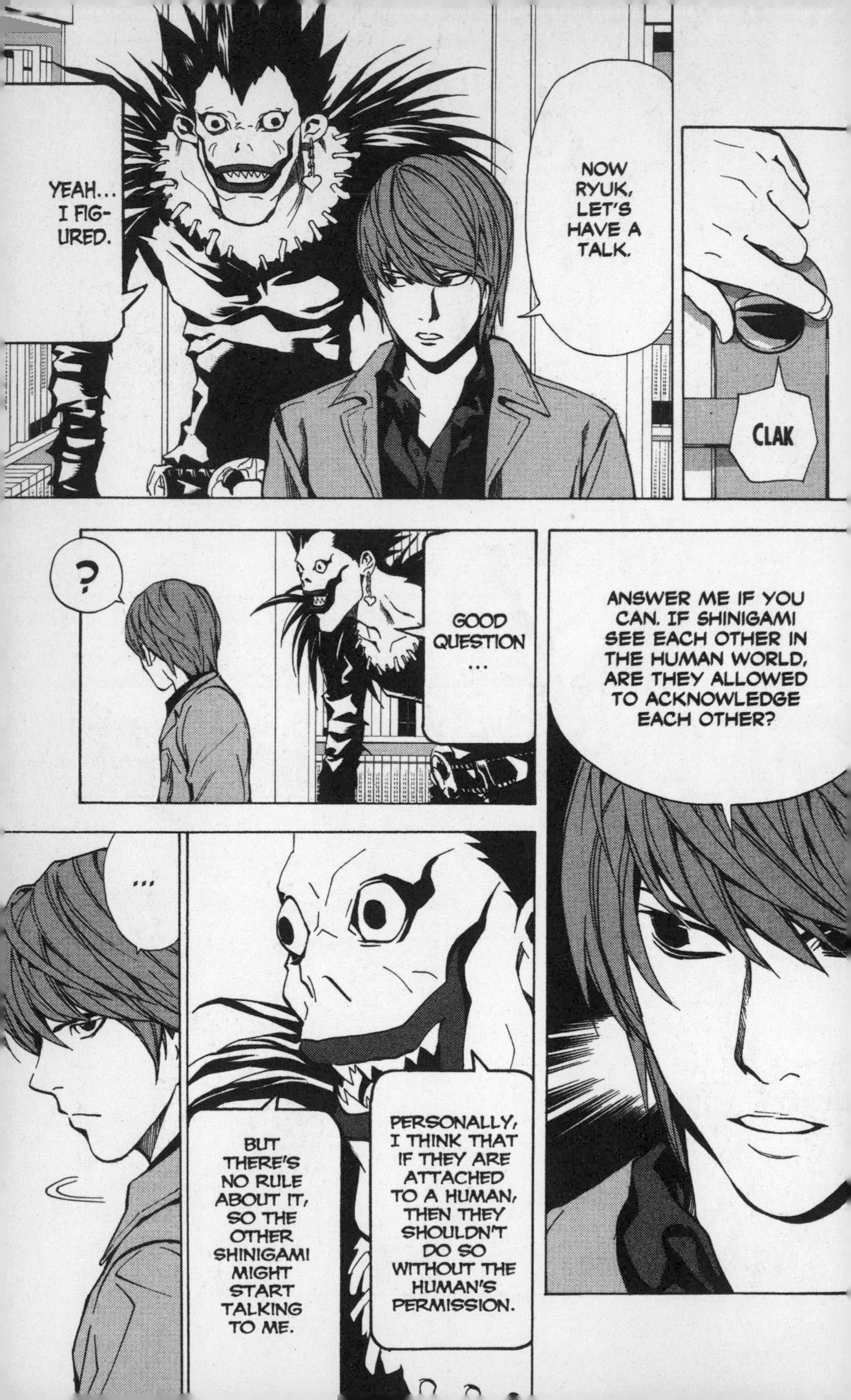
CLAK
NOW RYUK, LET'S HAVE A TALK.
YEAH... I FIG-URED.
ANSWER ME IF YOU CAN. IF SHINIGAMI SEE EACH OTHER IN THE HUMAN WORLD, ARE THEY ALLOWED TO ACKNOWLEDGE EACH OTHER?
GOOD QUESTION ...
?
PERSONALLY, I THINK THAT IF THEY ARE ATTACHED TO A HUMAN, THEN THEY SHOULDN'T DO SO WITHOUT THE HUMAN'S PERMISSION.
BUT THERE'S NO RULE ABOUT IT, SO THE OTHER SHINIGAMI MIGHT START TALKING TO ME.
...

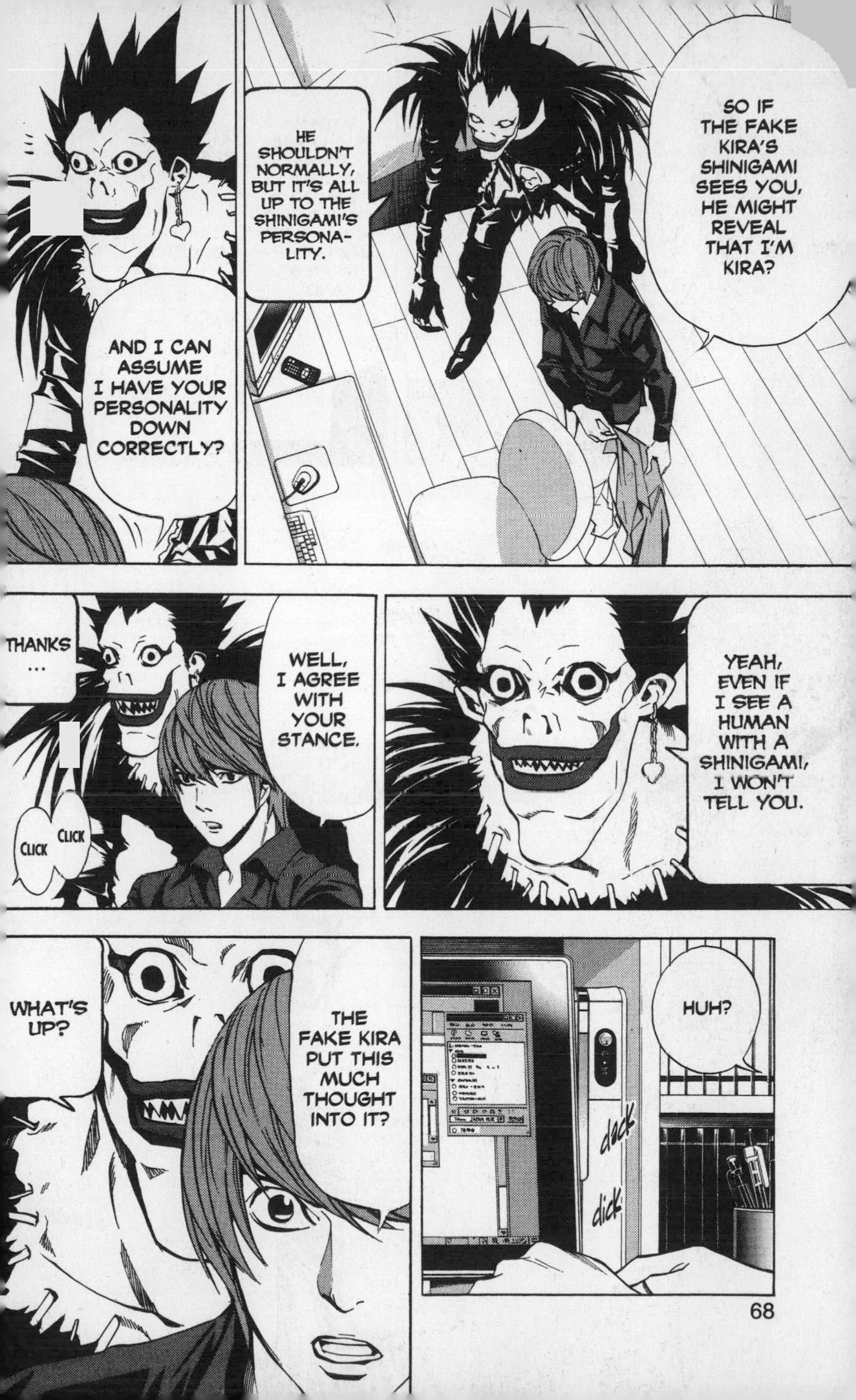
SO IF THE FAKE KIRA'S SHINIGAMI SEES YOU, HE MIGHT REVEAL THAT I'M KIRA?
HE SHOULDN'T NORMALLY, BUT IT'S ALL UP TO THE SHINIGAMI'S PERSONA-LITY.
AND I CAN ASSUME I HAVE YOUR PERSONALITY DOWN CORRECTLY?
YEAH, EVEN IF I SEE A HUMAN WITH A SHINIGAMI, I WON'T TELL YOU.
WELL, I AGREE WITH YOUR STANCE.
THANKS ...
CLICK
CLICK
HUH?
clack
click
THE FAKE KIRA PUT THIS MUCH THOUGHT INTO IT?
WHAT'S UP?

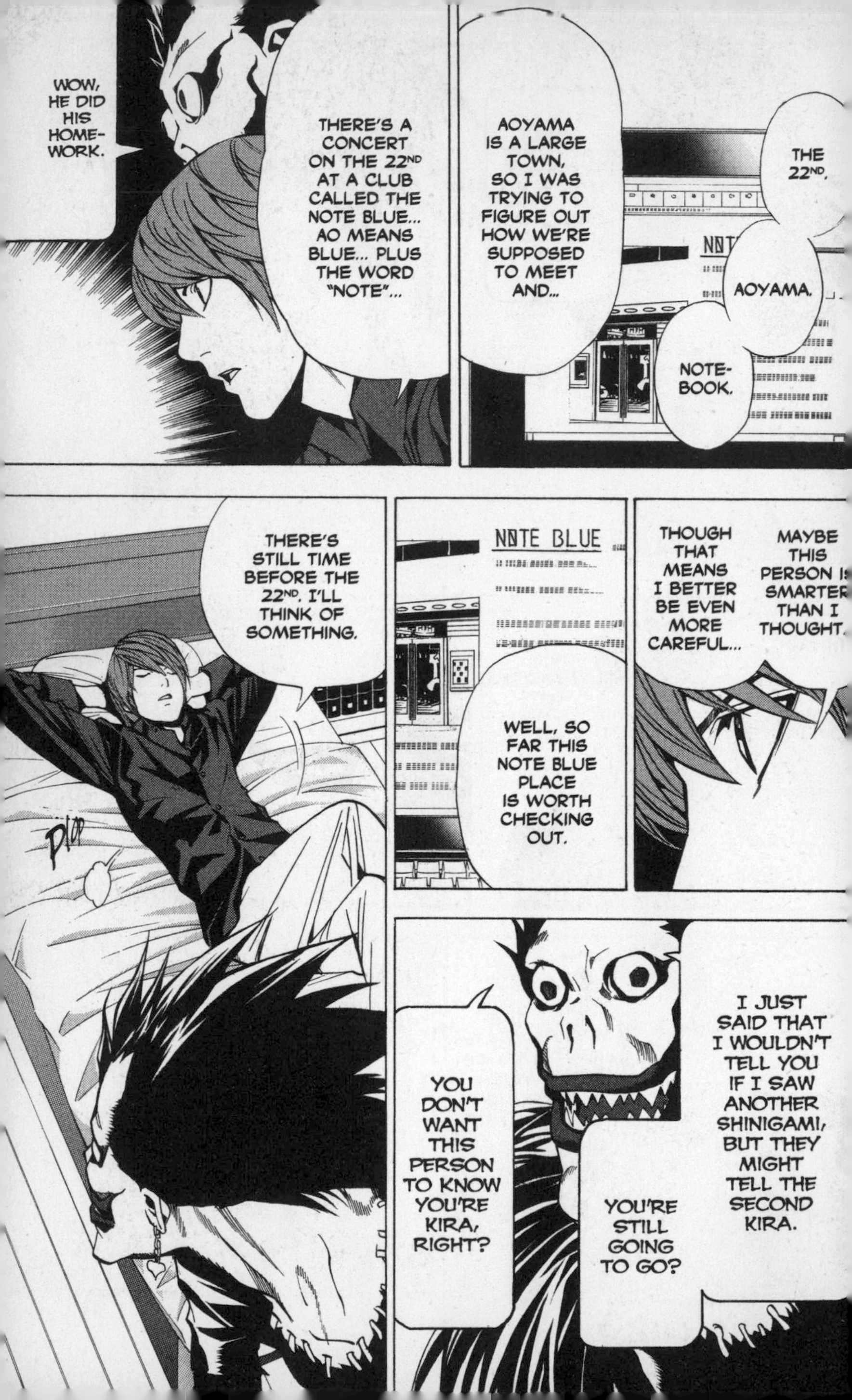
THE 22ND,
AOYAMA.
NOTEBOOK.
AOYAMA IS A LARGE TOWN, SO I WAS TRYING TO FIGURE OUT HOW WE'RE SUPPOSED TO MEET AND...
THERE'S A CONCERT ON THE 22ND AT A CLUB CALLED THE NOTE BLUE... AO MEANS BLUE... PLUS THE WORD "NOTE"...
WOW, HE DID HIS HOMEWORK.
MAYBE THIS PERSON IS SMARTER THAN I THOUGHT.
THOUGH THAT MEANS I BETTER BE EVEN MORE CAREFUL...
NOTE BLUE
WELL, SO FAR THIS NOTE BLUE PLACE IS WORTH CHECKING OUT.
YOU'RE STILL GOING TO GO?
I JUST SAID THAT I WOULDN'T TELL YOU IF I SAW ANOTHER SHINIGAMI, BUT THEY MIGHT TELL THE SECOND KIRA.
YOU DON'T WANT THIS PERSON TO KNOW YOU'RE KIRA, RIGHT?
THERE'S STILL TIME BEFORE THE 22ND. I'LL THINK OF SOMETHING.
PLOP

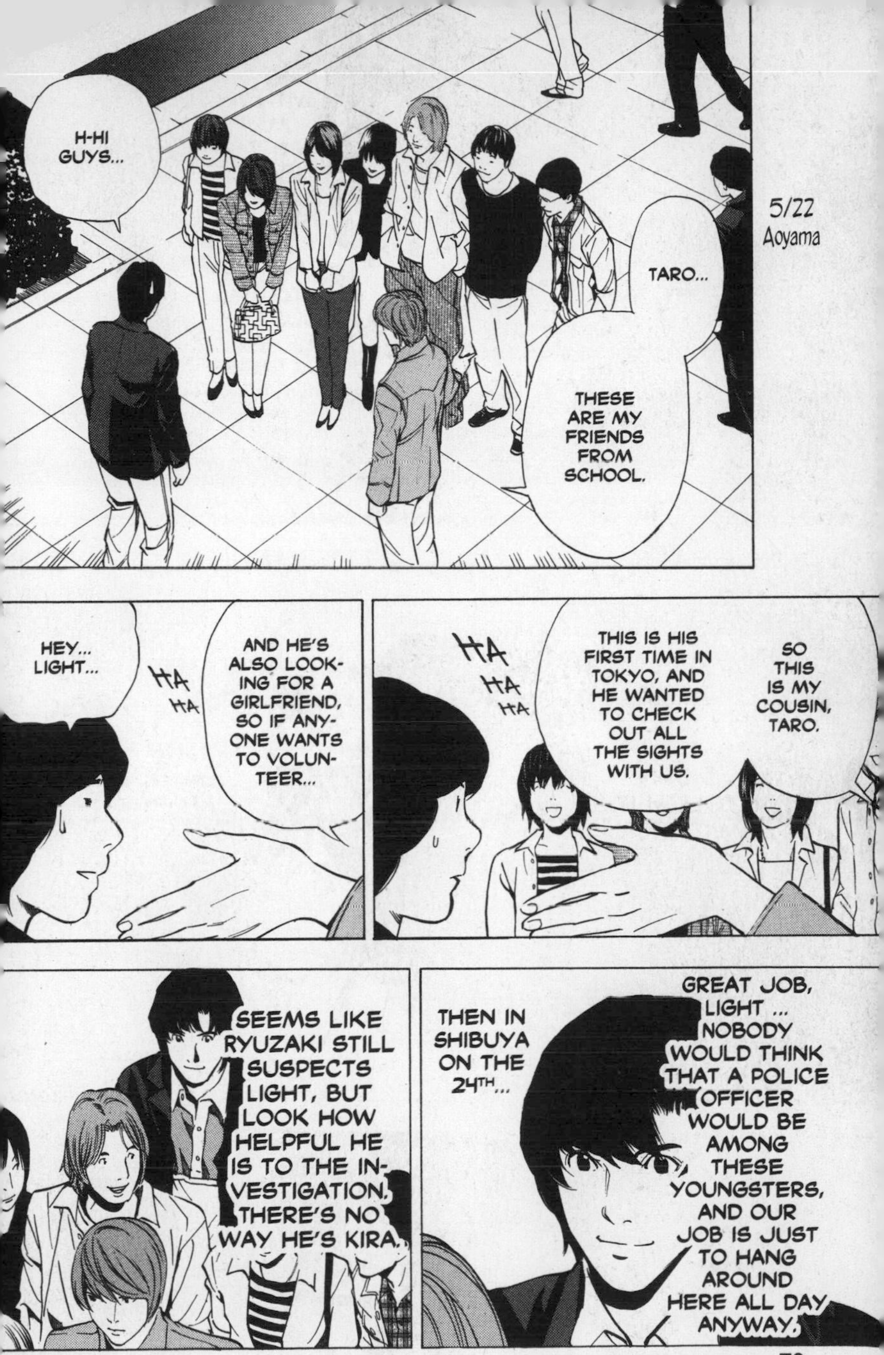
5/22 Aoyama
TARO...
THESE ARE MY FRIENDS FROM SCHOOL.
H-HI GUYS...
SO THIS IS MY COUSIN, TARO.
THIS IS HIS FIRST TIME IN TOKYO, AND HE WANTED TO CHECK OUT ALL THE SIGHTS WITH US.
HA HA HA
AND HE'S ALSO LOOKING FOR A GIRLFRIEND, SO IF ANYONE WANTS TO VOLUNTEER...
HA HA
HEY... LIGHT...
GREAT JOB, LIGHT ... NOBODY WOULD THINK THAT A POLICE OFFICER WOULD BE AMONG THESE YOUNGSTERS, AND OUR JOB IS JUST TO HANG AROUND HERE ALL DAY ANYWAY.
THEN IN SHIBUYA ON THE 24TH...
SEEMS LIKE RYUZAKI STILL SUSPECTS LIGHT, BUT LOOK HOW HELPFUL HE IS TO THE INVESTIGATION. THERE'S NO WAY HE'S KIRA.

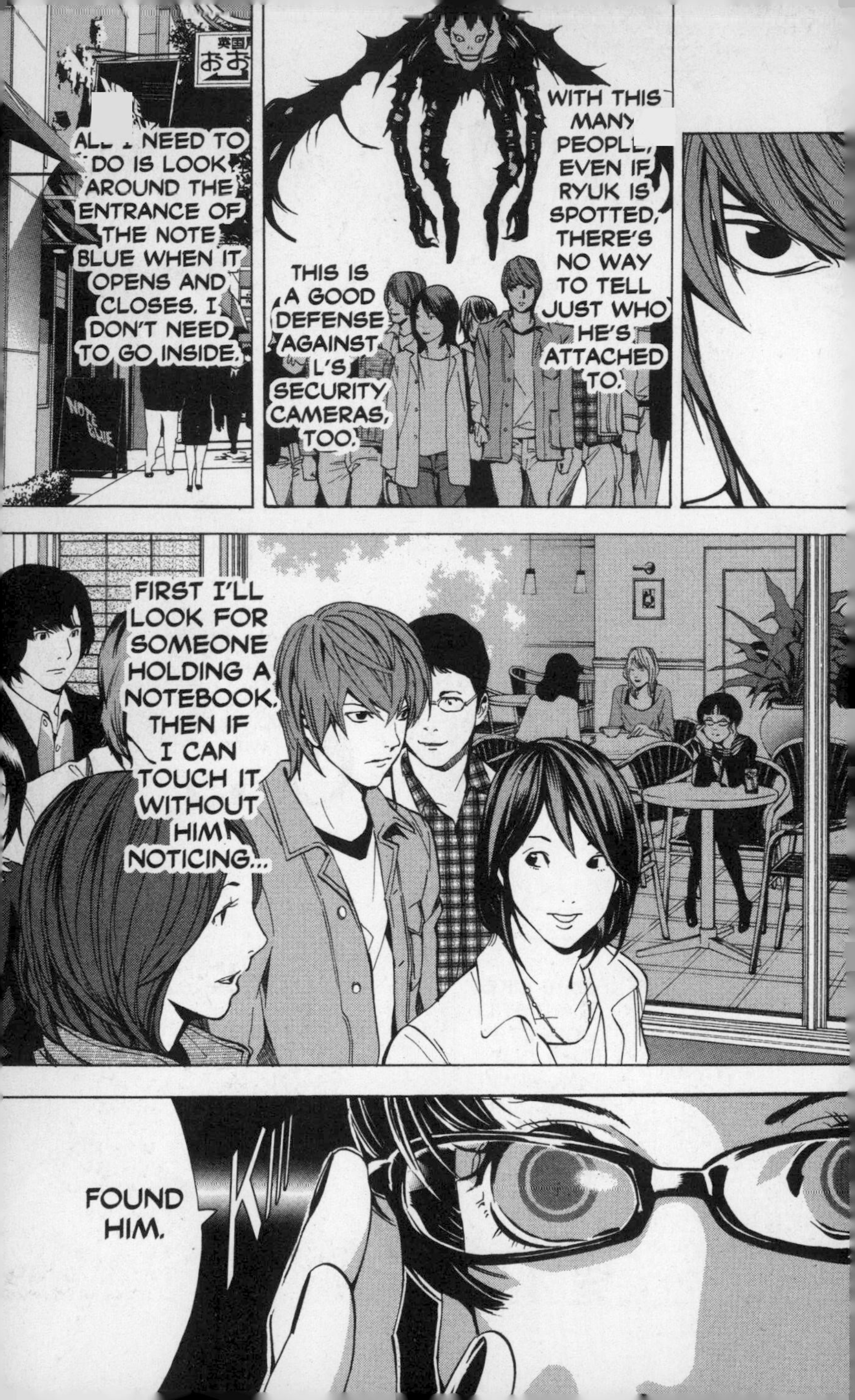
WITH THIS MANY PEOPLE, EVEN IF RYUK IS SPOTTED, THERE'S NO WAY TO TELL JUST WHO HE'S ATTACHED TO.
THIS IS A GOOD DEFENSE AGAINST L'S SECURITY CAMERAS, TOO.
ALL I NEED TO DO IS LOOK AROUND THE ENTRANCE OF THE NOTE BLUE WHEN IT OPENS AND CLOSES. I DON'T NEED TO GO INSIDE.
FIRST I'LL LOOK FOR SOMEONE HOLDING A NOTEBOOK. THEN IF I CAN TOUCH IT WITHOUT HIM NOTICING...
FOUND HIM.

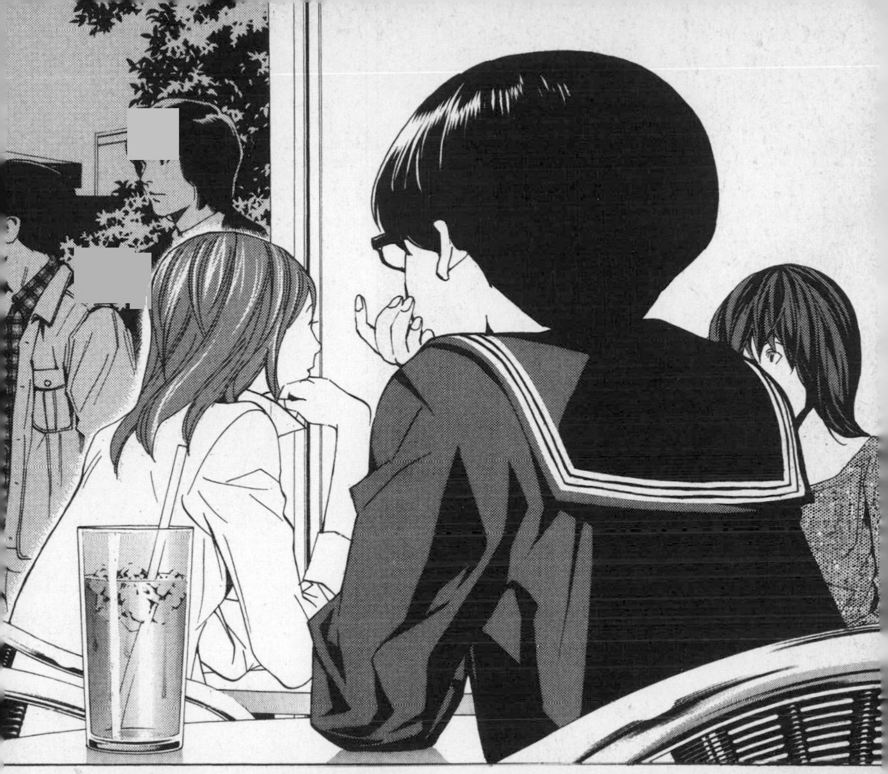

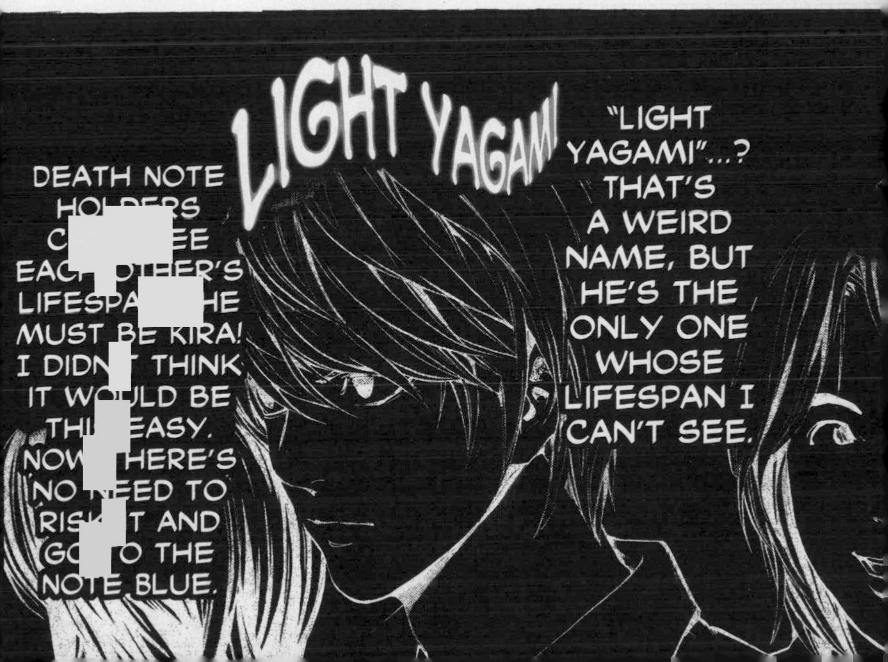
LIGHT YAGAMI
"LIGHT YAGAMI"...? THAT'S A WEIRD NAME, BUT HE'S THE ONLY ONE WHOSE LIFESPAN I CAN'T SEE.
DEATH NOTE HOLDERS [redacted] EE EAC[redacted] OTHER'S LIFESPA[redacted] HE MUST BE KIRA! I DIDN[redacted] THINK IT W[redacted] ULD BE THI[redacted] EASY. NOW[redacted] HERE'S NO [redacted] EED TO RIS[redacted] T AND GO[redacted] O THE NOTE BLUE.

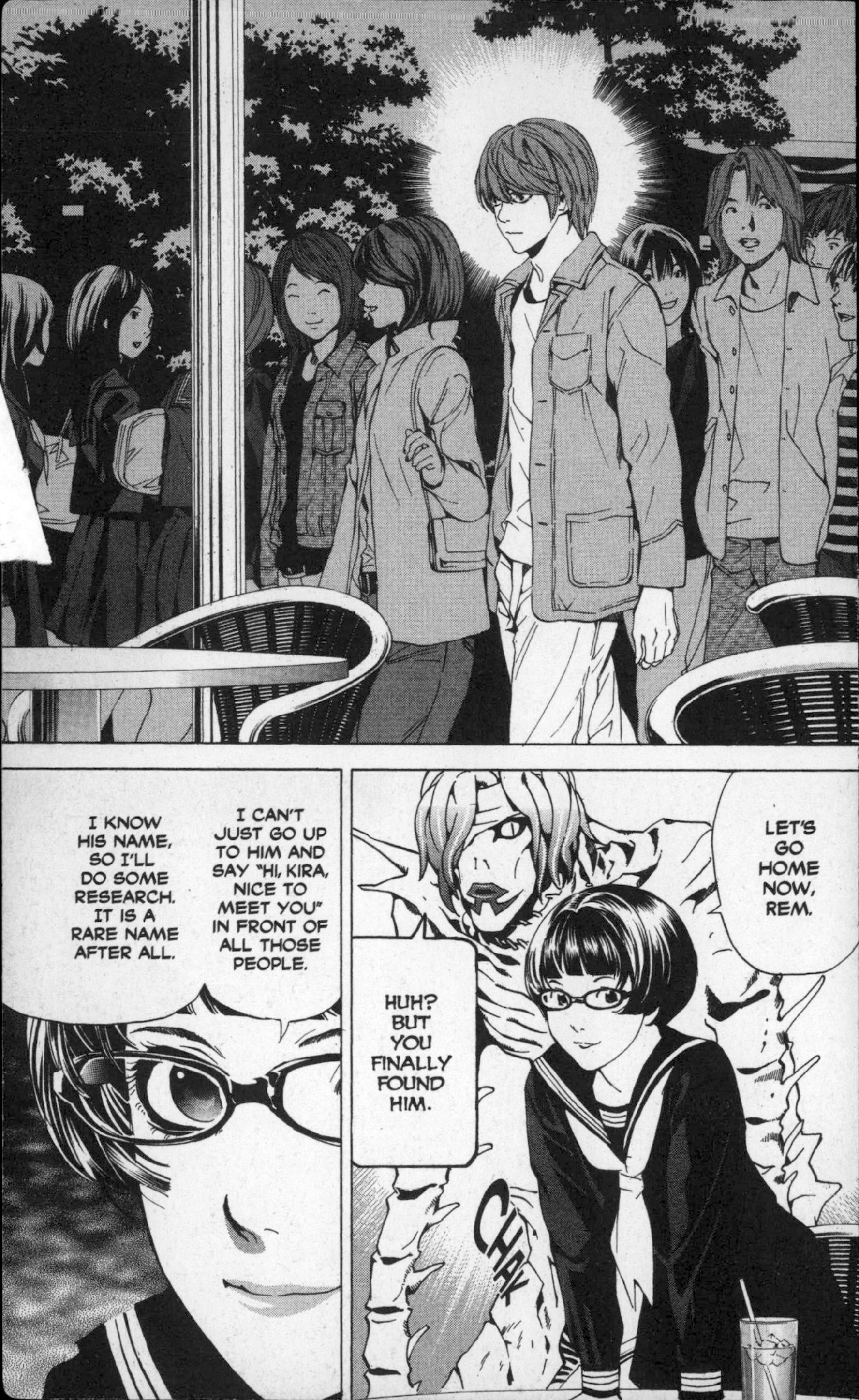
LET'S GO HOME NOW, REM.
HUH? BUT YOU FINALLY FOUND HIM.
CHAK
I CAN'T JUST GO UP TO HIM AND SAY "HI, KIRA, NICE TO MEET YOU" IN FRONT OF ALL THOSE PEOPLE.
I KNOW HIS NAME, SO I'LL DO SOME RESEARCH. IT IS A RARE NAME AFTER ALL.

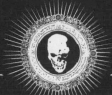

DEATH NOTE
HOW to USE It
XVⅢ

○ Only by touching each other's DEATH NOTE can human individuals who own the DEATH NOTE in the human world recognize the appearance or voice of each other's god of death.

人間界でデスノートを持った人間同士でも、相手のデスノートに触らなければ、相手に憑いている死神の姿や声は認知できない。

○ An individual with the eye power of a god of death can tell the name and life span of other humans by looking at that person's face.

By possessing the DEATH NOTE, an individual gains the ability to kill and stops being a victim. From this point, a person with the DEATH NOTE cannot see the life span of other DEATH NOTE owners, including him/herself. But, it is not really necessary for the individual to view the life span of him/herself nor other DEATH NOTE owners.

死神の目を持った人間は顔を見た人間の名前と寿命を見る事ができるが、デスノートを持つ事によって、命を取られる側から取る側になる為、殺す人間の寿命だけが見えていればいいという考え方から、自分を含め、他のデスノートを持った人間の寿命の方は見る事ができない。

○ The god of death must not tell humans the names or life spans of individuals he sees. This is to avoid confusion in the human world.

死神は人間に死神の目で見える名前や寿命を教えてはならない。これは人間界の混乱を避ける配慮である。

chapter 29 Weapon

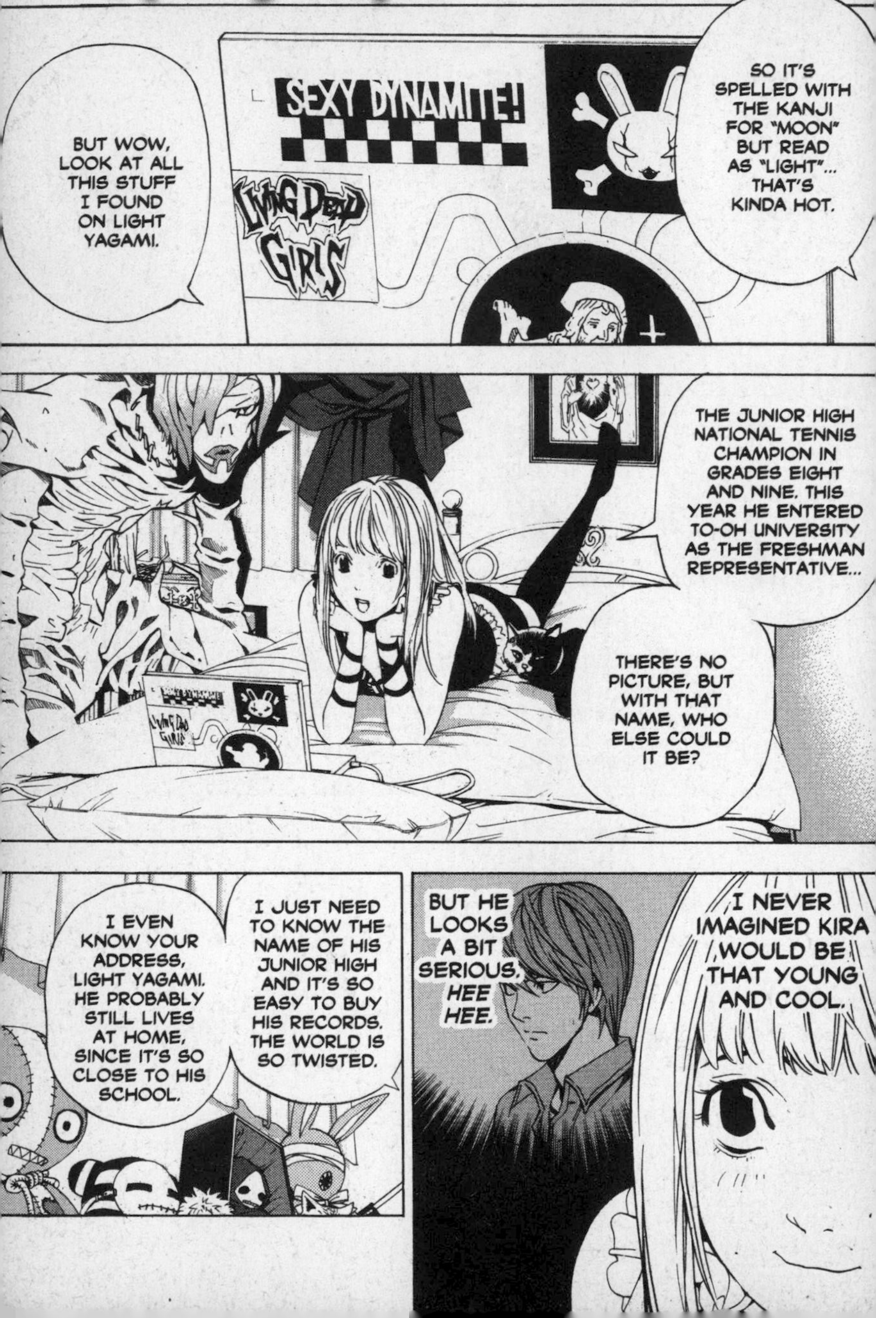
SO IT'S SPELLED WITH THE KANJI FOR "MOON" BUT READ AS "LIGHT"... THAT'S KINDA HOT.
SEXY DYNAMITE!
LIVING DEAD GIRLS
BUT WOW, LOOK AT ALL THIS STUFF I FOUND ON LIGHT YAGAMI.
THE JUNIOR HIGH NATIONAL TENNIS CHAMPION IN GRADES EIGHT AND NINE. THIS YEAR HE ENTERED TO-OH UNIVERSITY AS THE FRESHMAN REPRESENTATIVE...
THERE'S NO PICTURE, BUT WITH THAT NAME, WHO ELSE COULD IT BE?
I NEVER IMAGINED KIRA WOULD BE THAT YOUNG AND COOL.
BUT HE LOOKS A BIT SERIOUS. HEE HEE.
I JUST NEED TO KNOW THE NAME OF HIS JUNIOR HIGH AND IT'S SO EASY TO BUY HIS RECORDS. THE WORLD IS SO TWISTED.
I EVEN KNOW YOUR ADDRESS, LIGHT YAGAMI. HE PROBABLY STILL LIVES AT HOME, SINCE IT'S SO CLOSE TO HIS SCHOOL.

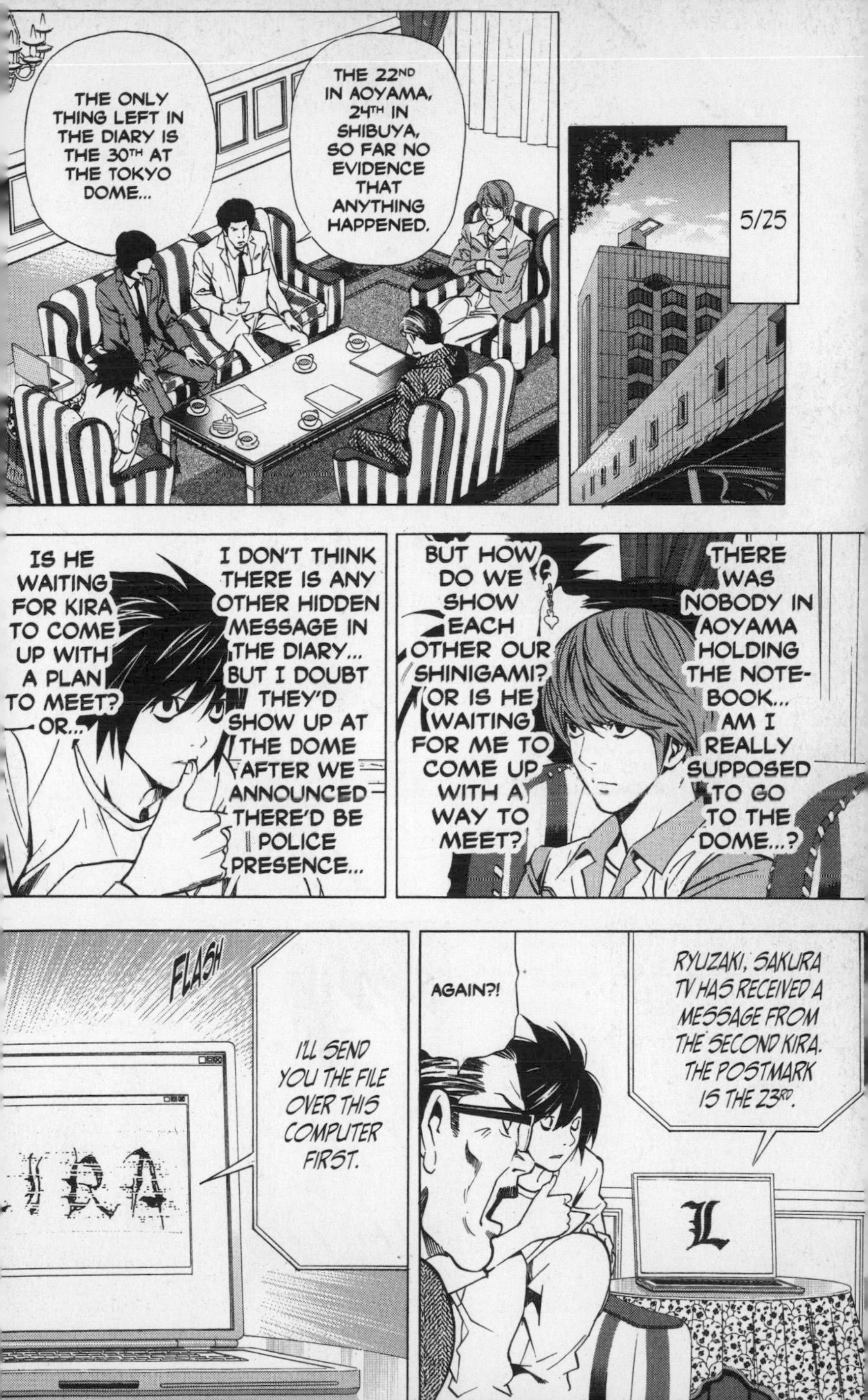
5/25
THE 22ND IN AOYAMA, 24TH IN SHIBUYA, SO FAR NO EVIDENCE THAT ANYTHING HAPPENED.
THE ONLY THING LEFT IN THE DIARY IS THE 30TH AT THE TOKYO DOME...
THERE WAS NOBODY IN AOYAMA HOLDING THE NOTEBOOK... AM I REALLY SUPPOSED TO GO TO THE DOME...?
BUT HOW DO WE SHOW EACH OTHER OUR SHINIGAMI? OR IS HE WAITING FOR ME TO COME UP WITH A WAY TO MEET?
I DON'T THINK THERE IS ANY OTHER HIDDEN MESSAGE IN THE DIARY... BUT I DOUBT THEY'D SHOW UP AT THE DOME AFTER WE ANNOUNCED THERE'D BE POLICE PRESENCE...
IS HE WAITING FOR KIRA TO COME UP WITH A PLAN TO MEET? OR...
RYUZAKI, SAKURA TV HAS RECEIVED A MESSAGE FROM THE SECOND KIRA. THE POSTMARK IS THE 23RD.
L
AGAIN?!
FLASH
I'LL SEND YOU THE FILE OVER THIS COMPUTER FIRST.

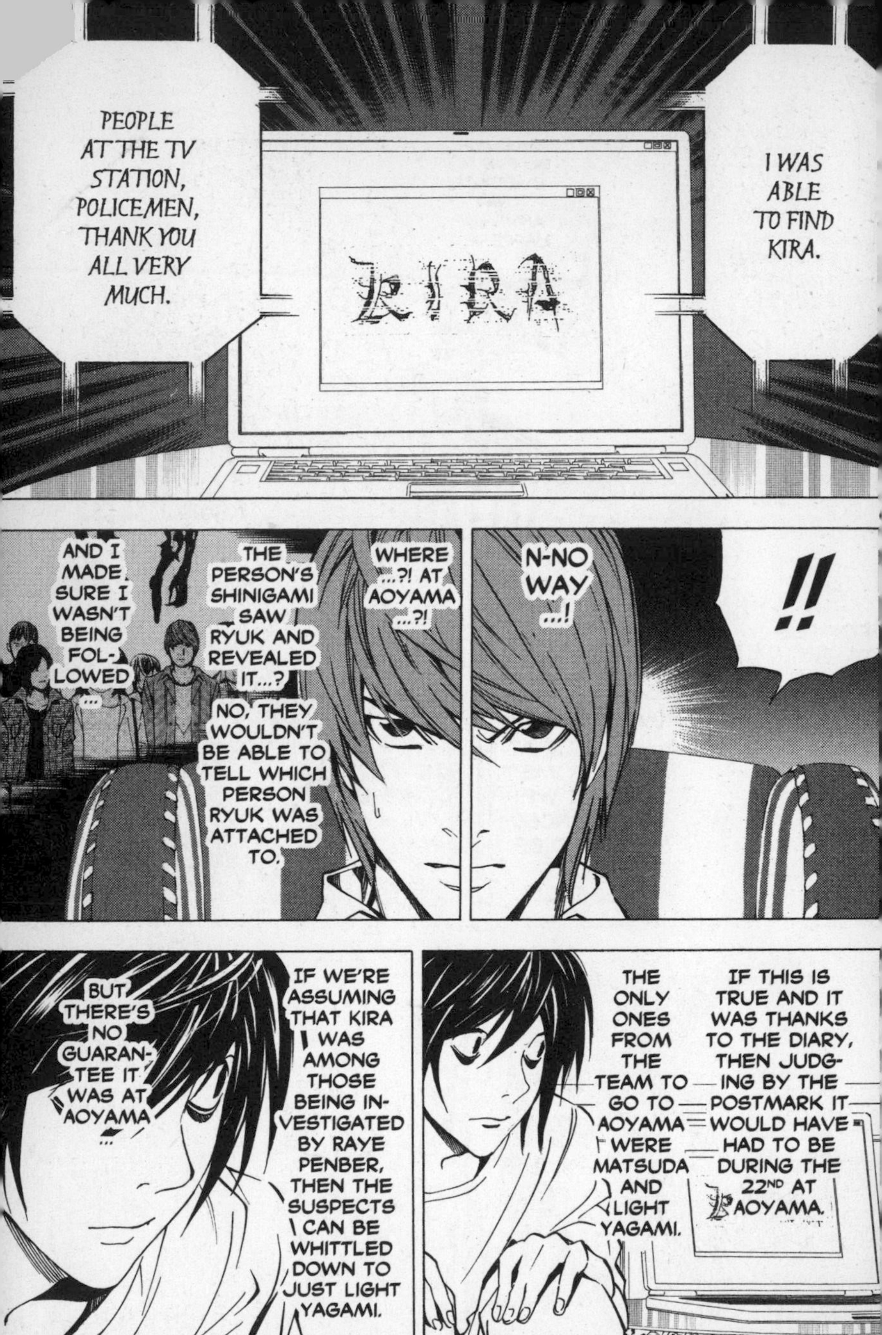
I WAS ABLE TO FIND KIRA.
KIRA
PEOPLE AT THE TV STATION, POLICEMEN, THANK YOU ALL VERY MUCH.
!!
N-NO WAY ...!
WHERE ...?! AT AOYAMA ...?!
THE PERSON'S SHINIGAMI SAW RYUK AND REVEALED IT...?
NO, THEY WOULDN'T BE ABLE TO TELL WHICH PERSON RYUK WAS ATTACHED TO.
AND I MADE SURE I WASN'T BEING FOL-LOWED...
IF THIS IS TRUE AND IT WAS THANKS TO THE DIARY, THEN JUDG-ING BY THE POSTMARK IT WOULD HAVE HAD TO BE DURING THE 22ND AT AOYAMA.
THE ONLY ONES FROM THE TEAM TO GO TO AOYAMA WERE MATSUDA AND LIGHT YAGAMI.
IF WE'RE ASSUMING THAT KIRA WAS AMONG THOSE BEING IN-VESTIGATED BY RAYE PENBER, THEN THE SUSPECTS CAN BE WHITTLED DOWN TO JUST LIGHT YAGAMI.
BUT THERE'S NO GUARAN-TEE IT WAS AT AOYAMA...

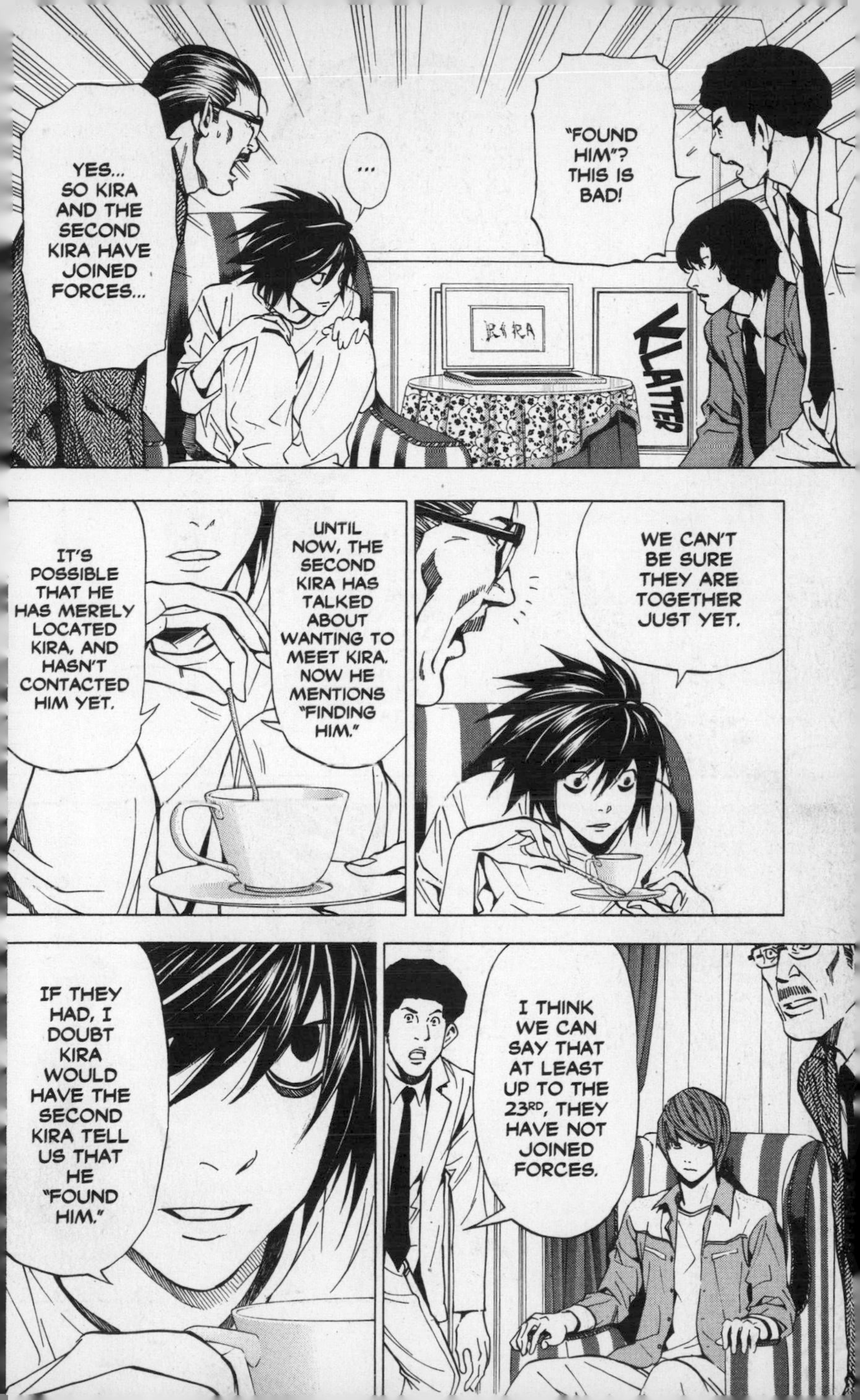
"FOUND HIM"? THIS IS BAD!
...
YES... SO KIRA AND THE SECOND KIRA HAVE JOINED FORCES...
KLATTER
WE CAN'T BE SURE THEY ARE TOGETHER JUST YET.
UNTIL NOW, THE SECOND KIRA HAS TALKED ABOUT WANTING TO MEET KIRA. NOW HE MENTIONS "FINDING HIM."
IT'S POSSIBLE THAT HE HAS MERELY LOCATED KIRA, AND HASN'T CONTACTED HIM YET.
I THINK WE CAN SAY THAT AT LEAST UP TO THE 23RD, THEY HAVE NOT JOINED FORCES.
IF THEY HAD, I DOUBT KIRA WOULD HAVE THE SECOND KIRA TELL US THAT HE "FOUND HIM."

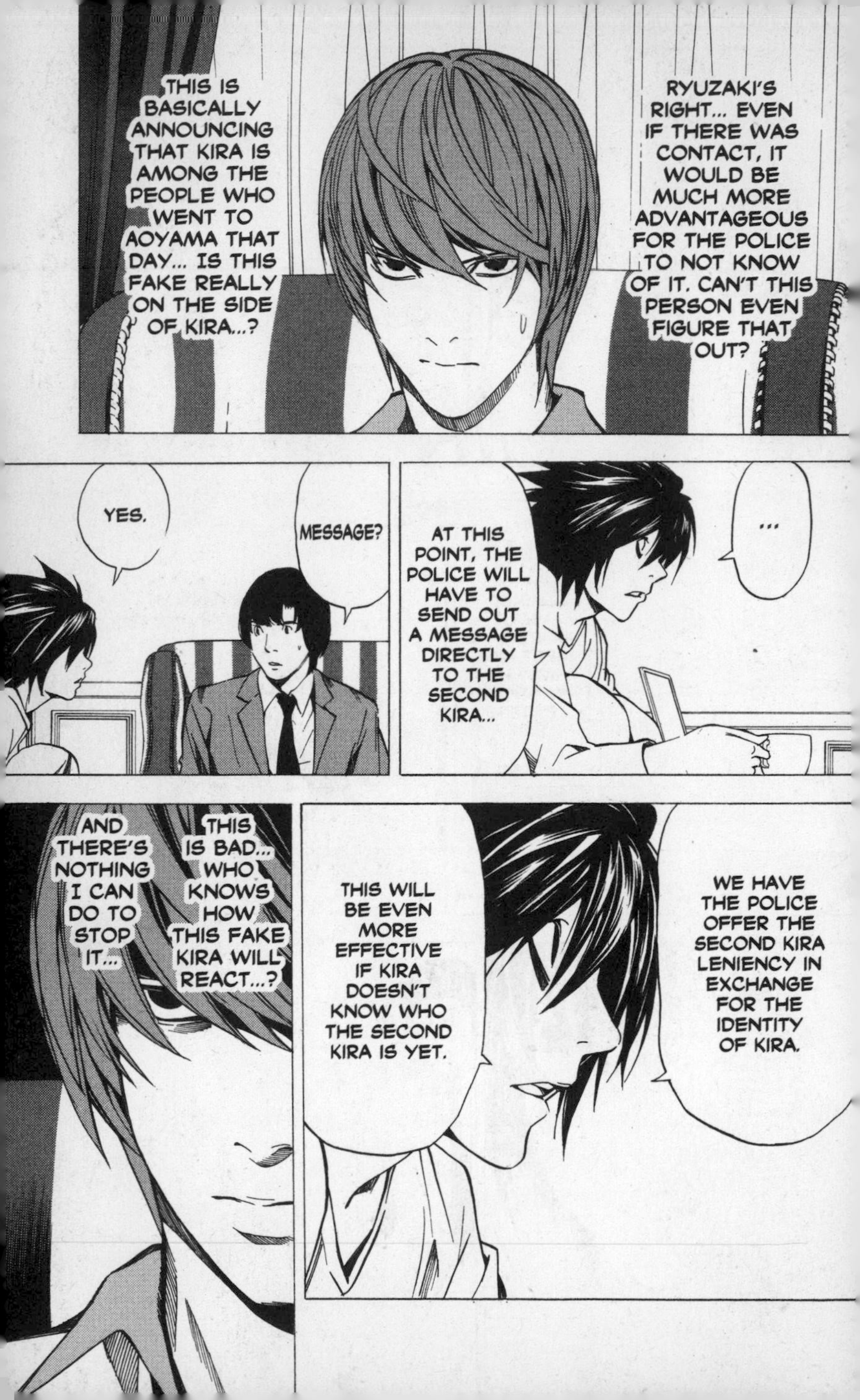
RYUZAKI'S RIGHT... EVEN IF THERE WAS CONTACT, IT WOULD BE MUCH MORE ADVANTAGEOUS FOR THE POLICE TO NOT KNOW OF IT. CAN'T THIS PERSON EVEN FIGURE THAT OUT?
THIS IS BASICALLY ANNOUNCING THAT KIRA IS AMONG THE PEOPLE WHO WENT TO AOYAMA THAT DAY... IS THIS FAKE REALLY ON THE SIDE OF KIRA...?
...
AT THIS POINT, THE POLICE WILL HAVE TO SEND OUT A MESSAGE DIRECTLY TO THE SECOND KIRA...
MESSAGE?
YES.
WE HAVE THE POLICE OFFER THE SECOND KIRA LENIENCY IN EXCHANGE FOR THE IDENTITY OF KIRA.
THIS WILL BE EVEN MORE EFFECTIVE IF KIRA DOESN'T KNOW WHO THE SECOND KIRA IS YET.
THIS IS BAD... WHO KNOWS HOW THIS FAKE KIRA WILL REACT...?
AND THERE'S NOTHING I CAN DO TO STOP IT...

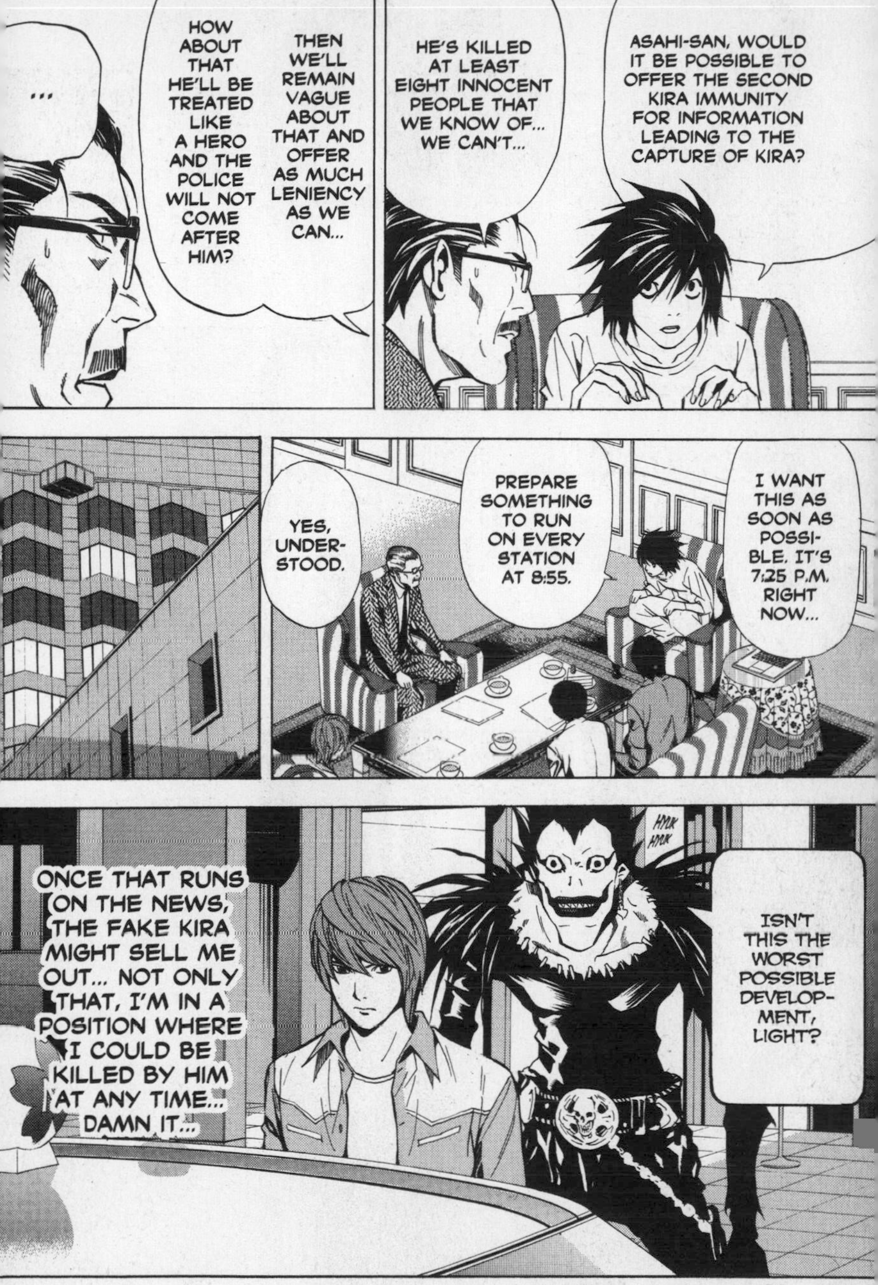
ASAHI-SAN, WOULD IT BE POSSIBLE TO OFFER THE SECOND KIRA IMMUNITY FOR INFORMATION LEADING TO THE CAPTURE OF KIRA?
HE'S KILLED AT LEAST EIGHT INNOCENT PEOPLE THAT WE KNOW OF... WE CAN'T...
THEN WE'LL REMAIN VAGUE ABOUT THAT AND OFFER AS MUCH LENIENCY AS WE CAN...
HOW ABOUT THAT HE'LL BE TREATED LIKE A HERO AND THE POLICE WILL NOT COME AFTER HIM?
...
I WANT THIS AS SOON AS POSSI-BLE. IT'S 7:25 P.M. RIGHT NOW...
PREPARE SOMETHING TO RUN ON EVERY STATION AT 8:55.
YES, UNDER-STOOD.
HYUK HYUK
ISN'T THIS THE WORST POSSIBLE DEVELOP-MENT, LIGHT?
ONCE THAT RUNS ON THE NEWS, THE FAKE KIRA MIGHT SELL ME OUT... NOT ONLY THAT, I'M IN A POSITION WHERE I COULD BE KILLED BY HIM AT ANY TIME... DAMN IT...

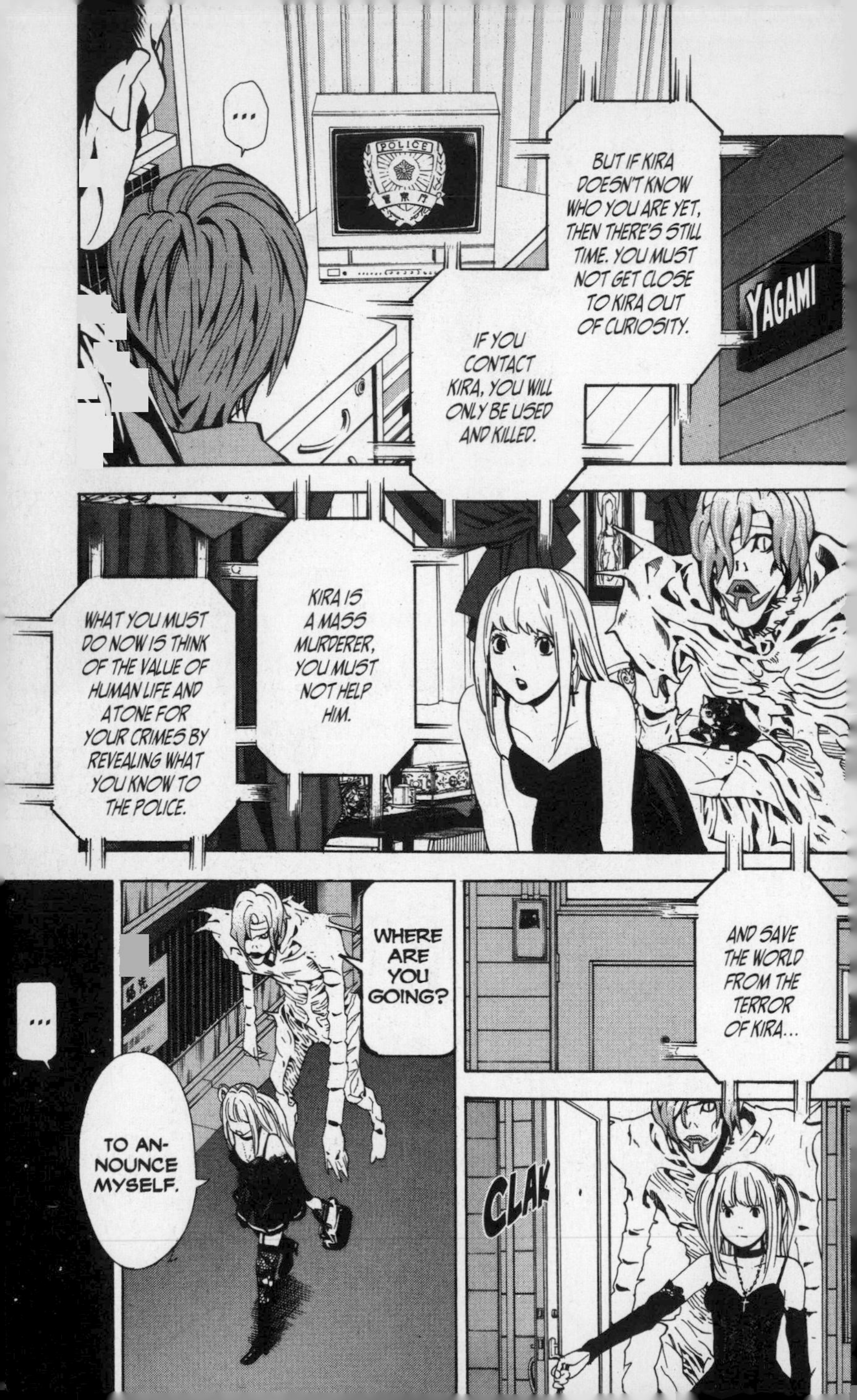

YAGAMI
BUT IF KIRA DOESN'T KNOW WHO YOU ARE YET, THEN THERE'S STILL TIME. YOU MUST NOT GET CLOSE TO KIRA OUT OF CURIOSITY.
IF YOU CONTACT KIRA, YOU WILL ONLY BE USED AND KILLED.
POLICE
...
KIRA IS A MASS MURDERER, YOU MUST NOT HELP HIM.
WHAT YOU MUST DO NOW IS THINK OF THE VALUE OF HUMAN LIFE AND ATONE FOR YOUR CRIMES BY REVEALING WHAT YOU KNOW TO THE POLICE.
AND SAVE THE WORLD FROM THE TERROR OF KIRA...
CLAK
WHERE ARE YOU GOING?
...
TO AN-NOUNCE MYSELF.

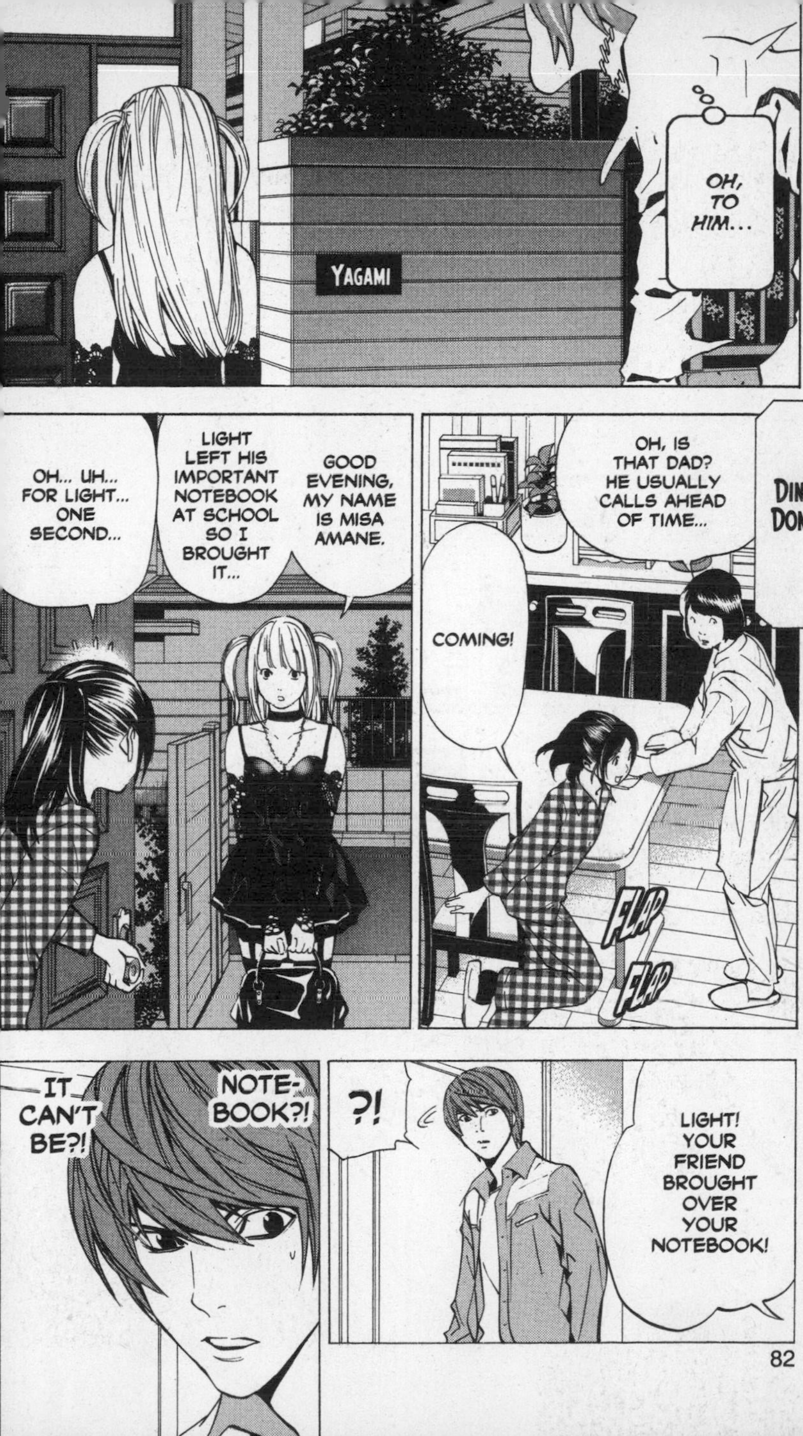
OH, TO HIM...
YAGAMI
DING DONG
OH, IS THAT DAD? HE USUALLY CALLS AHEAD OF TIME...
COMING!
FLAP
FLAP
GOOD EVENING, MY NAME IS MISA AMANE.
LIGHT LEFT HIS IMPORTANT NOTEBOOK AT SCHOOL SO I BROUGHT IT...
OH... UH... FOR LIGHT... ONE SECOND...
LIGHT! YOUR FRIEND BROUGHT OVER YOUR NOTEBOOK!
?!
NOTE-BOOK?!
IT CAN'T BE?!

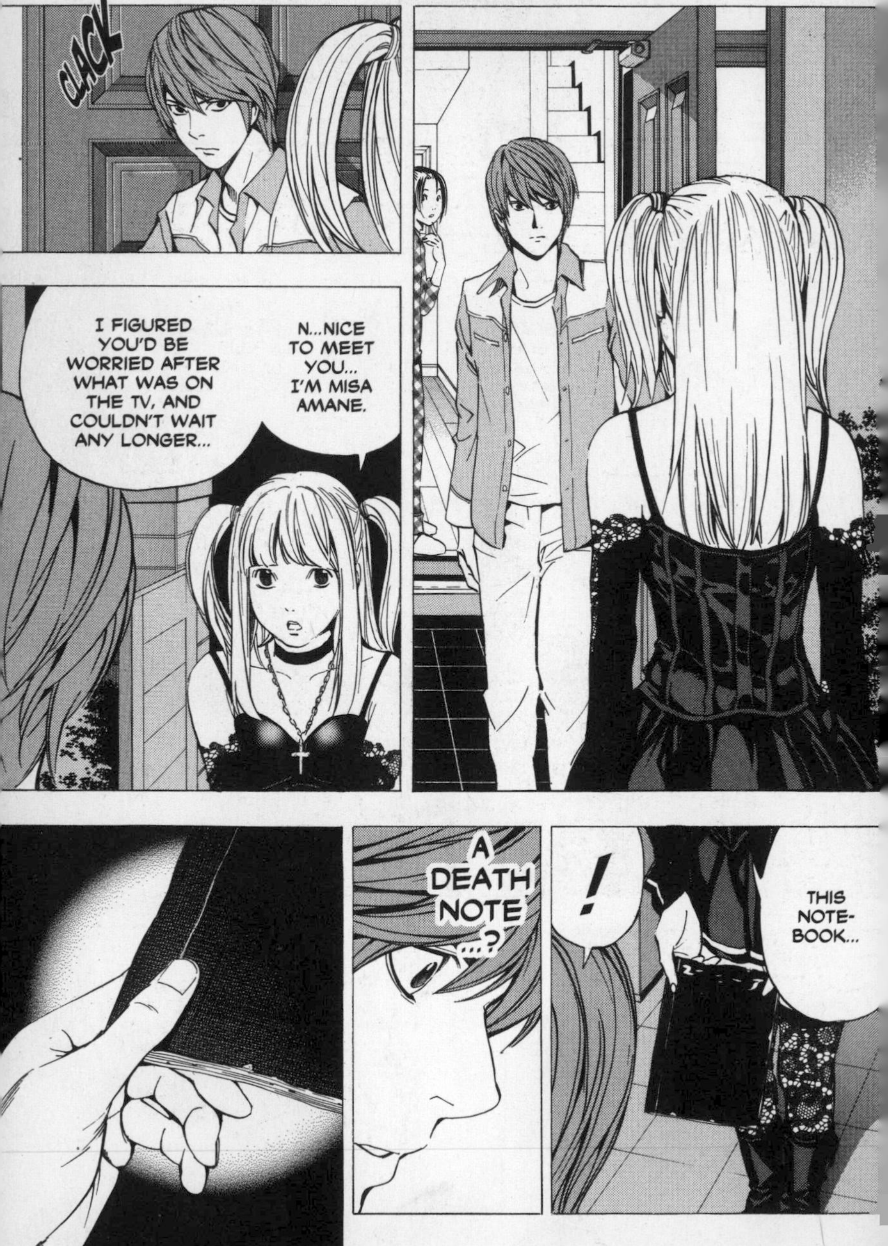
CLACK
N...NICE TO MEET YOU... I'M MISA AMANE.
I FIGURED YOU'D BE WORRIED AFTER WHAT WAS ON THE TV, AND COULDN'T WAIT ANY LONGER...
THIS NOTE-BOOK...
!
A DEATH NOTE ...?

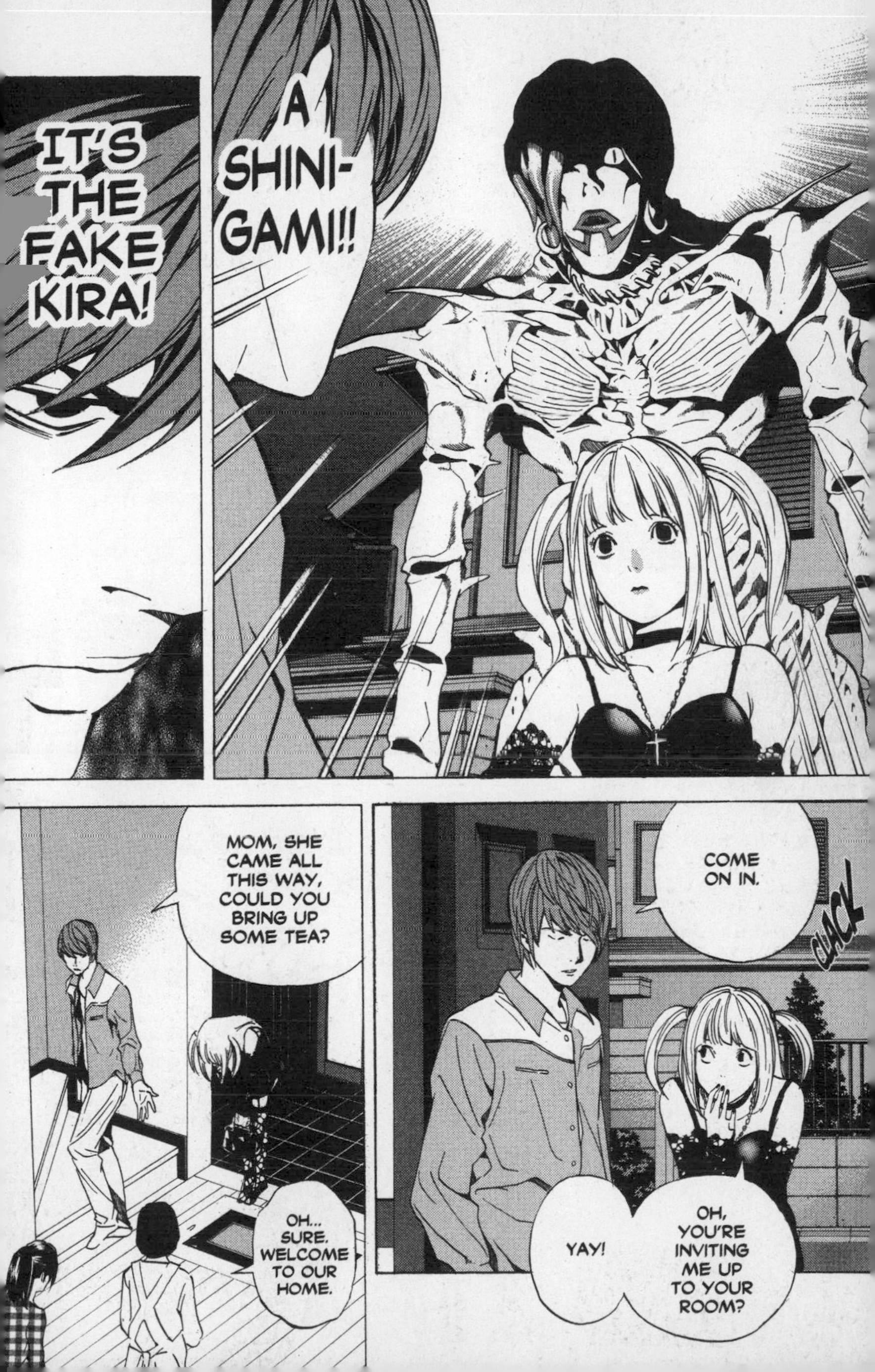
A SHINI-GAMI!!
IT'S THE FAKE KIRA!
COME ON IN.
CLACK
OH, YOU'RE INVITING ME UP TO YOUR ROOM?
YAY!
MOM, SHE CAME ALL THIS WAY, COULD YOU BRING UP SOME TEA?
OH... SURE. WELCOME TO OUR HOME.

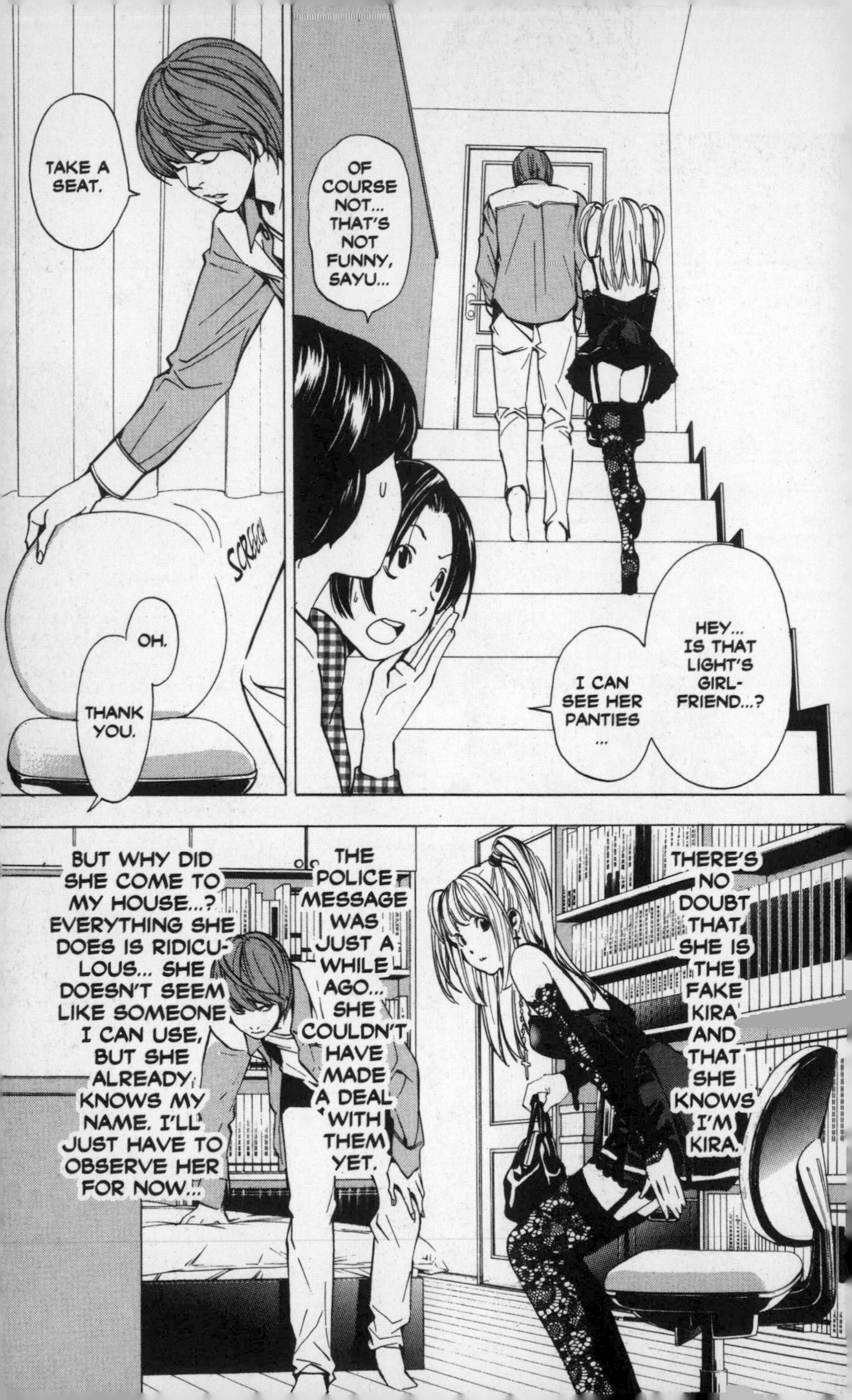
HEY... IS THAT LIGHT'S GIRL-FRIEND...?
I CAN SEE HER PANTIES ...
OF COURSE NOT... THAT'S NOT FUNNY, SAYU...
TAKE A SEAT.
SCREECH
OH.
THANK YOU.
THERE'S NO DOUBT THAT SHE IS THE FAKE KIRA AND THAT SHE KNOWS I'M KIRA.
THE POLICE MESSAGE WAS JUST A WHILE AGO... SHE COULDN'T HAVE MADE A DEAL WITH THEM YET.
BUT WHY DID SHE COME TO MY HOUSE...? EVERYTHING SHE DOES IS RIDICU-LOUS... SHE DOESN'T SEEM LIKE SOMEONE I CAN USE, BUT SHE ALREADY KNOWS MY NAME. I'LL JUST HAVE TO OBSERVE HER FOR NOW...

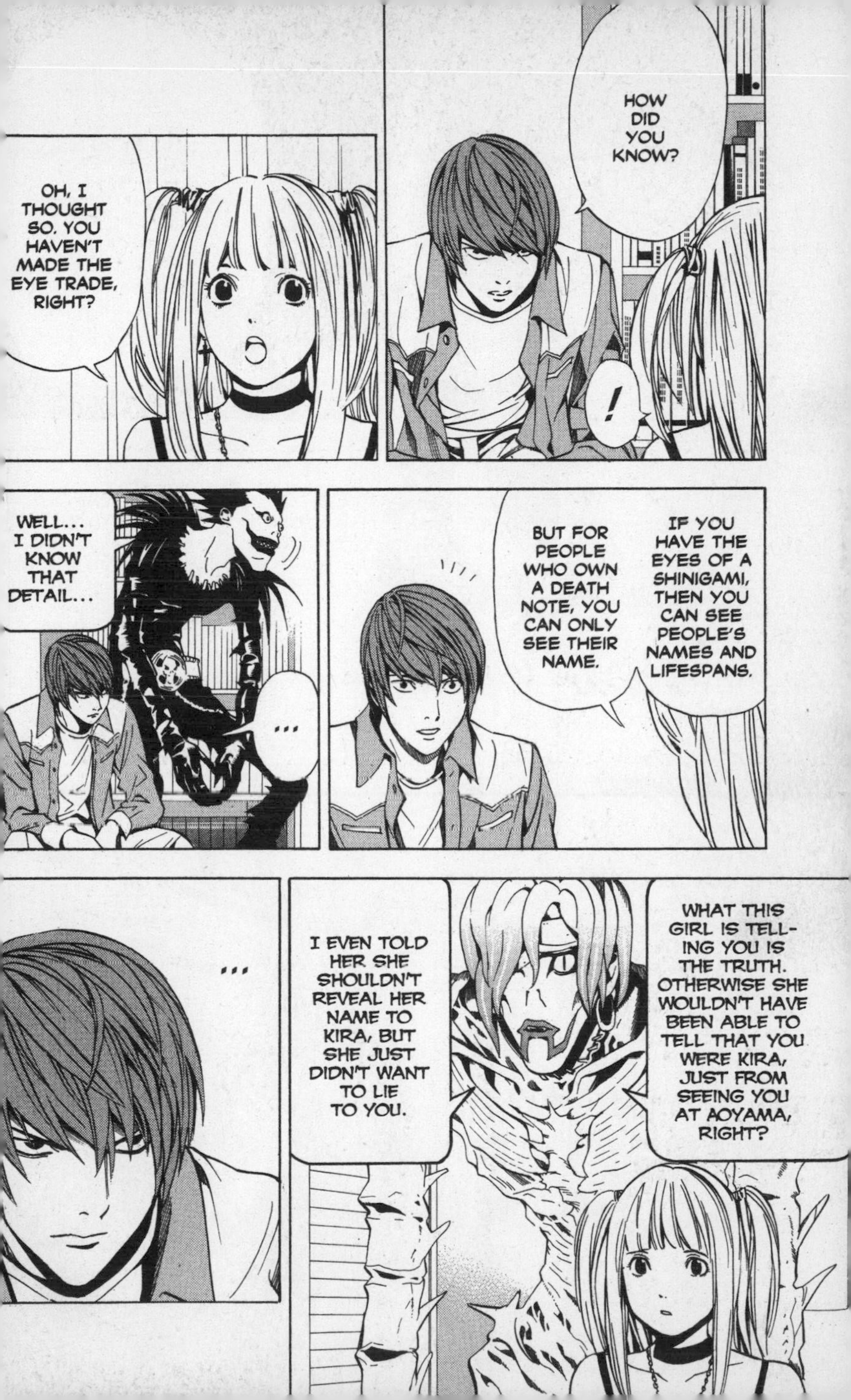
HOW DID YOU KNOW?
!
OH, I THOUGHT SO. YOU HAVEN'T MADE THE EYE TRADE, RIGHT?
IF YOU HAVE THE EYES OF A SHINIGAMI, THEN YOU CAN SEE PEOPLE'S NAMES AND LIFESPANS.
BUT FOR PEOPLE WHO OWN A DEATH NOTE, YOU CAN ONLY SEE THEIR NAME.
WELL... I DIDN'T KNOW THAT DETAIL...
...
WHAT THIS GIRL IS TELLING YOU IS THE TRUTH. OTHERWISE SHE WOULDN'T HAVE BEEN ABLE TO TELL THAT YOU WERE KIRA, JUST FROM SEEING YOU AT AOYAMA, RIGHT?
I EVEN TOLD HER SHE SHOULDN'T REVEAL HER NAME TO KIRA, BUT SHE JUST DIDN'T WANT TO LIE TO YOU.
...

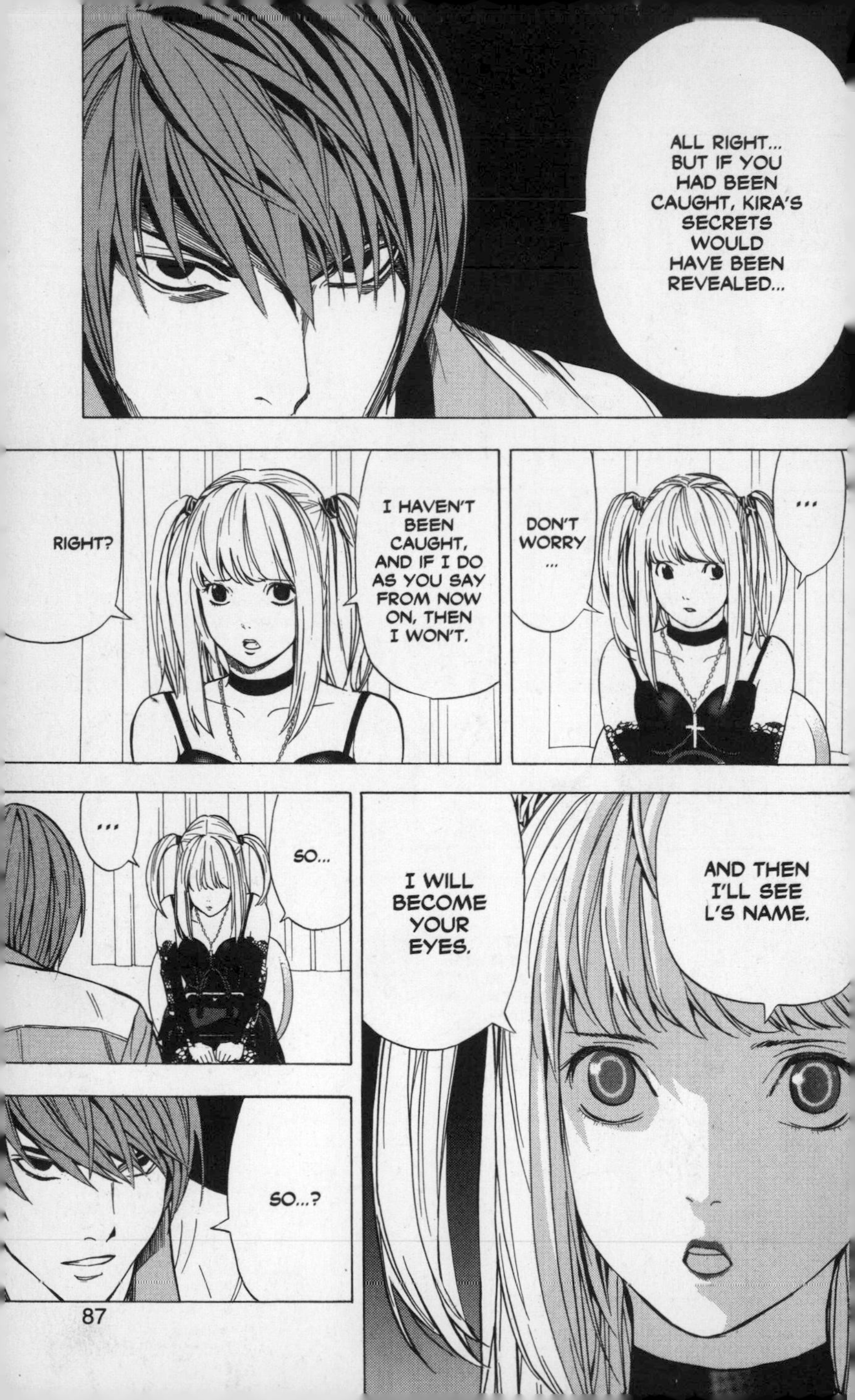
ALL RIGHT... BUT IF YOU HAD BEEN CAUGHT, KIRA'S SECRETS WOULD HAVE BEEN REVEALED...
...
DON'T WORRY ...
I HAVEN'T BEEN CAUGHT, AND IF I DO AS YOU SAY FROM NOW ON, THEN I WON'T.
RIGHT?
...
SO...
SO...?
I WILL BECOME YOUR EYES.
AND THEN I'LL SEE L'S NAME.

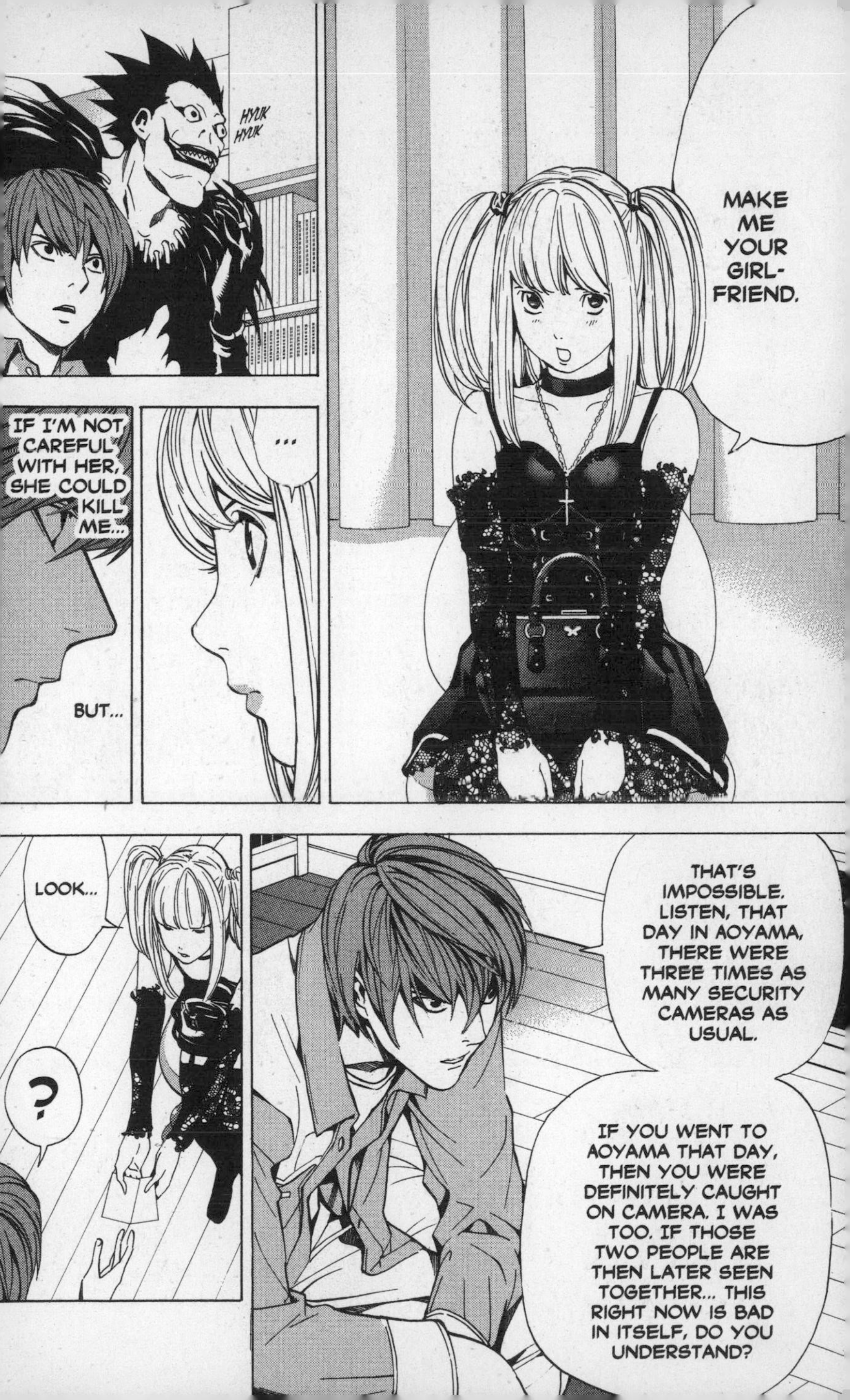
MAKE ME YOUR GIRL-FRIEND.
HYUK HYUK
...
IF I'M NOT CAREFUL WITH HER, SHE COULD KILL ME...
BUT...
THAT'S IMPOSSIBLE. LISTEN, THAT DAY IN AOYAMA, THERE WERE THREE TIMES AS MANY SECURITY CAMERAS AS USUAL.
IF YOU WENT TO AOYAMA THAT DAY, THEN YOU WERE DEFINITELY CAUGHT ON CAMERA. I WAS TOO. IF THOSE TWO PEOPLE ARE THEN LATER SEEN TOGETHER... THIS RIGHT NOW IS BAD IN ITSELF, DO YOU UNDERSTAND?
LOOK...
?

READ THIS WAY

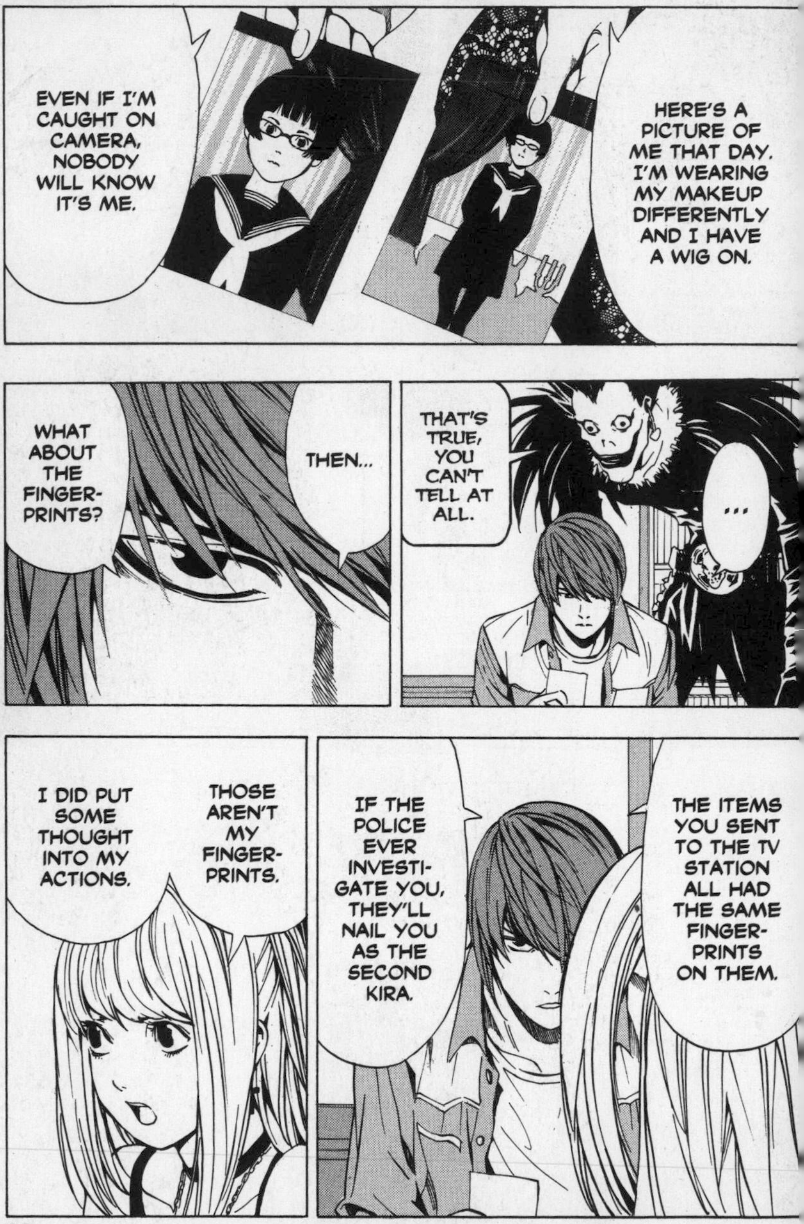
HERE'S A PICTURE OF ME THAT DAY. I'M WEARING MY MAKEUP DIFFERENTLY AND I HAVE A WIG ON.
EVEN IF I'M CAUGHT ON CAMERA, NOBODY WILL KNOW IT'S ME.
THAT'S TRUE, YOU CAN'T TELL AT ALL.
...
THEN...
WHAT ABOUT THE FINGER-PRINTS?
THE ITEMS YOU SENT TO THE TV STATION ALL HAD THE SAME FINGER-PRINTS ON THEM.
IF THE POLICE EVER INVESTI-GATE YOU, THEY'LL NAIL YOU AS THE SECOND KIRA.
THOSE AREN'T MY FINGER-PRINTS.
I DID PUT SOME THOUGHT INTO MY ACTIONS.

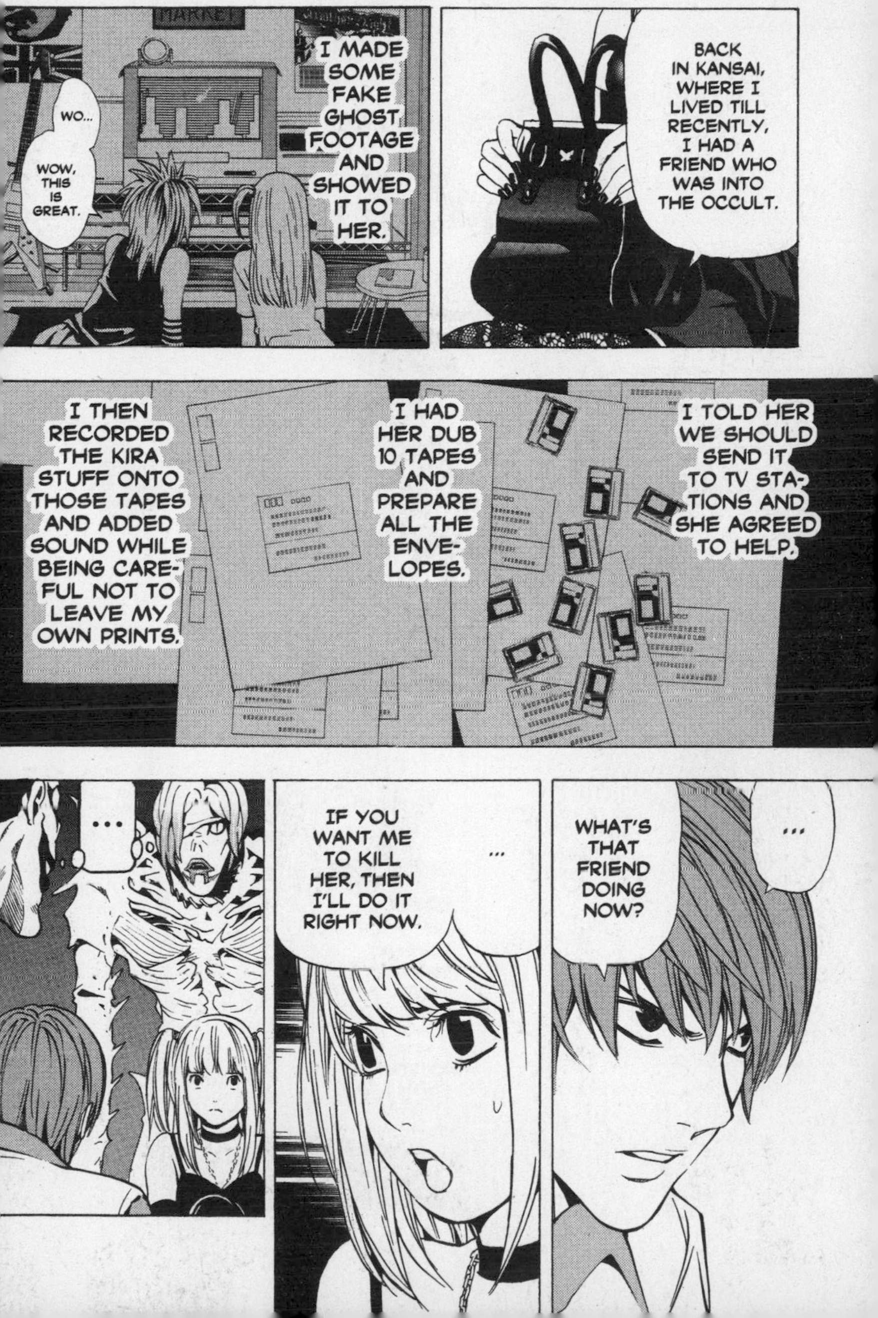
BACK IN KANSAI, WHERE I LIVED TILL RECENTLY, I HAD A FRIEND WHO WAS INTO THE OCCULT.
I MADE SOME FAKE GHOST FOOTAGE AND SHOWED IT TO HER.
WO...
WOW, THIS IS GREAT.
I TOLD HER WE SHOULD SEND IT TO TV STATIONS AND SHE AGREED TO HELP.
I HAD HER DUB 10 TAPES AND PREPARE ALL THE ENVELOPES.
I THEN RECORDED THE KIRA STUFF ONTO THOSE TAPES AND ADDED SOUND WHILE BEING CAREFUL NOT TO LEAVE MY OWN PRINTS.
...
WHAT'S THAT FRIEND DOING NOW?
...
IF YOU WANT ME TO KILL HER, THEN I'LL DO IT RIGHT NOW.
...

READ THIS WAY

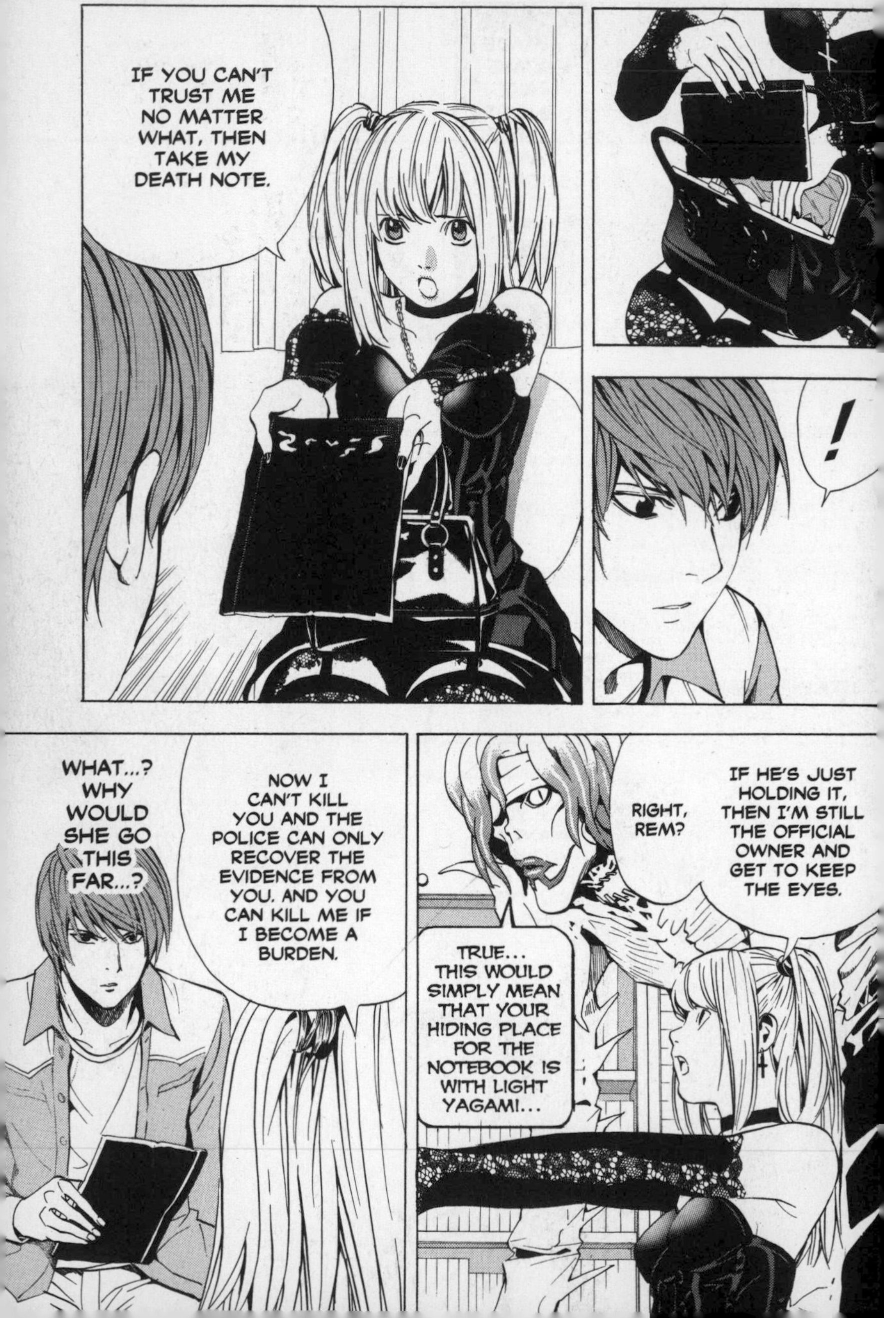
!
IF YOU CAN'T TRUST ME NO MATTER WHAT, THEN TAKE MY DEATH NOTE.
IF HE'S JUST HOLDING IT, THEN I'M STILL THE OFFICIAL OWNER AND GET TO KEEP THE EYES.
RIGHT, REM?
TRUE... THIS WOULD SIMPLY MEAN THAT YOUR HIDING PLACE FOR THE NOTEBOOK IS WITH LIGHT YAGAMI...
NOW I CAN'T KILL YOU AND THE POLICE CAN ONLY RECOVER THE EVIDENCE FROM YOU. AND YOU CAN KILL ME IF I BECOME A BURDEN.
WHAT...? WHY WOULD SHE GO THIS FAR...?

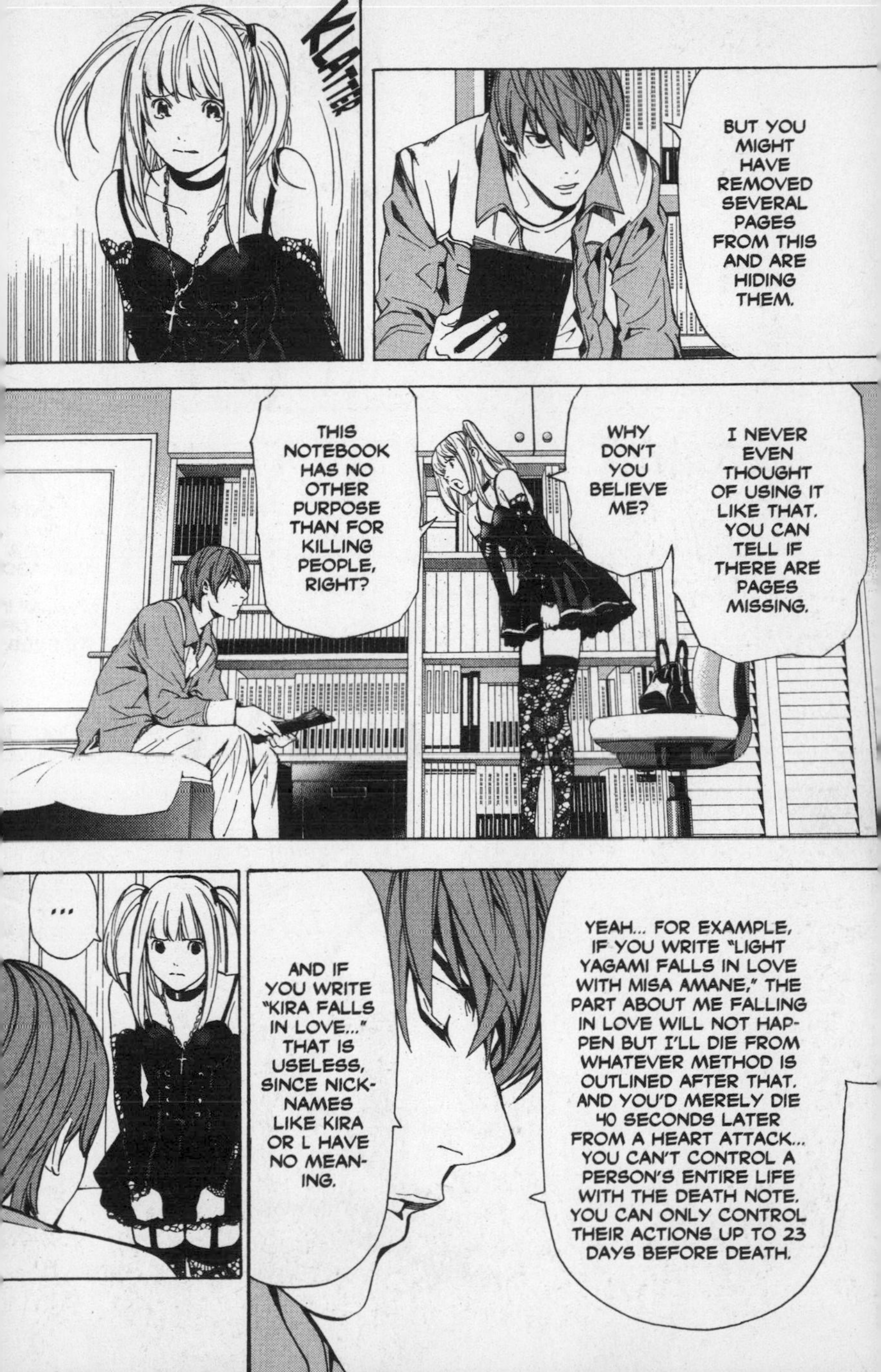
BUT YOU MIGHT HAVE REMOVED SEVERAL PAGES FROM THIS AND ARE HIDING THEM.
KLATTER
I NEVER EVEN THOUGHT OF USING IT LIKE THAT. YOU CAN TELL IF THERE ARE PAGES MISSING.
WHY DON'T YOU BELIEVE ME?
THIS NOTEBOOK HAS NO OTHER PURPOSE THAN FOR KILLING PEOPLE, RIGHT?
YEAH... FOR EXAMPLE, IF YOU WRITE "LIGHT YAGAMI FALLS IN LOVE WITH MISA AMANE," THE PART ABOUT ME FALLING IN LOVE WILL NOT HAPPEN BUT I'LL DIE FROM WHATEVER METHOD IS OUTLINED AFTER THAT. AND YOU'D MERELY DIE 40 SECONDS LATER FROM A HEART ATTACK... YOU CAN'T CONTROL A PERSON'S ENTIRE LIFE WITH THE DEATH NOTE. YOU CAN ONLY CONTROL THEIR ACTIONS UP TO 23 DAYS BEFORE DEATH.
AND IF YOU WRITE "KIRA FALLS IN LOVE..." THAT IS USELESS, SINCE NICKNAMES LIKE KIRA OR L HAVE NO MEANING.
...

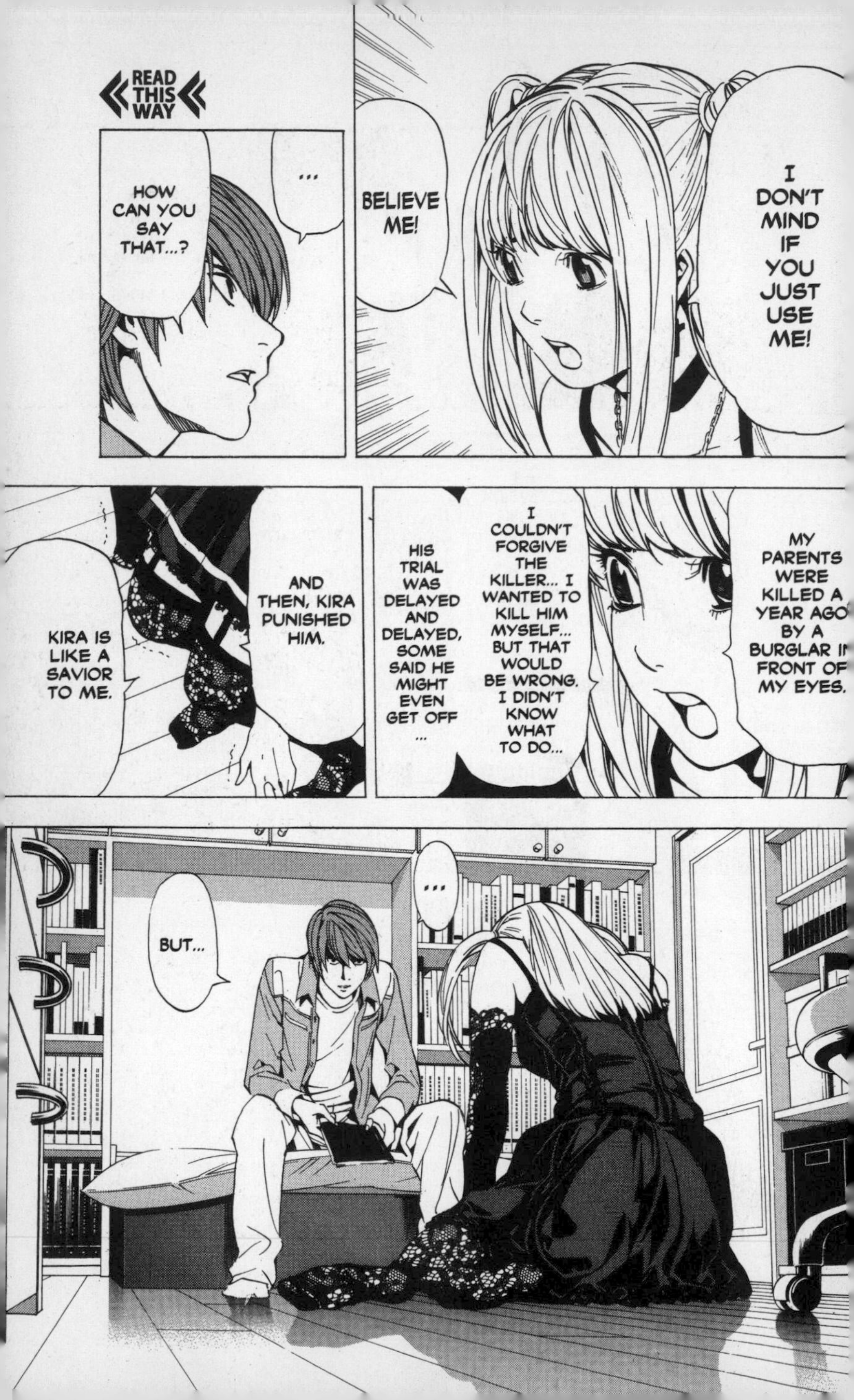
READ THIS WAY
I DON'T MIND IF YOU JUST USE ME!
BELIEVE ME!
...
HOW CAN YOU SAY THAT...?
MY PARENTS WERE KILLED A YEAR AGO BY A BURGLAR IN FRONT OF MY EYES.
I COULDN'T FORGIVE THE KILLER... I WANTED TO KILL HIM MYSELF... BUT THAT WOULD BE WRONG. I DIDN'T KNOW WHAT TO DO...
HIS TRIAL WAS DELAYED AND DELAYED, SOME SAID HE MIGHT EVEN GET OFF ...
AND THEN, KIRA PUNISHED HIM.
KIRA IS LIKE A SAVIOR TO ME.
...
BUT...

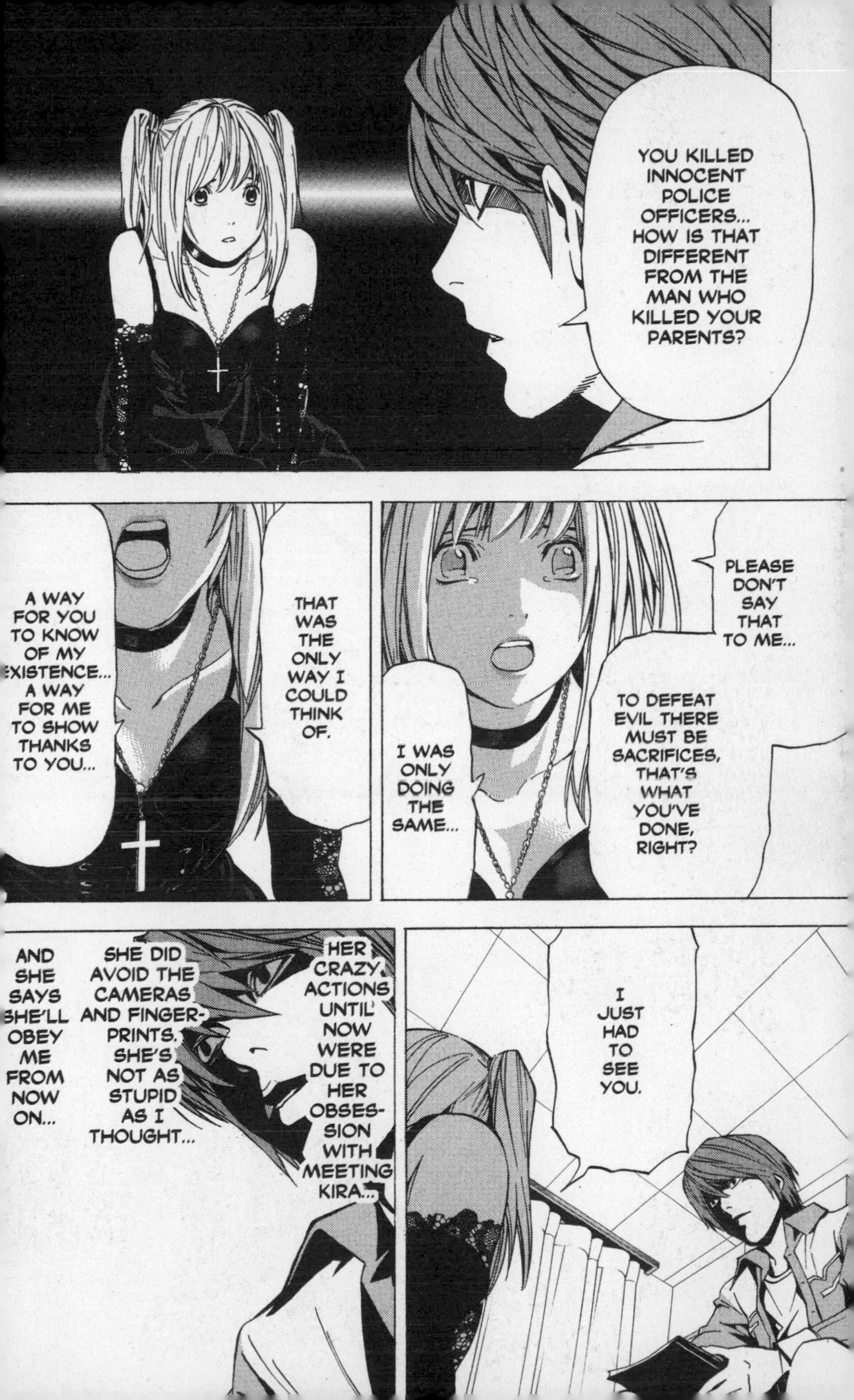
YOU KILLED INNOCENT POLICE OFFICERS... HOW IS THAT DIFFERENT FROM THE MAN WHO KILLED YOUR PARENTS?
PLEASE DON'T SAY THAT TO ME...
TO DEFEAT EVIL THERE MUST BE SACRIFICES, THAT'S WHAT YOU'VE DONE, RIGHT?
I WAS ONLY DOING THE SAME...
THAT WAS THE ONLY WAY I COULD THINK OF.
A WAY FOR YOU TO KNOW OF MY EXISTENCE... A WAY FOR ME TO SHOW THANKS TO YOU...
I JUST HAD TO SEE YOU.
HER CRAZY ACTIONS UNTIL NOW WERE DUE TO HER OBSESSION WITH MEETING KIRA...
SHE DID AVOID THE CAMERAS AND FINGER-PRINTS. SHE'S NOT AS STUPID AS I THOUGHT...
AND SHE SAYS SHE'LL OBEY ME FROM NOW ON...

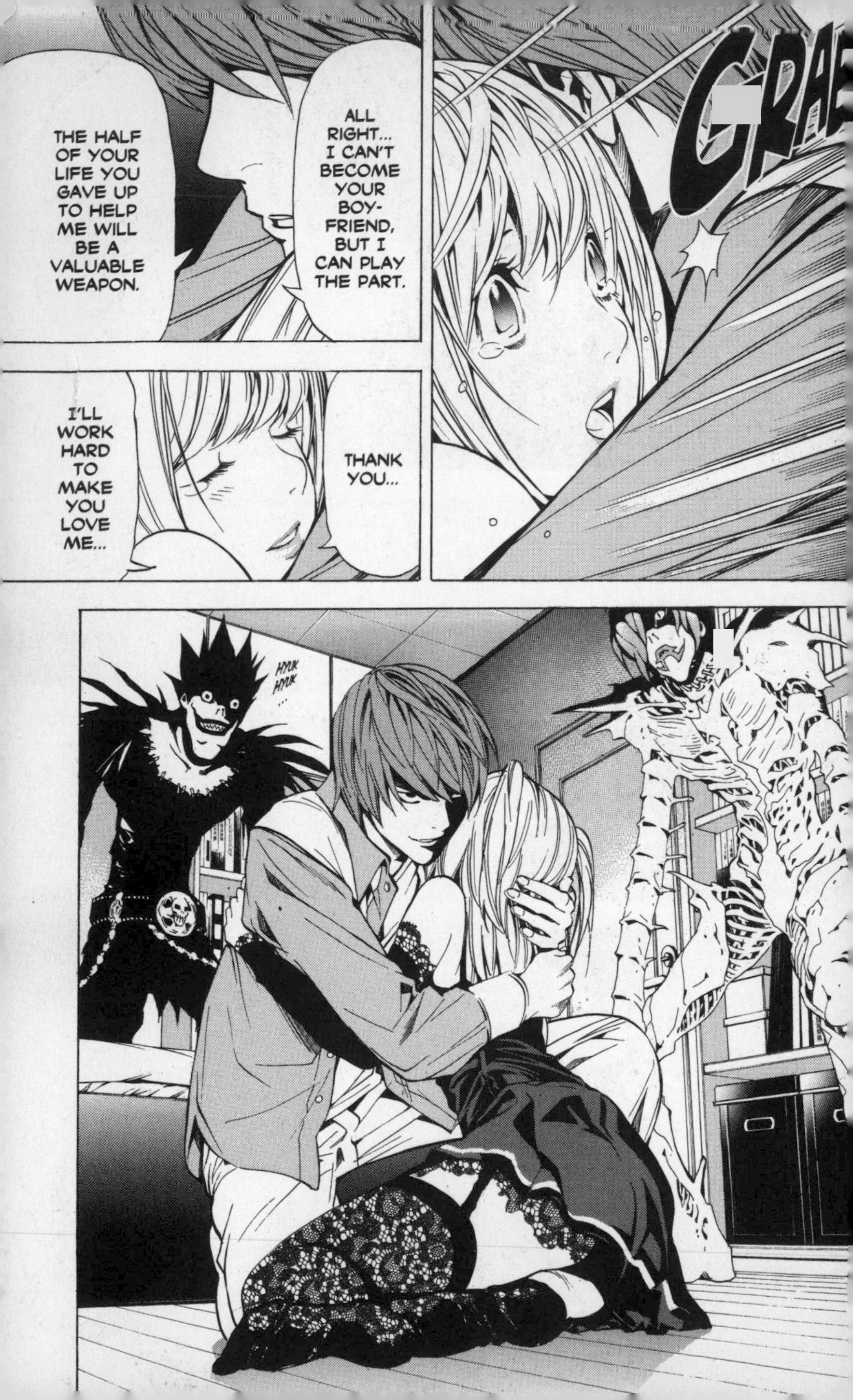

GRA
ALL RIGHT... I CAN'T BECOME YOUR BOY-FRIEND, BUT I CAN PLAY THE PART.
THE HALF OF YOUR LIFE YOU GAVE UP TO HELP ME WILL BE A VALUABLE WEAPON.
THANK YOU...
I'LL WORK HARD TO MAKE YOU LOVE ME...
HYUK HYUK ...

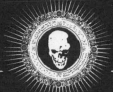

DEATH NOTE
How to use it
XVN

○ It is prerequisite for the DEATH NOTE used in the human world that a living god of death makes sure that the humans in the human world use it.

人間界で使われるデスノートには、生きた死神の人間界で人間に使わせる という意思が始めになければならない。

○ It is very difficult to consider that a god of death who has possessed a human could die, but if he should die, the DEATH NOTE that he brought into the human world will not lose its power.

その後、人間に憑いた死神が死ぬ事は考えにくいが、 死んだ場合、その死神が人間界に持ち込んだデスノートの効力に 変化は生じない。

chapter 30 Bomb

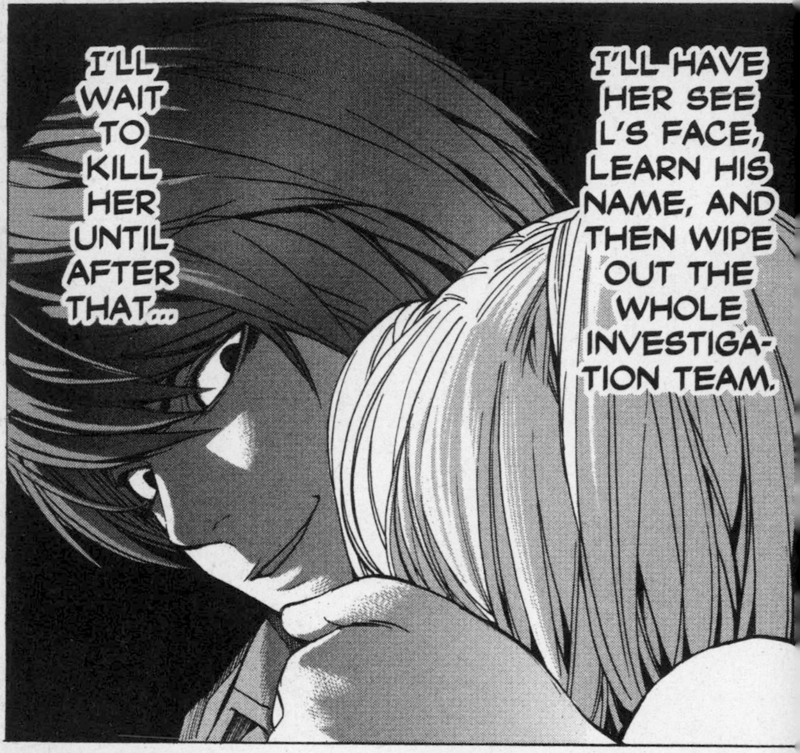
I'LL HAVE HER SEE L'S FACE, LEARN HIS NAME, AND THEN WIPE OUT THE WHOLE INVESTIGA-TION TEAM.
I'LL WAIT TO KILL HER UNTIL AFTER THAT...

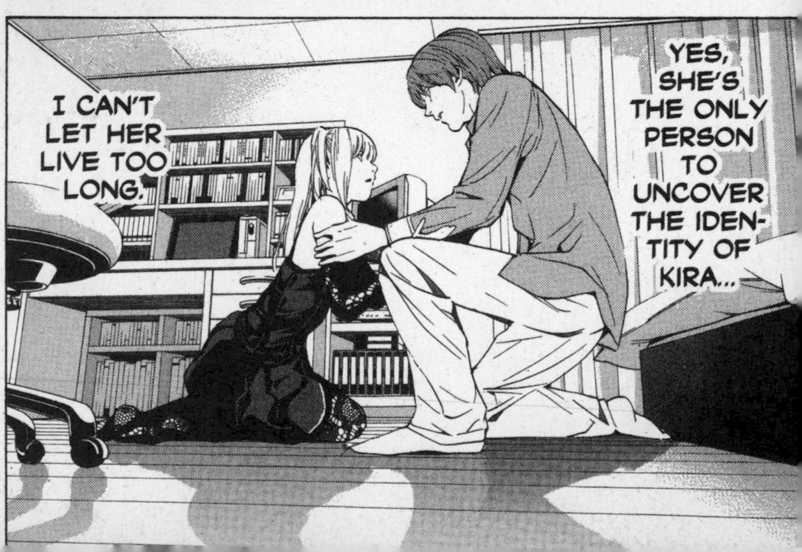
YES, SHE'S THE ONLY PERSON TO UNCOVER THE IDEN-TITY OF KIRA...
I CAN'T LET HER LIVE TOO LONG.

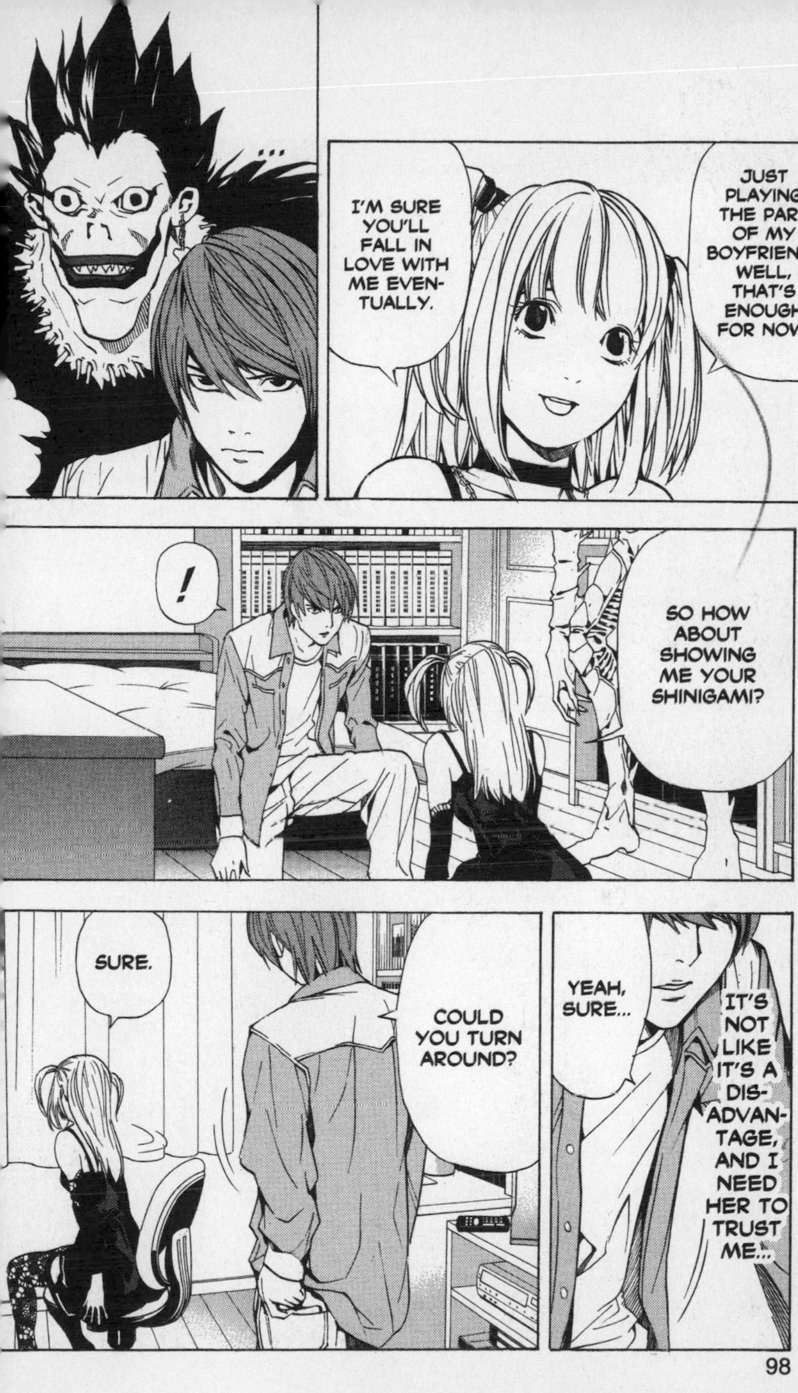
JUST PLAYING THE PART OF MY BOYFRIEND? WELL, THAT'S ENOUGH FOR NOW.
I'M SURE YOU'LL FALL IN LOVE WITH ME EVENTUALLY.
...
SO HOW ABOUT SHOWING ME YOUR SHINIGAMI?
!
YEAH, SURE...
IT'S NOT LIKE IT'S A DISADVANTAGE, AND I NEED HER TO TRUST ME...
COULD YOU TURN AROUND?
SURE.

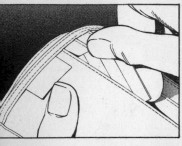

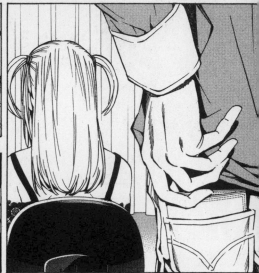

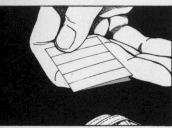

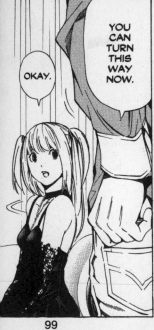

YOU CAN TURN THIS WAY NOW.

OKAY.

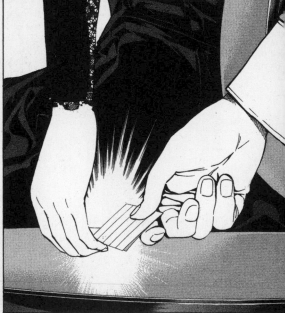

99

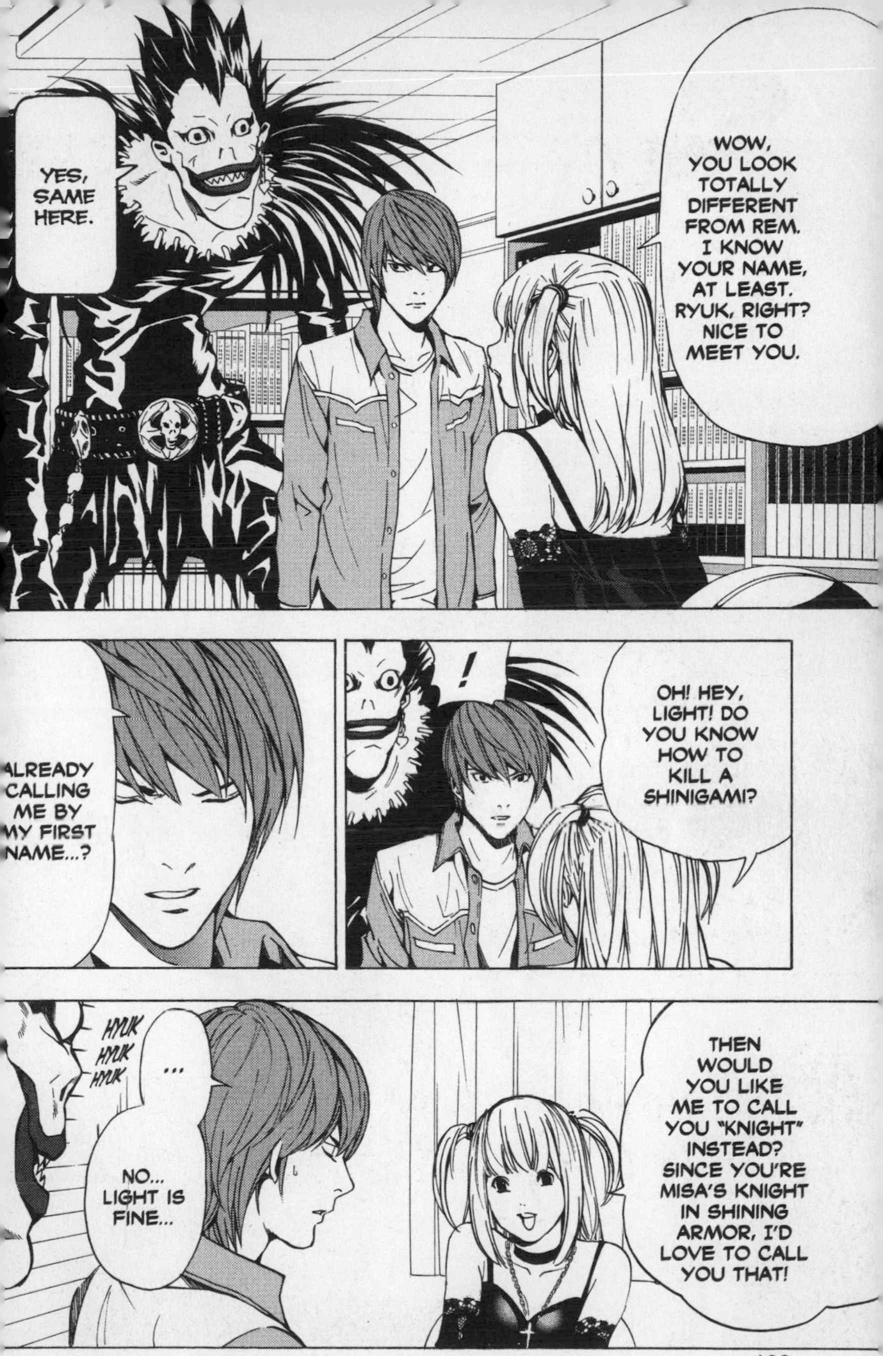
WOW, YOU LOOK TOTALLY DIFFERENT FROM REM. I KNOW YOUR NAME, AT LEAST. RYUK, RIGHT? NICE TO MEET YOU.
YES, SAME HERE.
!
OH! HEY, LIGHT! DO YOU KNOW HOW TO KILL A SHINIGAMI?
ALREADY CALLING ME BY MY FIRST NAME...?
THEN WOULD YOU LIKE ME TO CALL YOU "KNIGHT" INSTEAD? SINCE YOU'RE MISA'S KNIGHT IN SHINING ARMOR, I'D LOVE TO CALL YOU THAT!
...
NO... LIGHT IS FINE...
HYUK HYUK HYUK

READ THIS WAY

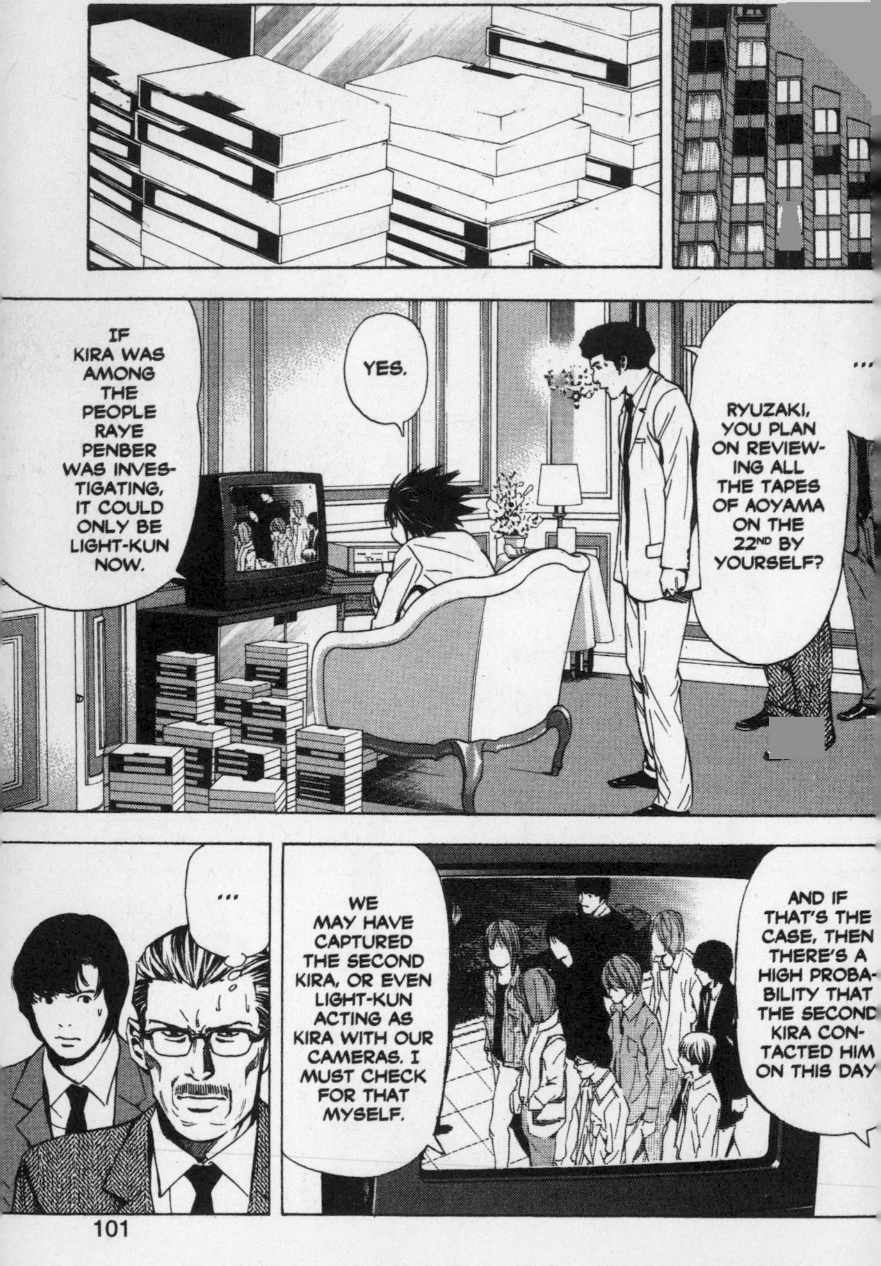
...
RYUZAKI, YOU PLAN ON REVIEWING ALL THE TAPES OF AOYAMA ON THE 22ND BY YOURSELF?
YES.
IF KIRA WAS AMONG THE PEOPLE RAYE PENBER WAS INVESTIGATING, IT COULD ONLY BE LIGHT-KUN NOW.
AND IF THAT'S THE CASE, THEN THERE'S A HIGH PROBABILITY THAT THE SECOND KIRA CONTACTED HIM ON THIS DAY
WE MAY HAVE CAPTURED THE SECOND KIRA, OR EVEN LIGHT-KUN ACTING AS KIRA WITH OUR CAMERAS. I MUST CHECK FOR THAT MYSELF.
...

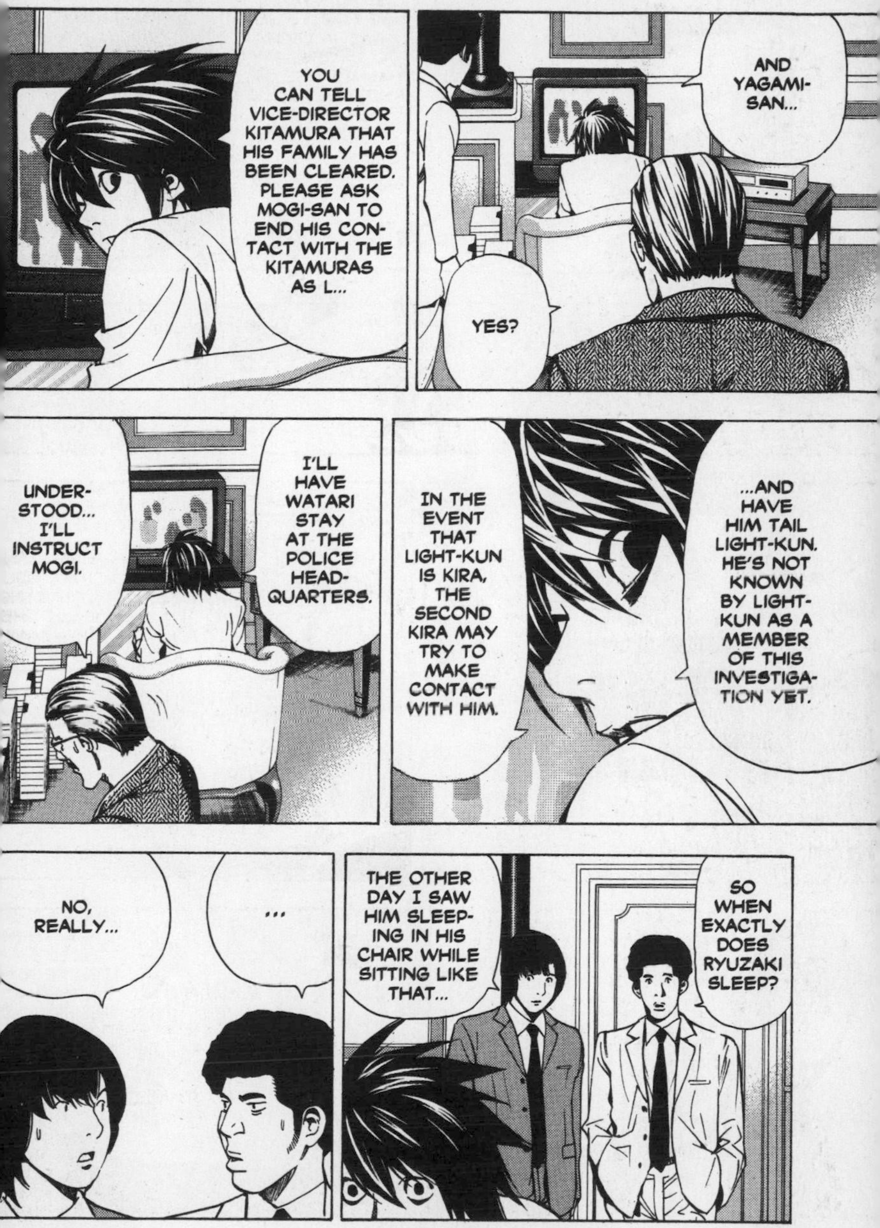
AND YAGAMI-SAN...
YES?
YOU CAN TELL VICE-DIRECTOR KITAMURA THAT HIS FAMILY HAS BEEN CLEARED. PLEASE ASK MOGI-SAN TO END HIS CONTACT WITH THE KITAMURAS AS L...
...AND HAVE HIM TAIL LIGHT-KUN. HE'S NOT KNOWN BY LIGHT-KUN AS A MEMBER OF THIS INVESTIGATION YET.
IN THE EVENT THAT LIGHT-KUN IS KIRA, THE SECOND KIRA MAY TRY TO MAKE CONTACT WITH HIM.
I'LL HAVE WATARI STAY AT THE POLICE HEADQUARTERS.
UNDERSTOOD... I'LL INSTRUCT MOGI.
SO WHEN EXACTLY DOES RYUZAKI SLEEP?
THE OTHER DAY I SAW HIM SLEEPING IN HIS CHAIR WHILE SITTING LIKE THAT...
...
NO, REALLY...

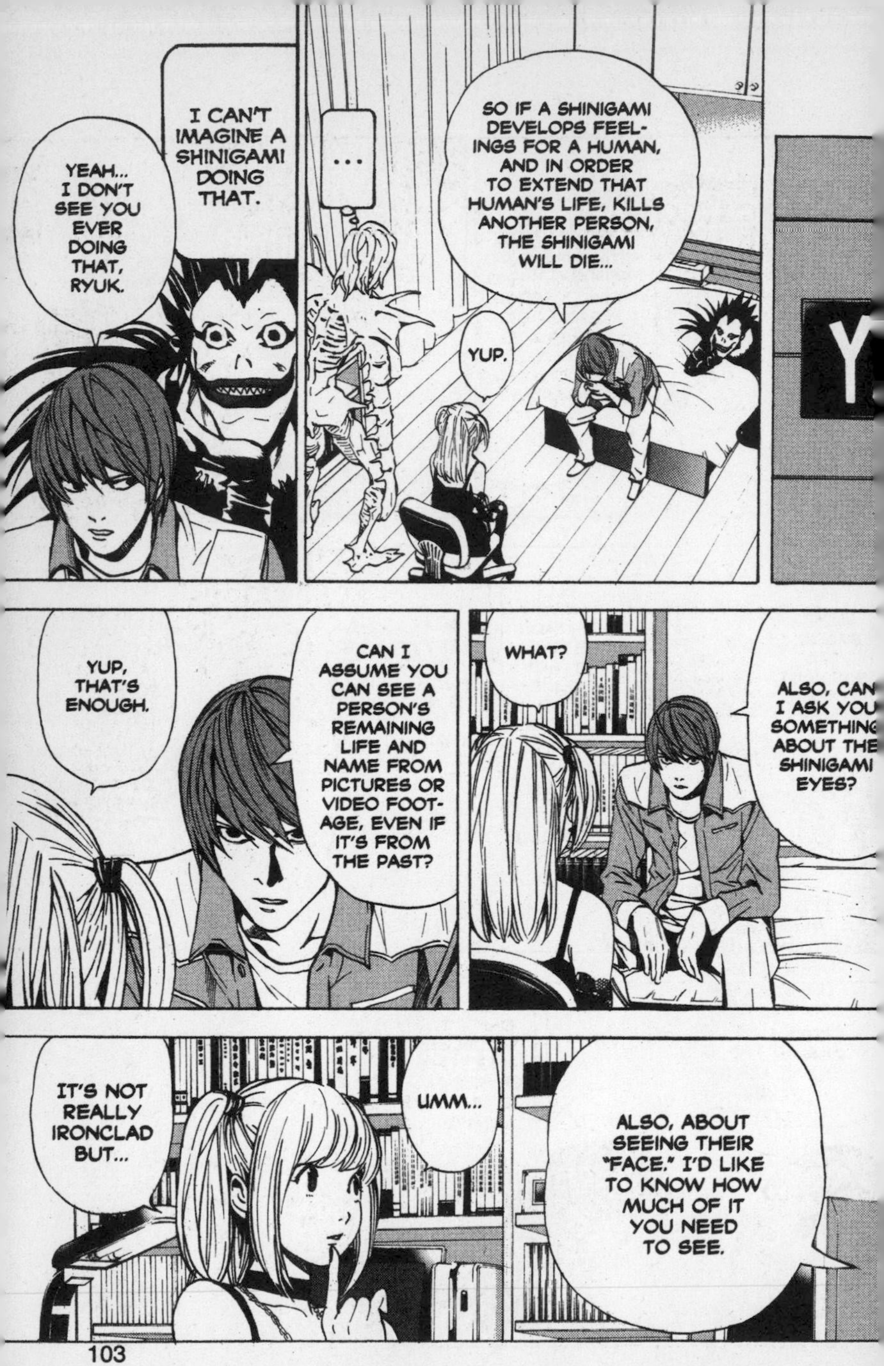
SO IF A SHINIGAMI DEVELOPS FEEL-INGS FOR A HUMAN, AND IN ORDER TO EXTEND THAT HUMAN'S LIFE, KILLS ANOTHER PERSON, THE SHINIGAMI WILL DIE...
...
YUP.
I CAN'T IMAGINE A SHINIGAMI DOING THAT.
YEAH... I DON'T SEE YOU EVER DOING THAT, RYUK.
ALSO, CAN I ASK YOU SOMETHING ABOUT THE SHINIGAMI EYES?
WHAT?
CAN I ASSUME YOU CAN SEE A PERSON'S REMAINING LIFE AND NAME FROM PICTURES OR VIDEO FOOT-AGE, EVEN IF IT'S FROM THE PAST?
YUP, THAT'S ENOUGH.
ALSO, ABOUT SEEING THEIR "FACE," I'D LIKE TO KNOW HOW MUCH OF IT YOU NEED TO SEE.
UMM...
IT'S NOT REALLY IRONCLAD BUT...

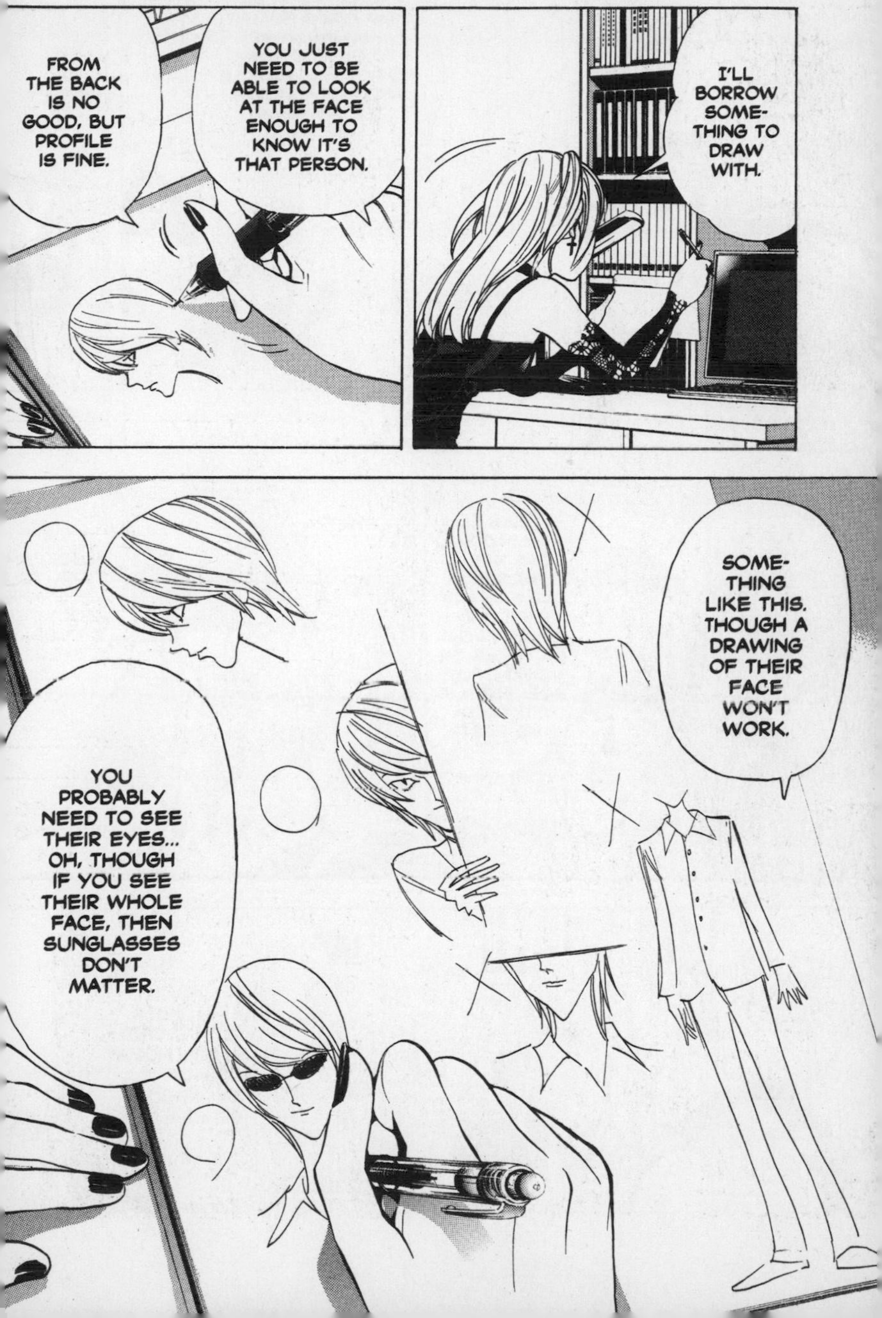
I'LL BORROW SOME-THING TO DRAW WITH.
YOU JUST NEED TO BE ABLE TO LOOK AT THE FACE ENOUGH TO KNOW IT'S THAT PERSON.
FROM THE BACK IS NO GOOD, BUT PROFILE IS FINE.
SOME-THING LIKE THIS. THOUGH A DRAWING OF THEIR FACE WON'T WORK.
YOU PROBABLY NEED TO SEE THEIR EYES... OH, THOUGH IF YOU SEE THEIR WHOLE FACE, THEN SUNGLASSES DON'T MATTER.

READ THIS WAY

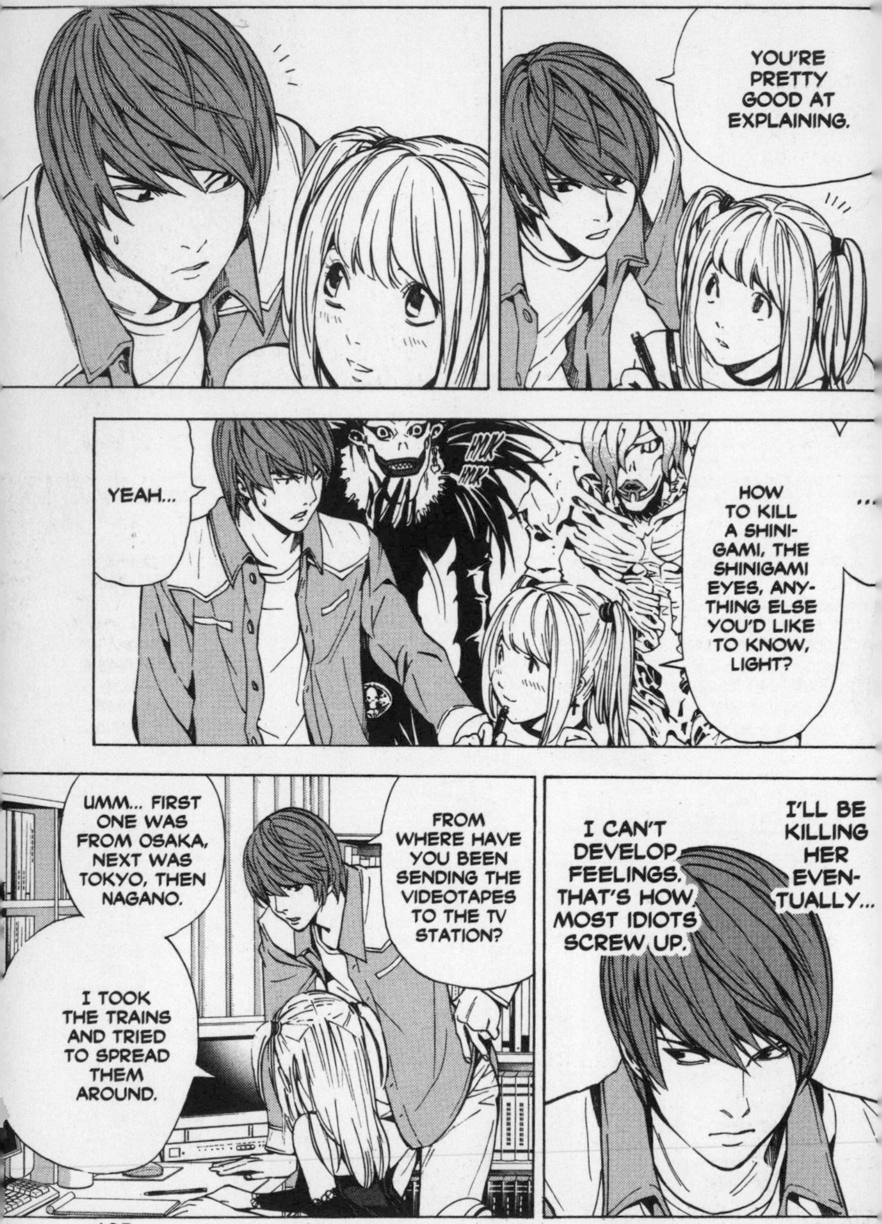
YOU'RE PRETTY GOOD AT EXPLAINING.
HOW TO KILL A SHINIGAMI, THE SHINIGAMI EYES, ANYTHING ELSE YOU'D LIKE TO KNOW, LIGHT?
...
HYUK HYUK
YEAH...
I'LL BE KILLING HER EVENTUALLY...
I CAN'T DEVELOP FEELINGS. THAT'S HOW MOST IDIOTS SCREW UP.
FROM WHERE HAVE YOU BEEN SENDING THE VIDEOTAPES TO THE TV STATION?
UMM... FIRST ONE WAS FROM OSAKA, NEXT WAS TOKYO, THEN NAGANO.
I TOOK THE TRAINS AND TRIED TO SPREAD THEM AROUND.

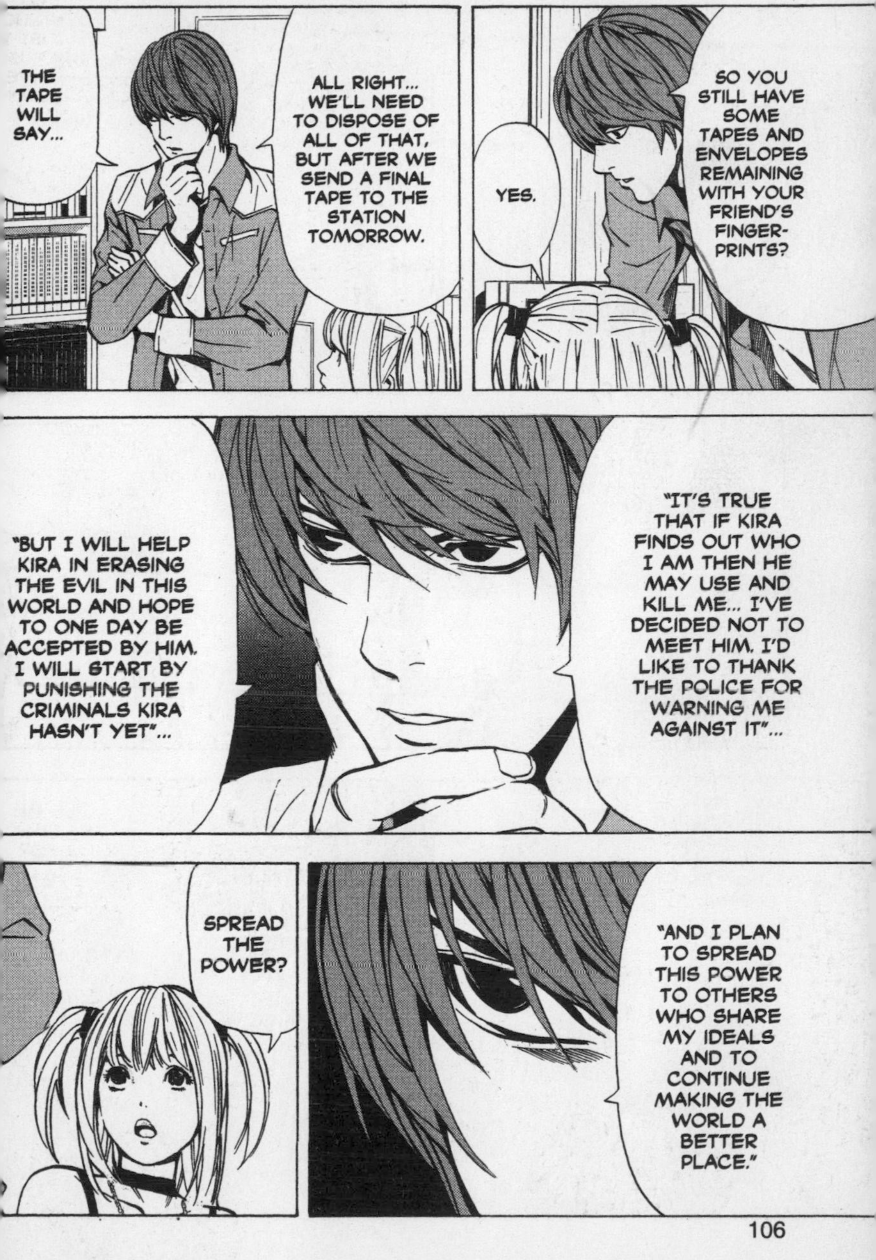
SO YOU STILL HAVE SOME TAPES AND ENVELOPES REMAINING WITH YOUR FRIEND'S FINGER-PRINTS?
YES.
ALL RIGHT... WE'LL NEED TO DISPOSE OF ALL OF THAT, BUT AFTER WE SEND A FINAL TAPE TO THE STATION TOMORROW.
THE TAPE WILL SAY...
"IT'S TRUE THAT IF KIRA FINDS OUT WHO I AM THEN HE MAY USE AND KILL ME... I'VE DECIDED NOT TO MEET HIM. I'D LIKE TO THANK THE POLICE FOR WARNING ME AGAINST IT"...
"BUT I WILL HELP KIRA IN ERASING THE EVIL IN THIS WORLD AND HOPE TO ONE DAY BE ACCEPTED BY HIM. I WILL START BY PUNISHING THE CRIMINALS KIRA HASN'T YET"...
"AND I PLAN TO SPREAD THIS POWER TO OTHERS WHO SHARE MY IDEALS AND TO CONTINUE MAKING THE WORLD A BETTER PLACE."
SPREAD THE POWER?

READ THIS WAY

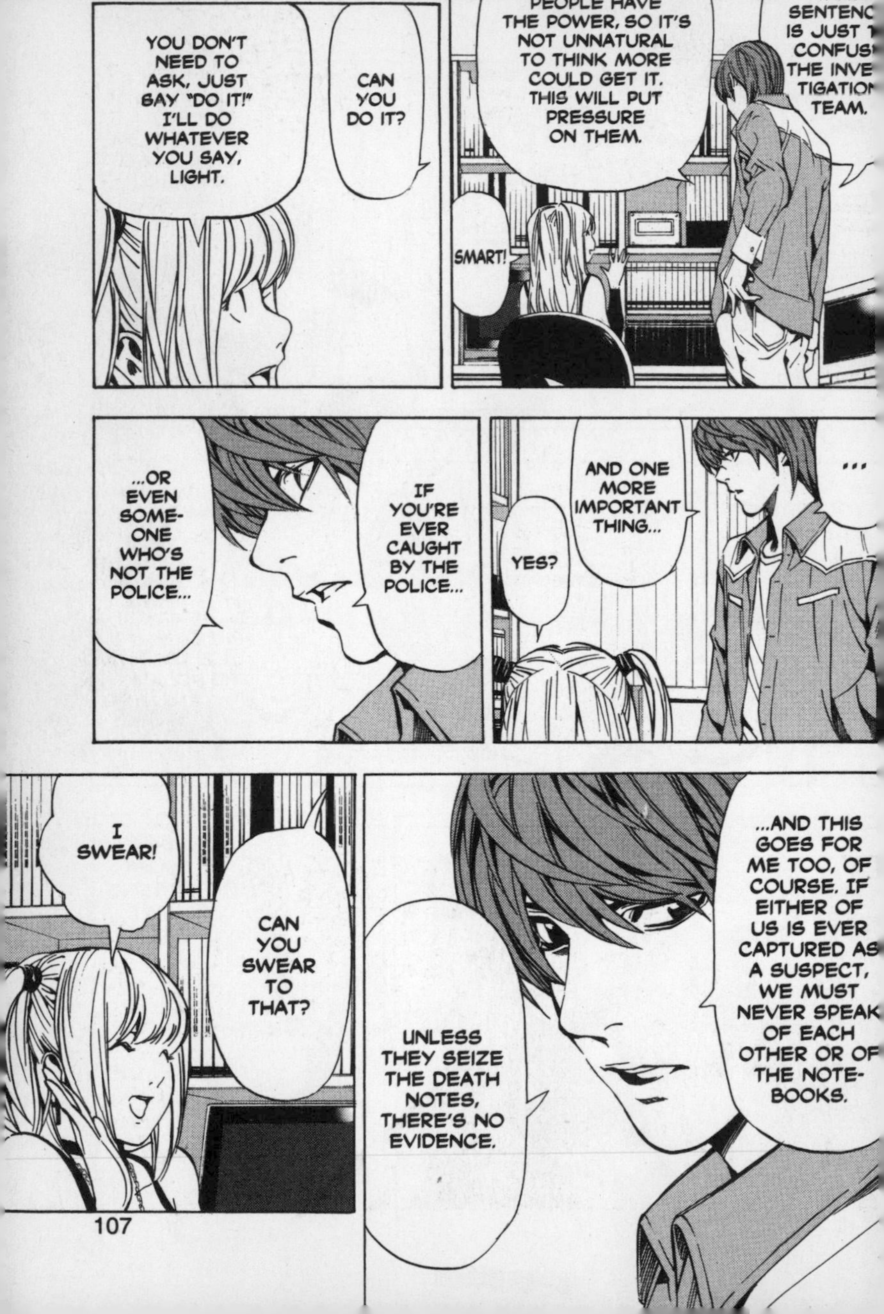
THAT SENTENC IS JUST T CONFUS THE INVE TIGATION TEAM.
ALREADY TWO PEOPLE HAVE THE POWER, SO IT'S NOT UNNATURAL TO THINK MORE COULD GET IT. THIS WILL PUT PRESSURE ON THEM.
SMART!
CAN YOU DO IT?
YOU DON'T NEED TO ASK, JUST SAY "DO IT!" I'LL DO WHATEVER YOU SAY, LIGHT.
...
AND ONE MORE IMPORTANT THING...
YES?
IF YOU'RE EVER CAUGHT BY THE POLICE...
...OR EVEN SOME-ONE WHO'S NOT THE POLICE...
...AND THIS GOES FOR ME TOO, OF COURSE. IF EITHER OF US IS EVER CAPTURED AS A SUSPECT, WE MUST NEVER SPEAK OF EACH OTHER OR OF THE NOTE-BOOKS.
UNLESS THEY SEIZE THE DEATH NOTES, THERE'S NO EVIDENCE.
CAN YOU SWEAR TO THAT?
I SWEAR!

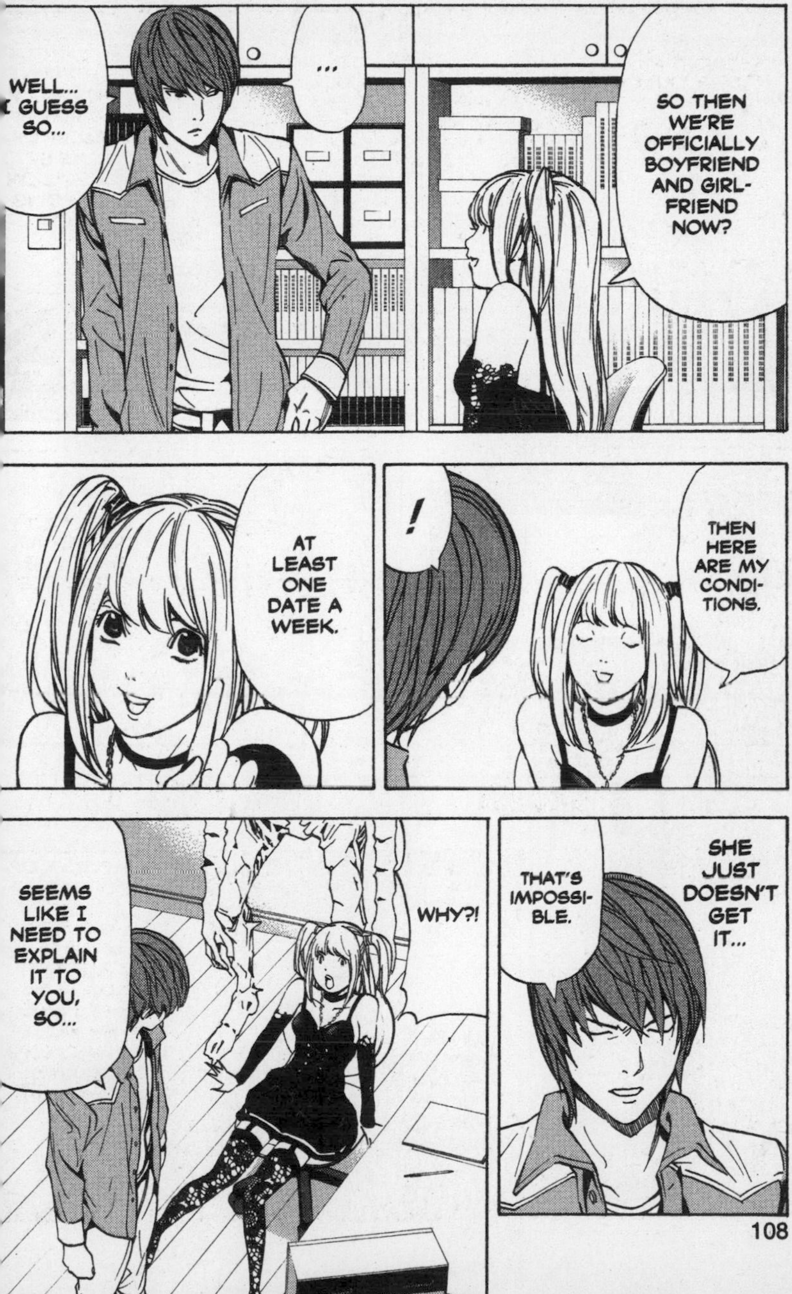
SO THEN WE'RE OFFICIALLY BOYFRIEND AND GIRL-FRIEND NOW?
...
WELL... I GUESS SO...
THEN HERE ARE MY CONDI-TIONS.
!
AT LEAST ONE DATE A WEEK.
SHE JUST DOESN'T GET IT...
THAT'S IMPOSSI-BLE.
WHY?!
SEEMS LIKE I NEED TO EXPLAIN IT TO YOU, SO...

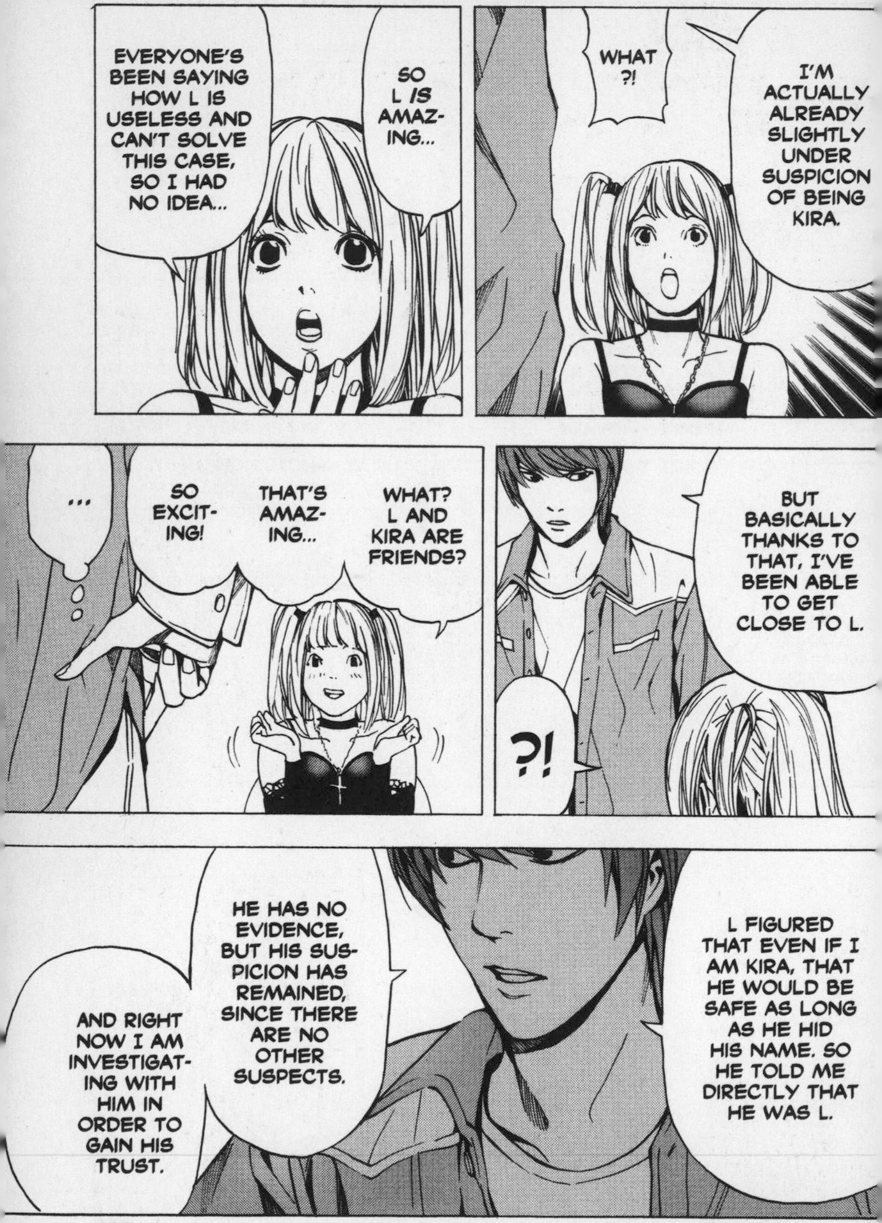
I'M ACTUALLY ALREADY SLIGHTLY UNDER SUSPICION OF BEING KIRA.
WHAT ?!
SO L IS AMAZING...
EVERYONE'S BEEN SAYING HOW L IS USELESS AND CAN'T SOLVE THIS CASE, SO I HAD NO IDEA...
BUT BASICALLY THANKS TO THAT, I'VE BEEN ABLE TO GET CLOSE TO L.
?!
WHAT? L AND KIRA ARE FRIENDS?
THAT'S AMAZING...
SO EXCITING!
...
L FIGURED THAT EVEN IF I AM KIRA, THAT HE WOULD BE SAFE AS LONG AS HE HID HIS NAME. SO HE TOLD ME DIRECTLY THAT HE WAS L.
HE HAS NO EVIDENCE, BUT HIS SUSPICION HAS REMAINED, SINCE THERE ARE NO OTHER SUSPECTS.
AND RIGHT NOW I AM INVESTIGATING WITH HIM IN ORDER TO GAIN HIS TRUST.

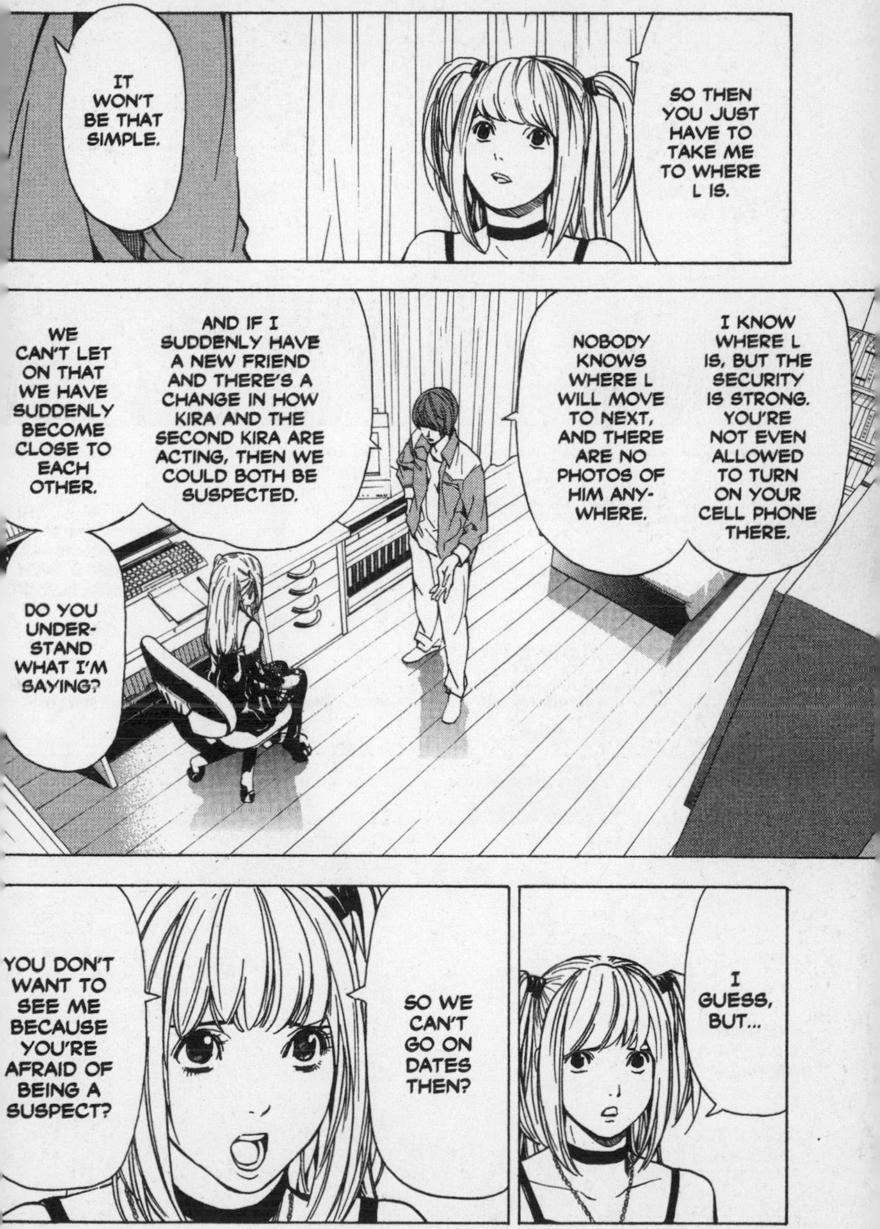
SO THEN YOU JUST HAVE TO TAKE ME TO WHERE L IS.
IT WON'T BE THAT SIMPLE.
I KNOW WHERE L IS, BUT THE SECURITY IS STRONG. YOU'RE NOT EVEN ALLOWED TO TURN ON YOUR CELL PHONE THERE.
NOBODY KNOWS WHERE L WILL MOVE TO NEXT, AND THERE ARE NO PHOTOS OF HIM ANY-WHERE.
AND IF I SUDDENLY HAVE A NEW FRIEND AND THERE'S A CHANGE IN HOW KIRA AND THE SECOND KIRA ARE ACTING, THEN WE COULD BOTH BE SUSPECTED.
WE CAN'T LET ON THAT WE HAVE SUDDENLY BECOME CLOSE TO EACH OTHER.
DO YOU UNDER-STAND WHAT I'M SAYING?
I GUESS, BUT...
SO WE CAN'T GO ON DATES THEN?
YOU DON'T WANT TO SEE ME BECAUSE YOU'RE AFRAID OF BEING A SUSPECT?

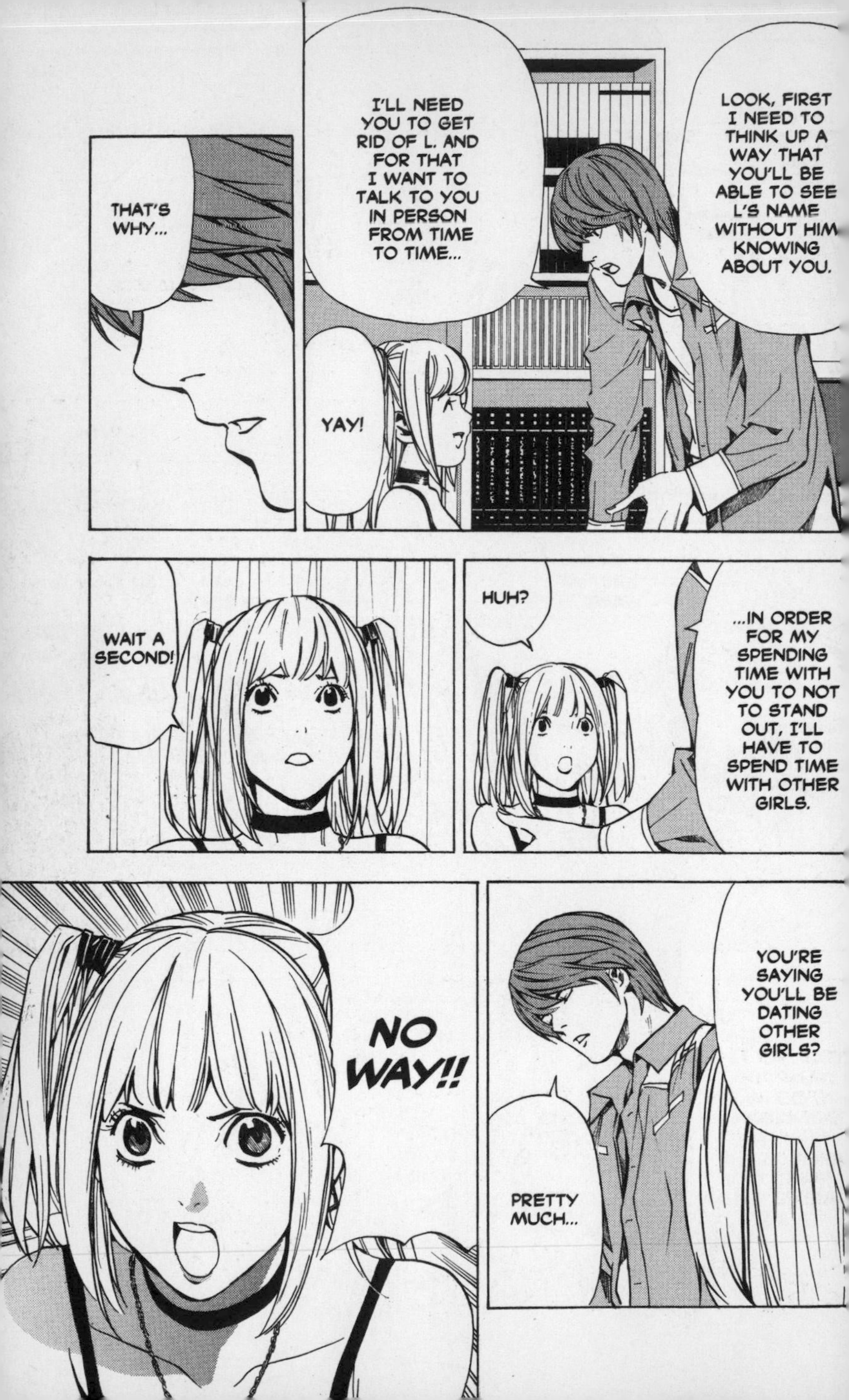
LOOK, FIRST I NEED TO THINK UP A WAY THAT YOU'LL BE ABLE TO SEE L'S NAME WITHOUT HIM KNOWING ABOUT YOU.
I'LL NEED YOU TO GET RID OF L. AND FOR THAT I WANT TO TALK TO YOU IN PERSON FROM TIME TO TIME...
YAY!
THAT'S WHY...
...IN ORDER FOR MY SPENDING TIME WITH YOU TO NOT TO STAND OUT, I'LL HAVE TO SPEND TIME WITH OTHER GIRLS.
HUH?
WAIT A SECOND!
YOU'RE SAYING YOU'LL BE DATING OTHER GIRLS?
PRETTY MUCH...
NO WAY!!

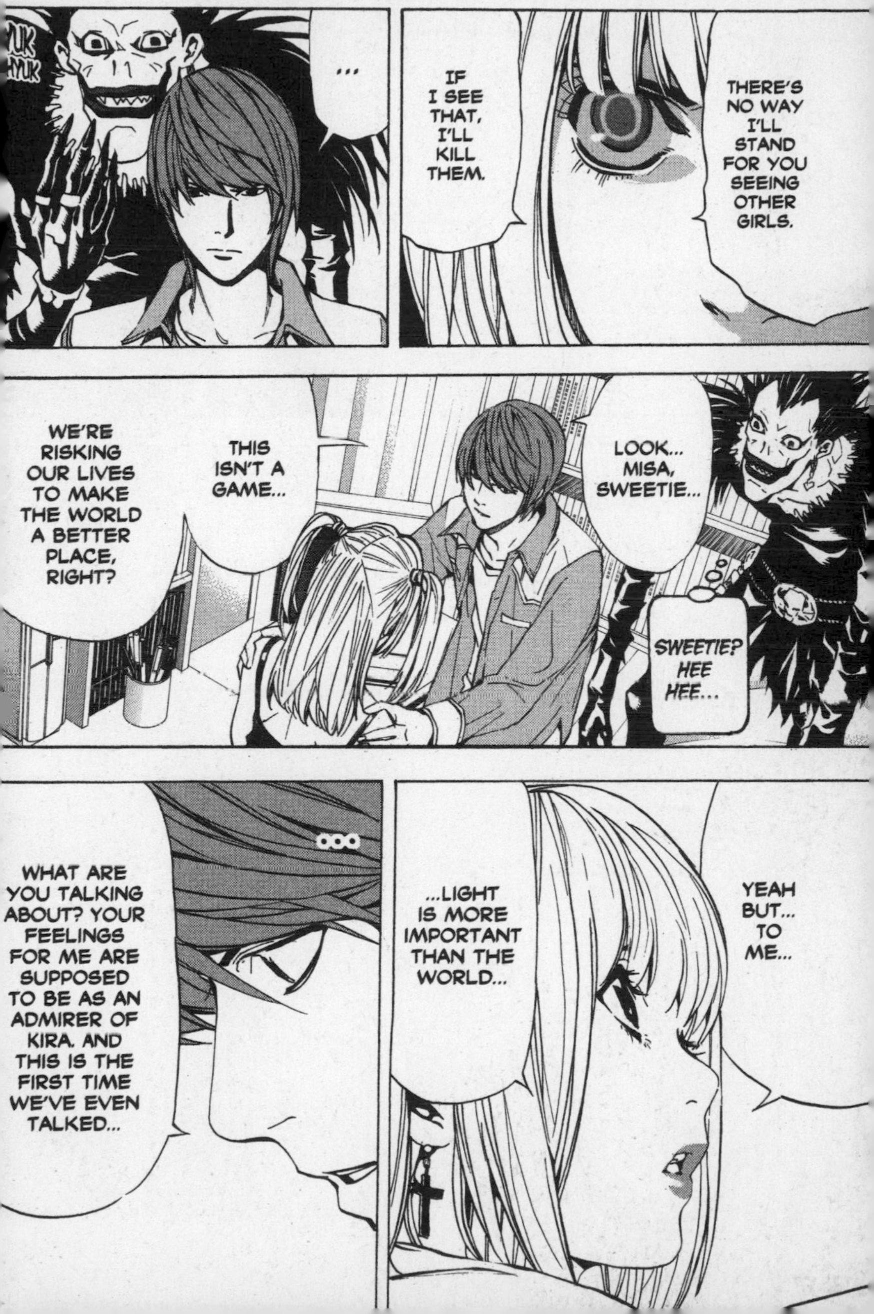
THERE'S NO WAY I'LL STAND FOR YOU SEEING OTHER GIRLS.
IF I SEE THAT, I'LL KILL THEM.
...
LOOK... MISA, SWEETIE...
SWEETIE? HEE HEE...
THIS ISN'T A GAME...
WE'RE RISKING OUR LIVES TO MAKE THE WORLD A BETTER PLACE, RIGHT?
YEAH BUT... TO ME...
...LIGHT IS MORE IMPORTANT THAN THE WORLD...
WHAT ARE YOU TALKING ABOUT? YOUR FEELINGS FOR ME ARE SUPPOSED TO BE AS AN ADMIRER OF KIRA. AND THIS IS THE FIRST TIME WE'VE EVEN TALKED...

READ THIS WAY

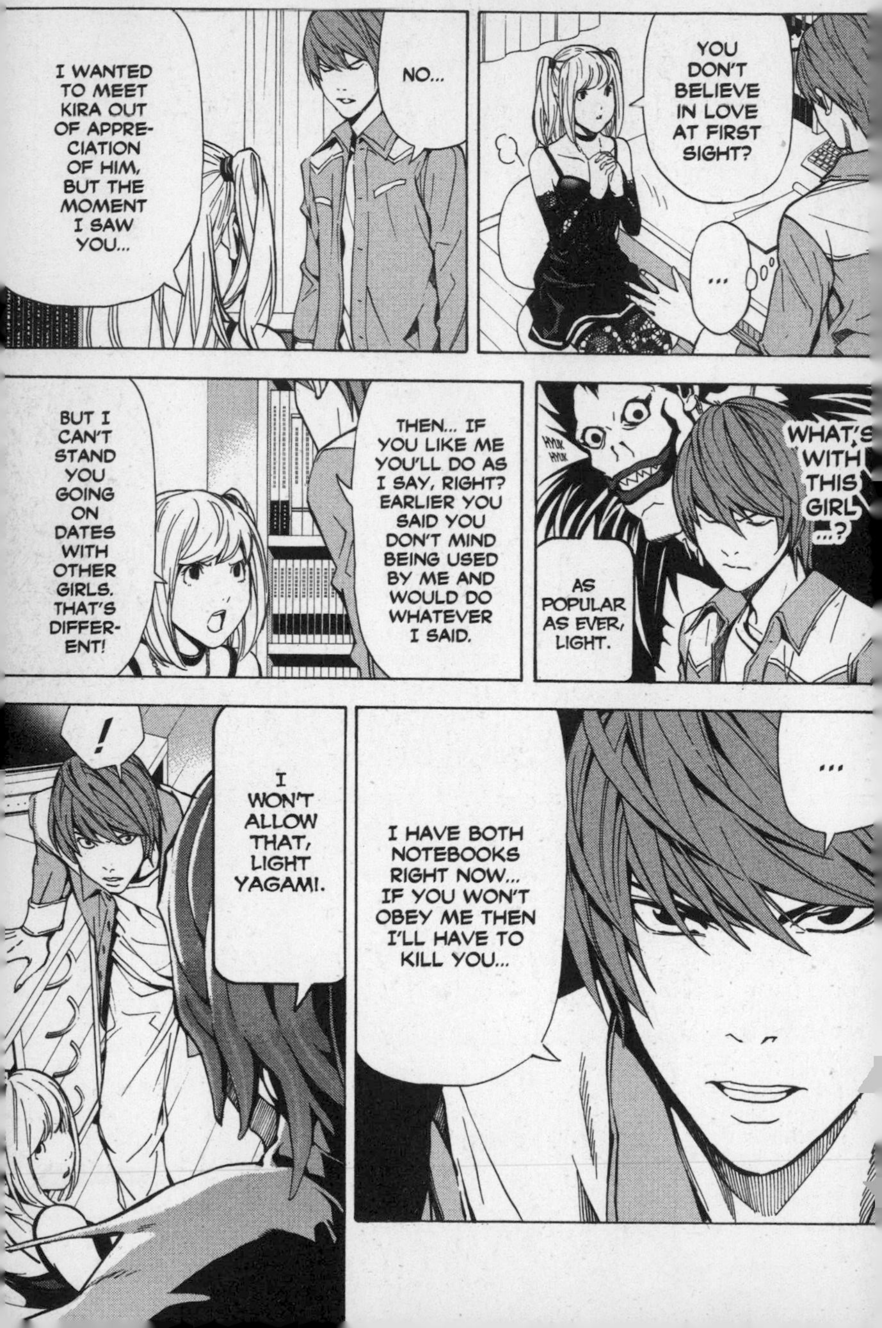
YOU DON'T BELIEVE IN LOVE AT FIRST SIGHT?
...
NO...
I WANTED TO MEET KIRA OUT OF APPRE-CIATION OF HIM, BUT THE MOMENT I SAW YOU...
WHAT'S WITH THIS GIRL ...?
HYUK HYUK
AS POPULAR AS EVER, LIGHT.
THEN... IF YOU LIKE ME YOU'LL DO AS I SAY, RIGHT? EARLIER YOU SAID YOU DON'T MIND BEING USED BY ME AND WOULD DO WHATEVER I SAID.
BUT I CAN'T STAND YOU GOING ON DATES WITH OTHER GIRLS. THAT'S DIFFER-ENT!
...
I HAVE BOTH NOTEBOOKS RIGHT NOW... IF YOU WON'T OBEY ME THEN I'LL HAVE TO KILL YOU...
!
I WON'T ALLOW THAT, LIGHT YAGAMI.

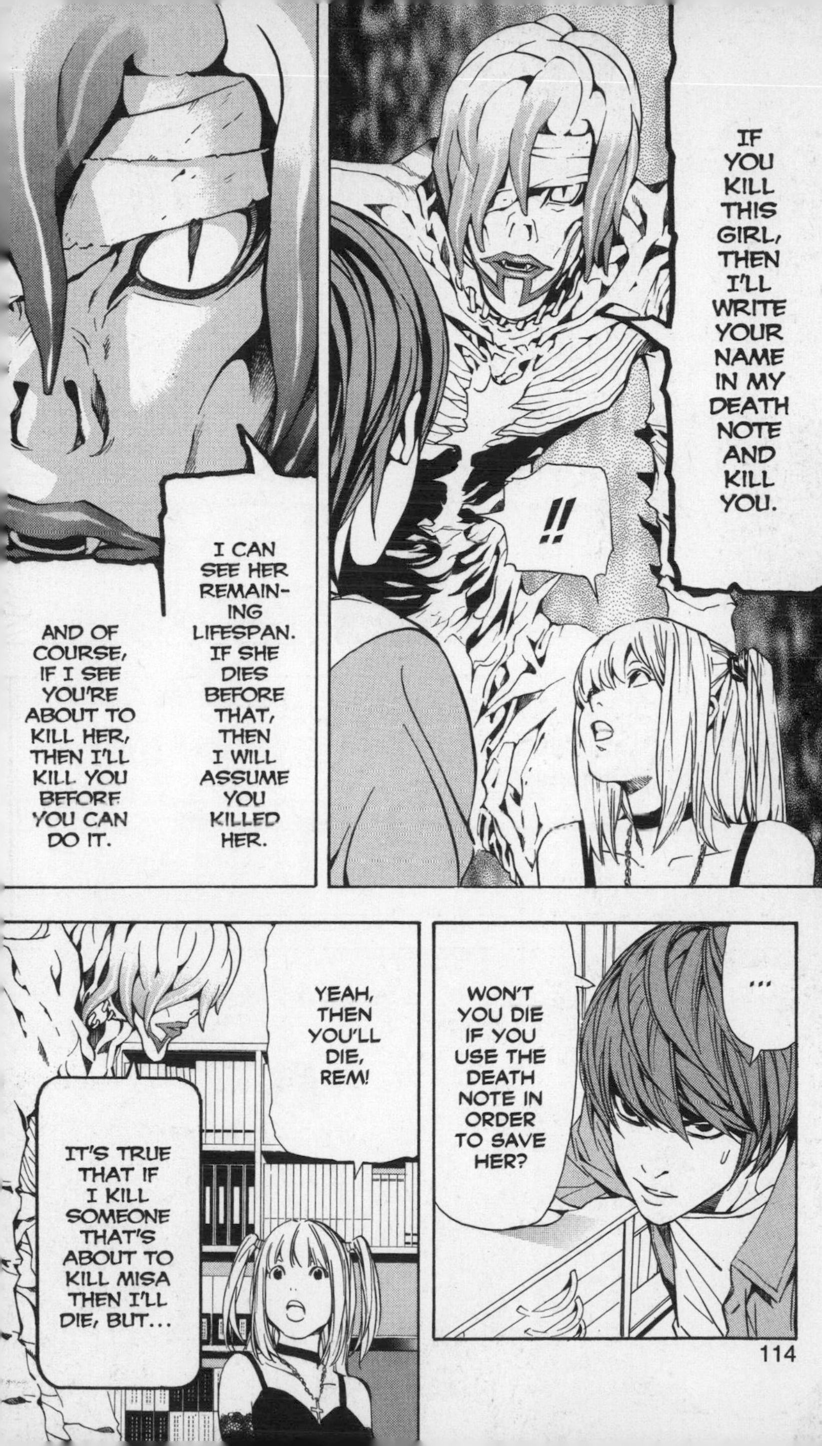
IF YOU KILL THIS GIRL, THEN I'LL WRITE YOUR NAME IN MY DEATH NOTE AND KILL YOU.
!!
I CAN SEE HER REMAINING LIFESPAN. IF SHE DIES BEFORE THAT, THEN I WILL ASSUME YOU KILLED HER.
AND OF COURSE, IF I SEE YOU'RE ABOUT TO KILL HER, THEN I'LL KILL YOU BEFORE YOU CAN DO IT.
...
WON'T YOU DIE IF YOU USE THE DEATH NOTE IN ORDER TO SAVE HER?
YEAH, THEN YOU'LL DIE, REM!
IT'S TRUE THAT IF I KILL SOMEONE THAT'S ABOUT TO KILL MISA THEN I'LL DIE, BUT...

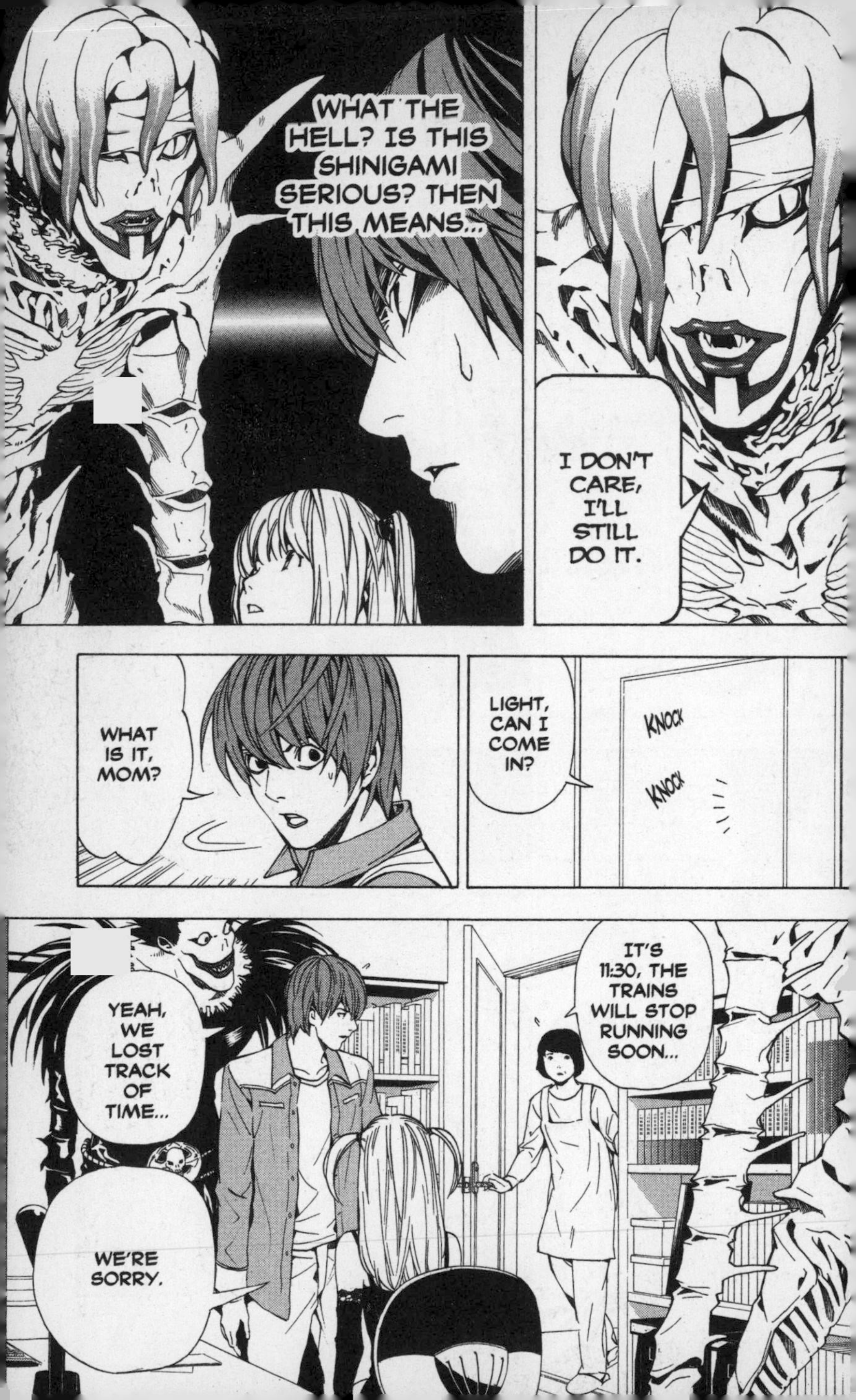
I DON'T CARE, I'LL STILL DO IT.
WHAT THE HELL? IS THIS SHINIGAMI SERIOUS? THEN THIS MEANS...
KNOCK
KNOCK
LIGHT, CAN I COME IN?
WHAT IS IT, MOM?
IT'S 11:30, THE TRAINS WILL STOP RUNNING SOON...
YEAH, WE LOST TRACK OF TIME...
WE'RE SORRY.

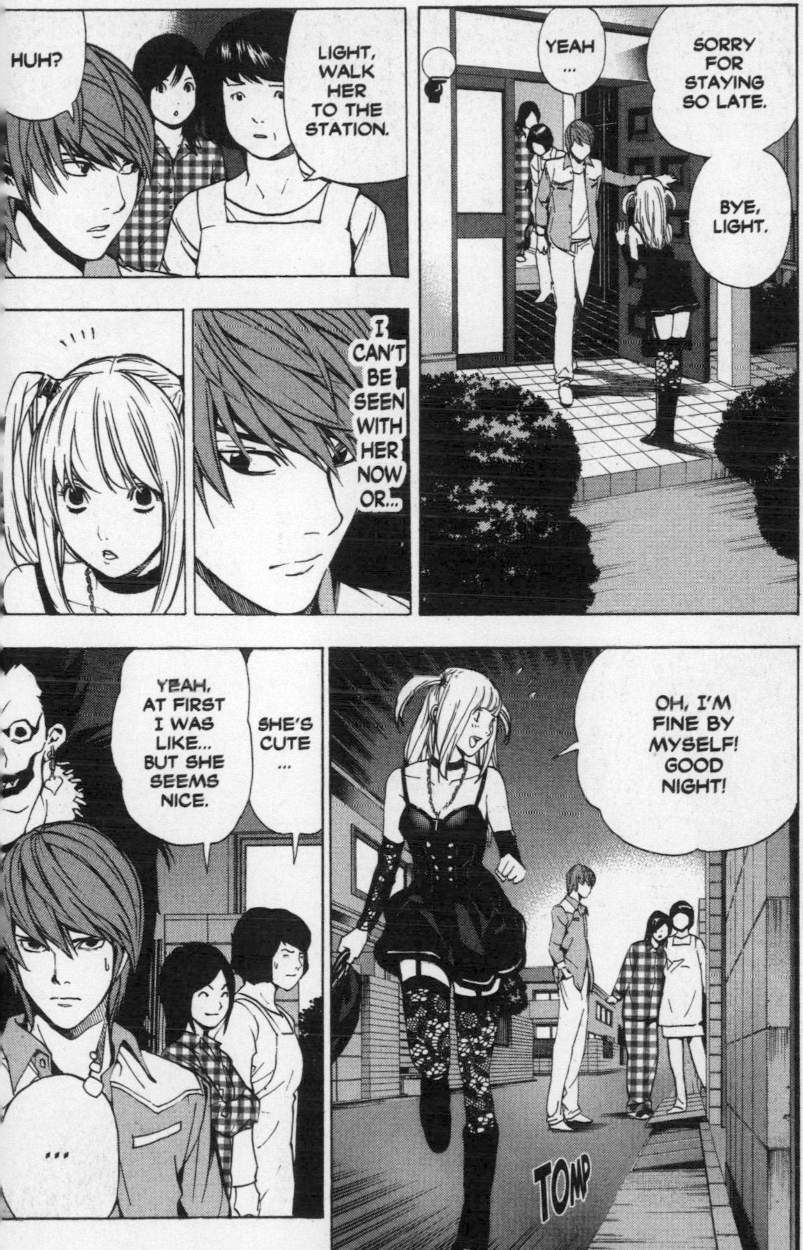
SORRY FOR STAYING SO LATE.
BYE, LIGHT.
YEAH ...
LIGHT, WALK HER TO THE STATION.
HUH?
I CAN'T BE SEEN WITH HER NOW OR...
OH, I'M FINE BY MYSELF! GOOD NIGHT!
TOMP
SHE'S CUTE ...
YEAH, AT FIRST I WAS LIKE... BUT SHE SEEMS NICE.
...

READ THIS WAY

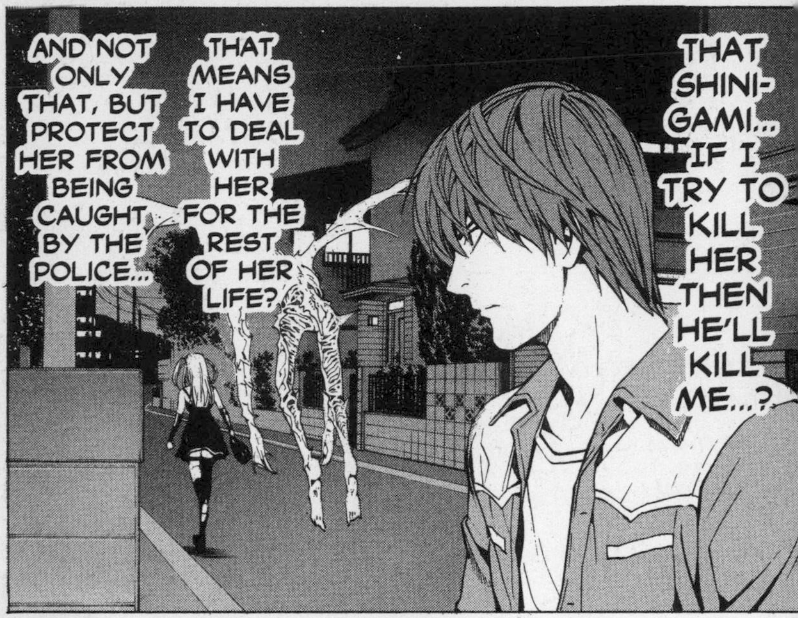
THAT SHINI-GAMI... IF I TRY TO KILL HER THEN HE'LL KILL ME...?
THAT MEANS I HAVE TO DEAL WITH HER FOR THE REST OF HER LIFE?
AND NOT ONLY THAT, BUT PROTECT HER FROM BEING CAUGHT BY THE POLICE...

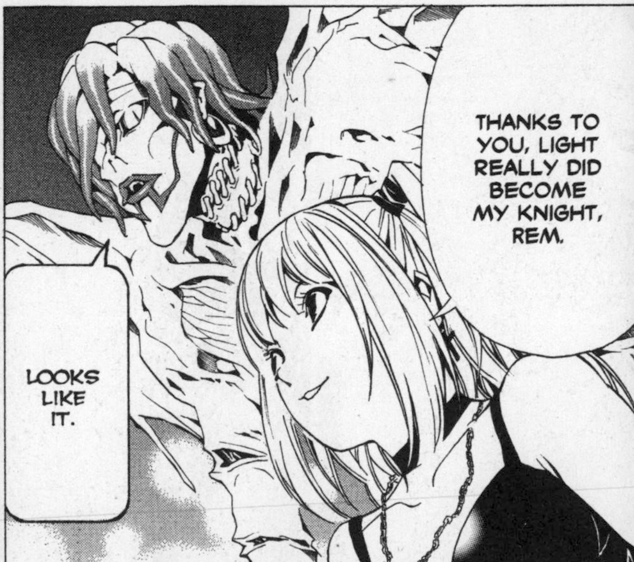
THANKS TO YOU, LIGHT REALLY DID BECOME MY KNIGHT, REM.
LOOKS LIKE IT.

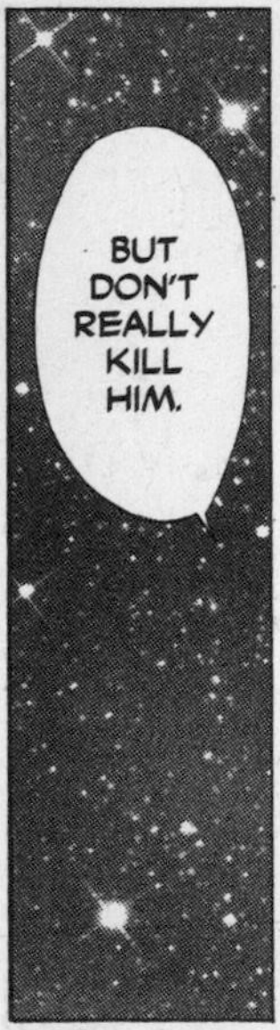
BUT DON'T REALLY KILL HIM.

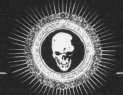

DEATH NOTE
How to Use It

XX

○ In order to see the names and life spans of humans by using the eye power of the god of death, the owner must look at more than half of that person's face. When looking from top to bottom, he must look at least from the head to the nose. If he looks at only the eyes and under, he will not be able to see the person's name and life span. Also, even though some parts of the face, for example the eyes, nose or mouth are hidden, if he can basically see the whole face, he will be able to see the person's name and life span. It is still not clear how much exposure is needed to tell the name and life span, and this needs to be verified.

死神の目で人間の名前・寿命を見るには、その人間の顔の左右の半分以上を見なければならず、上下の場合は頭から鼻まで見る必要があり、目より下だけを見ても名前・寿命は見えない。また、顔の一部、目・鼻・口等が隠れていても顔全体が見えていれば、名前・寿命を見る事ができる。隠された部分が顔の何％を占めると名前・寿命が見えなくなるかは検証していくしかない。

◎ If above conditions are met, names and life spans can be seen through photos and pictures, no matter how old they are. But this is sometimes influenced by the vividness and size. Also, names and life spans cannot be seen by face drawings, however realistic they may be.

上記の条件をクリアーしていれば、どんなに過去の物であろうと写真や映像でも名前・寿命を見る事ができるが、写真・映像の場合はその大きさや鮮明度で見えない事がある。また、どんなに写実であろうとも顔の絵では名前や寿命は見えない。

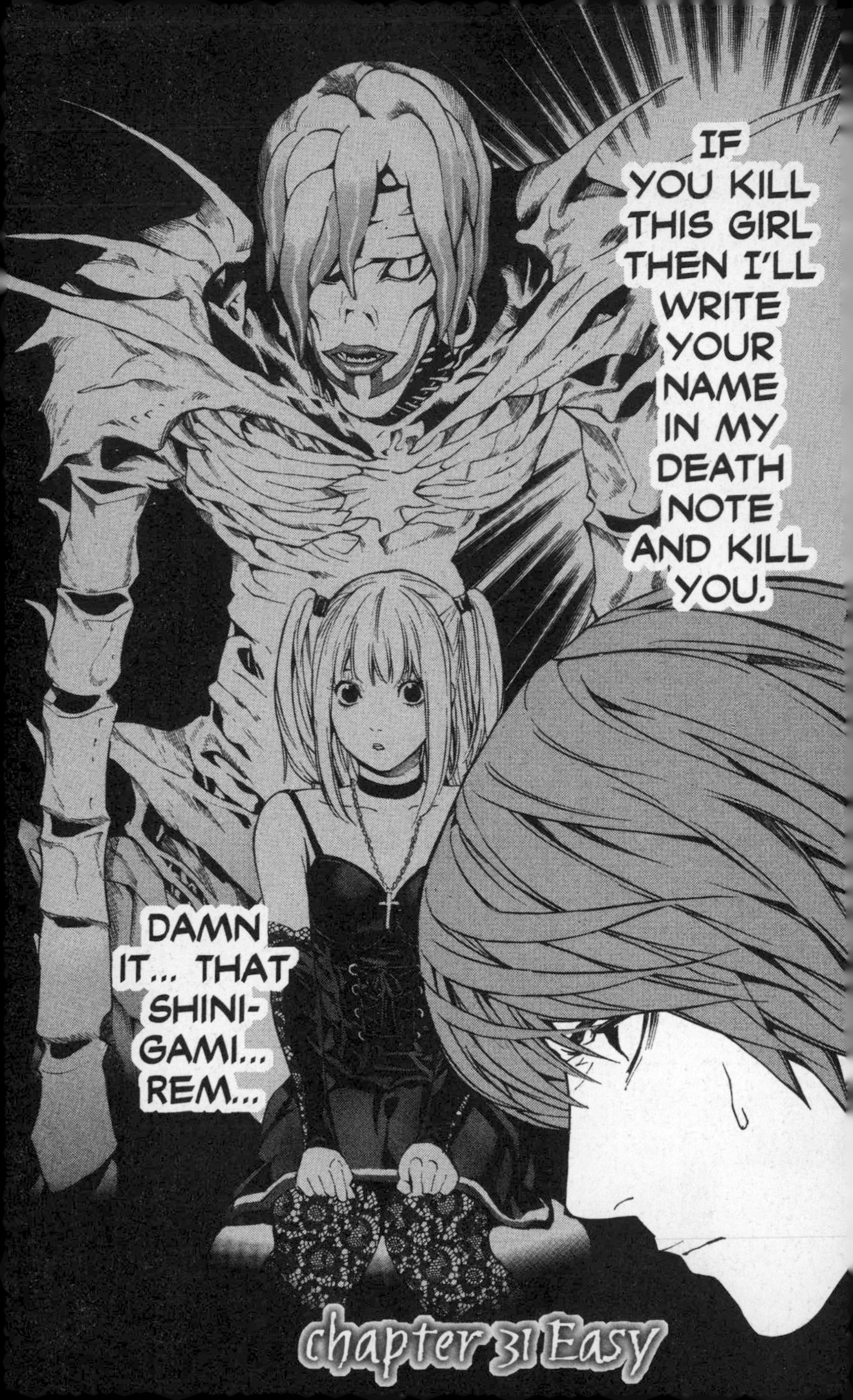
IF YOU KILL THIS GIRL THEN I'LL WRITE YOUR NAME IN MY DEATH NOTE AND KILL YOU.
DAMN IT... THAT SHINI-GAMI... REM...
chapter 31 Easy

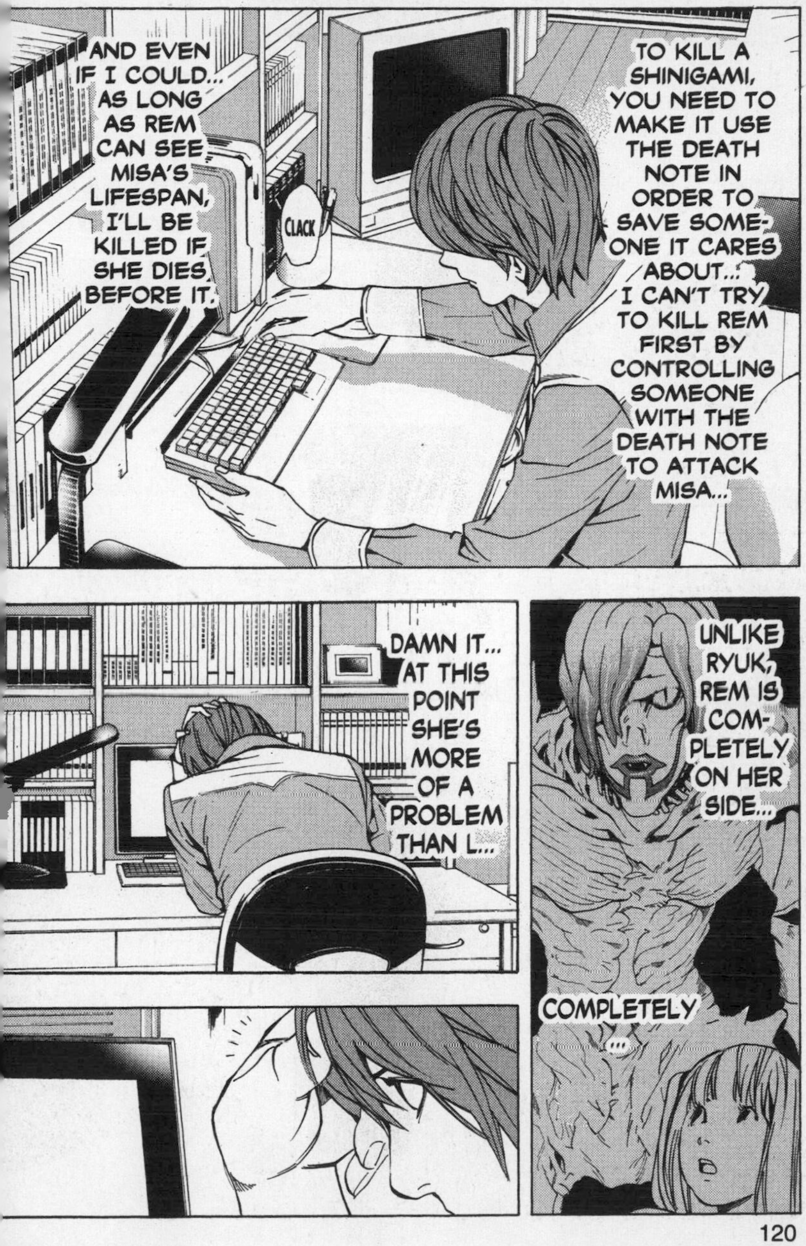
TO KILL A SHINIGAMI, YOU NEED TO MAKE IT USE THE DEATH NOTE IN ORDER TO SAVE SOME-ONE IT CARES ABOUT... I CAN'T TRY TO KILL REM FIRST BY CONTROLLING SOMEONE WITH THE DEATH NOTE TO ATTACK MISA...
AND EVEN IF I COULD... AS LONG AS REM CAN SEE MISA'S LIFESPAN, I'LL BE KILLED IF SHE DIES BEFORE IT.
CLACK
DAMN IT... AT THIS POINT SHE'S MORE OF A PROBLEM THAN L...
UNLIKE RYUK, REM IS COM-PLETELY ON HER SIDE...
COMPLETELY ...

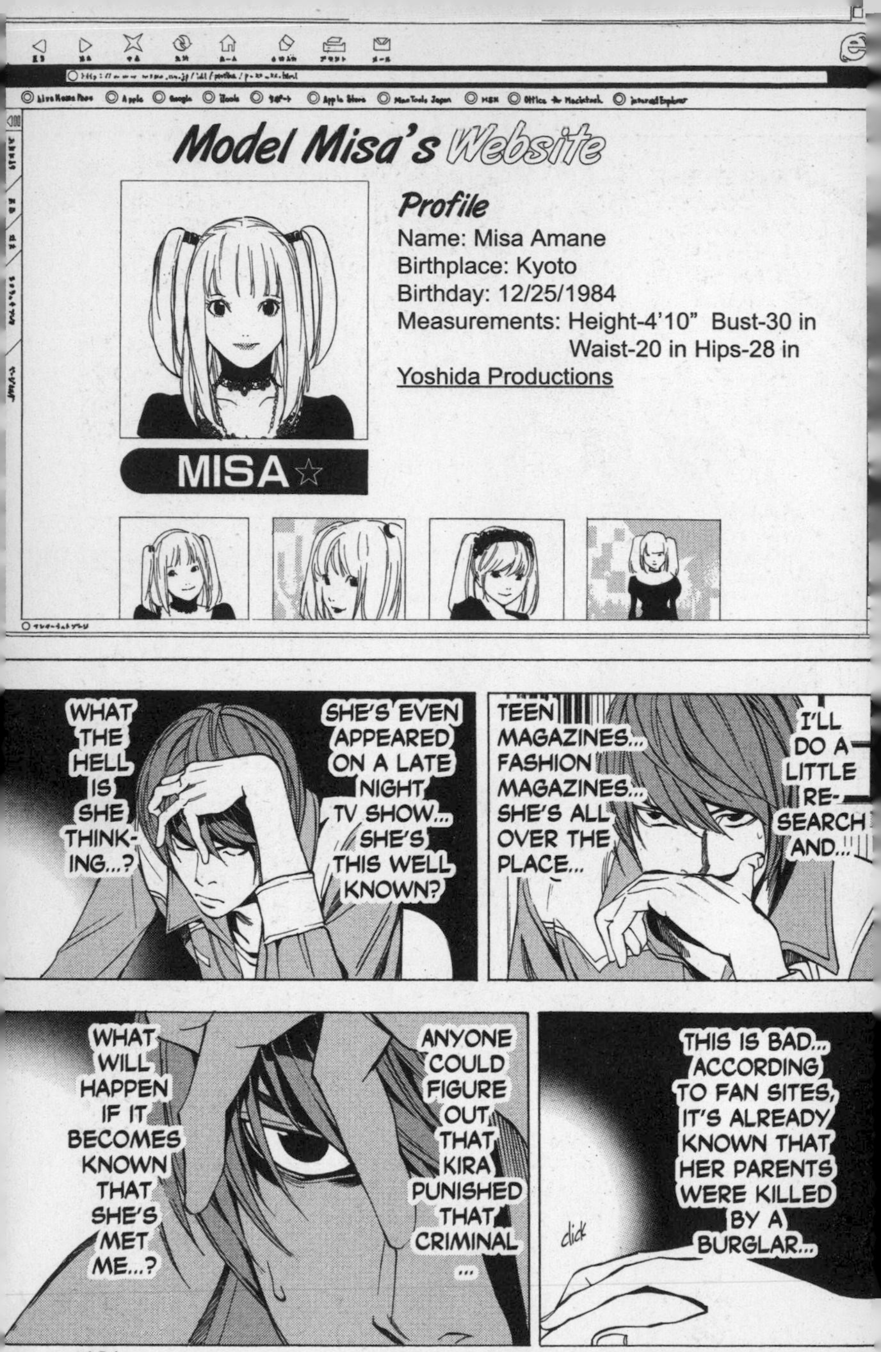
Model Misa's Website
Profile
Name: Misa Amane
Birthplace: Kyoto
Birthday: 12/25/1984
Measurements: Height-4'10" Bust-30 in Waist-20 in Hips-28 in
Yoshida Productions
MISA☆
I'LL DO A LITTLE RE-SEARCH AND..!!
TEEN MAGAZINES... FASHION MAGAZINES... SHE'S ALL OVER THE PLACE...
SHE'S EVEN APPEARED ON A LATE NIGHT TV SHOW... SHE'S THIS WELL KNOWN?
WHAT THE HELL IS SHE THINKING...?
THIS IS BAD... ACCORDING TO FAN SITES, IT'S ALREADY KNOWN THAT HER PARENTS WERE KILLED BY A BURGLAR...
click
ANYONE COULD FIGURE OUT THAT KIRA PUNISHED THAT CRIMINAL...
WHAT WILL HAPPEN IF IT BECOMES KNOWN THAT SHE'S MET ME...?

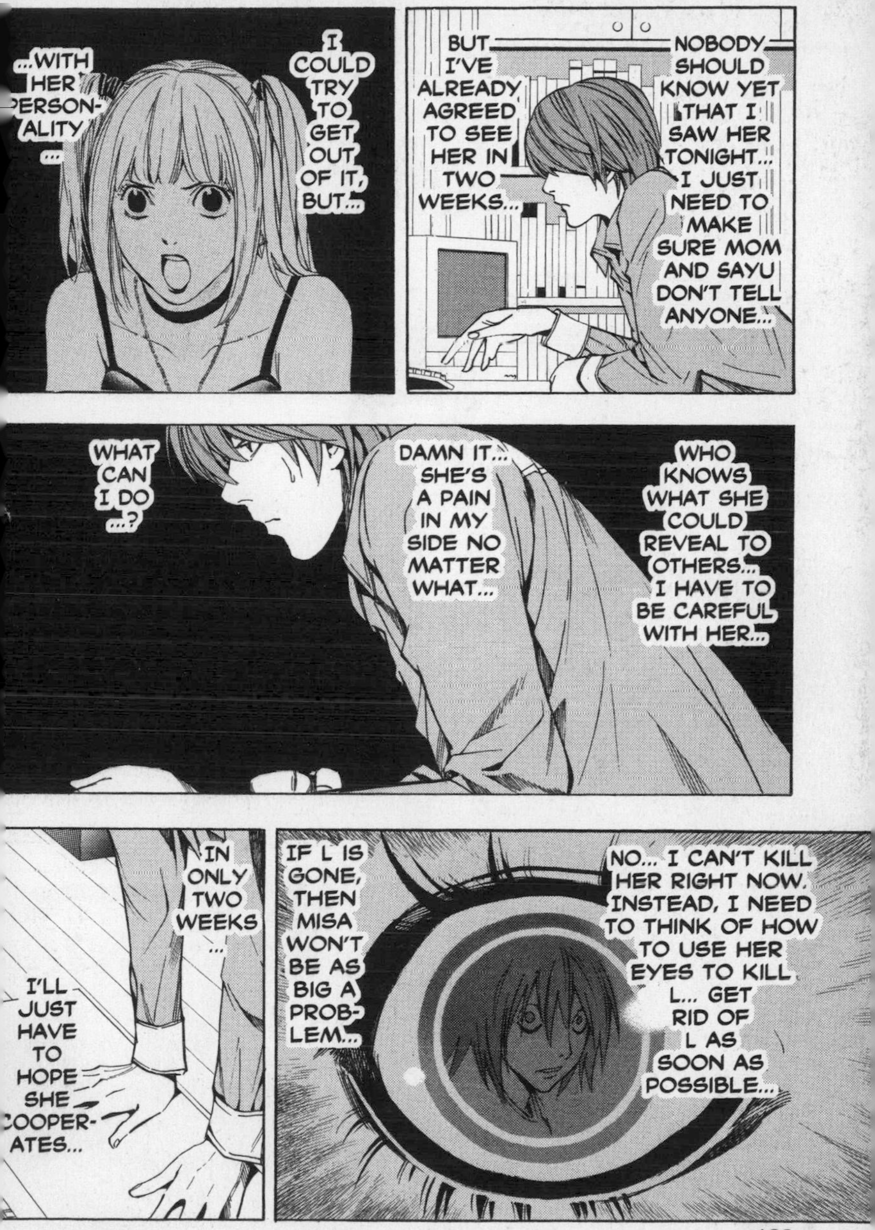
NOBODY SHOULD KNOW YET THAT I SAW HER TONIGHT... I JUST NEED TO MAKE SURE MOM AND SAYU DON'T TELL ANYONE...
BUT I'VE ALREADY AGREED TO SEE HER IN TWO WEEKS...
I COULD TRY TO GET OUT OF IT, BUT...
...WITH HER PERSONALITY...
WHO KNOWS WHAT SHE COULD REVEAL TO OTHERS... I HAVE TO BE CAREFUL WITH HER...
DAMN IT... SHE'S A PAIN IN MY SIDE NO MATTER WHAT...
WHAT CAN I DO ...?
NO... I CAN'T KILL HER RIGHT NOW. INSTEAD, I NEED TO THINK OF HOW TO USE HER EYES TO KILL L... GET RID OF L AS SOON AS POSSIBLE...
IF L IS GONE, THEN MISA WON'T BE AS BIG A PROBLEM...
IN ONLY TWO WEEKS...
I'LL JUST HAVE TO HOPE SHE COOPERATES...

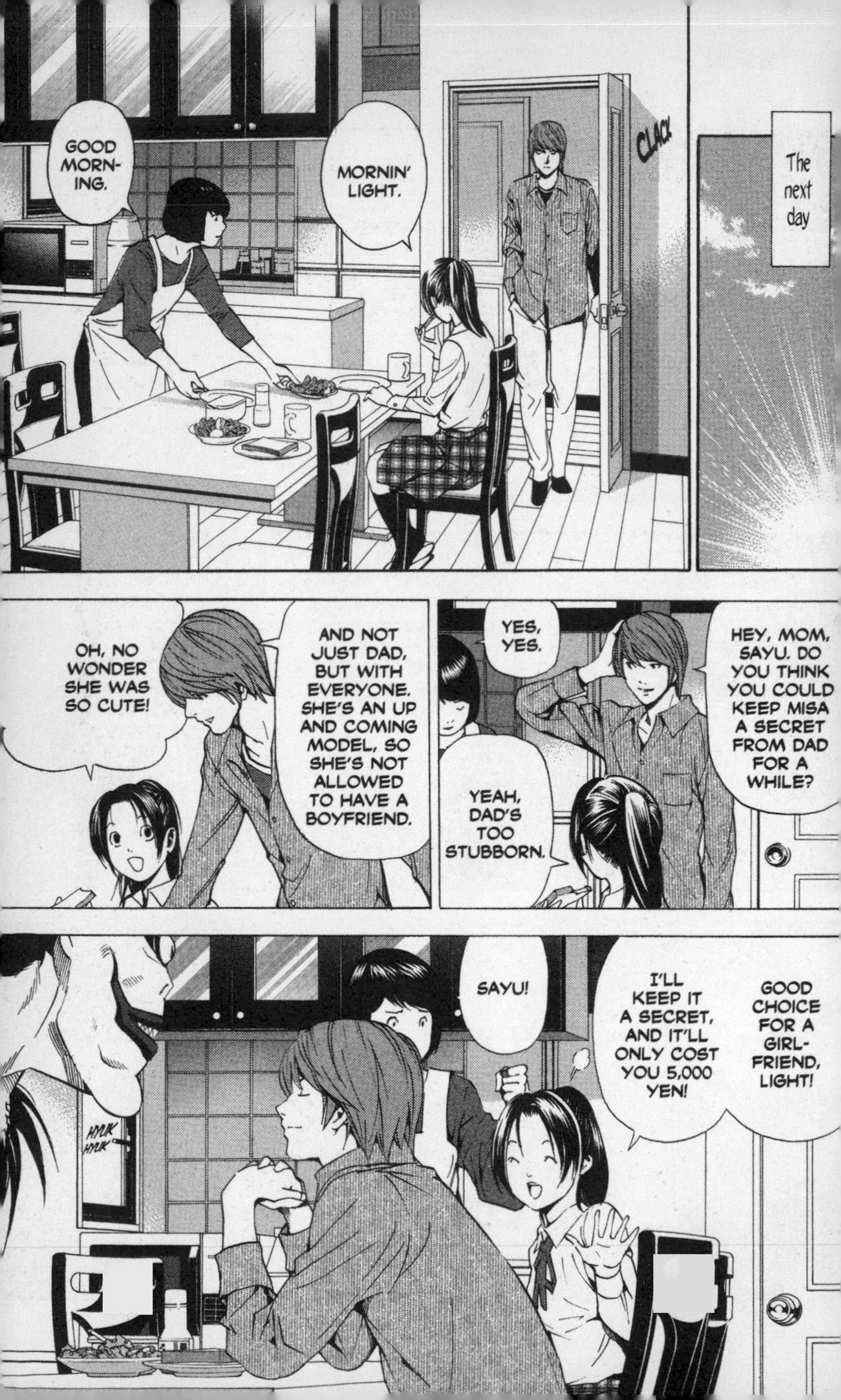
The next day
CLACK
MORNIN' LIGHT.
GOOD MORNING.
HEY, MOM, SAYU. DO YOU THINK YOU COULD KEEP MISA A SECRET FROM DAD FOR A WHILE?
YES, YES.
YEAH, DAD'S TOO STUBBORN.
AND NOT JUST DAD, BUT WITH EVERYONE. SHE'S AN UP AND COMING MODEL, SO SHE'S NOT ALLOWED TO HAVE A BOYFRIEND.
OH, NO WONDER SHE WAS SO CUTE!
GOOD CHOICE FOR A GIRLFRIEND, LIGHT!
I'LL KEEP IT A SECRET, AND IT'LL ONLY COST YOU 5,000 YEN!
SAYU!
HYUK HYUK

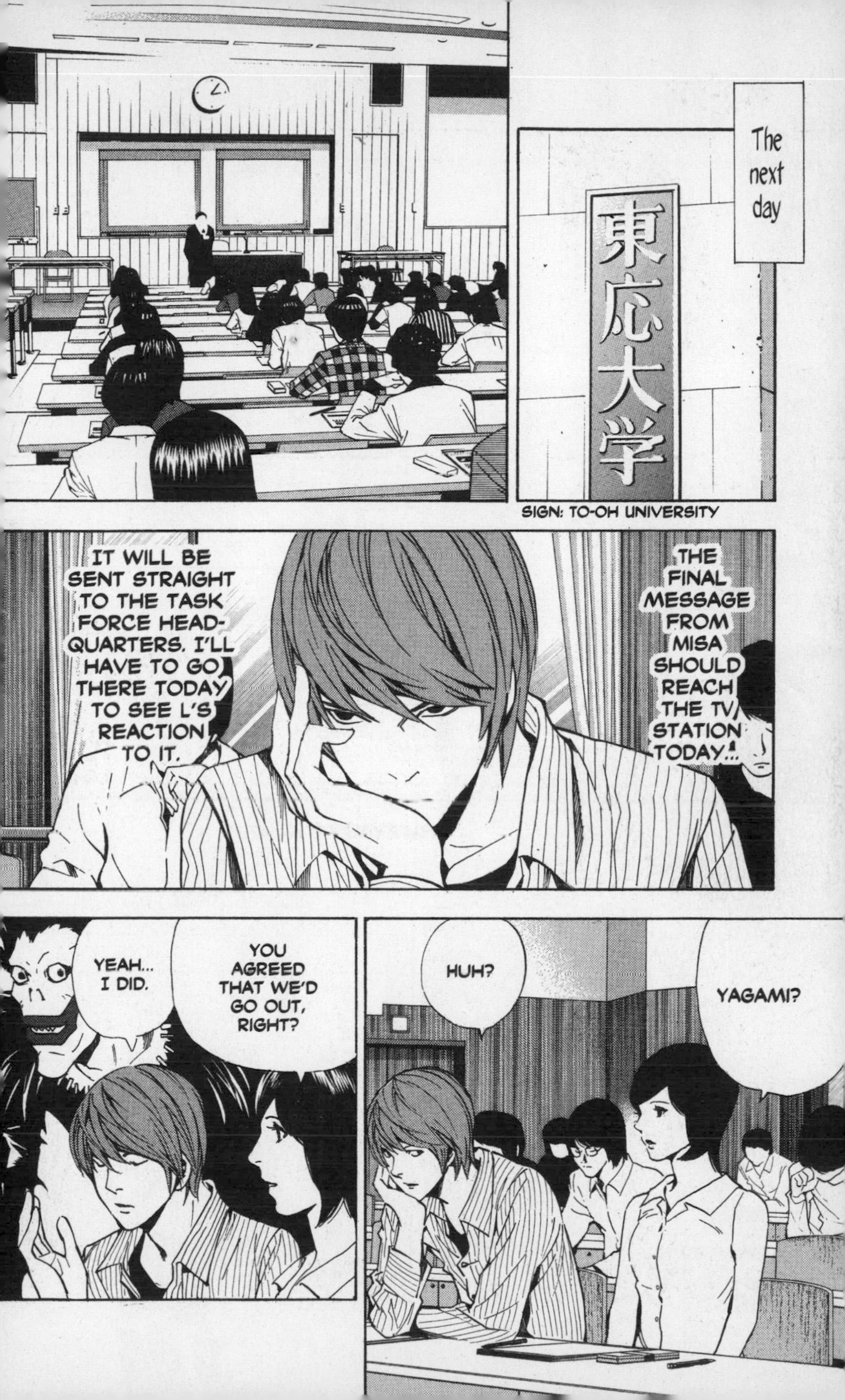
The next day
東応大学
SIGN: TO-OH UNIVERSITY
THE FINAL MESSAGE FROM MISA SHOULD REACH THE TV STATION TODAY...
IT WILL BE SENT STRAIGHT TO THE TASK FORCE HEAD-QUARTERS. I'LL HAVE TO GO THERE TODAY TO SEE L'S REACTION TO IT.
YAGAMI?
HUH?
YOU AGREED THAT WE'D GO OUT, RIGHT?
YEAH... I DID.

READ THIS WAY

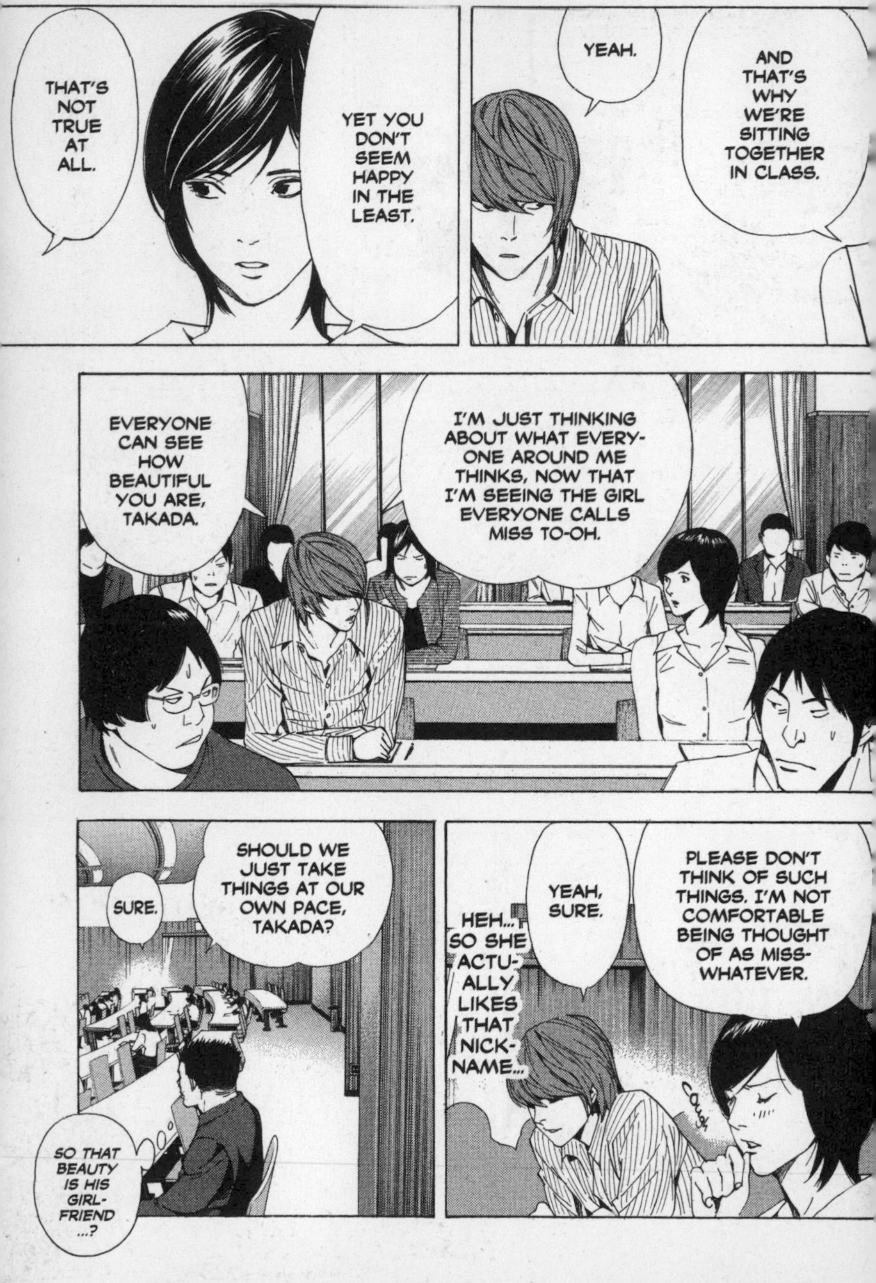
AND THAT'S WHY WE'RE SITTING TOGETHER IN CLASS.
YEAH.
YET YOU DON'T SEEM HAPPY IN THE LEAST.
THAT'S NOT TRUE AT ALL.
I'M JUST THINKING ABOUT WHAT EVERY-ONE AROUND ME THINKS, NOW THAT I'M SEEING THE GIRL EVERYONE CALLS MISS TO-OH.
EVERYONE CAN SEE HOW BEAUTIFUL YOU ARE, TAKADA.
PLEASE DON'T THINK OF SUCH THINGS. I'M NOT COMFORTABLE BEING THOUGHT OF AS MISS-WHATEVER.
YEAH, SURE.
HEH... SO SHE ACTU-ALLY LIKES THAT NICK-NAME...
COUGH
SHOULD WE JUST TAKE THINGS AT OUR OWN PACE, TAKADA?
SURE.
SO THAT BEAUTY IS HIS GIRL-FRIEND ...?

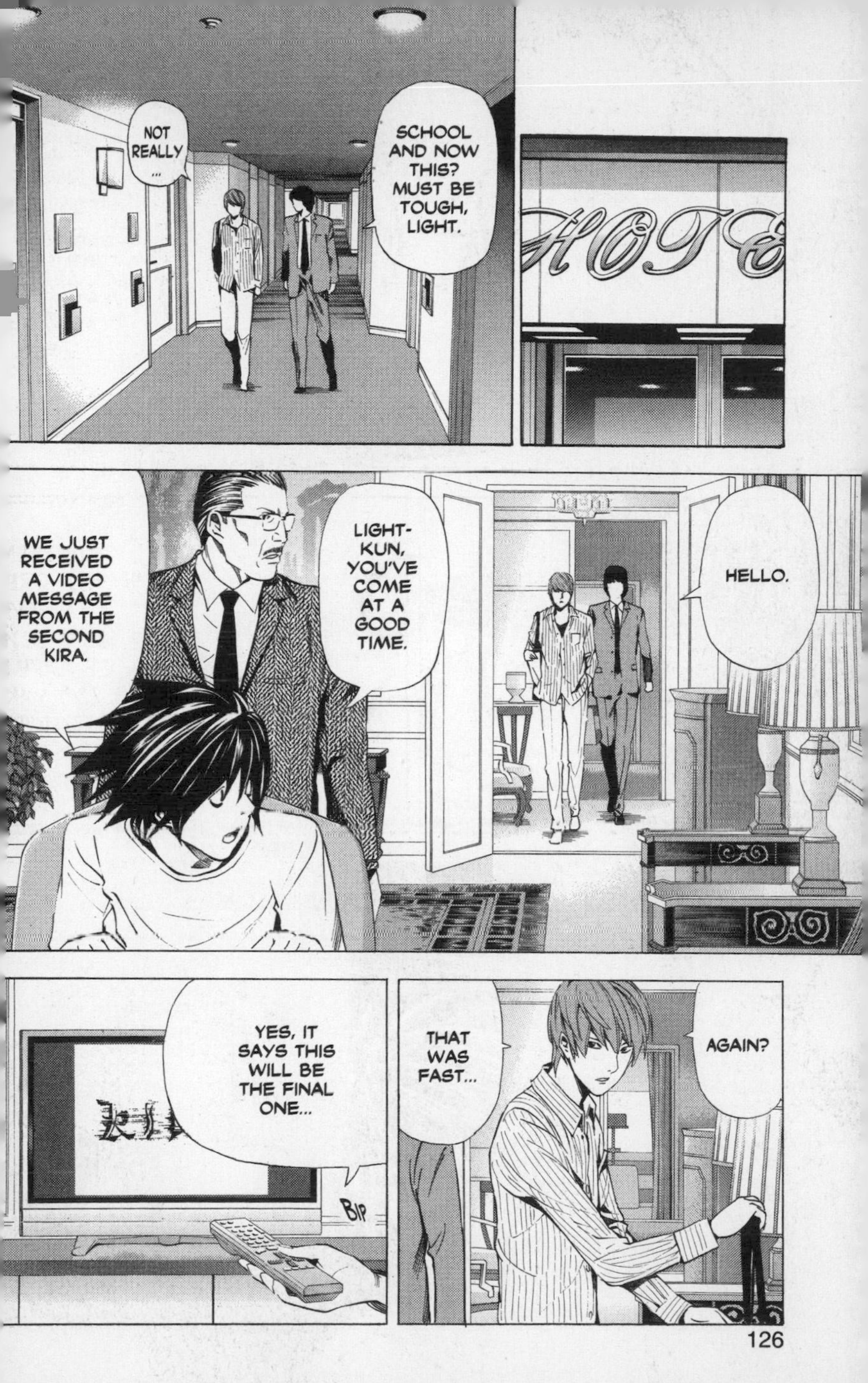
SCHOOL AND NOW THIS? MUST BE TOUGH, LIGHT.
NOT REALLY ...
HELLO.
LIGHT-KUN, YOU'VE COME AT A GOOD TIME.
WE JUST RECEIVED A VIDEO MESSAGE FROM THE SECOND KIRA.
AGAIN?
THAT WAS FAST...
YES, IT SAYS THIS WILL BE THE FINAL ONE...
BIP

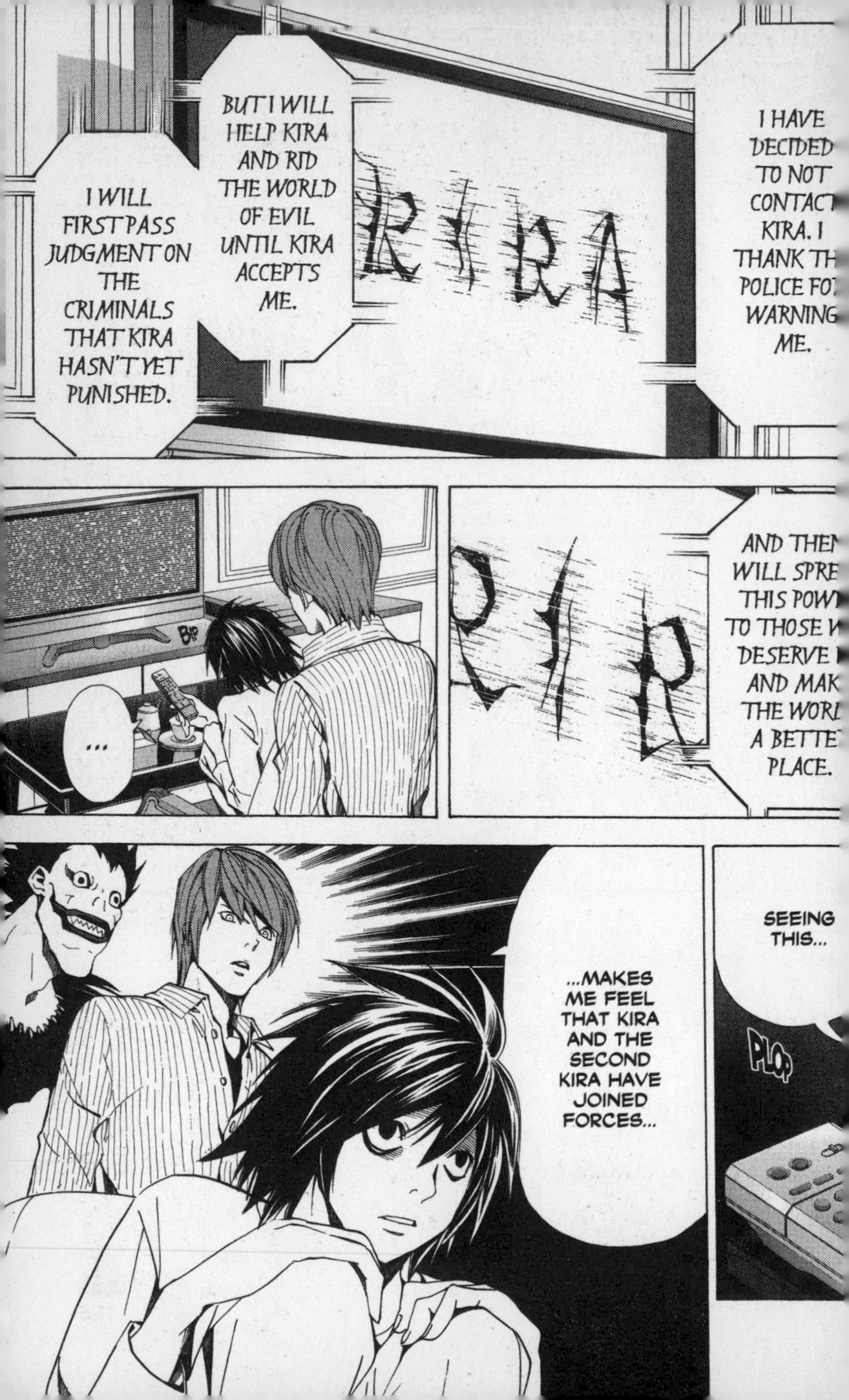
I HAVE DECIDED TO NOT CONTAC KIRA. I THANK TH POLICE FO WARNING ME.
KIRA
BUT I WILL HELP KIRA AND RID THE WORLD OF EVIL UNTIL KIRA ACCEPTS ME.
I WILL FIRST PASS JUDGMENT ON THE CRIMINALS THAT KIRA HASN'T YET PUNISHED.
AND THEN WILL SPRE THIS POW TO THOSE W DESERVE AND MAK THE WORL A BETTE PLACE.
BIP
...
SEEING THIS...
PLOP
...MAKES ME FEEL THAT KIRA AND THE SECOND KIRA HAVE JOINED FORCES...

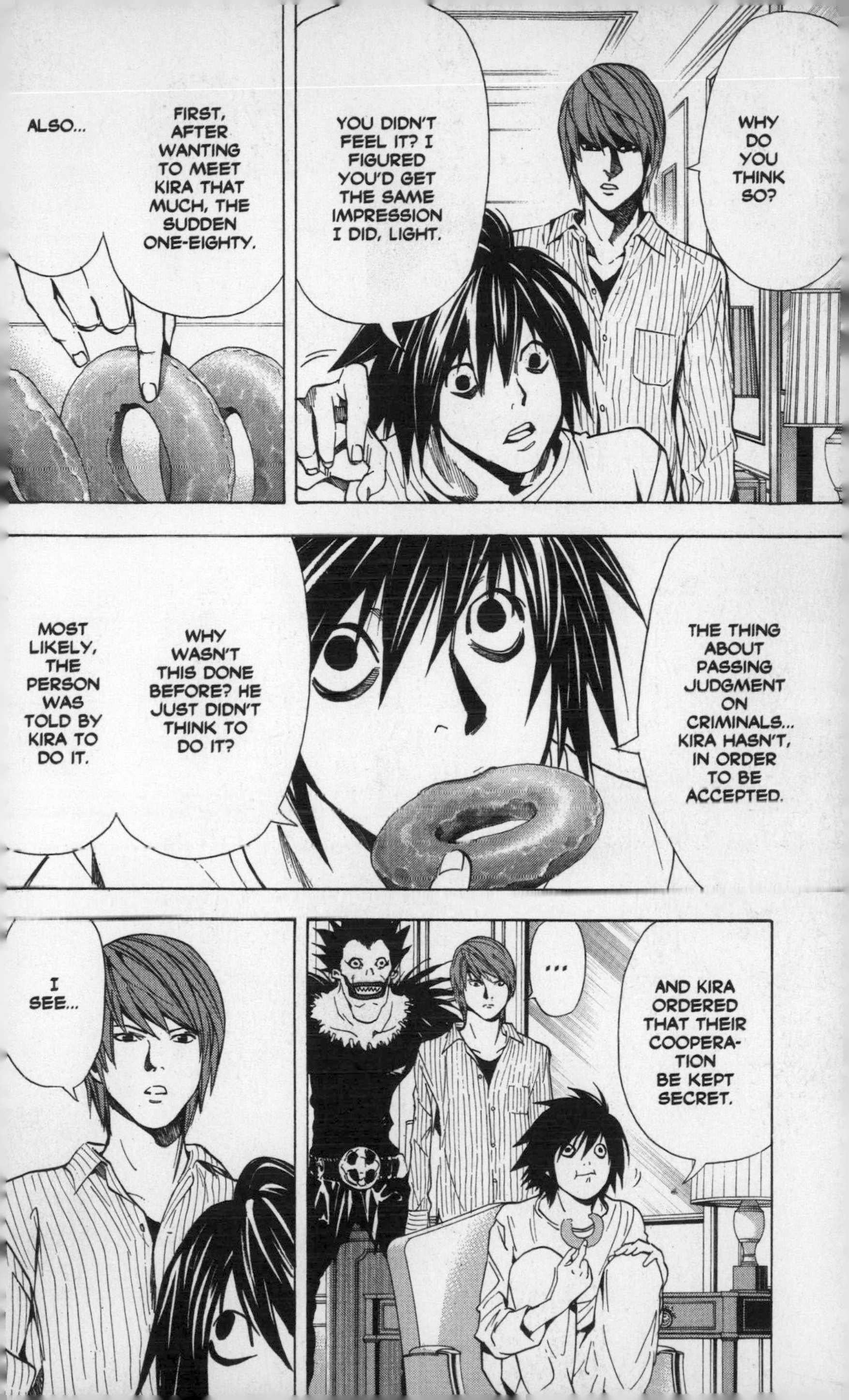
WHY DO YOU THINK SO?
YOU DIDN'T FEEL IT? I FIGURED YOU'D GET THE SAME IMPRESSION I DID, LIGHT.
FIRST, AFTER WANTING TO MEET KIRA THAT MUCH, THE SUDDEN ONE-EIGHTY.
ALSO...
THE THING ABOUT PASSING JUDGMENT ON CRIMINALS... KIRA HASN'T, IN ORDER TO BE ACCEPTED.
WHY WASN'T THIS DONE BEFORE? HE JUST DIDN'T THINK TO DO IT?
MOST LIKELY, THE PERSON WAS TOLD BY KIRA TO DO IT.
AND KIRA ORDERED THAT THEIR COOPERATION BE KEPT SECRET.
...
I SEE...

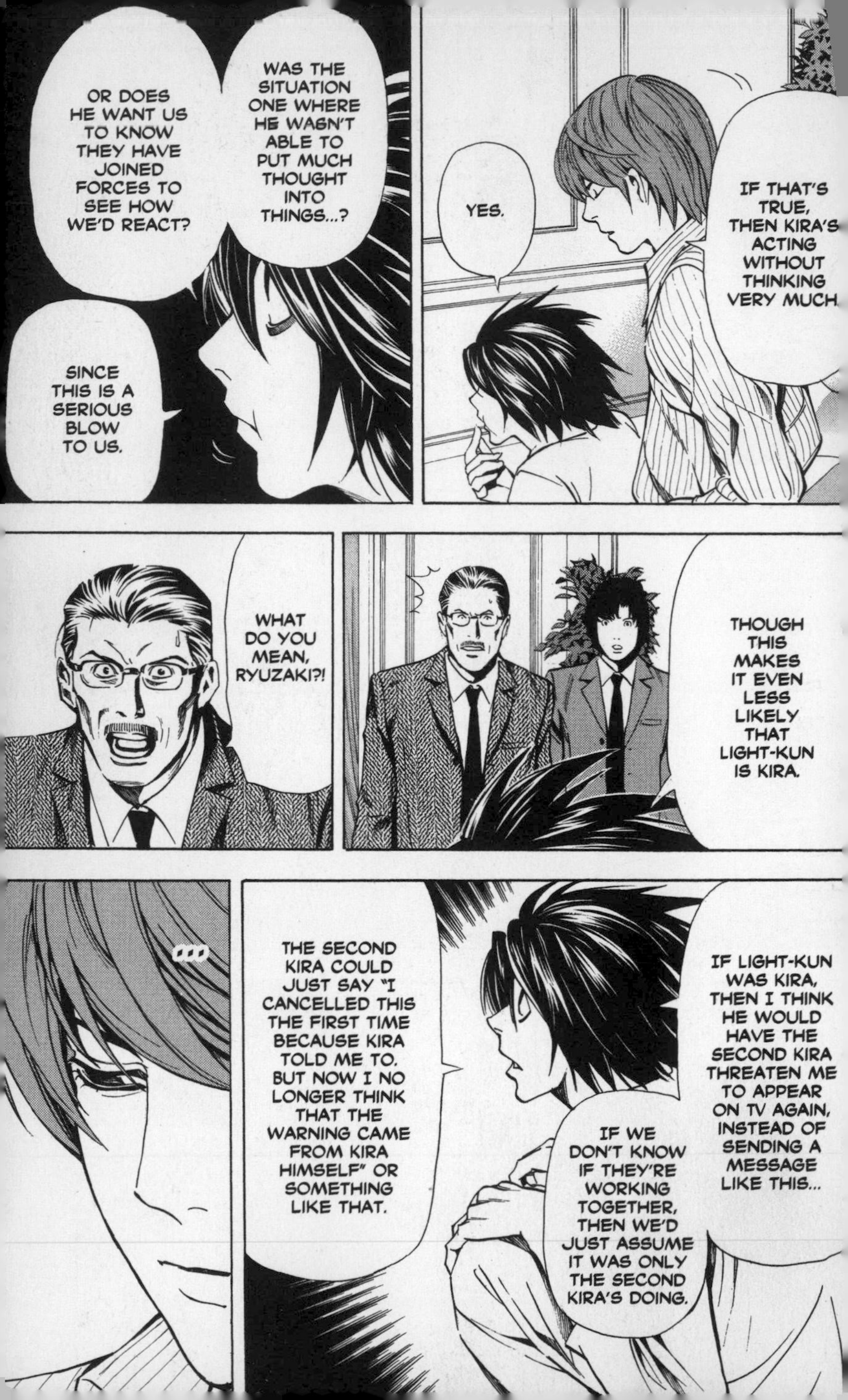
IF THAT'S TRUE, THEN KIRA'S ACTING WITHOUT THINKING VERY MUCH.
YES.
WAS THE SITUATION ONE WHERE HE WASN'T ABLE TO PUT MUCH THOUGHT INTO THINGS...?
OR DOES HE WANT US TO KNOW THEY HAVE JOINED FORCES TO SEE HOW WE'D REACT?
SINCE THIS IS A SERIOUS BLOW TO US.
THOUGH THIS MAKES IT EVEN LESS LIKELY THAT LIGHT-KUN IS KIRA.
WHAT DO YOU MEAN, RYUZAKI?!
IF LIGHT-KUN WAS KIRA, THEN I THINK HE WOULD HAVE THE SECOND KIRA THREATEN ME TO APPEAR ON TV AGAIN, INSTEAD OF SENDING A MESSAGE LIKE THIS...
IF WE DON'T KNOW IF THEY'RE WORKING TOGETHER, THEN WE'D JUST ASSUME IT WAS ONLY THE SECOND KIRA'S DOING.
THE SECOND KIRA COULD JUST SAY "I CANCELLED THIS THE FIRST TIME BECAUSE KIRA TOLD ME TO. BUT NOW I NO LONGER THINK THAT THE WARNING CAME FROM KIRA HIMSELF" OR SOMETHING LIKE THAT.
...

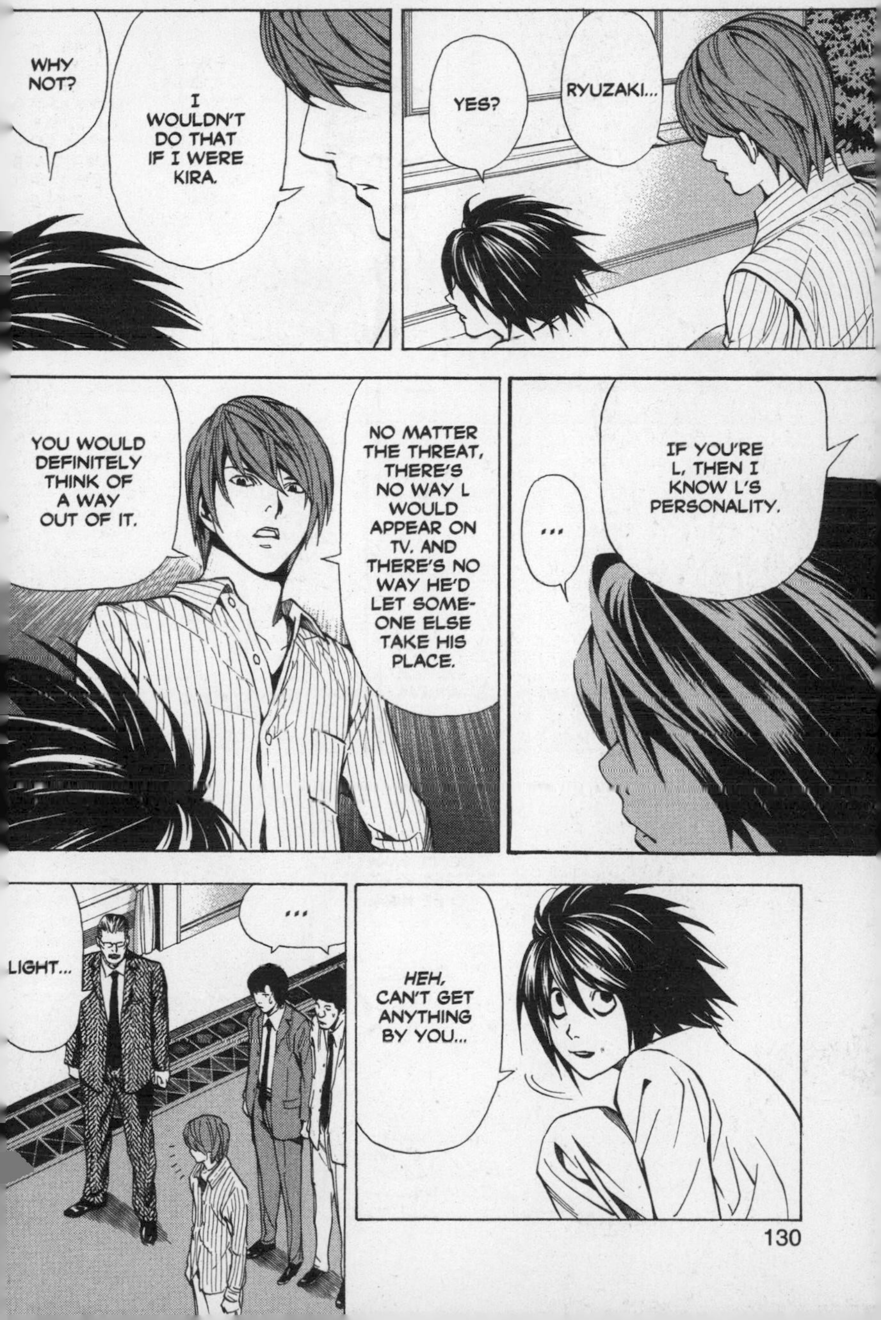
RYUZAKI...
YES?
I WOULDN'T DO THAT IF I WERE KIRA.
WHY NOT?
IF YOU'RE L, THEN I KNOW L'S PERSONALITY.
...
NO MATTER THE THREAT, THERE'S NO WAY L WOULD APPEAR ON TV. AND THERE'S NO WAY HE'D LET SOME-ONE ELSE TAKE HIS PLACE.
YOU WOULD DEFINITELY THINK OF A WAY OUT OF IT.
HEH, CAN'T GET ANYTHING BY YOU...
...
LIGHT...

READ THIS WAY

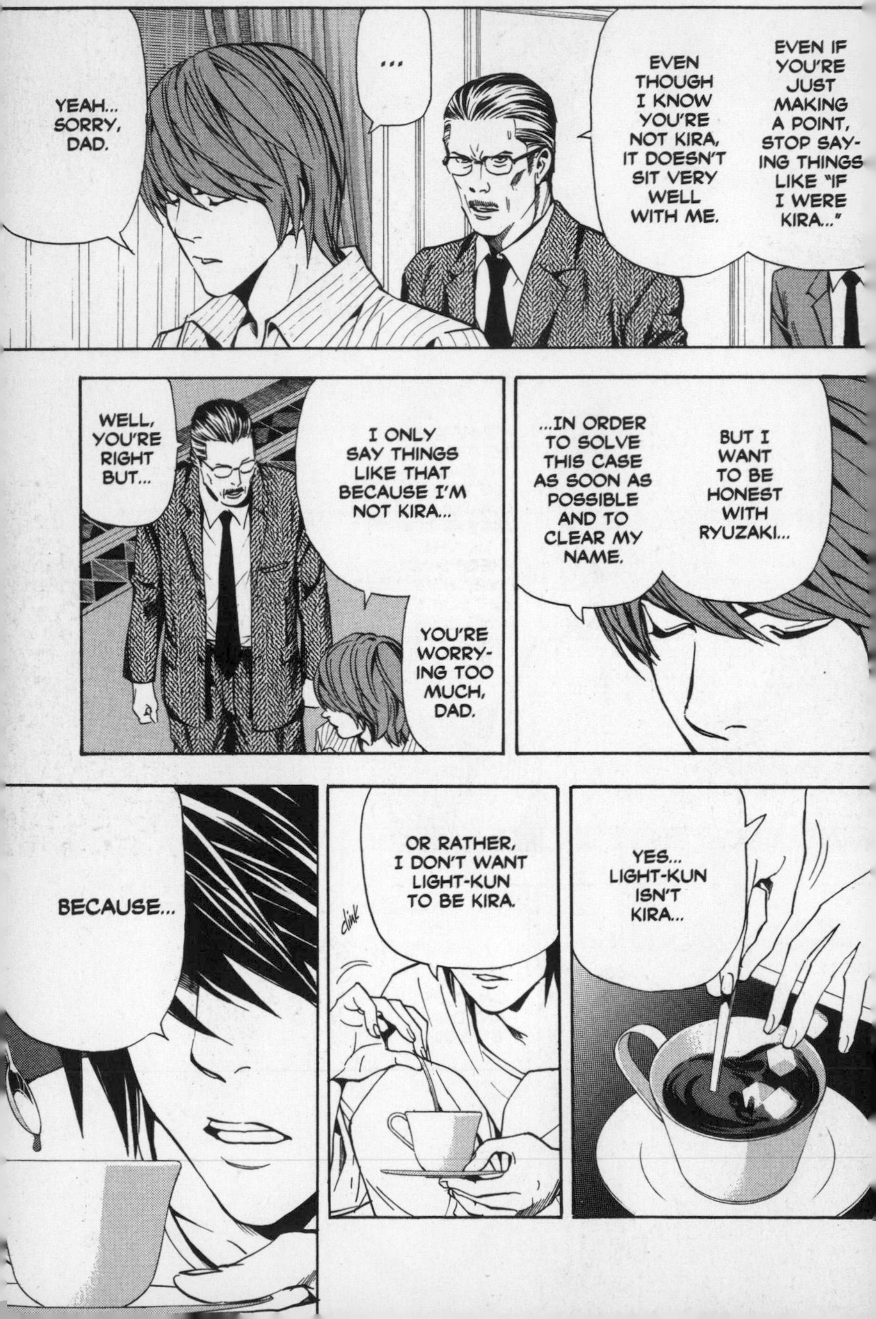
EVEN IF YOU'RE JUST MAKING A POINT, STOP SAYING THINGS LIKE "IF I WERE KIRA..."
EVEN THOUGH I KNOW YOU'RE NOT KIRA, IT DOESN'T SIT VERY WELL WITH ME.
...
YEAH... SORRY, DAD.
BUT I WANT TO BE HONEST WITH RYUZAKI...
...IN ORDER TO SOLVE THIS CASE AS SOON AS POSSIBLE AND TO CLEAR MY NAME.
I ONLY SAY THINGS LIKE THAT BECAUSE I'M NOT KIRA...
YOU'RE WORRYING TOO MUCH, DAD.
WELL, YOU'RE RIGHT BUT...
YES... LIGHT-KUN ISN'T KIRA...
OR RATHER, I DON'T WANT LIGHT-KUN TO BE KIRA.
clink
BECAUSE...

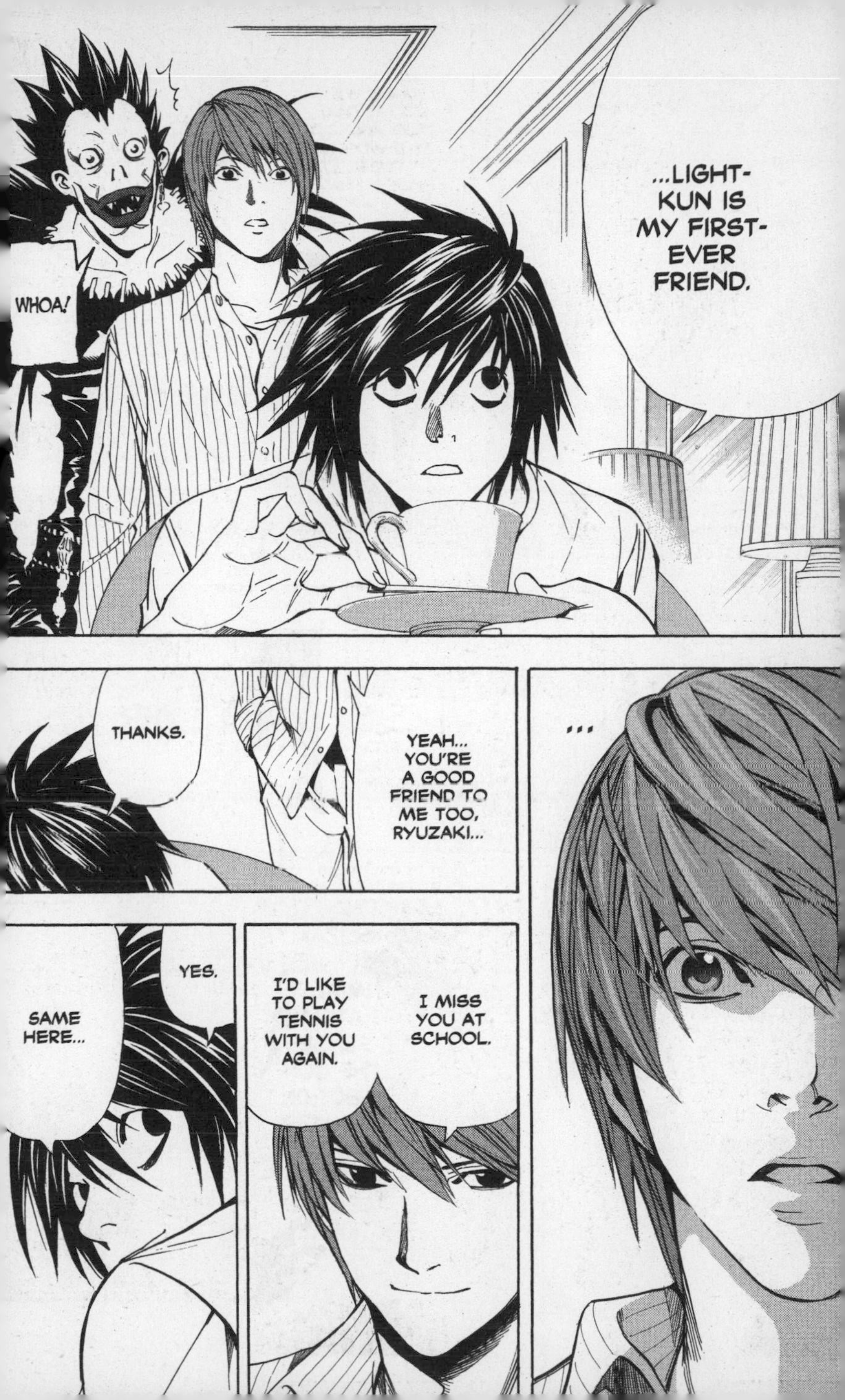
...LIGHT-KUN IS MY FIRST-EVER FRIEND.
WHOA!
YEAH... YOU'RE A GOOD FRIEND TO ME TOO, RYUZAKI...
THANKS.
I MISS YOU AT SCHOOL.
I'D LIKE TO PLAY TENNIS WITH YOU AGAIN.
YES.
SAME HERE...
...

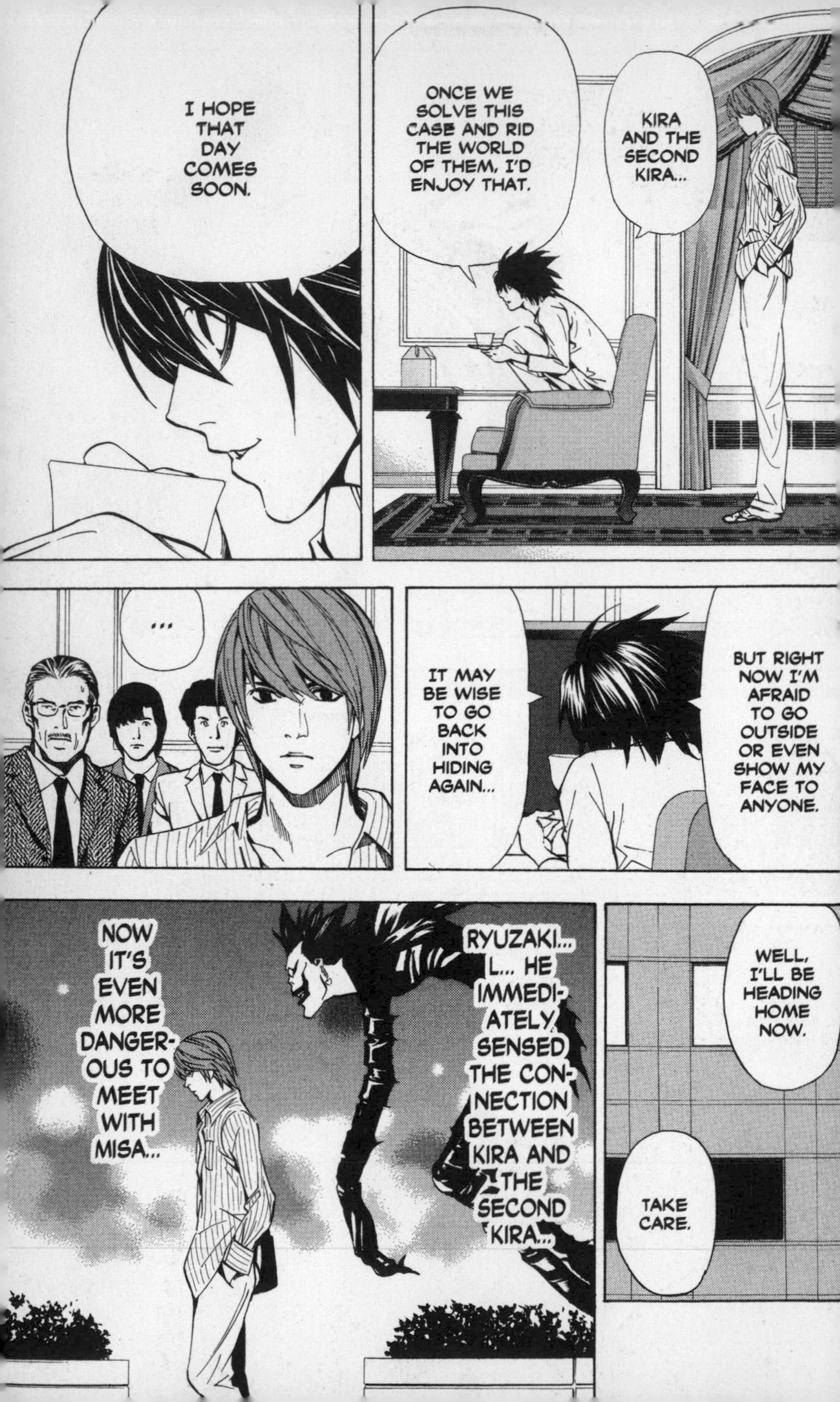
KIRA AND THE SECOND KIRA...
ONCE WE SOLVE THIS CASE AND RID THE WORLD OF THEM, I'D ENJOY THAT.
I HOPE THAT DAY COMES SOON.
BUT RIGHT NOW I'M AFRAID TO GO OUTSIDE OR EVEN SHOW MY FACE TO ANYONE.
IT MAY BE WISE TO GO BACK INTO HIDING AGAIN...
...
WELL, I'LL BE HEADING HOME NOW.
TAKE CARE.
RYUZAKI... L... HE IMMEDIATELY SENSED THE CONNECTION BETWEEN KIRA AND THE SECOND KIRA...
NOW IT'S EVEN MORE DANGEROUS TO MEET WITH MISA...

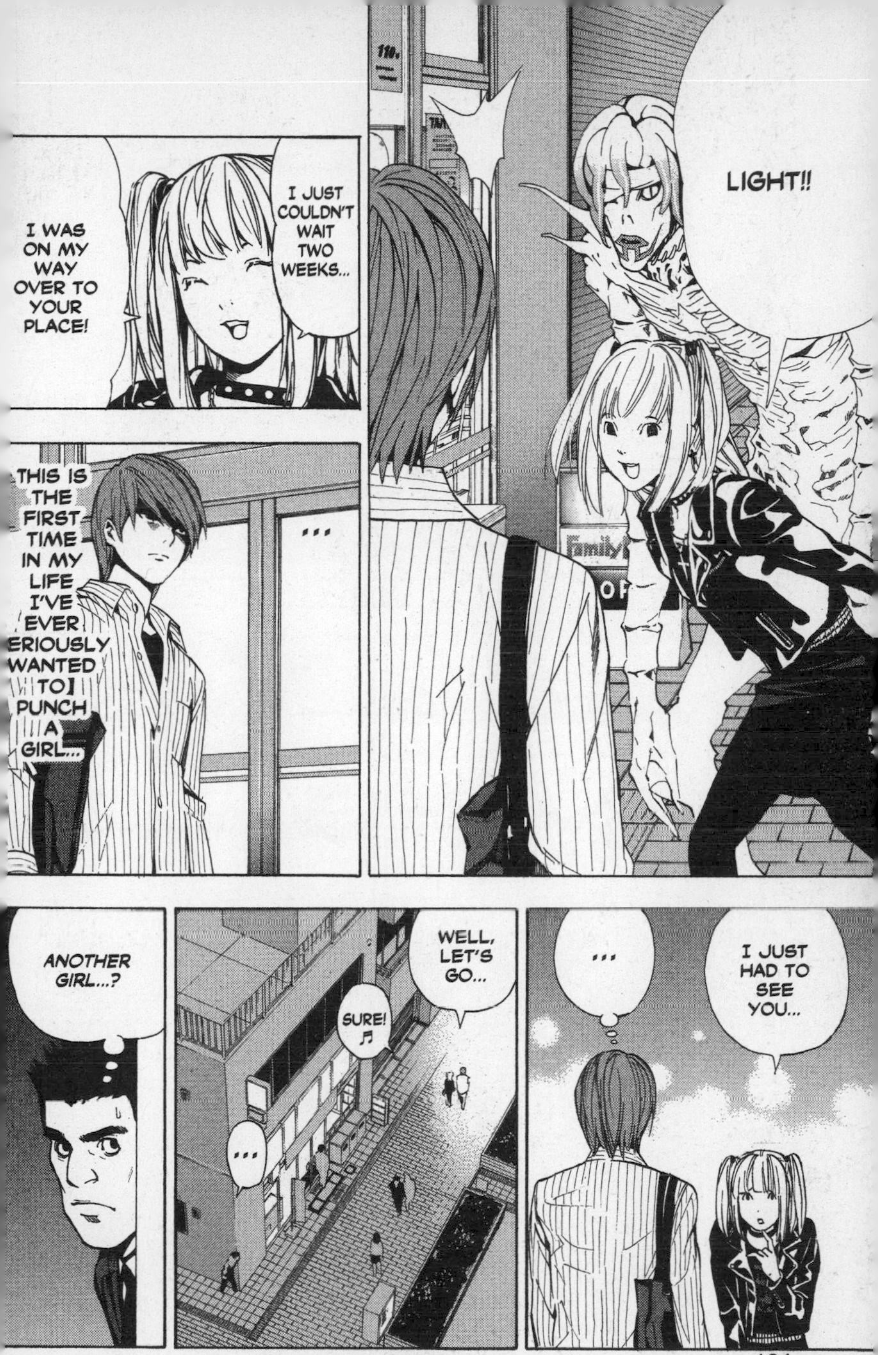
LIGHT!!
I JUST COULDN'T WAIT TWO WEEKS...
I WAS ON MY WAY OVER TO YOUR PLACE!
...
THIS IS THE FIRST TIME IN MY LIFE I'VE EVER ERIOUSLY WANTED TO PUNCH A GIRL...
I JUST HAD TO SEE YOU...
...
WELL, LET'S GO...
SURE! ♪
...
ANOTHER GIRL...?

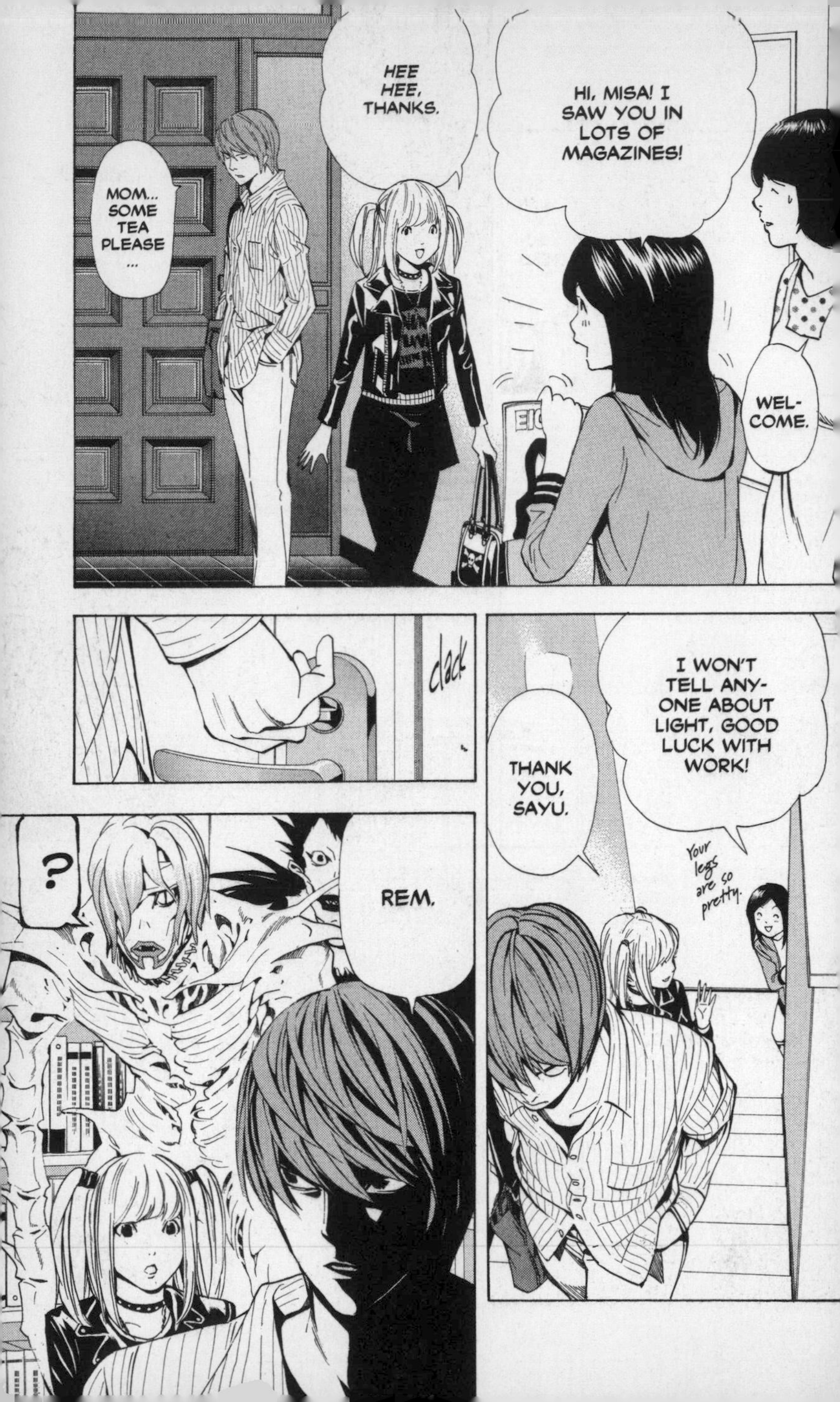
WEL-
COME.
HI, MISA! I SAW YOU IN LOTS OF MAGAZINES!
HEE HEE, THANKS.
MOM... SOME TEA PLEASE ...
I WON'T TELL ANY-
ONE ABOUT LIGHT, GOOD LUCK WITH WORK!
THANK YOU, SAYU.
Your legs are so pretty.
clack
REM.
?

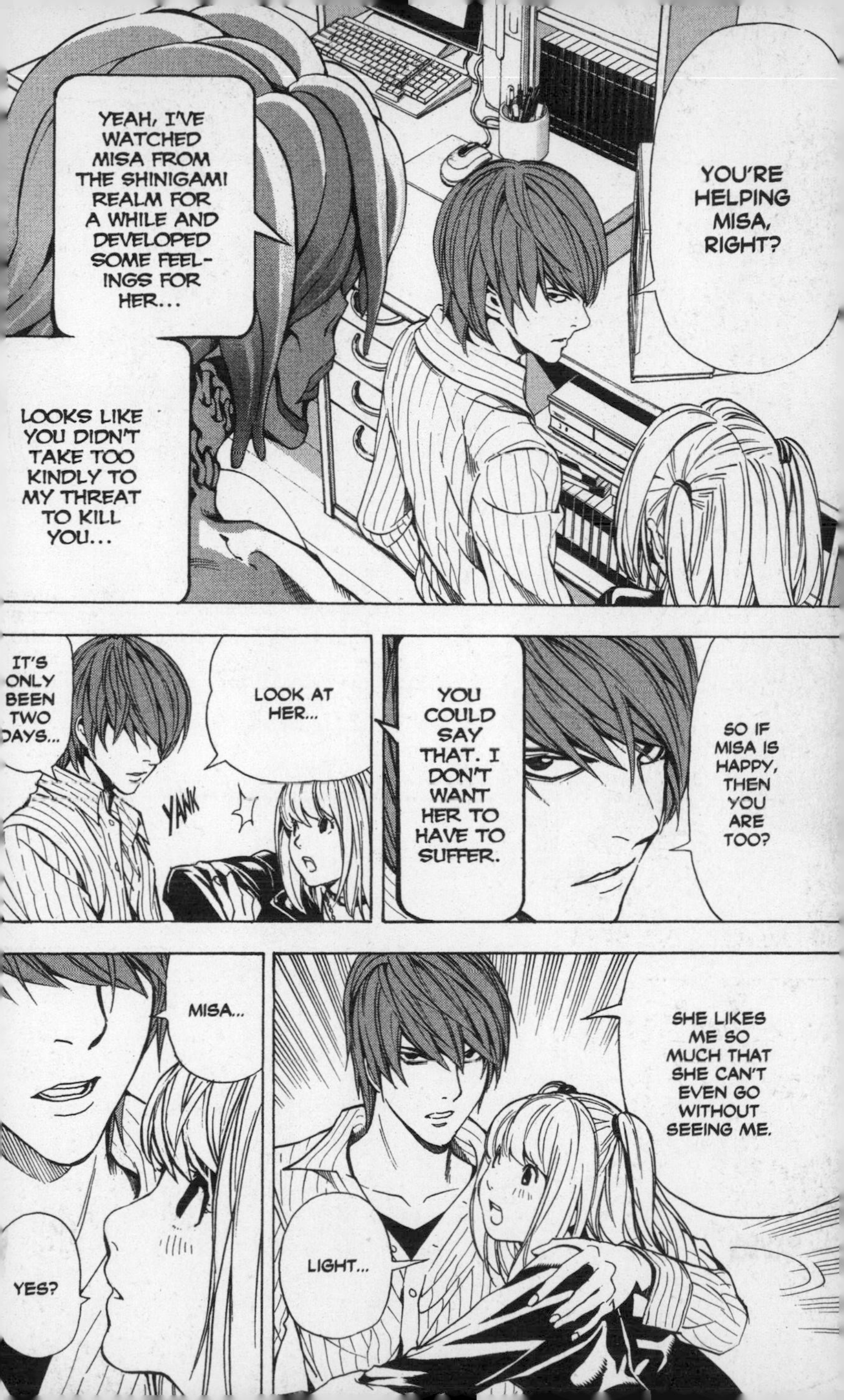
YOU'RE HELPING MISA, RIGHT?
YEAH, I'VE WATCHED MISA FROM THE SHINIGAMI REALM FOR A WHILE AND DEVELOPED SOME FEEL-INGS FOR HER...
LOOKS LIKE YOU DIDN'T TAKE TOO KINDLY TO MY THREAT TO KILL YOU...
SO IF MISA IS HAPPY, THEN YOU ARE TOO?
YOU COULD SAY THAT. I DON'T WANT HER TO HAVE TO SUFFER.
LOOK AT HER...
IT'S ONLY BEEN TWO DAYS...
YANK
SHE LIKES ME SO MUCH THAT SHE CAN'T EVEN GO WITHOUT SEEING ME.
LIGHT...
MISA...
YES?

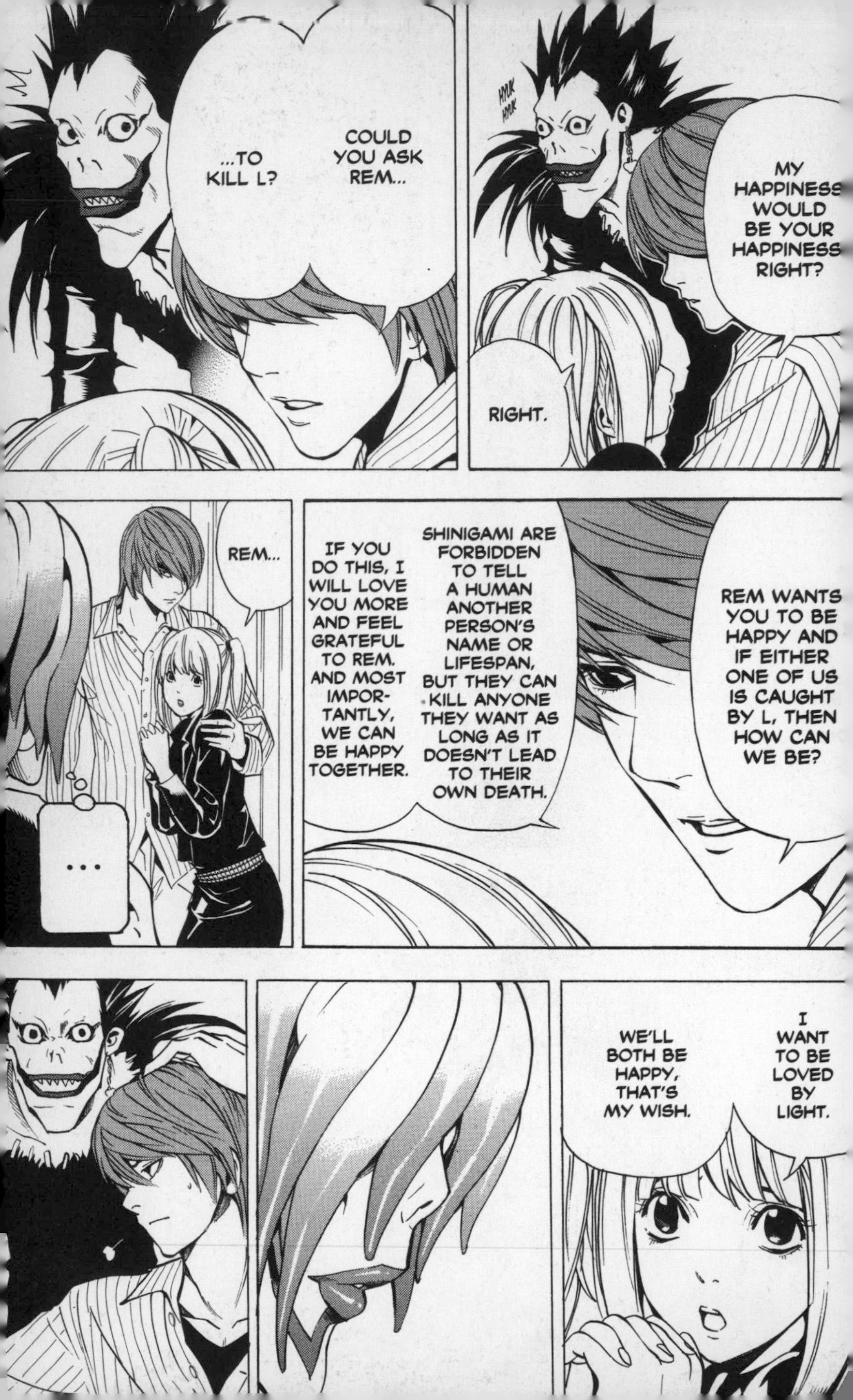
HYUK HYUK
MY HAPPINESS WOULD BE YOUR HAPPINESS RIGHT?
RIGHT.
COULD YOU ASK REM...
...TO KILL L?
REM WANTS YOU TO BE HAPPY AND IF EITHER ONE OF US IS CAUGHT BY L, THEN HOW CAN WE BE?
SHINIGAMI ARE FORBIDDEN TO TELL A HUMAN ANOTHER PERSON'S NAME OR LIFESPAN, BUT THEY CAN KILL ANYONE THEY WANT AS LONG AS IT DOESN'T LEAD TO THEIR OWN DEATH.
IF YOU DO THIS, I WILL LOVE YOU MORE AND FEEL GRATEFUL TO REM. AND MOST IMPORTANTLY, WE CAN BE HAPPY TOGETHER.
REM...
...
I WANT TO BE LOVED BY LIGHT.
WE'LL BOTH BE HAPPY, THAT'S MY WISH.

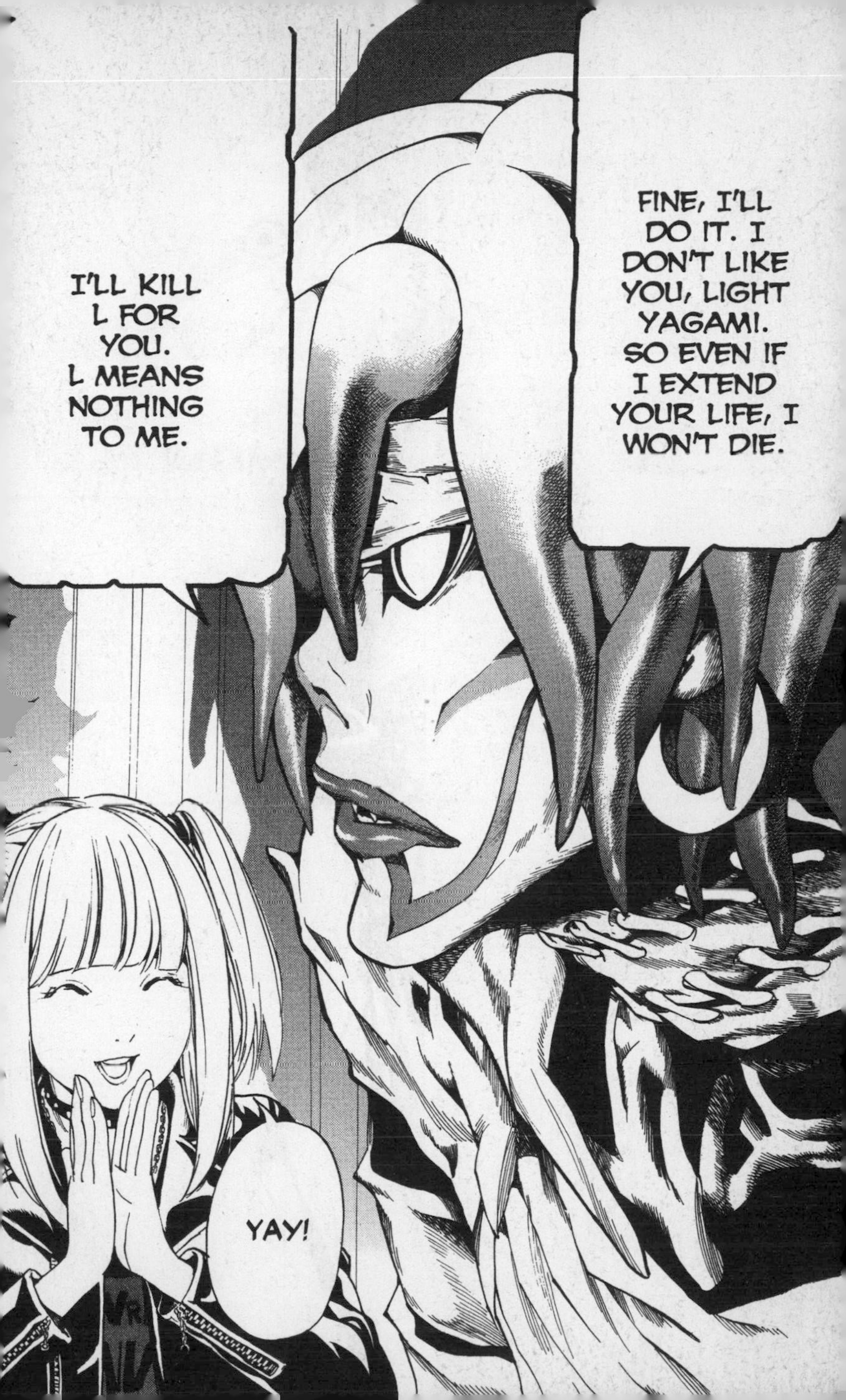
FINE, I'LL DO IT. I DON'T LIKE YOU, LIGHT YAGAMI. SO EVEN IF I EXTEND YOUR LIFE, I WON'T DIE.
I'LL KILL L FOR YOU. L MEANS NOTHING TO ME.
YAY!

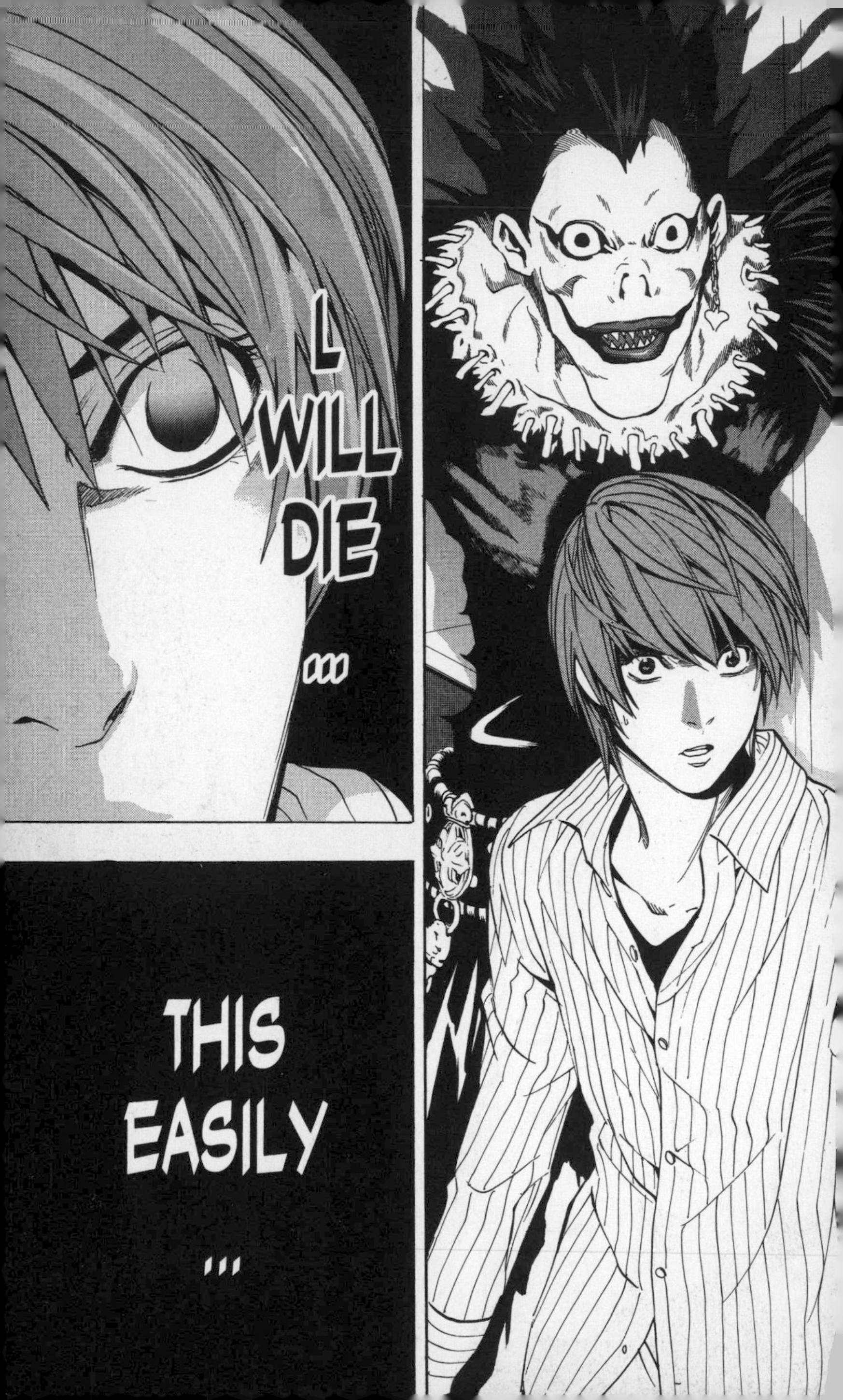
L WILL DIE ...
THIS EASILY ...

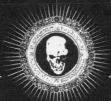

DEATH NOTE
HOW TO USE IT
XI

Those with the eye power of the god of death will have the eyesight of over 3.6 in the human measurement, regardless of their original eyesight.

死神の目を持った人間は、元の視力に拘らず、人間界でいう 3.6以上の視力になる。

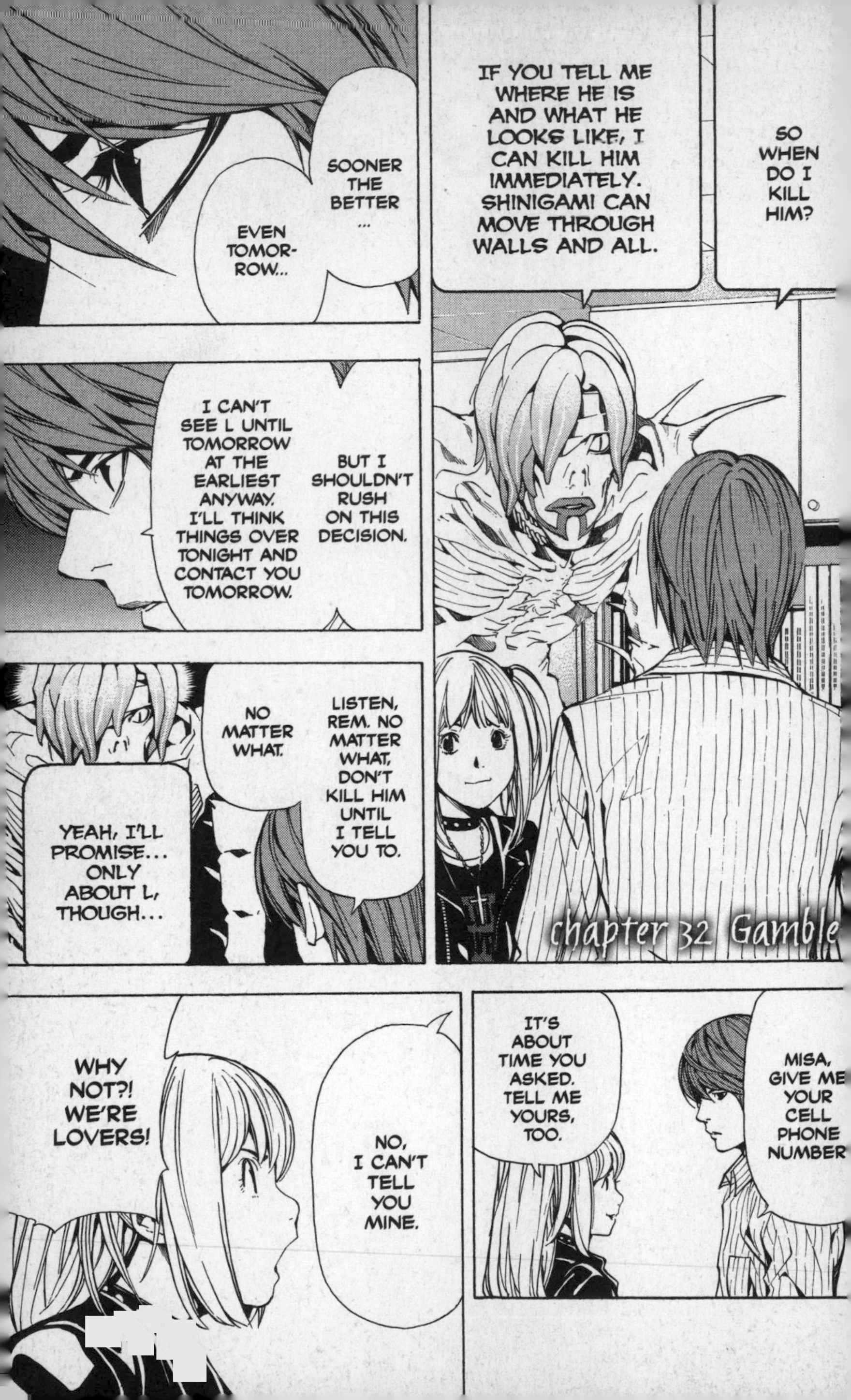
SO WHEN DO I KILL HIM?
IF YOU TELL ME WHERE HE IS AND WHAT HE LOOKS LIKE, I CAN KILL HIM IMMEDIATELY. SHINIGAMI CAN MOVE THROUGH WALLS AND ALL.
chapter 32 Gamble
SOONER THE BETTER ...
EVEN TOMORROW...
BUT I SHOULDN'T RUSH ON THIS DECISION.
I CAN'T SEE L UNTIL TOMORROW AT THE EARLIEST ANYWAY. I'LL THINK THINGS OVER TONIGHT AND CONTACT YOU TOMORROW.
LISTEN, REM. NO MATTER WHAT, DON'T KILL HIM UNTIL I TELL YOU TO.
NO MATTER WHAT.
YEAH, I'LL PROMISE... ONLY ABOUT L, THOUGH...
MISA, GIVE ME YOUR CELL PHONE NUMBER
IT'S ABOUT TIME YOU ASKED. TELL ME YOURS, TOO.
NO, I CAN'T TELL YOU MINE.
WHY NOT?! WE'RE LOVERS!

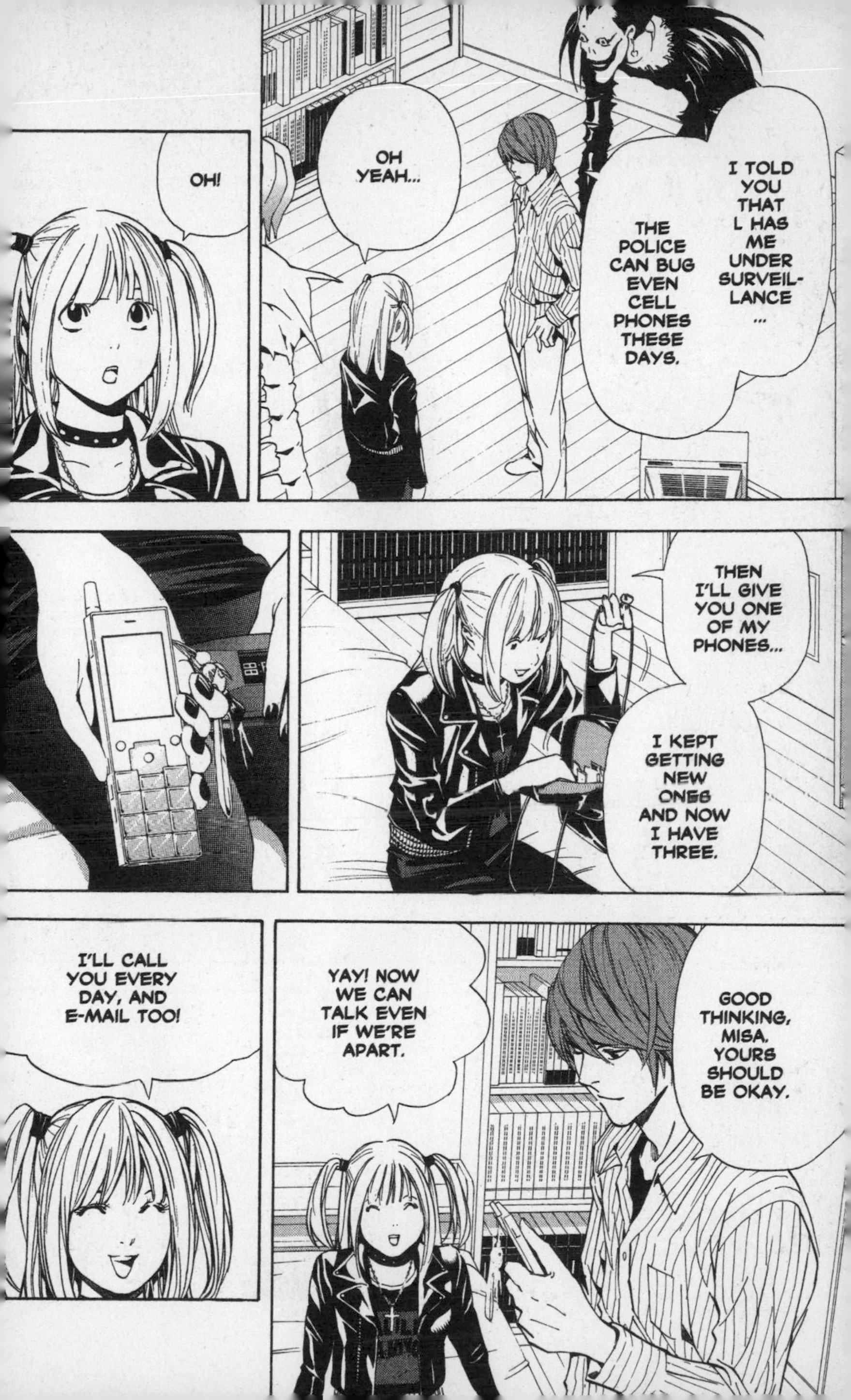
I TOLD YOU THAT L HAS ME UNDER SURVEIL-LANCE...
THE POLICE CAN BUG EVEN CELL PHONES THESE DAYS.
OH YEAH...
OH!
THEN I'LL GIVE YOU ONE OF MY PHONES...
I KEPT GETTING NEW ONES AND NOW I HAVE THREE.
GOOD THINKING, MISA. YOURS SHOULD BE OKAY.
YAY! NOW WE CAN TALK EVEN IF WE'RE APART.
I'LL CALL YOU EVERY DAY, AND E-MAIL TOO!

READ THIS WAY

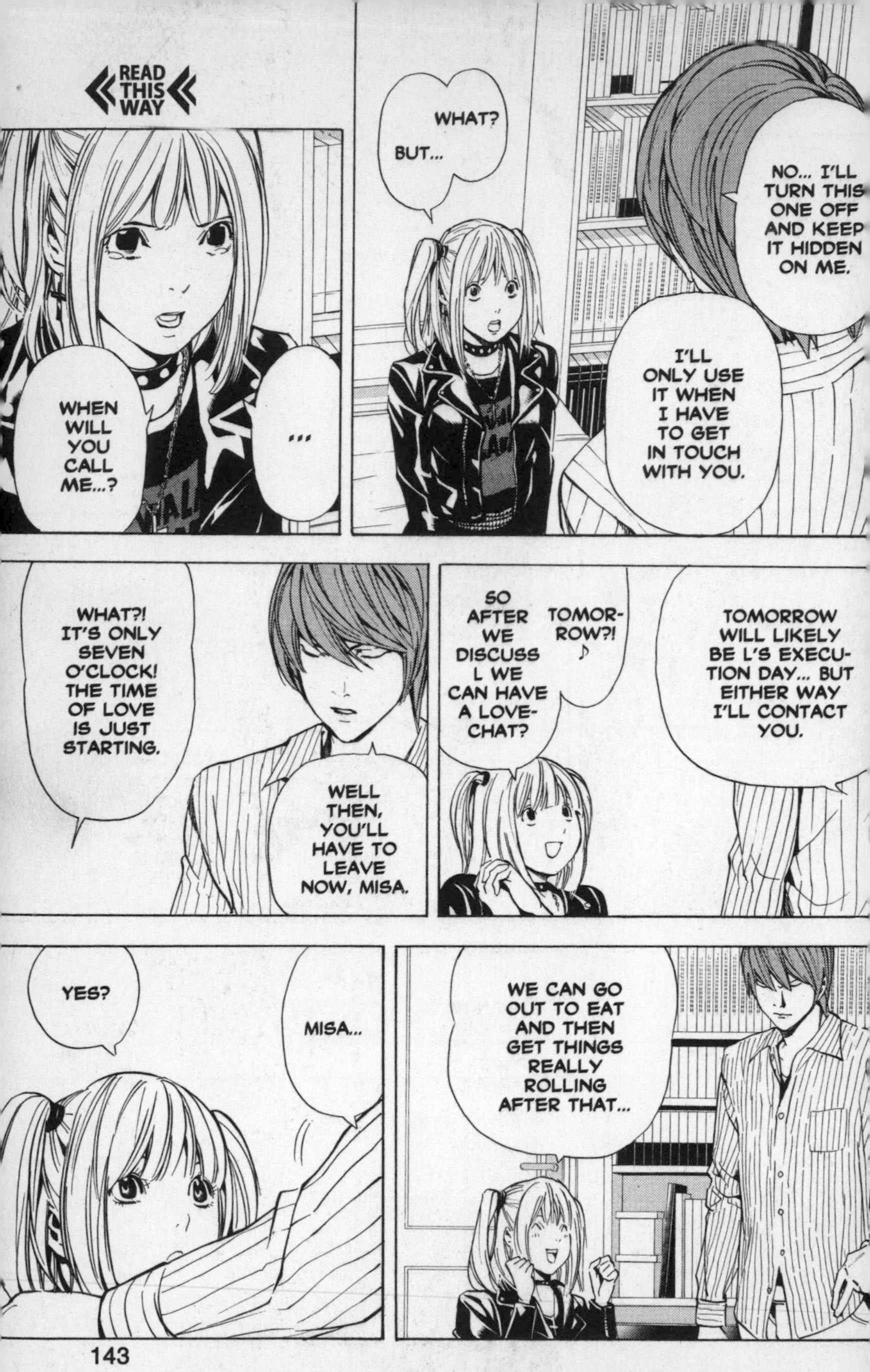
NO... I'LL TURN THIS ONE OFF AND KEEP IT HIDDEN ON ME.
I'LL ONLY USE IT WHEN I HAVE TO GET IN TOUCH WITH YOU.
WHAT? BUT...
...
WHEN WILL YOU CALL ME...?
TOMORROW WILL LIKELY BE L'S EXECUTION DAY... BUT EITHER WAY I'LL CONTACT YOU.
TOMORROW?! ♪
SO AFTER WE DISCUSS L WE CAN HAVE A LOVE-CHAT?
WELL THEN, YOU'LL HAVE TO LEAVE NOW, MISA.
WHAT?! IT'S ONLY SEVEN O'CLOCK! THE TIME OF LOVE IS JUST STARTING.
WE CAN GO OUT TO EAT AND THEN GET THINGS REALLY ROLLING AFTER THAT...
MISA...
YES?

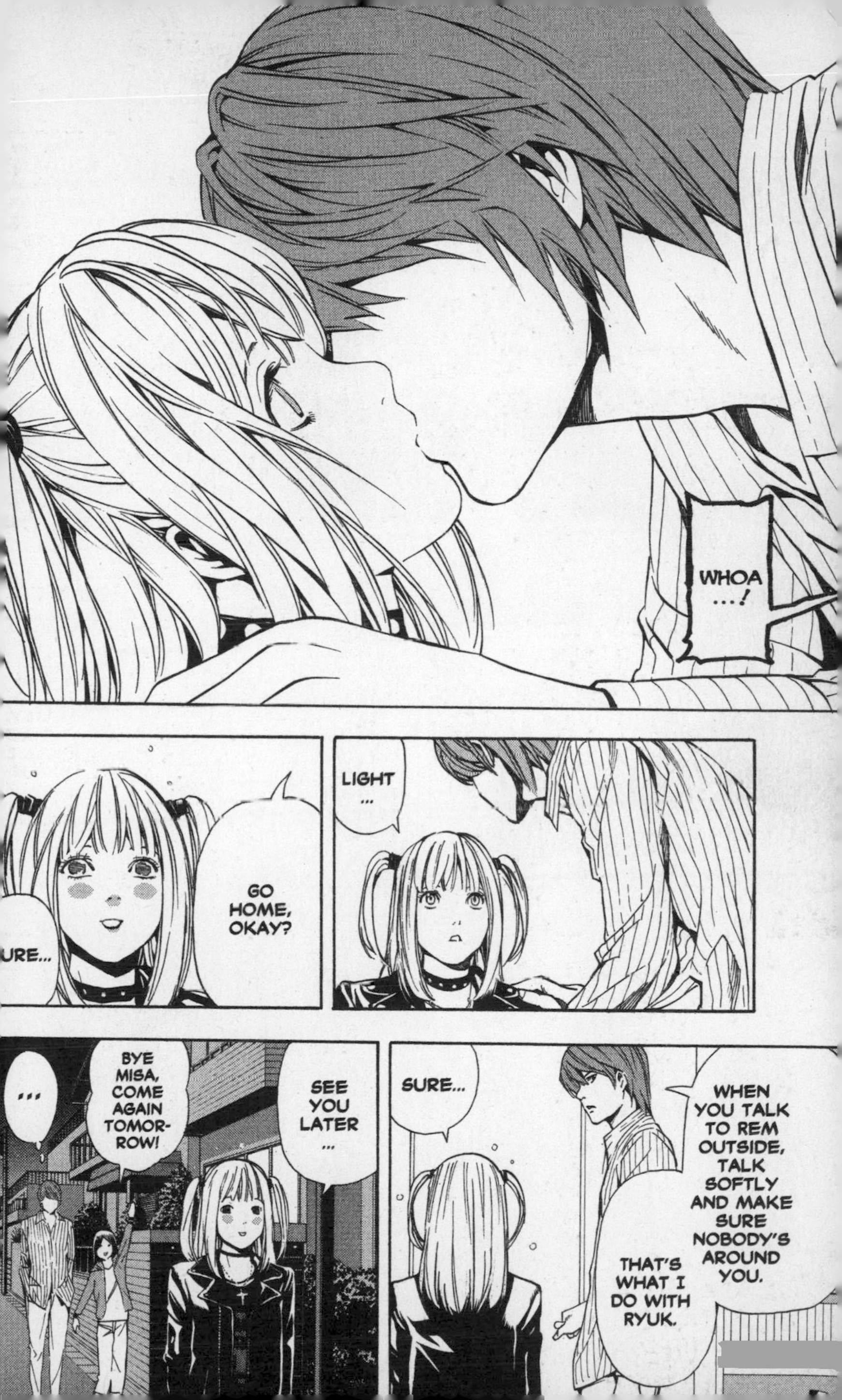
WHOA ...!
LIGHT ...
GO HOME, OKAY?
URE...
WHEN YOU TALK TO REM OUTSIDE, TALK SOFTLY AND MAKE SURE NOBODY'S AROUND YOU.
THAT'S WHAT I DO WITH RYUK.
SURE...
SEE YOU LATER ...
BYE MISA, COME AGAIN TOMOR-ROW!
...

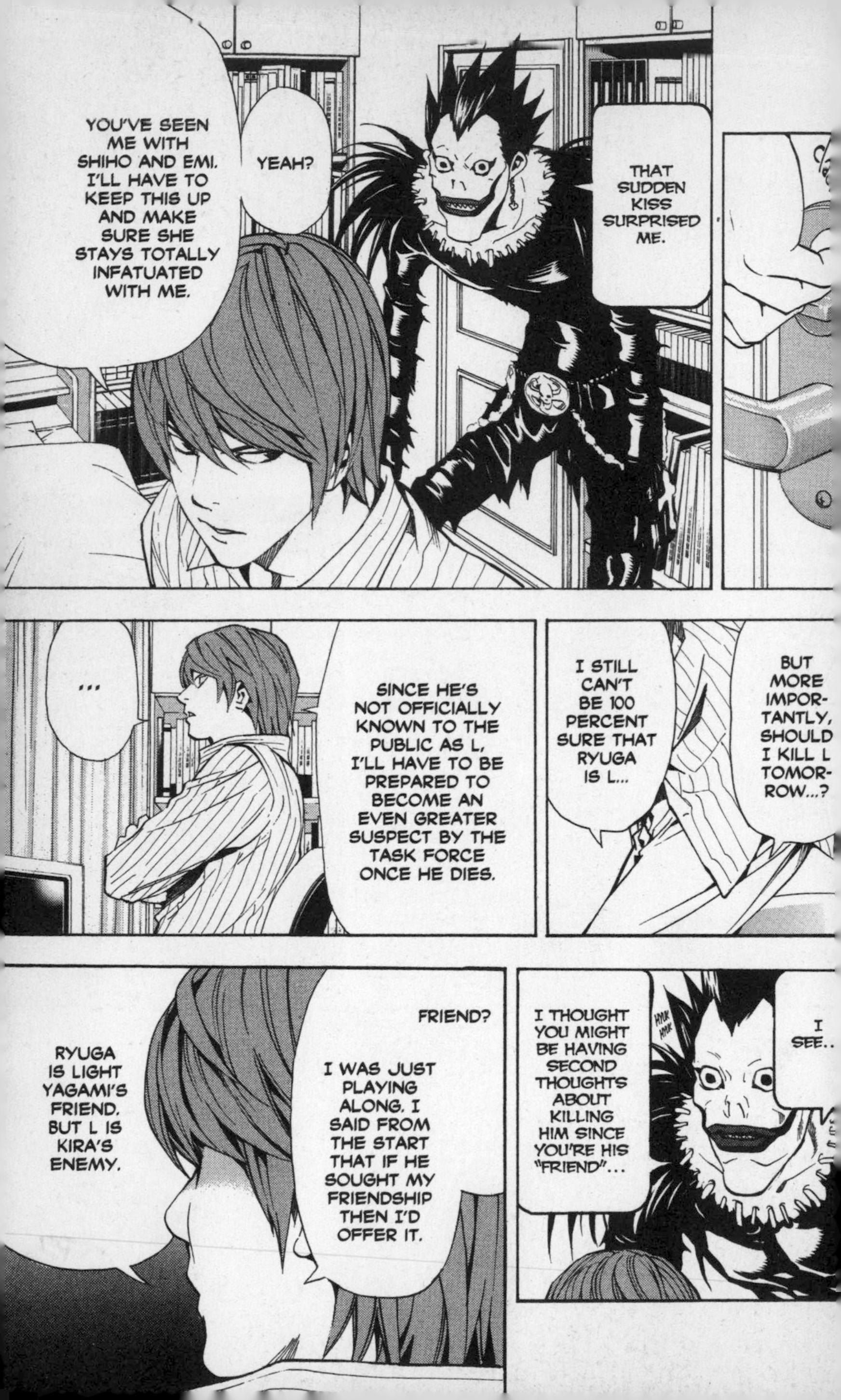

THAT SUDDEN KISS SURPRISED ME.
YEAH?
YOU'VE SEEN ME WITH SHIHO AND EMI. I'LL HAVE TO KEEP THIS UP AND MAKE SURE SHE STAYS TOTALLY INFATUATED WITH ME.
BUT MORE IMPORTANTLY, SHOULD I KILL L TOMORROW...?
I STILL CAN'T BE 100 PERCENT SURE THAT RYUGA IS L...
SINCE HE'S NOT OFFICIALLY KNOWN TO THE PUBLIC AS L, I'LL HAVE TO BE PREPARED TO BECOME AN EVEN GREATER SUSPECT BY THE TASK FORCE ONCE HE DIES.
...
I SEE..
HYUK HYUK
I THOUGHT YOU MIGHT BE HAVING SECOND THOUGHTS ABOUT KILLING HIM SINCE YOU'RE HIS "FRIEND"...
FRIEND?
I WAS JUST PLAYING ALONG. I SAID FROM THE START THAT IF HE SOUGHT MY FRIENDSHIP THEN I'D OFFER IT.
RYUGA IS LIGHT YAGAMI'S FRIEND. BUT L IS KIRA'S ENEMY.

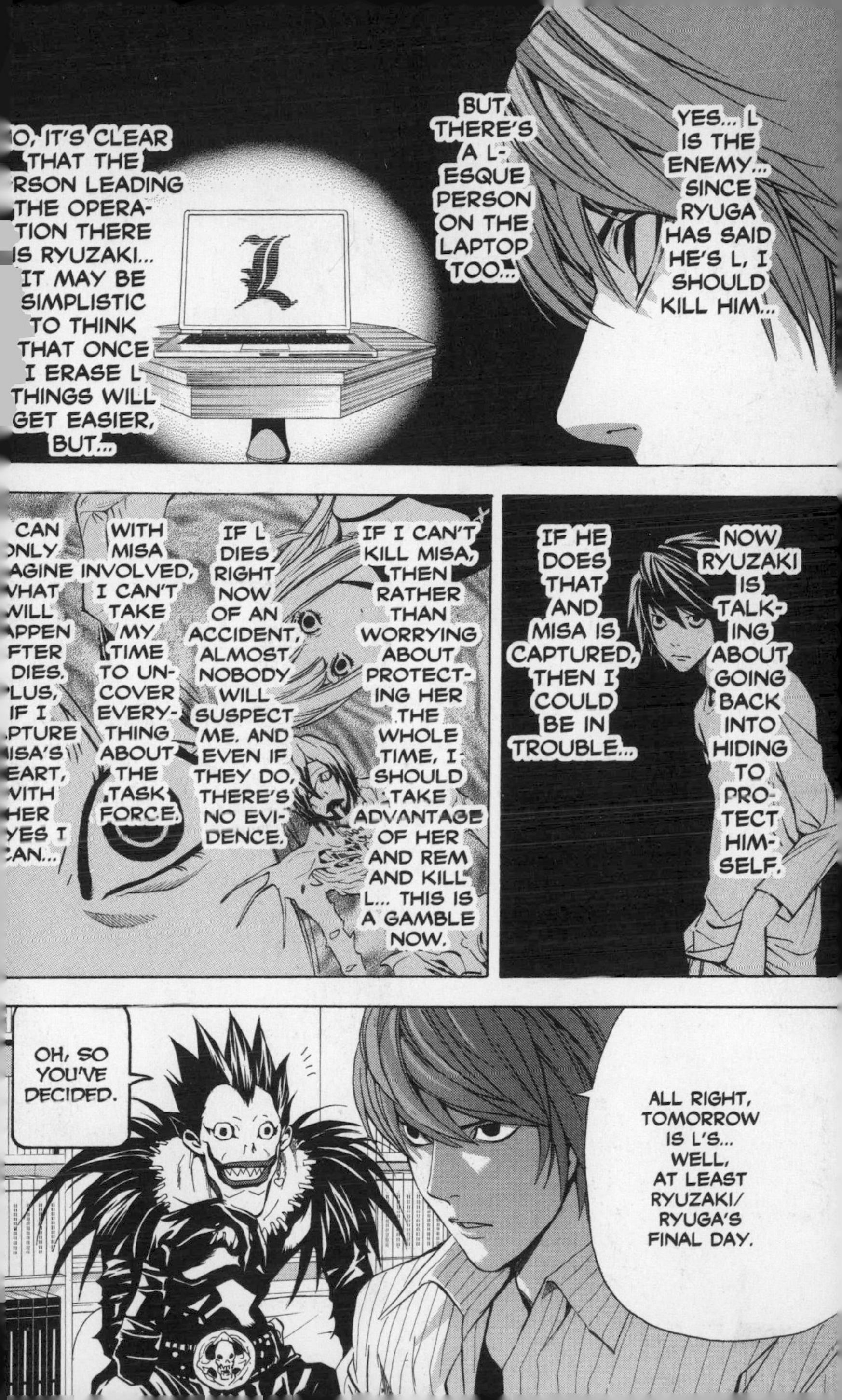

YES... L IS THE ENEMY... SINCE RYUGA HAS SAID HE'S L, I SHOULD KILL HIM...
BUT THERE'S A L-ESQUE PERSON ON THE LAPTOP TOO...
O, IT'S CLEAR THAT THE RSON LEADING THE OPERA-TION THERE S RYUZAKI... IT MAY BE SIMPLISTIC TO THINK THAT ONCE I ERASE L THINGS WILL GET EASIER, BUT...
NOW RYUZAKI IS TALK-ING ABOUT GOING BACK INTO HIDING TO PRO-TECT HIM-SELF.
IF HE DOES THAT AND MISA IS CAPTURED, THEN I COULD BE IN TROUBLE...
IF I CAN'T KILL MISA, THEN RATHER THAN WORRYING ABOUT PROTECT-ING HER THE WHOLE TIME, I SHOULD TAKE ADVANTAGE OF HER AND REM AND KILL L... THIS IS A GAMBLE NOW.
IF L DIES RIGHT NOW OF AN ACCIDENT, ALMOST NOBODY WILL SUSPECT ME. AND EVEN IF THEY DO, THERE'S NO EVI-DENCE.
WITH MISA INVOLVED, I CAN'T TAKE MY TIME TO UN-COVER EVERY-THING ABOUT THE TASK FORCE.
CAN NLY AGINE VHAT WILL APPEN FTER DIES. LUS, IF I PTURE ISA'S EART, WITH HER YES I CAN...
ALL RIGHT, TOMORROW IS L'S... WELL, AT LEAST RYUZAKI/ RYUGA'S FINAL DAY.
OH, SO YOU'VE DECIDED.

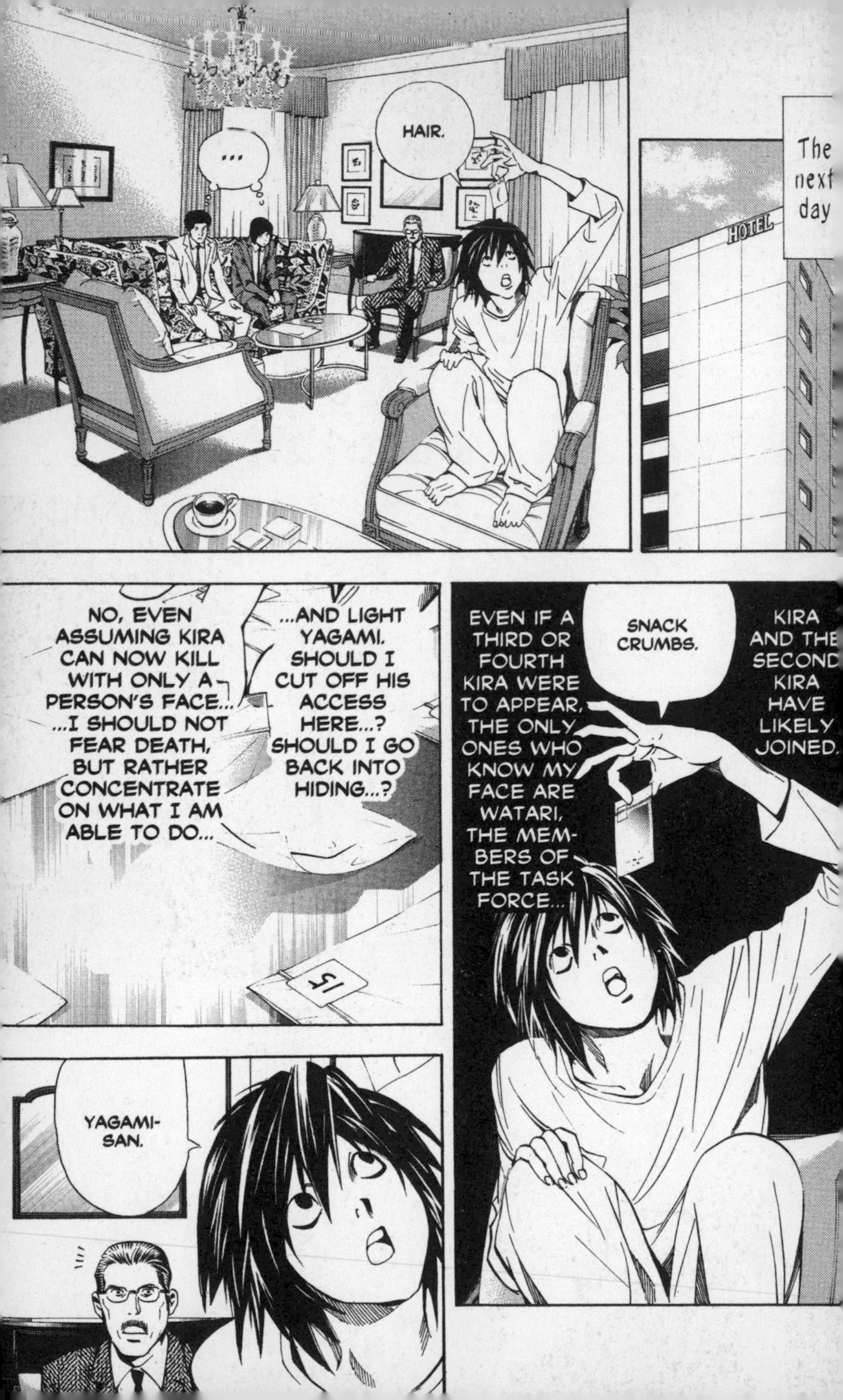
The next day
HOTEL
HAIR.
...
KIRA AND THE SECOND KIRA HAVE LIKELY JOINED.
SNACK CRUMBS.
EVEN IF A THIRD OR FOURTH KIRA WERE TO APPEAR, THE ONLY ONES WHO KNOW MY FACE ARE WATARI, THE MEMBERS OF THE TASK FORCE...
...AND LIGHT YAGAMI. SHOULD I CUT OFF HIS ACCESS HERE...? SHOULD I GO BACK INTO HIDING...?
NO, EVEN ASSUMING KIRA CAN NOW KILL WITH ONLY A PERSON'S FACE... ...I SHOULD NOT FEAR DEATH, BUT RATHER CONCENTRATE ON WHAT I AM ABLE TO DO...
YAGAMI-SAN.

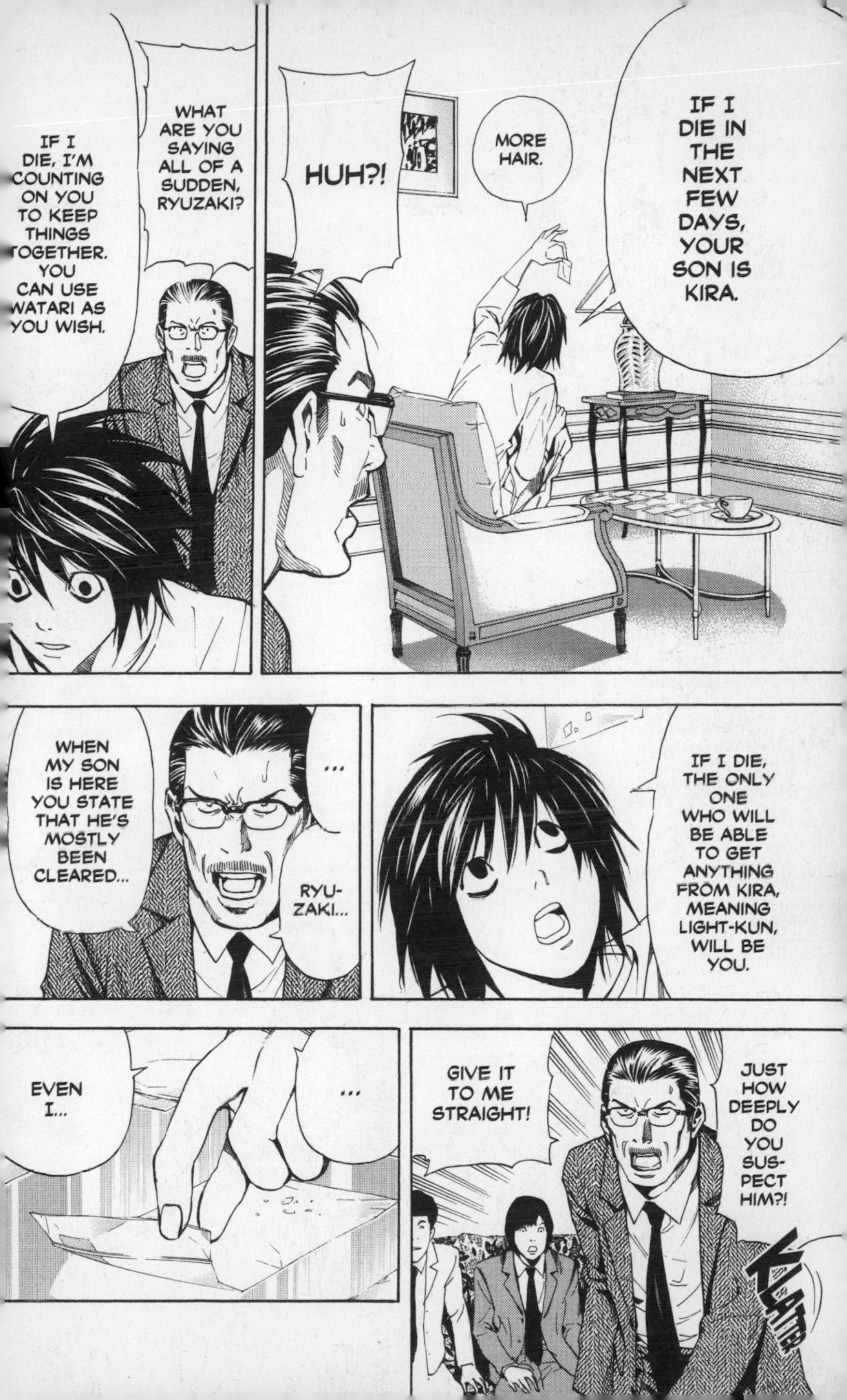
IF I DIE IN THE NEXT FEW DAYS, YOUR SON IS KIRA.
MORE HAIR.
HUH?!
WHAT ARE YOU SAYING ALL OF A SUDDEN, RYUZAKI?
IF I DIE, I'M COUNTING ON YOU TO KEEP THINGS TOGETHER. YOU CAN USE WATARI AS YOU WISH.
IF I DIE, THE ONLY ONE WHO WILL BE ABLE TO GET ANYTHING FROM KIRA, MEANING LIGHT-KUN, WILL BE YOU.
...
RYU-ZAKI...
WHEN MY SON IS HERE YOU STATE THAT HE'S MOSTLY BEEN CLEARED...
JUST HOW DEEPLY DO YOU SUS-PECT HIM?!
GIVE IT TO ME STRAIGHT!
KLATTER
...
EVEN I...

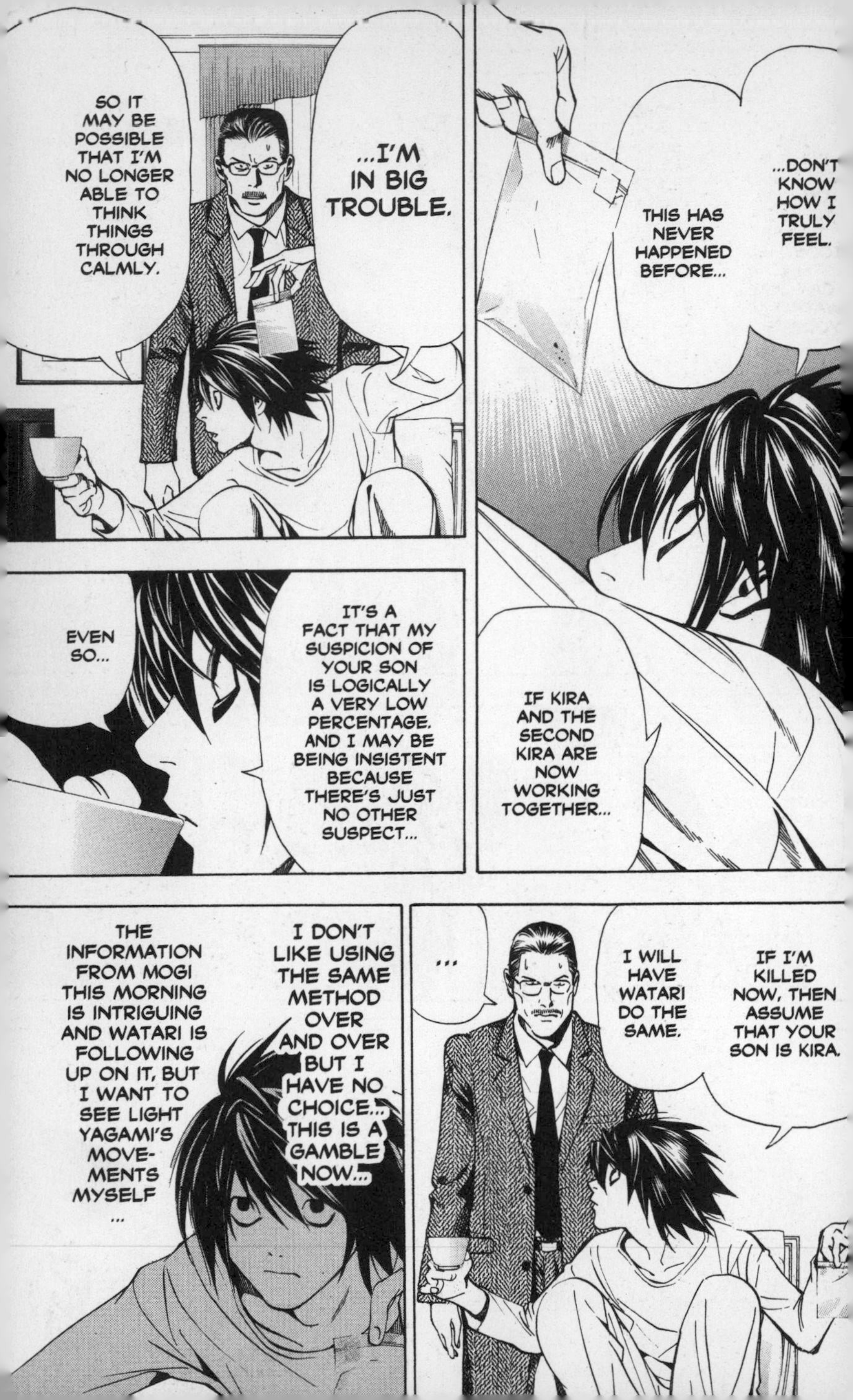
...DON'T KNOW HOW I TRULY FEEL.
THIS HAS NEVER HAPPENED BEFORE...
IF KIRA AND THE SECOND KIRA ARE NOW WORKING TOGETHER...
...I'M IN BIG TROUBLE.
SO IT MAY BE POSSIBLE THAT I'M NO LONGER ABLE TO THINK THINGS THROUGH CALMLY.
IT'S A FACT THAT MY SUSPICION OF YOUR SON IS LOGICALLY A VERY LOW PERCENTAGE. AND I MAY BE BEING INSISTENT BECAUSE THERE'S JUST NO OTHER SUSPECT...
EVEN SO...
IF I'M KILLED NOW, THEN ASSUME THAT YOUR SON IS KIRA.
I WILL HAVE WATARI DO THE SAME.
...
I DON'T LIKE USING THE SAME METHOD OVER AND OVER BUT I HAVE NO CHOICE... THIS IS A GAMBLE NOW...
THE INFORMATION FROM MOGI THIS MORNING IS INTRIGUING AND WATARI IS FOLLOWING UP ON IT, BUT I WANT TO SEE LIGHT YAGAMI'S MOVE-MENTS MYSELF ...

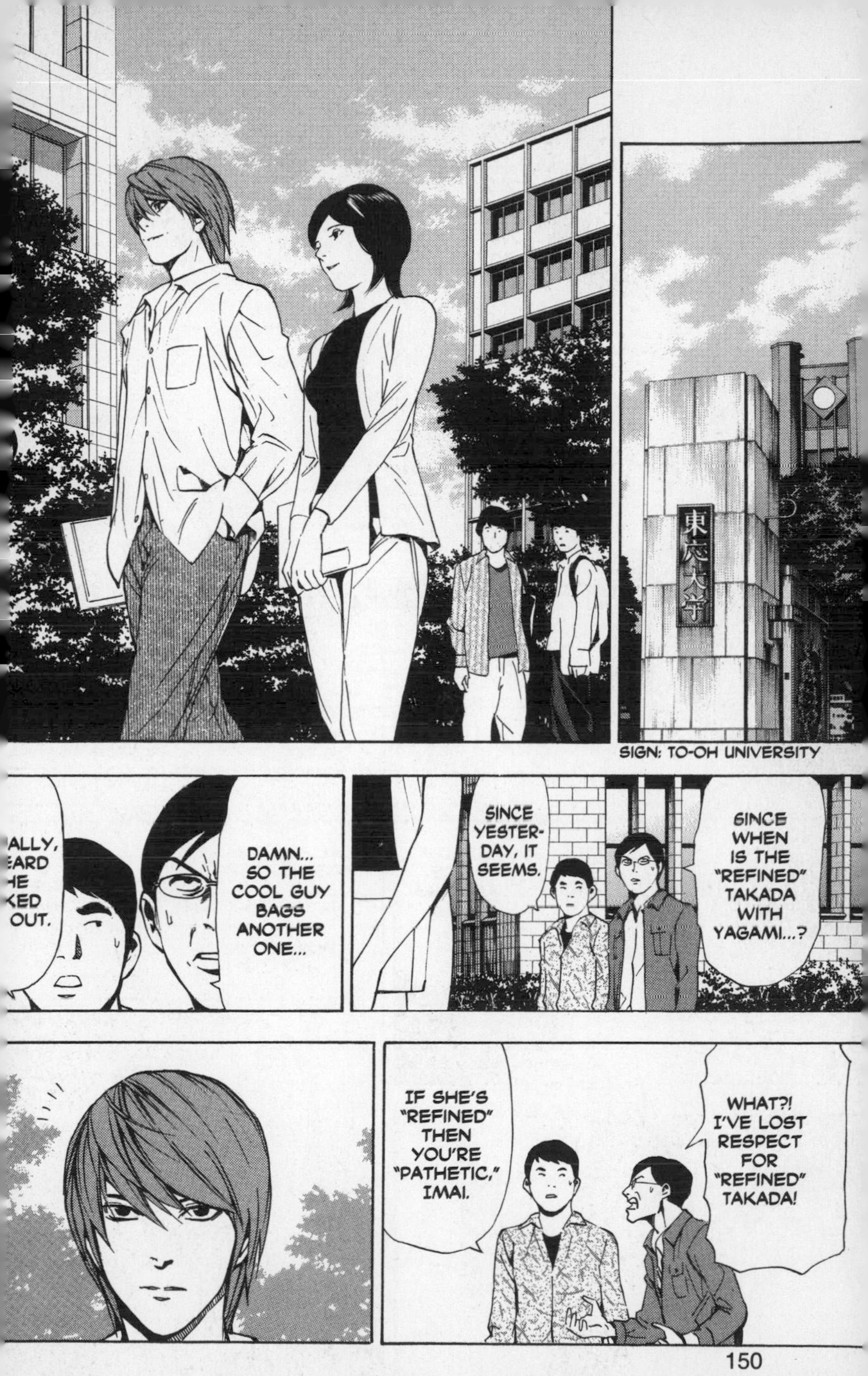
東応大学
SIGN: TO-OH UNIVERSITY
SINCE WHEN IS THE "REFINED" TAKADA WITH YAGAMI...?
SINCE YESTERDAY, IT SEEMS.
DAMN... SO THE COOL GUY BAGS ANOTHER ONE...
WHAT?! I'VE LOST RESPECT FOR "REFINED" TAKADA!
IF SHE'S "REFINED" THEN YOU'RE "PATHETIC," IMAI.

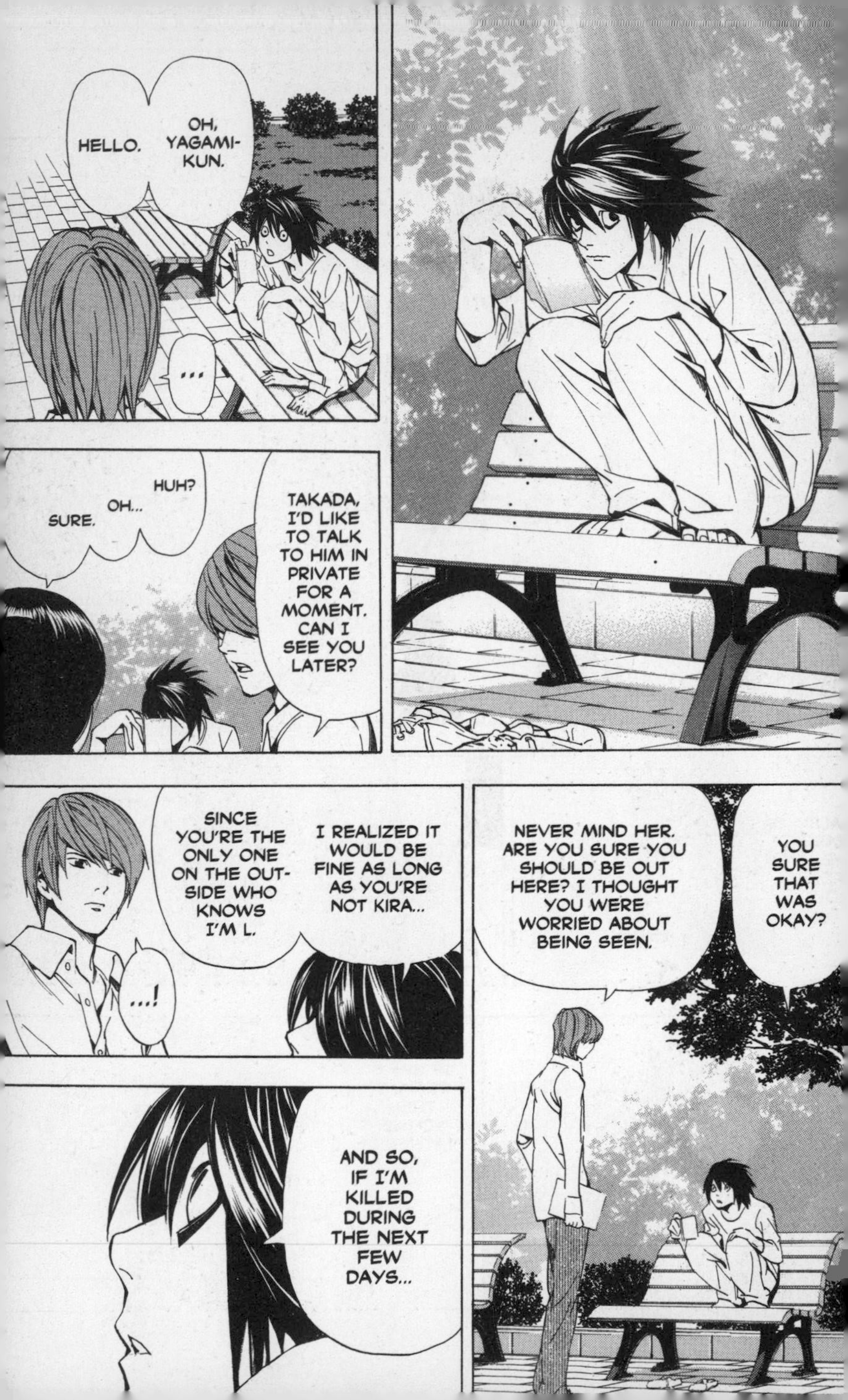
OH, YAGAMI-KUN.
HELLO.
...
TAKADA, I'D LIKE TO TALK TO HIM IN PRIVATE FOR A MOMENT. CAN I SEE YOU LATER?
HUH? OH... SURE.
YOU SURE THAT WAS OKAY?
NEVER MIND HER. ARE YOU SURE YOU SHOULD BE OUT HERE? I THOUGHT YOU WERE WORRIED ABOUT BEING SEEN.
I REALIZED IT WOULD BE FINE AS LONG AS YOU'RE NOT KIRA...
SINCE YOU'RE THE ONLY ONE ON THE OUT-SIDE WHO KNOWS I'M L.
...!
AND SO, IF I'M KILLED DURING THE NEXT FEW DAYS...

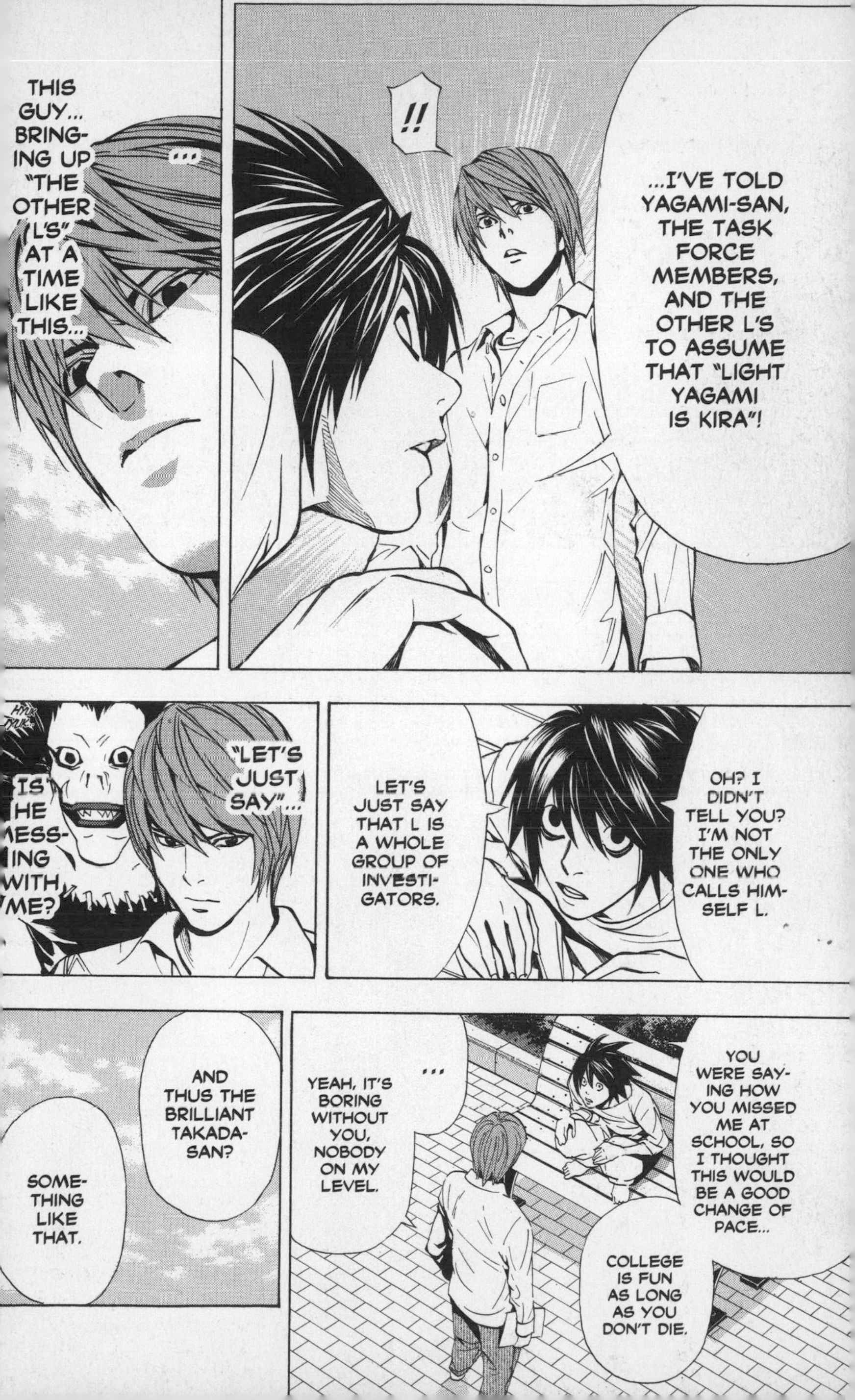
...I'VE TOLD YAGAMI-SAN, THE TASK FORCE MEMBERS, AND THE OTHER L'S TO ASSUME THAT "LIGHT YAGAMI IS KIRA"!
!!
...
THIS GUY... BRINGING UP "THE OTHER L'S" AT A TIME LIKE THIS...
OH? I DIDN'T TELL YOU? I'M NOT THE ONLY ONE WHO CALLS HIMSELF L.
LET'S JUST SAY THAT L IS A WHOLE GROUP OF INVESTIGATORS.
"LET'S JUST SAY"...
IS HE MESSING WITH ME?
YOU WERE SAYING HOW YOU MISSED ME AT SCHOOL, SO I THOUGHT THIS WOULD BE A GOOD CHANGE OF PACE...
COLLEGE IS FUN AS LONG AS YOU DON'T DIE.
...
YEAH, IT'S BORING WITHOUT YOU, NOBODY ON MY LEVEL.
AND THUS THE BRILLIANT TAKADA-SAN?
SOMETHING LIKE THAT.

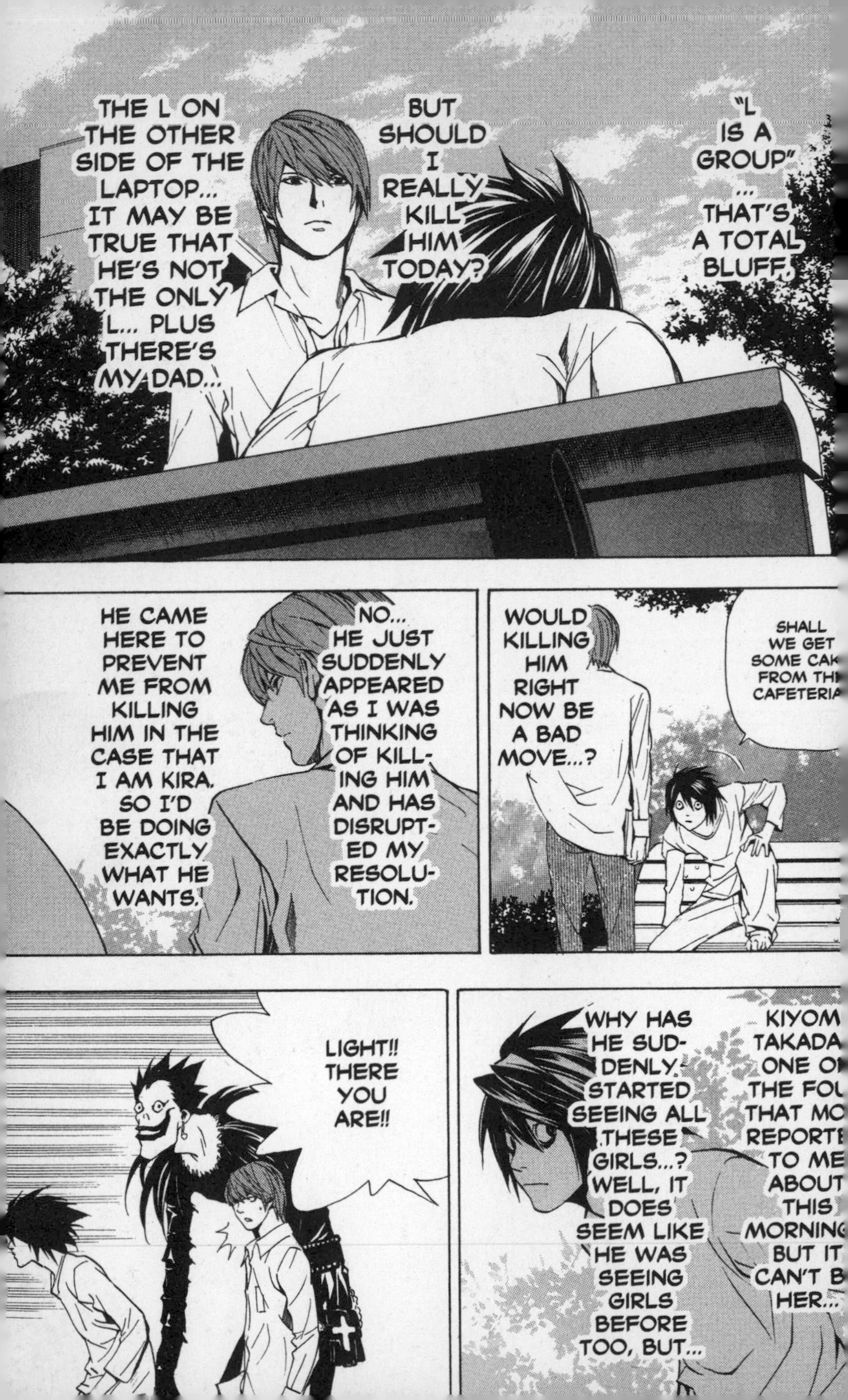
"L IS A GROUP" ... THAT'S A TOTAL BLUFF.
BUT SHOULD I REALLY KILL HIM TODAY?
THE L ON THE OTHER SIDE OF THE LAPTOP... IT MAY BE TRUE THAT HE'S NOT THE ONLY L... PLUS THERE'S MY DAD...
SHALL WE GET SOME CAK FROM TH CAFETERIA
WOULD KILLING HIM RIGHT NOW BE A BAD MOVE...?
NO... HE JUST SUDDENLY APPEARED AS I WAS THINKING OF KILLING HIM AND HAS DISRUPTED MY RESOLUTION.
HE CAME HERE TO PREVENT ME FROM KILLING HIM IN THE CASE THAT I AM KIRA. SO I'D BE DOING EXACTLY WHAT HE WANTS.
KIYOM TAKADA ONE O THE FOU THAT MO REPORTE TO ME ABOUT THIS MORNING BUT IT CAN'T B HER...
WHY HAS HE SUDDENLY STARTED SEEING ALL THESE GIRLS...? WELL, IT DOES SEEM LIKE HE WAS SEEING GIRLS BEFORE TOO, BUT...
LIGHT!! THERE YOU ARE!!

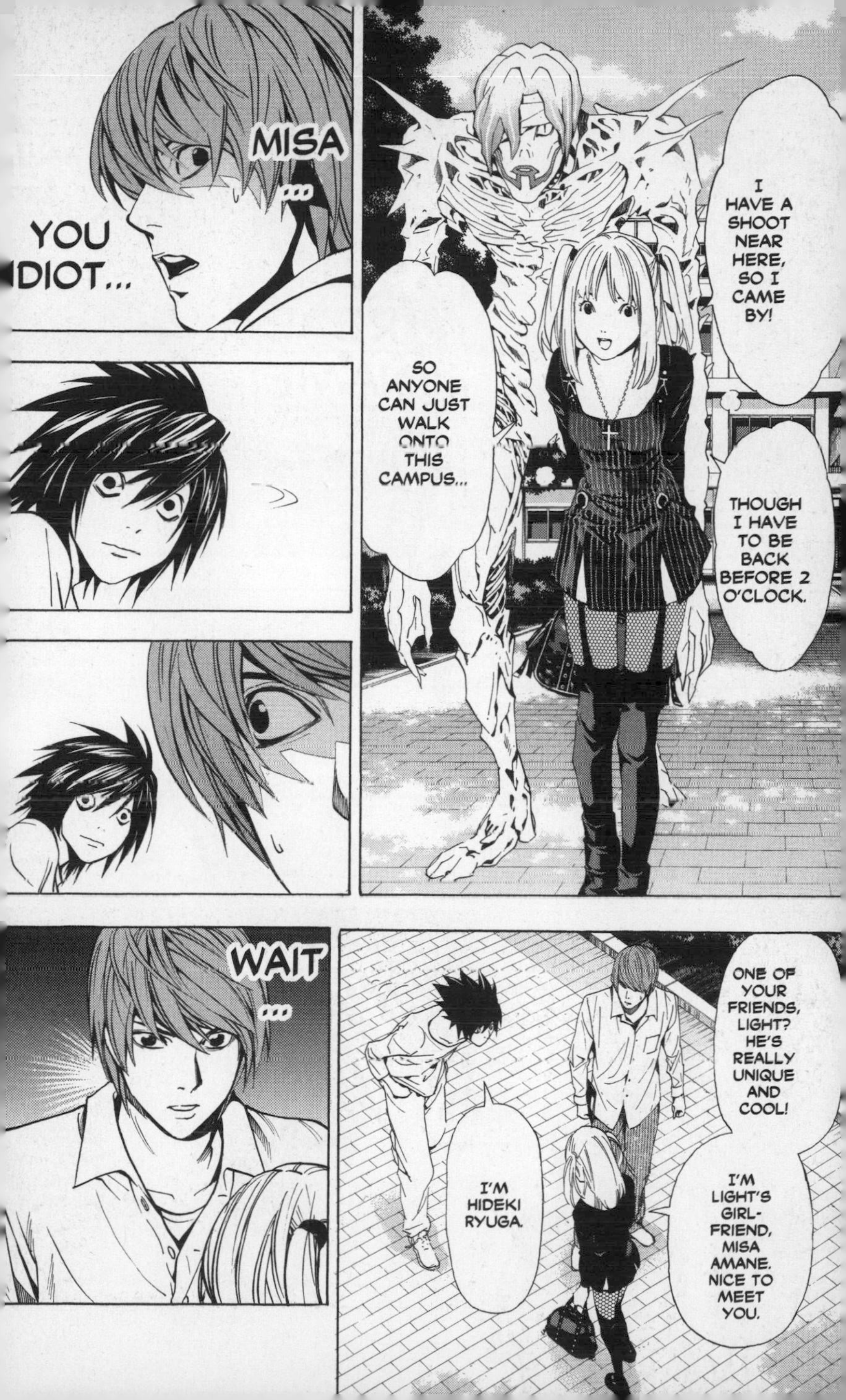
I HAVE A SHOOT NEAR HERE, SO I CAME BY!
THOUGH I HAVE TO BE BACK BEFORE 2 O'CLOCK.
SO ANYONE CAN JUST WALK ONTO THIS CAMPUS...
MISA ...
YOU IDIOT...
ONE OF YOUR FRIENDS, LIGHT? HE'S REALLY UNIQUE AND COOL!
I'M LIGHT'S GIRL-FRIEND, MISA AMANE. NICE TO MEET YOU.
I'M HIDEKI RYUGA.
WAIT ...

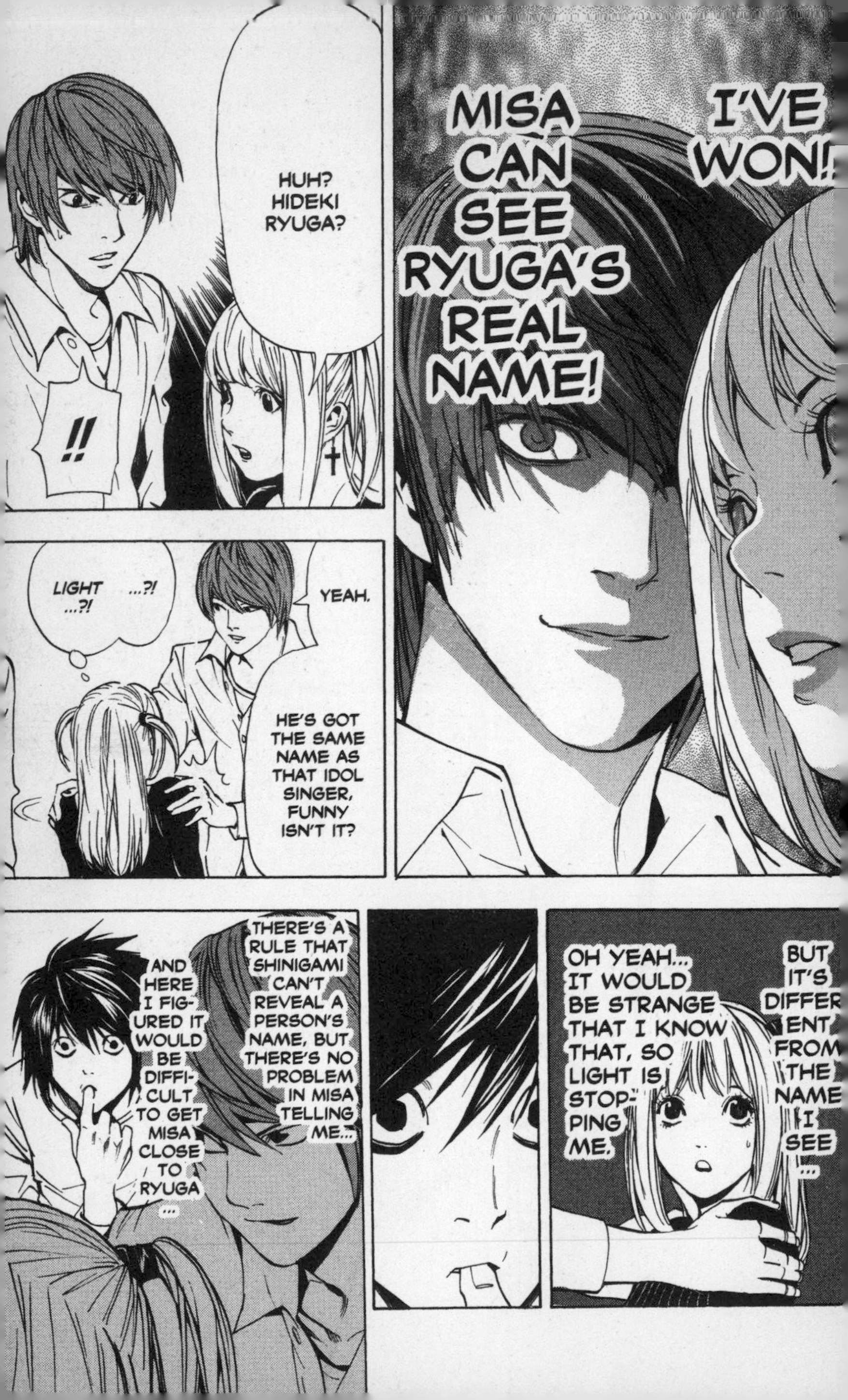
I'VE WON!
MISA CAN SEE RYUGA'S REAL NAME!
HUH? HIDEKI RYUGA?
!!
YEAH.
LIGHT ...?! ...?!
HE'S GOT THE SAME NAME AS THAT IDOL SINGER, FUNNY ISN'T IT?
BUT IT'S DIFFERENT FROM THE NAME I SEE...
OH YEAH... IT WOULD BE STRANGE THAT I KNOW THAT, SO LIGHT IS STOPPING ME.
THERE'S A RULE THAT SHINIGAMI CAN'T REVEAL A PERSON'S NAME, BUT THERE'S NO PROBLEM IN MISA TELLING ME...
AND HERE I FIGURED IT WOULD BE DIFFICULT TO GET MISA CLOSE TO RYUGA...

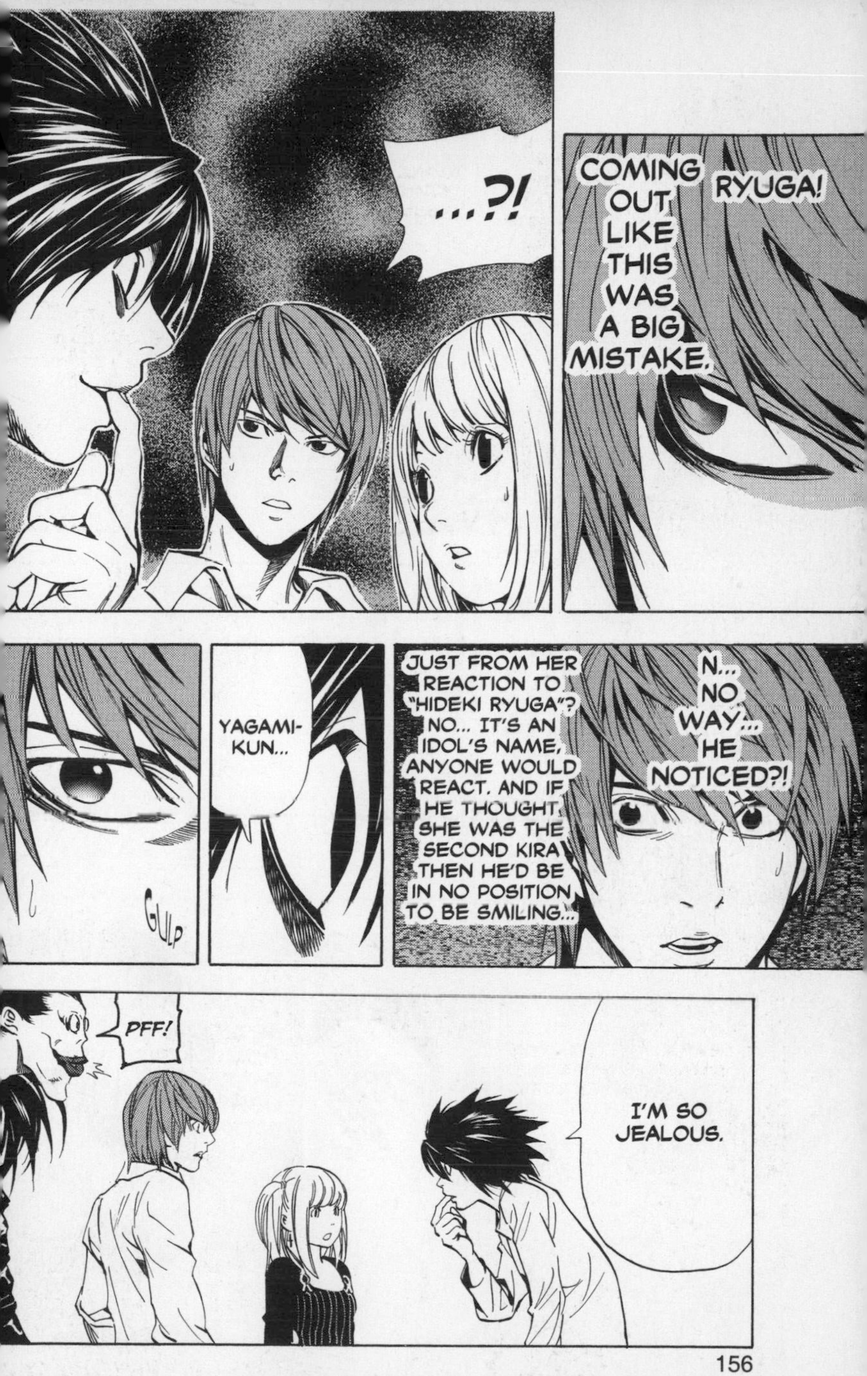
RYUGA!
COMING OUT LIKE THIS WAS A BIG MISTAKE.
...?!
N... NO WAY... HE NOTICED?!
JUST FROM HER REACTION TO "HIDEKI RYUGA"? NO... IT'S AN IDOL'S NAME, ANYONE WOULD REACT. AND IF HE THOUGHT SHE WAS THE SECOND KIRA THEN HE'D BE IN NO POSITION TO BE SMILING...
YAGAMI-KUN...
GULP
I'M SO JEALOUS.
PFF!

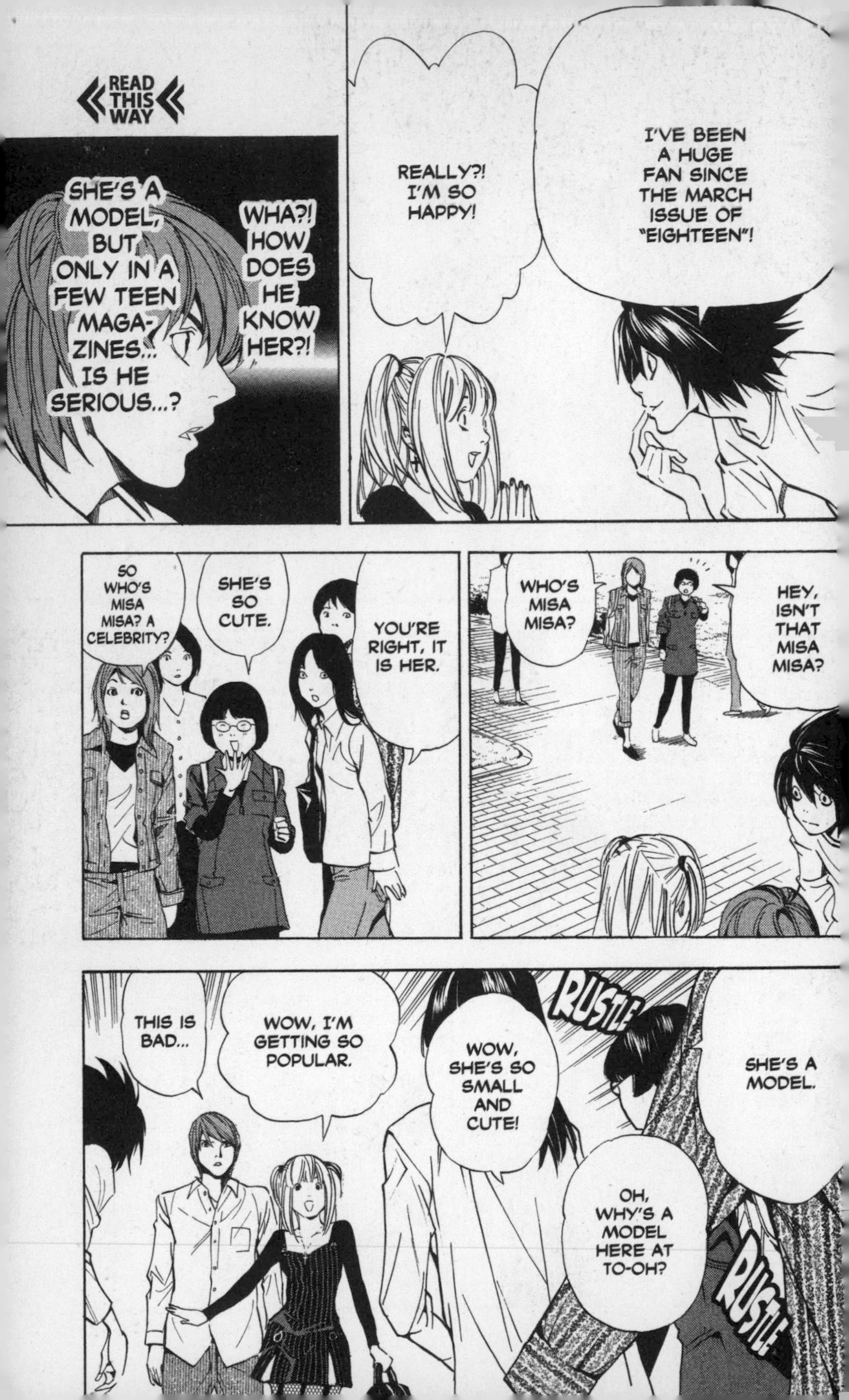
READ THIS WAY
I'VE BEEN A HUGE FAN SINCE THE MARCH ISSUE OF "EIGHTEEN"!
REALLY?! I'M SO HAPPY!
WHA?! HOW DOES HE KNOW HER?!
SHE'S A MODEL, BUT ONLY IN A FEW TEEN MAGA-ZINES... IS HE SERIOUS...?
HEY, ISN'T THAT MISA MISA?
WHO'S MISA MISA?
YOU'RE RIGHT, IT IS HER.
SHE'S SO CUTE.
SO WHO'S MISA MISA? A CELEBRITY?
SHE'S A MODEL.
RUSTLE
OH, WHY'S A MODEL HERE AT TO-OH?
RUSTLE
WOW, SHE'S SO SMALL AND CUTE!
WOW, I'M GETTING SO POPULAR.
THIS IS BAD...

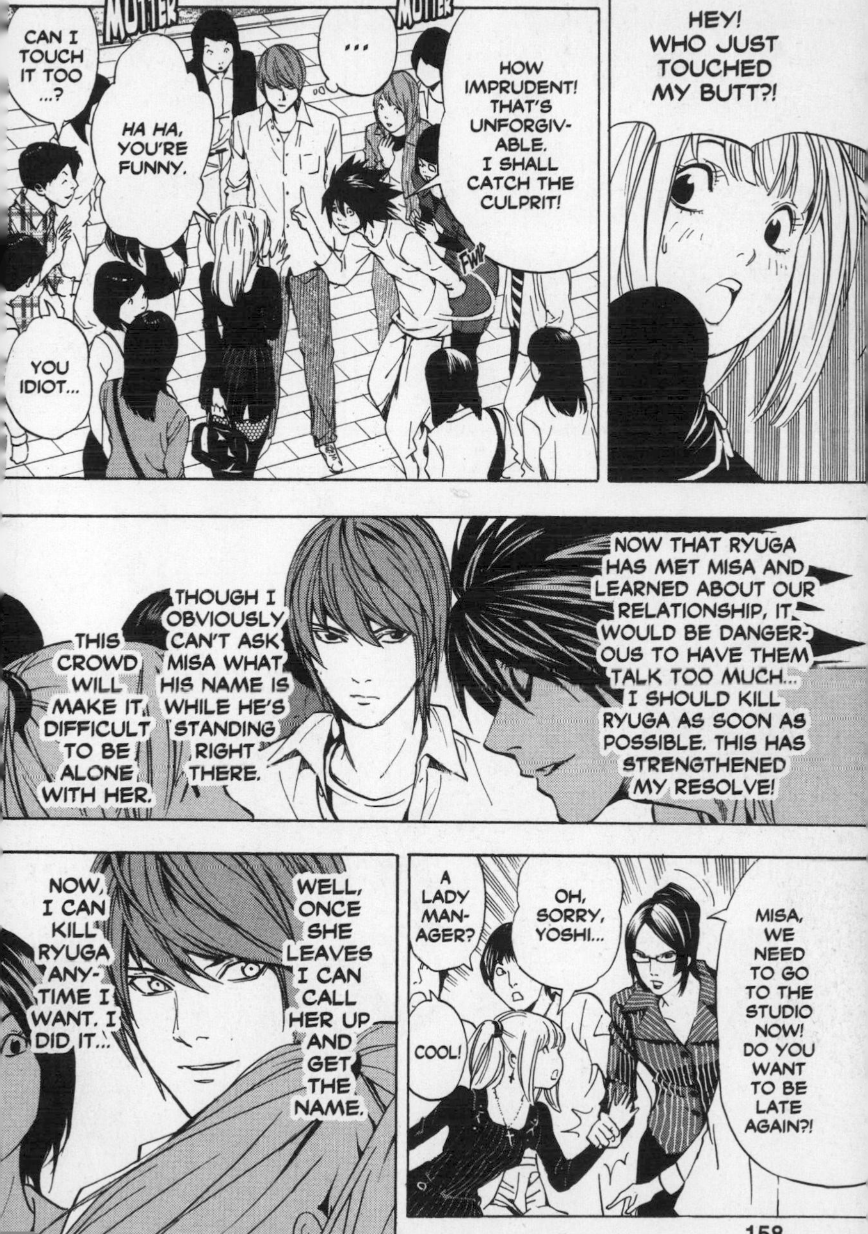
HEY! WHO JUST TOUCHED MY BUTT?!
MUTTER
HOW IMPRUDENT! THAT'S UNFORGIV-ABLE. I SHALL CATCH THE CULPRIT!
...
FWIP
MUTTER
HA HA, YOU'RE FUNNY.
CAN I TOUCH IT TOO ...?
YOU IDIOT...
NOW THAT RYUGA HAS MET MISA AND LEARNED ABOUT OUR RELATIONSHIP, IT WOULD BE DANGER-OUS TO HAVE THEM TALK TOO MUCH... I SHOULD KILL RYUGA AS SOON AS POSSIBLE. THIS HAS STRENGTHENED MY RESOLVE!
THOUGH I OBVIOUSLY CAN'T ASK MISA WHAT HIS NAME IS WHILE HE'S STANDING RIGHT THERE.
THIS CROWD WILL MAKE IT DIFFICULT TO BE ALONE WITH HER.
MISA, WE NEED TO GO TO THE STUDIO NOW! DO YOU WANT TO BE LATE AGAIN?!
OH, SORRY, YOSHI...
A LADY MAN-AGER?
COOL!
WELL, ONCE SHE LEAVES I CAN CALL HER UP AND GET THE NAME.
NOW, I CAN KILL RYUGA ANY-TIME I WANT. I DID IT...

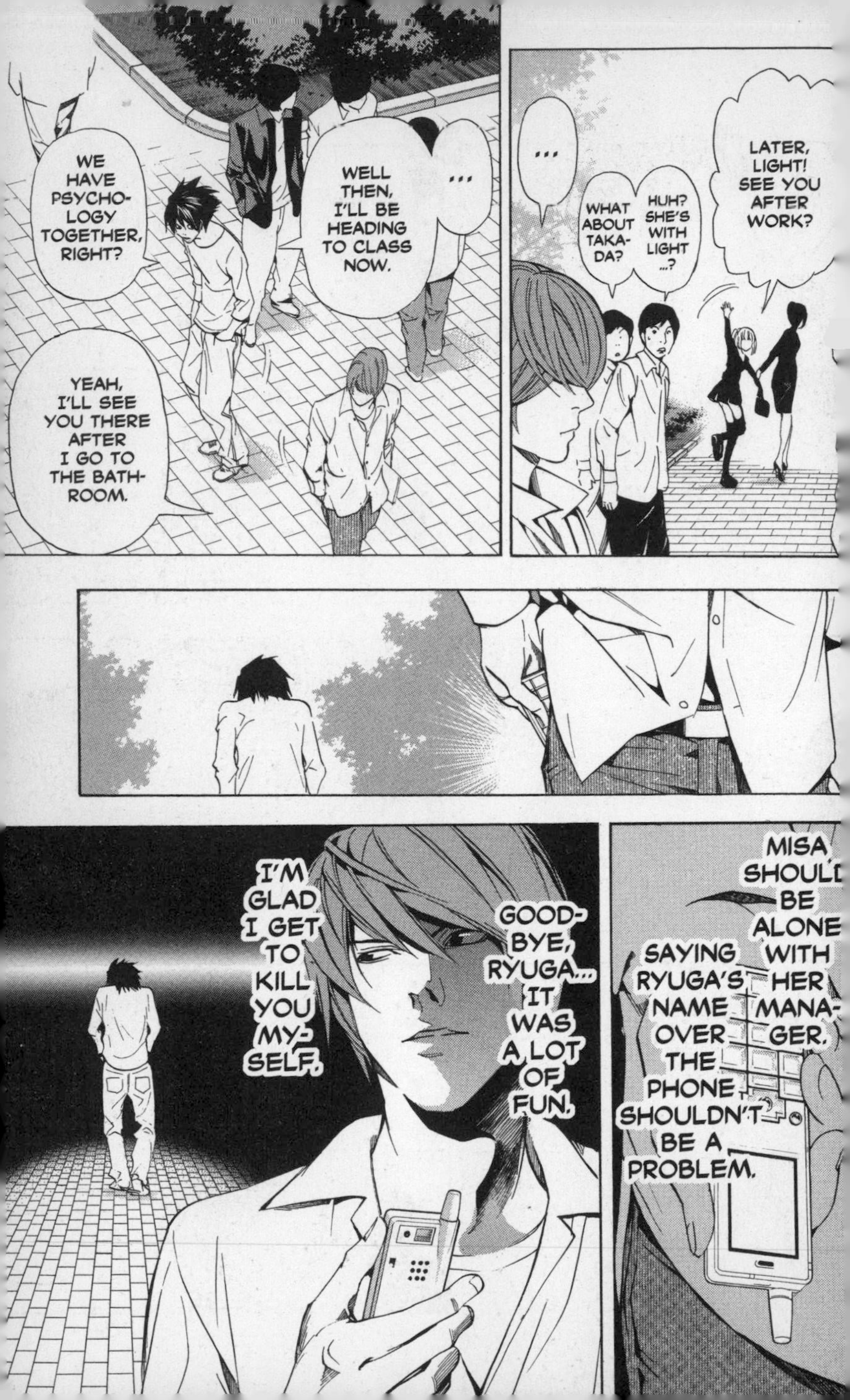
LATER, LIGHT! SEE YOU AFTER WORK?
HUH? SHE'S WITH LIGHT ...?
WHAT ABOUT TAKADA?
...
...
WELL THEN, I'LL BE HEADING TO CLASS NOW.
WE HAVE PSYCHOLOGY TOGETHER, RIGHT?
YEAH, I'LL SEE YOU THERE AFTER I GO TO THE BATHROOM.
MISA SHOULD BE ALONE WITH HER MANAGER.
SAYING RYUGA'S NAME OVER THE PHONE SHOULDN'T BE A PROBLEM.
GOOD-BYE, RYUGA... IT WAS A LOT OF FUN.
I'M GLAD I GET TO KILL YOU MYSELF.

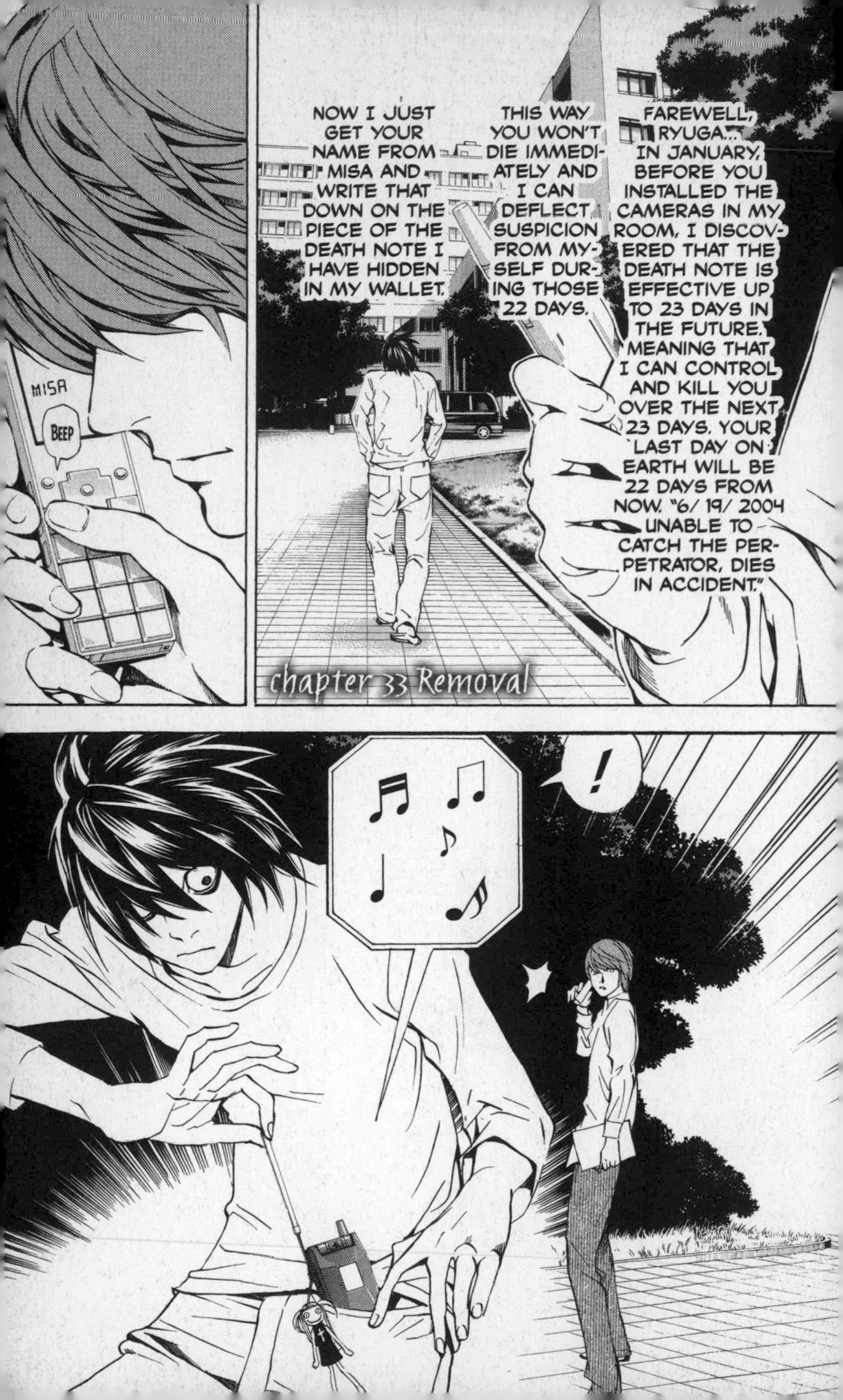
FAREWELL, RYUGA... IN JANUARY, BEFORE YOU INSTALLED THE CAMERAS IN MY ROOM, I DISCOVERED THAT THE DEATH NOTE IS EFFECTIVE UP TO 23 DAYS IN THE FUTURE. MEANING THAT I CAN CONTROL AND KILL YOU OVER THE NEXT 23 DAYS. YOUR LAST DAY ON EARTH WILL BE 22 DAYS FROM NOW. "6/ 19/ 2004 UNABLE TO CATCH THE PERPETRATOR, DIES IN ACCIDENT."
NOW I JUST GET YOUR NAME FROM MISA AND WRITE THAT DOWN ON THE PIECE OF THE DEATH NOTE I HAVE HIDDEN IN MY WALLET.
THIS WAY YOU WON'T DIE IMMEDIATELY AND I CAN DEFLECT SUSPICION FROM MYSELF DURING THOSE 22 DAYS.
MISA
BEEP
chapter 33 Removal
!

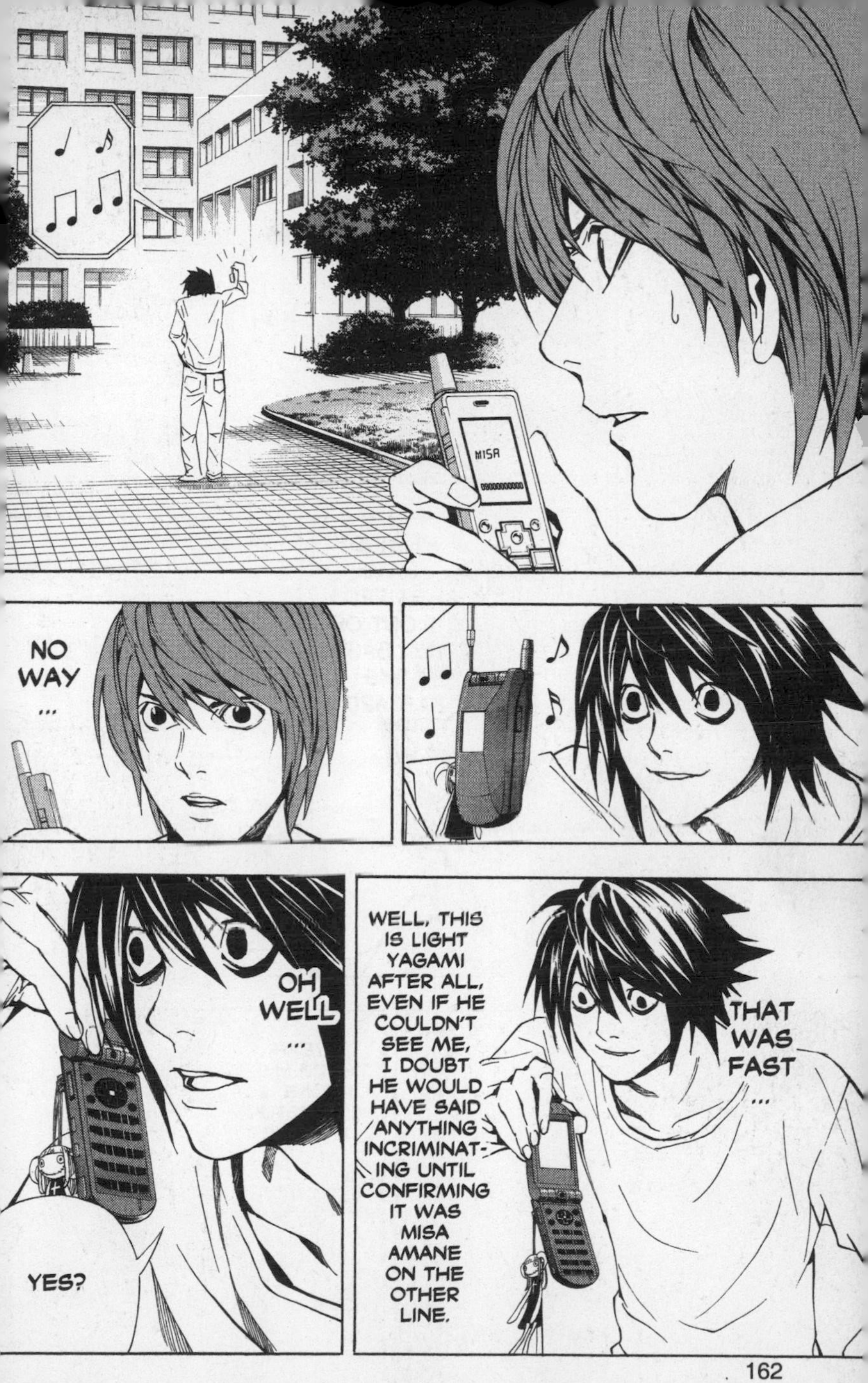
MISA
NO WAY ...
THAT WAS FAST ...
WELL, THIS IS LIGHT YAGAMI AFTER ALL, EVEN IF HE COULDN'T SEE ME, I DOUBT HE WOULD HAVE SAID ANYTHING INCRIMINATING UNTIL CONFIRMING IT WAS MISA AMANE ON THE OTHER LINE.
OH WELL ...
YES?

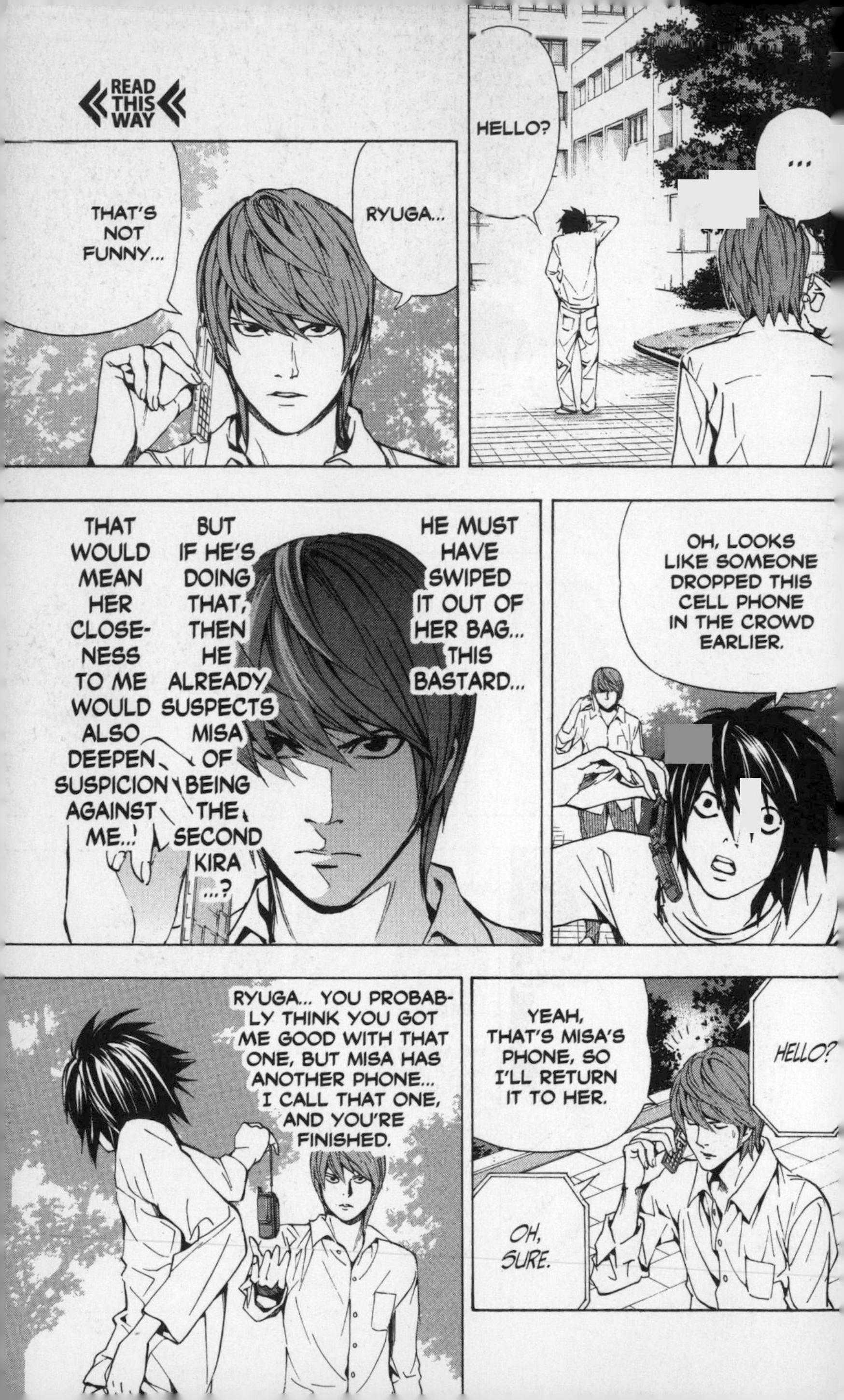
READ THIS WAY
HELLO?
...
RYUGA...
THAT'S NOT FUNNY...
OH, LOOKS LIKE SOMEONE DROPPED THIS CELL PHONE IN THE CROWD EARLIER.
HE MUST HAVE SWIPED IT OUT OF HER BAG... THIS BASTARD...
BUT IF HE'S DOING THAT, THEN HE ALREADY SUSPECTS MISA OF BEING THE SECOND KIRA ...?
THAT WOULD MEAN HER CLOSE-NESS TO ME WOULD ALSO DEEPEN SUSPICION AGAINST ME...!
HELLO?
YEAH, THAT'S MISA'S PHONE, SO I'LL RETURN IT TO HER.
OH, SURE.
RYUGA... YOU PROBAB-LY THINK YOU GOT ME GOOD WITH THAT ONE, BUT MISA HAS ANOTHER PHONE... I CALL THAT ONE, AND YOU'RE FINISHED.

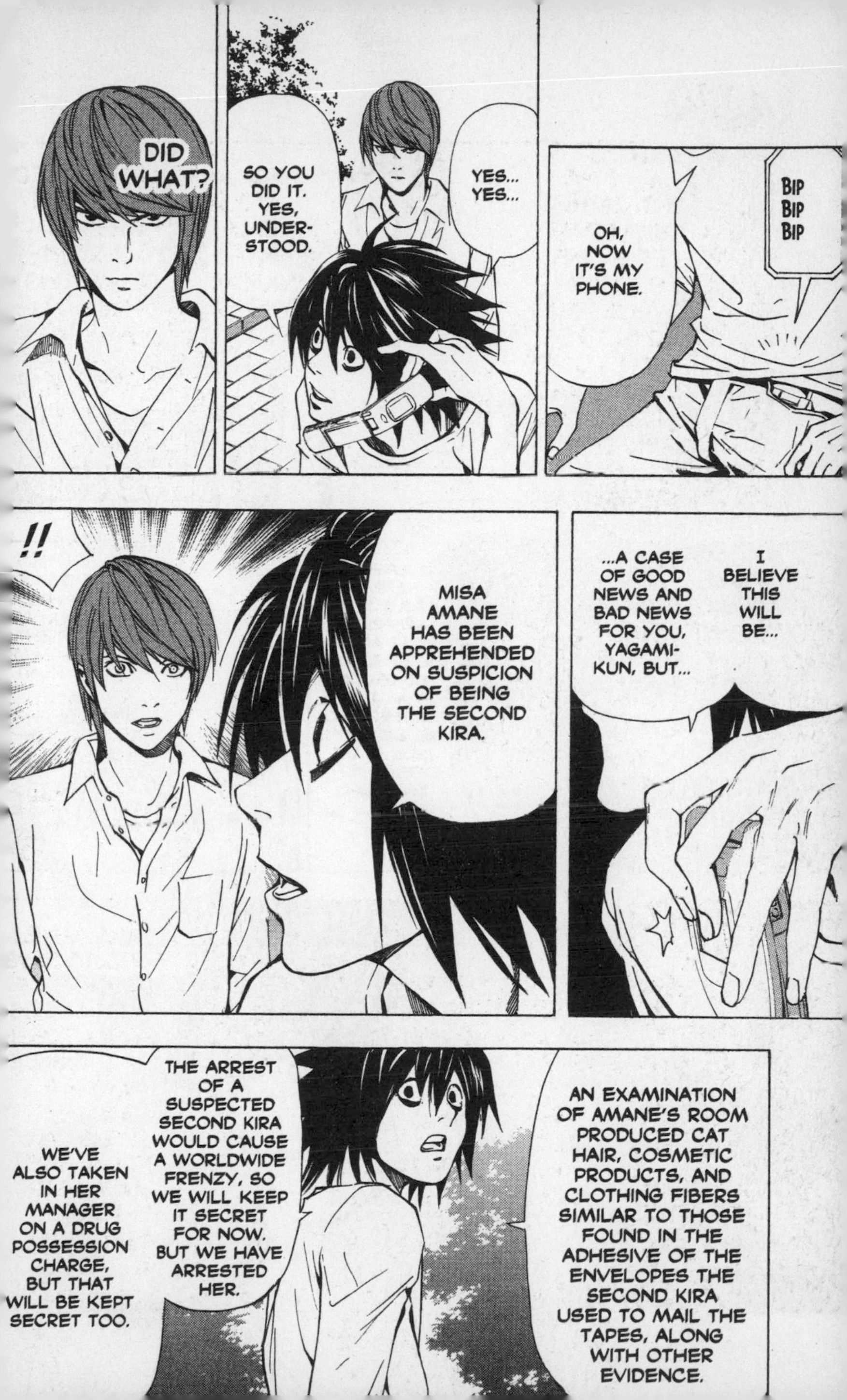
BIP BIP BIP
OH, NOW IT'S MY PHONE.
YES... YES...
SO YOU DID IT. YES, UNDERSTOOD.
DID WHAT?
I BELIEVE THIS WILL BE...
...A CASE OF GOOD NEWS AND BAD NEWS FOR YOU, YAGAMI-KUN, BUT...
MISA AMANE HAS BEEN APPREHENDED ON SUSPICION OF BEING THE SECOND KIRA.
!!
AN EXAMINATION OF AMANE'S ROOM PRODUCED CAT HAIR, COSMETIC PRODUCTS, AND CLOTHING FIBERS SIMILAR TO THOSE FOUND IN THE ADHESIVE OF THE ENVELOPES THE SECOND KIRA USED TO MAIL THE TAPES, ALONG WITH OTHER EVIDENCE.
THE ARREST OF A SUSPECTED SECOND KIRA WOULD CAUSE A WORLDWIDE FRENZY, SO WE WILL KEEP IT SECRET FOR NOW. BUT WE HAVE ARRESTED HER.
WE'VE ALSO TAKEN IN HER MANAGER ON A DRUG POSSESSION CHARGE, BUT THAT WILL BE KEPT SECRET TOO.

READ THIS WAY

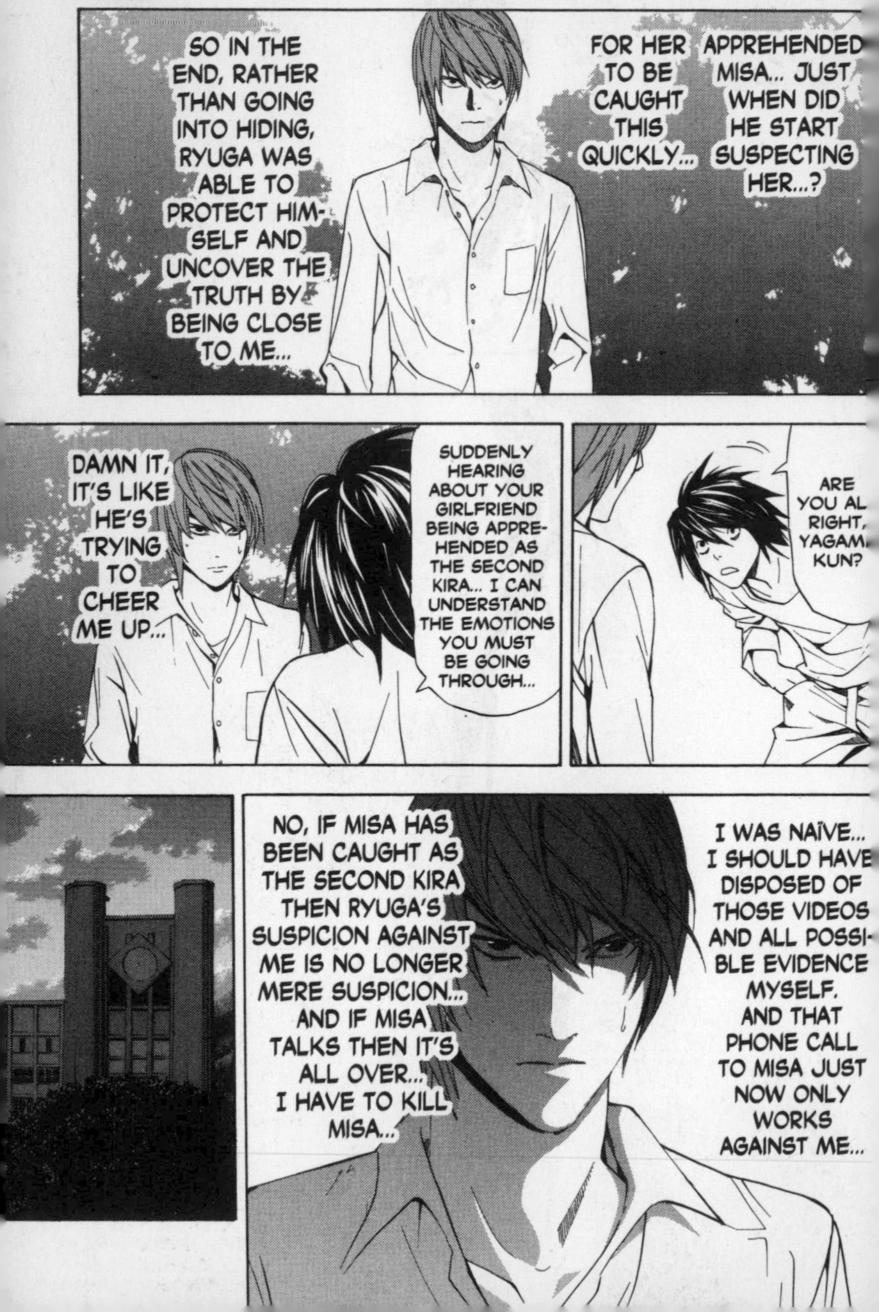
APPREHENDED MISA... JUST WHEN DID HE START SUSPECTING HER...?
FOR HER TO BE CAUGHT THIS QUICKLY...
SO IN THE END, RATHER THAN GOING INTO HIDING, RYUGA WAS ABLE TO PROTECT HIM-SELF AND UNCOVER THE TRUTH BY BEING CLOSE TO ME...
ARE YOU AL RIGHT, YAGAM KUN?
SUDDENLY HEARING ABOUT YOUR GIRLFRIEND BEING APPRE-HENDED AS THE SECOND KIRA... I CAN UNDERSTAND THE EMOTIONS YOU MUST BE GOING THROUGH...
DAMN IT, IT'S LIKE HE'S TRYING TO CHEER ME UP...
I WAS NAÏVE... I SHOULD HAVE DISPOSED OF THOSE VIDEOS AND ALL POSSI-BLE EVIDENCE MYSELF. AND THAT PHONE CALL TO MISA JUST NOW ONLY WORKS AGAINST ME...
NO, IF MISA HAS BEEN CAUGHT AS THE SECOND KIRA THEN RYUGA'S SUSPICION AGAINST ME IS NO LONGER MERE SUSPICION... AND IF MISA TALKS THEN IT'S ALL OVER... I HAVE TO KILL MISA...

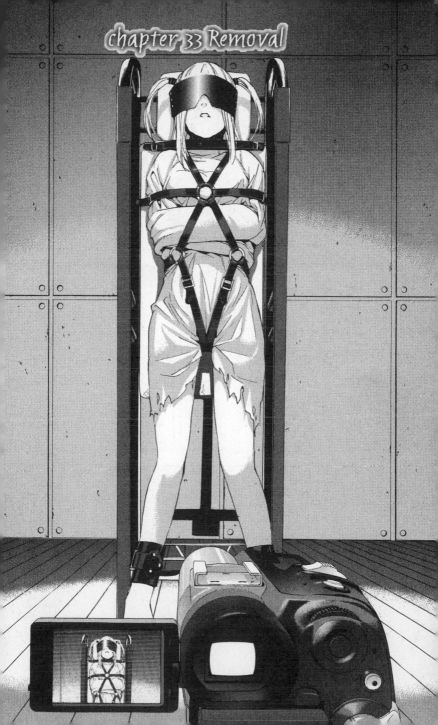

chapter 33 Removal

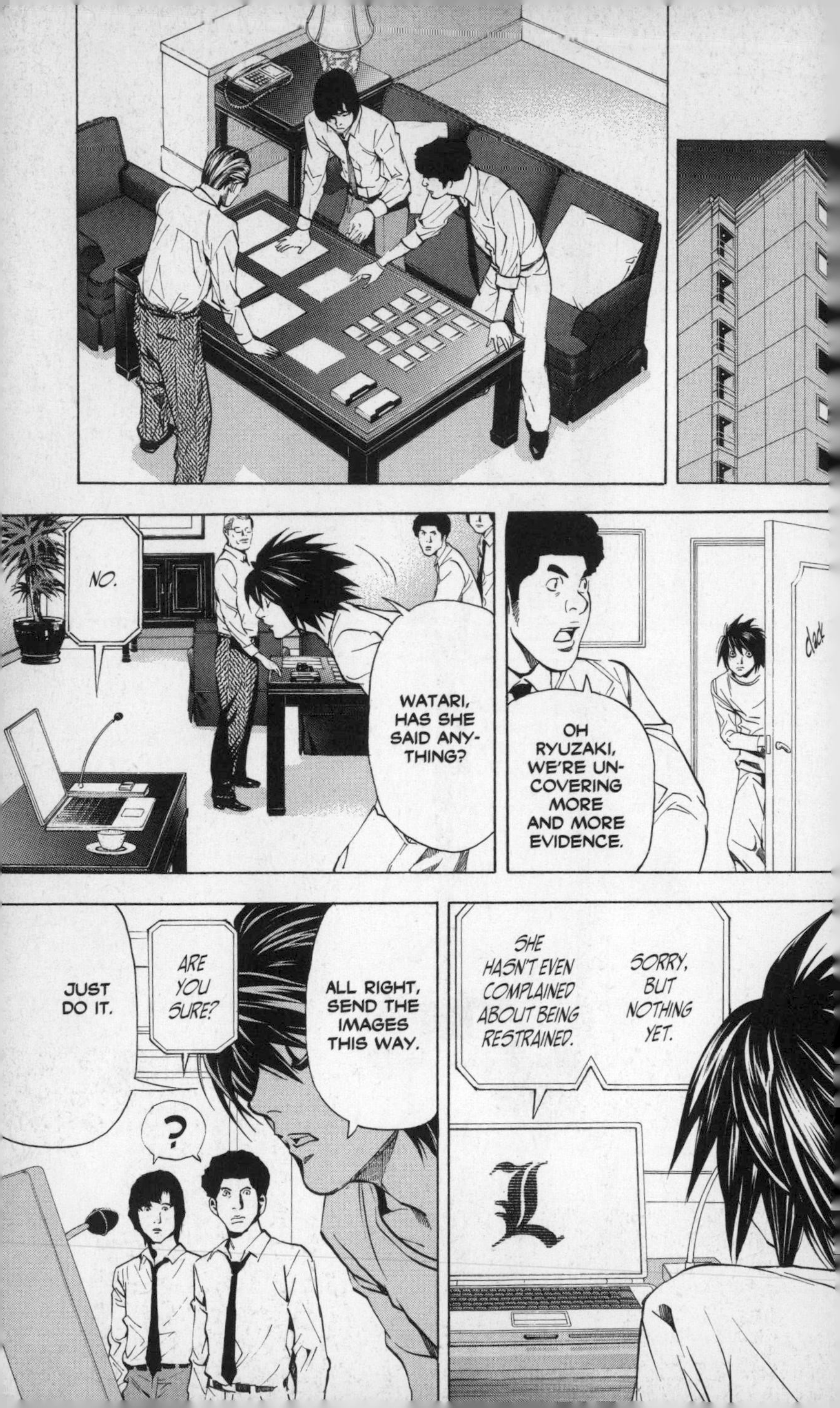
clack
OH RYUZAKI, WE'RE UNCOVERING MORE AND MORE EVIDENCE.
WATARI, HAS SHE SAID ANYTHING?
NO.
SORRY, BUT NOTHING YET.
SHE HASN'T EVEN COMPLAINED ABOUT BEING RESTRAINED.
ALL RIGHT, SEND THE IMAGES THIS WAY.
ARE YOU SURE?
JUST DO IT.
?

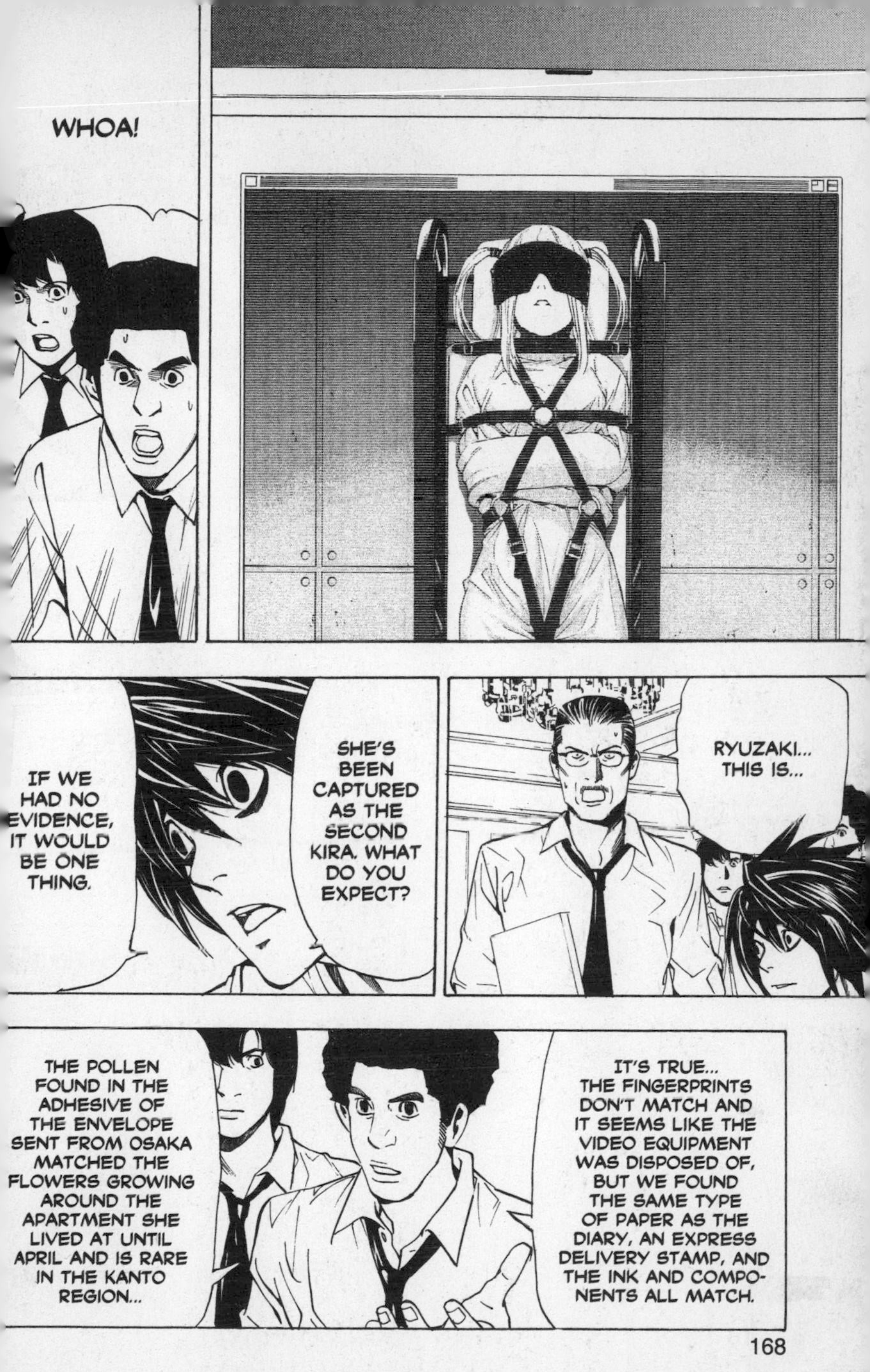
WHOA!
RYUZAKI... THIS IS...
SHE'S BEEN CAPTURED AS THE SECOND KIRA. WHAT DO YOU EXPECT?
IF WE HAD NO EVIDENCE, IT WOULD BE ONE THING.
IT'S TRUE... THE FINGERPRINTS DON'T MATCH AND IT SEEMS LIKE THE VIDEO EQUIPMENT WAS DISPOSED OF, BUT WE FOUND THE SAME TYPE OF PAPER AS THE DIARY, AN EXPRESS DELIVERY STAMP, AND THE INK AND COMPONENTS ALL MATCH.
THE POLLEN FOUND IN THE ADHESIVE OF THE ENVELOPE SENT FROM OSAKA MATCHED THE FLOWERS GROWING AROUND THE APARTMENT SHE LIVED AT UNTIL APRIL AND IS RARE IN THE KANTO REGION...

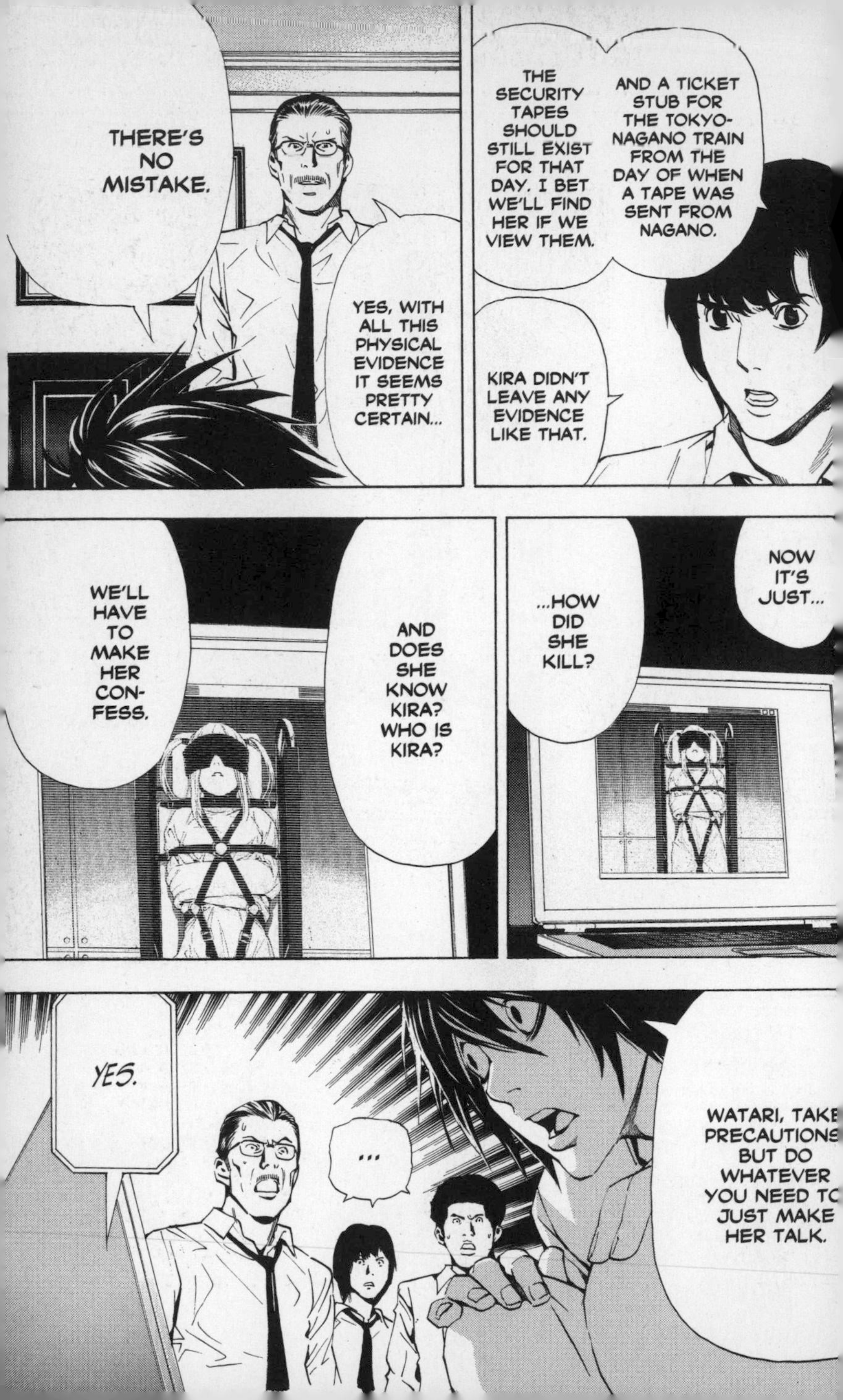
AND A TICKET STUB FOR THE TOKYO-NAGANO TRAIN FROM THE DAY OF WHEN A TAPE WAS SENT FROM NAGANO.
THE SECURITY TAPES SHOULD STILL EXIST FOR THAT DAY. I BET WE'LL FIND HER IF WE VIEW THEM.
KIRA DIDN'T LEAVE ANY EVIDENCE LIKE THAT.
THERE'S NO MISTAKE.
YES, WITH ALL THIS PHYSICAL EVIDENCE IT SEEMS PRETTY CERTAIN...
NOW IT'S JUST...
...HOW DID SHE KILL?
AND DOES SHE KNOW KIRA? WHO IS KIRA?
WE'LL HAVE TO MAKE HER CON-FESS.
WATARI, TAKE PRECAUTIONS BUT DO WHATEVER YOU NEED TO JUST MAKE HER TALK.
...
YES.

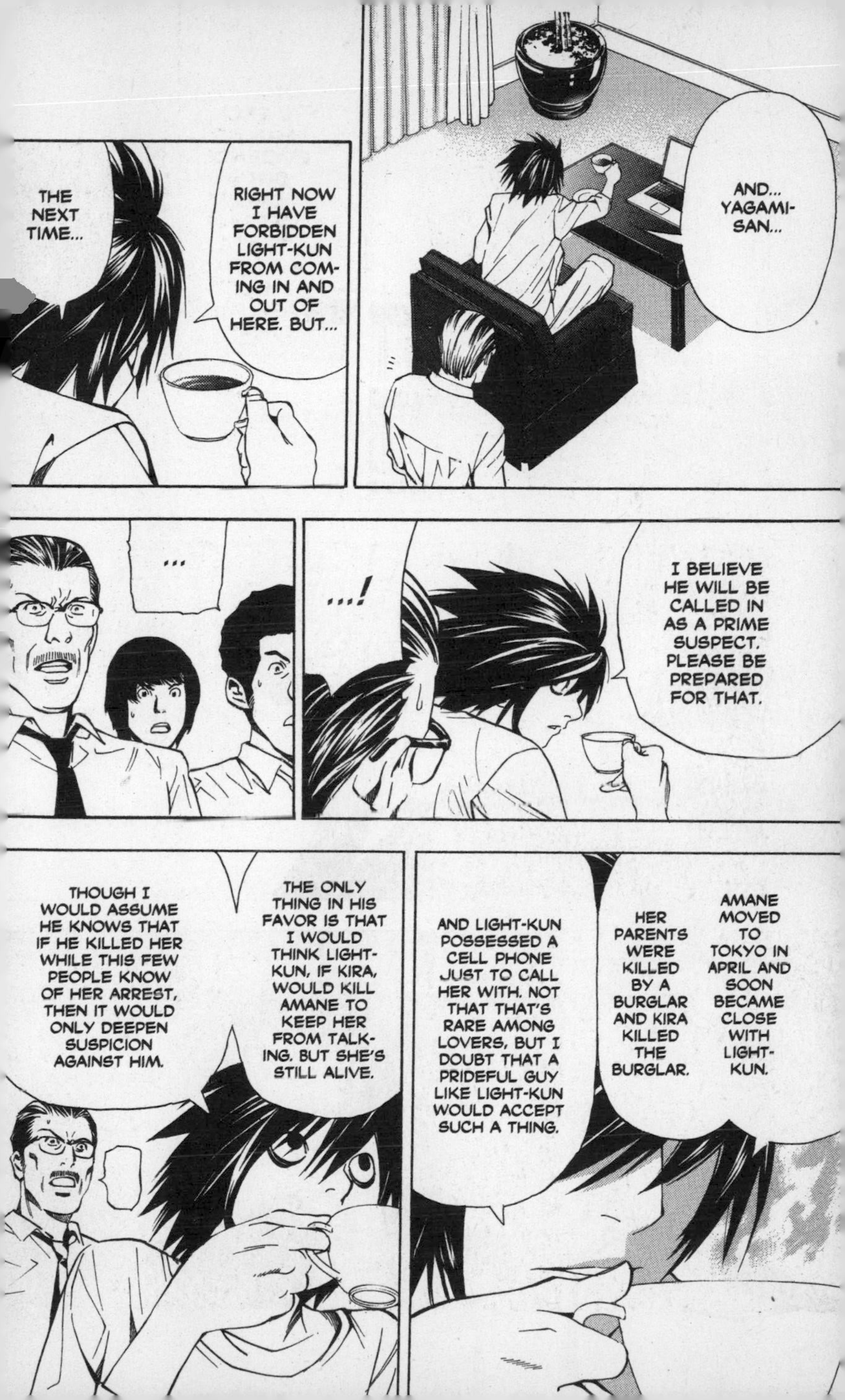
AND... YAGAMI-SAN...
RIGHT NOW I HAVE FORBIDDEN LIGHT-KUN FROM COMING IN AND OUT OF HERE. BUT...
THE NEXT TIME...
I BELIEVE HE WILL BE CALLED IN AS A PRIME SUSPECT. PLEASE BE PREPARED FOR THAT.
...!
...
AMANE MOVED TO TOKYO IN APRIL AND SOON BECAME CLOSE WITH LIGHT-KUN.
HER PARENTS WERE KILLED BY A BURGLAR AND KIRA KILLED THE BURGLAR.
AND LIGHT-KUN POSSESSED A CELL PHONE JUST TO CALL HER WITH. NOT THAT THAT'S RARE AMONG LOVERS, BUT I DOUBT THAT A PRIDEFUL GUY LIKE LIGHT-KUN WOULD ACCEPT SUCH A THING.
THE ONLY THING IN HIS FAVOR IS THAT I WOULD THINK LIGHT-KUN, IF KIRA, WOULD KILL AMANE TO KEEP HER FROM TALKING. BUT SHE'S STILL ALIVE.
THOUGH I WOULD ASSUME HE KNOWS THAT IF HE KILLED HER WHILE THIS FEW PEOPLE KNOW OF HER ARREST, THEN IT WOULD ONLY DEEPEN SUSPICION AGAINST HIM.
...

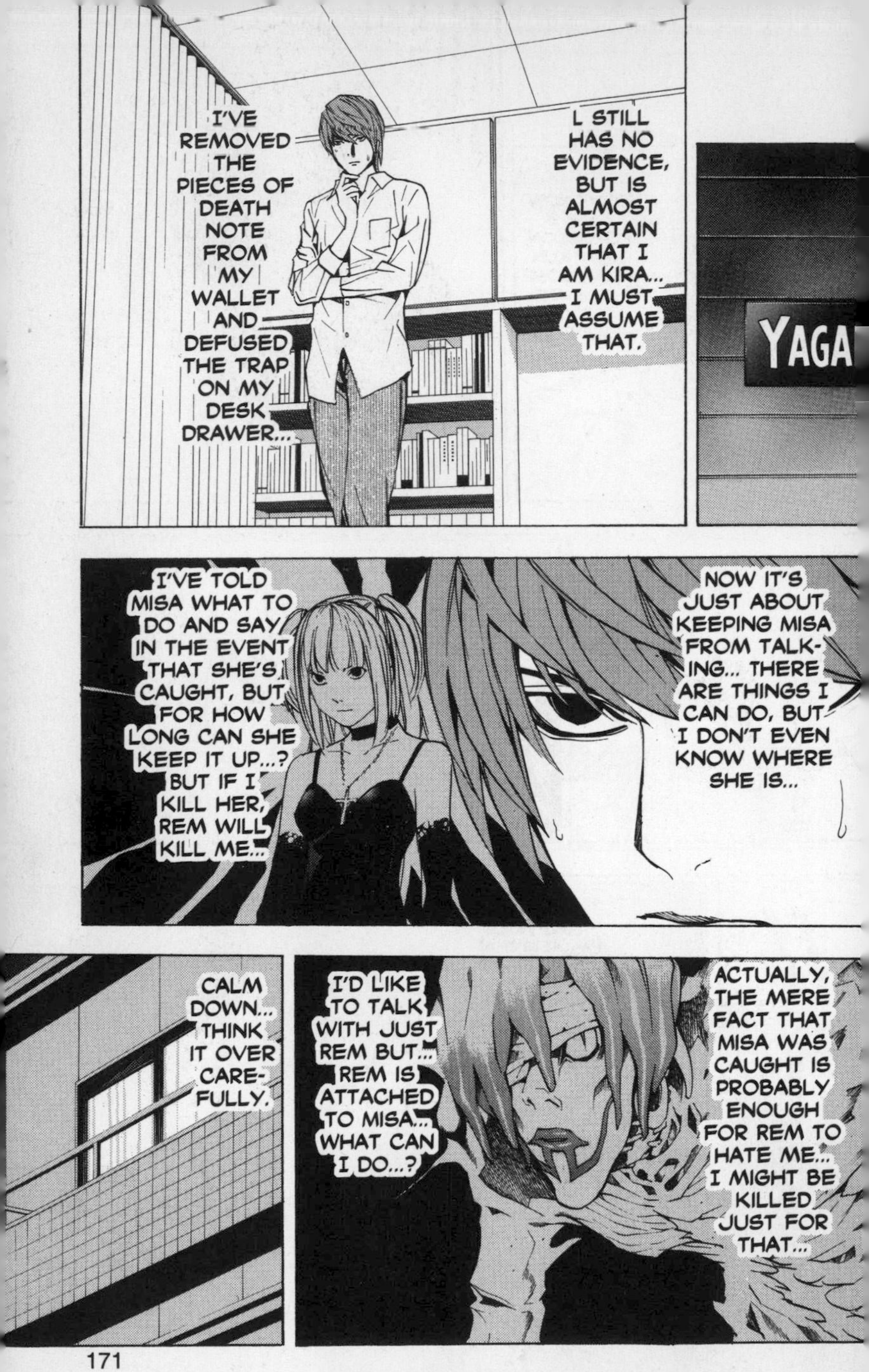
L STILL HAS NO EVIDENCE, BUT IS ALMOST CERTAIN THAT I AM KIRA... I MUST ASSUME THAT.
I'VE REMOVED THE PIECES OF DEATH NOTE FROM MY WALLET AND DEFUSED THE TRAP ON MY DESK DRAWER...
YAGA
NOW IT'S JUST ABOUT KEEPING MISA FROM TALK-ING... THERE ARE THINGS I CAN DO, BUT I DON'T EVEN KNOW WHERE SHE IS...
I'VE TOLD MISA WHAT TO DO AND SAY IN THE EVENT THAT SHE'S CAUGHT, BUT FOR HOW LONG CAN SHE KEEP IT UP...? BUT IF I KILL HER, REM WILL KILL ME...
ACTUALLY, THE MERE FACT THAT MISA WAS CAUGHT IS PROBABLY ENOUGH FOR REM TO HATE ME... I MIGHT BE KILLED JUST FOR THAT...
I'D LIKE TO TALK WITH JUST REM BUT... REM IS ATTACHED TO MISA... WHAT CAN I DO...?
CALM DOWN... THINK IT OVER CARE-FULLY.

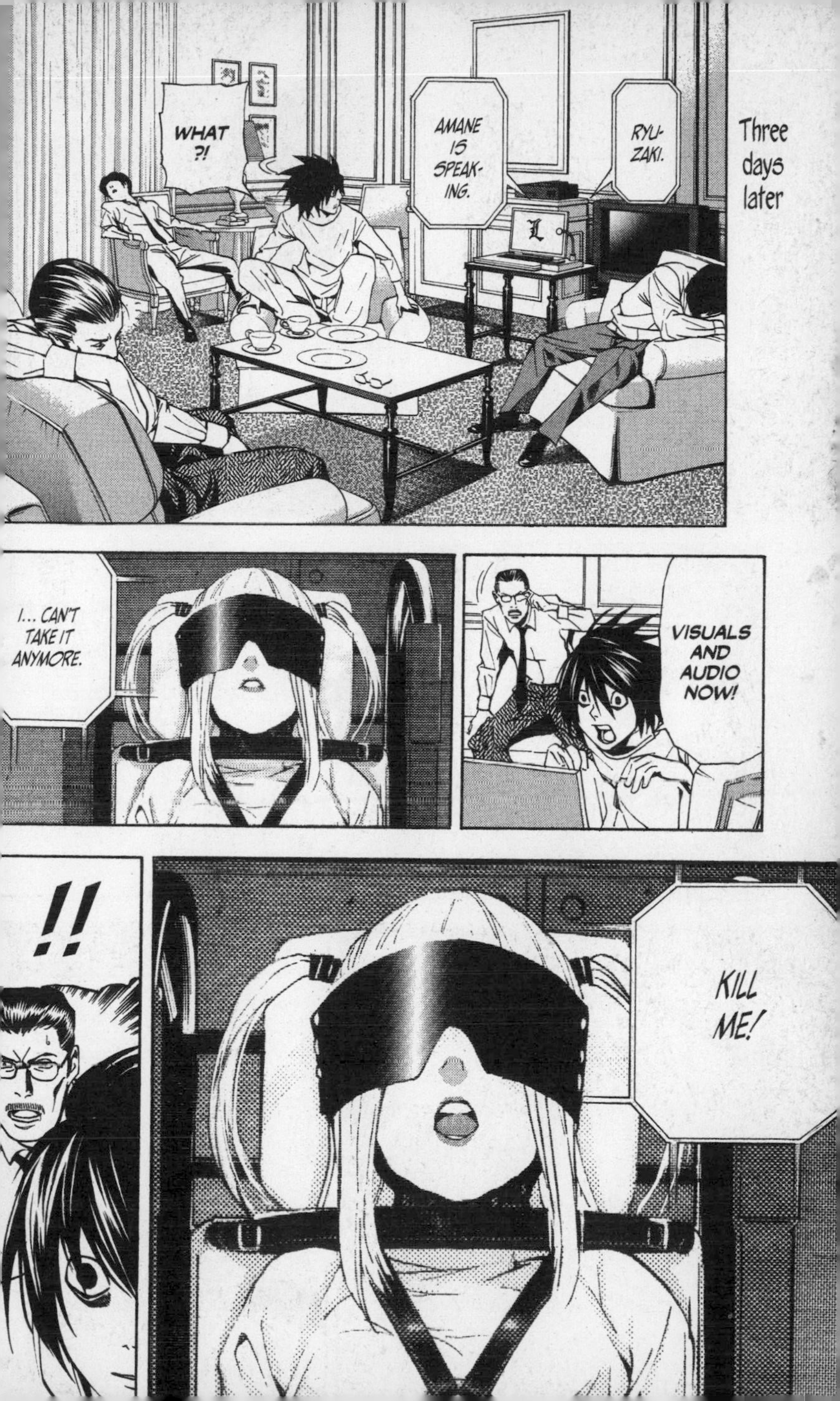
Three days later
RYU-ZAKI.
AMANE IS SPEAK-ING.
WHAT ?!
VISUALS AND AUDIO NOW!
I... CAN'T TAKE IT ANYMORE.
KILL ME!
!!

KILL ME.
HURRY UP AND KILL ME.
YOU SAID SHE HASN'T HAD WATER IN THREE DAYS, RIGHT...?
THAT'S TOO MUCH FOR A TWENTY-YEAR OLD GIRL... SHE MUST BE AT HER LIMIT...
...
Click
MISA AMANE, CAN YOU HEAR ME?
YES...

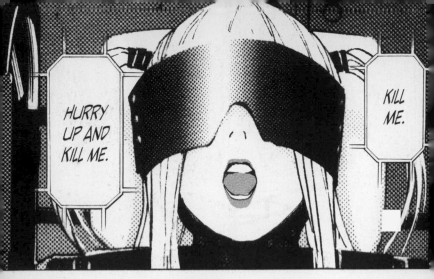

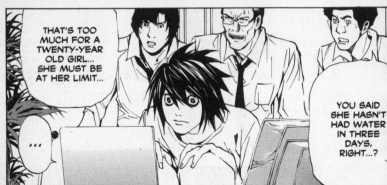

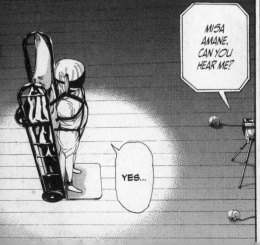

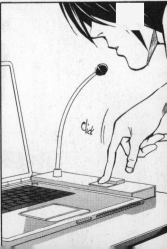

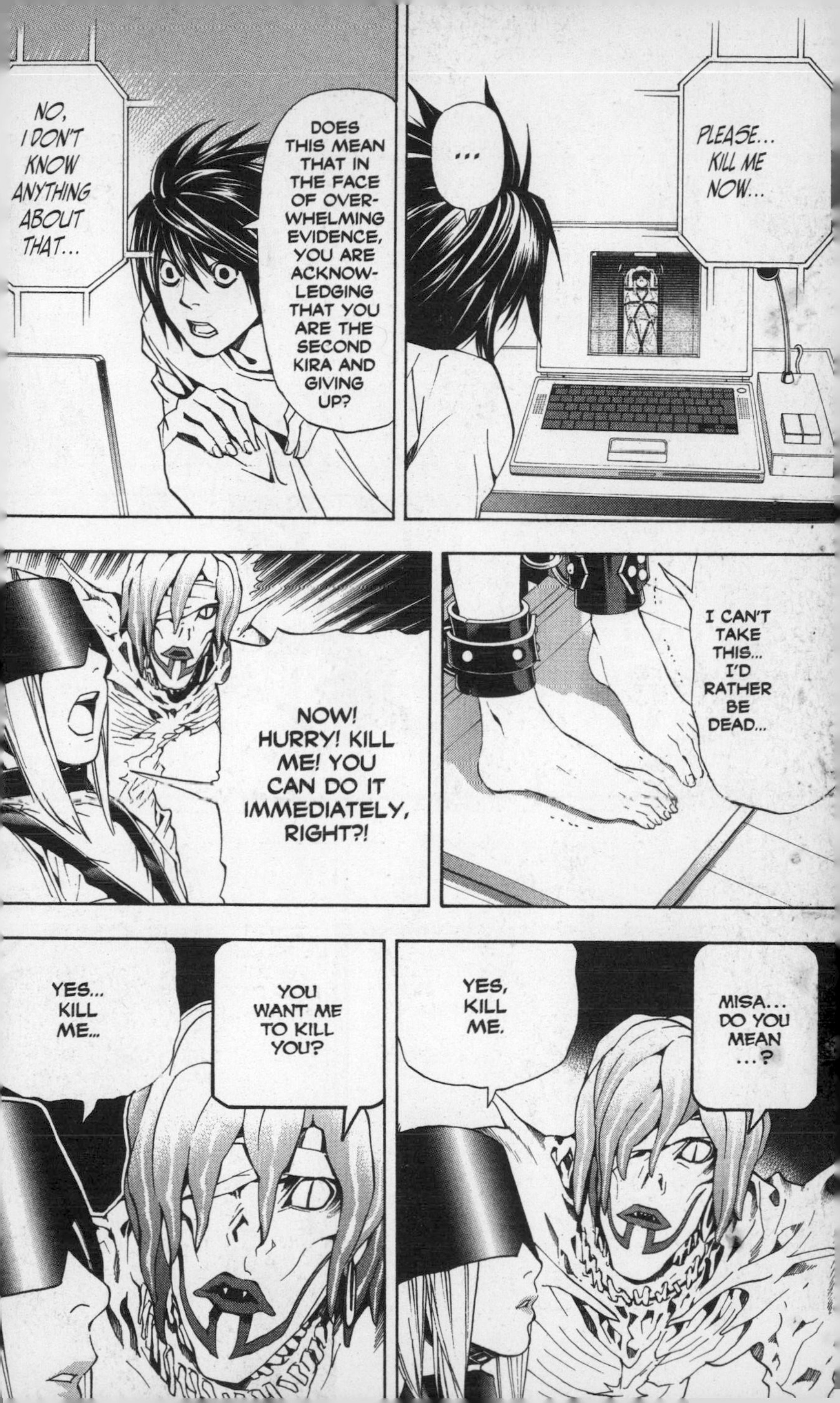
PLEASE... KILL ME NOW...
...
DOES THIS MEAN THAT IN THE FACE OF OVER-WHELMING EVIDENCE, YOU ARE ACKNOW-LEDGING THAT YOU ARE THE SECOND KIRA AND GIVING UP?
NO, I DON'T KNOW ANYTHING ABOUT THAT...
I CAN'T TAKE THIS... I'D RATHER BE DEAD...
NOW! HURRY! KILL ME! YOU CAN DO IT IMMEDIATELY, RIGHT?!
MISA... DO YOU MEAN ...?
YES, KILL ME.
YOU WANT ME TO KILL YOU?
YES... KILL ME...

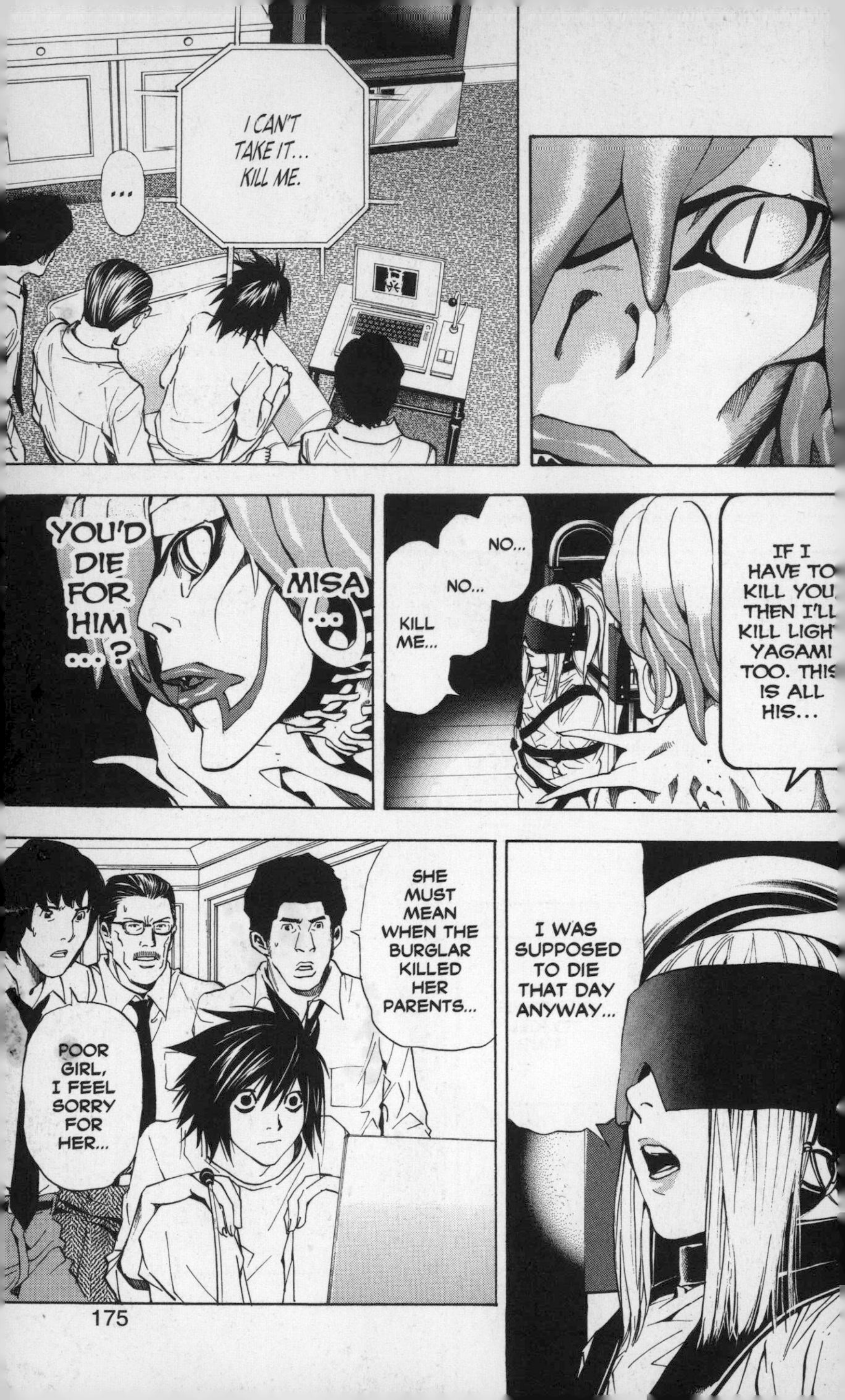
I CAN'T TAKE IT... KILL ME.
...
IF I HAVE TO KILL YOU, THEN I'LL KILL LIGHT YAGAMI TOO. THIS IS ALL HIS...
NO...
NO...
KILL ME...
MISA...
YOU'D DIE FOR HIM...?
I WAS SUPPOSED TO DIE THAT DAY ANYWAY...
SHE MUST MEAN WHEN THE BURGLAR KILLED HER PARENTS...
POOR GIRL, I FEEL SORRY FOR HER...

NOW THAT I THINK ABOUT IT, HAD I NOT GIVEN YOU THAT NOTEBOOK... "HUMANS POSSESSED BY SHINIGAMI MEET MISFORTUNE"... MAYBE IT'S TRUE.

I'M SORRY, MISA.

...WHILE I'M STILL YOUNG AND PRETTY... KILL ME...

I WOULD DIE HAPPY NOW...

MISA...

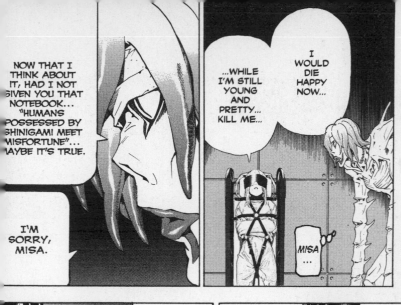

WATARI, MAKE SURE SHE CAN'T BITE HER TONGUE OFF.

YES.

IF YOU WON'T KILL ME, THEN...

I DON'T CARE, JUST KILL ME!!

...

COULD THESE ALREADY BE THE ACTIONS BEFORE DEATH, CONTROLLED BY KIRA...?

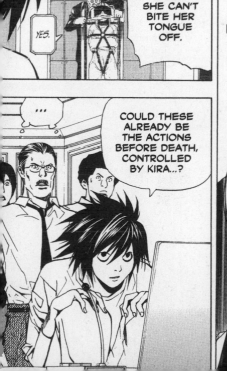

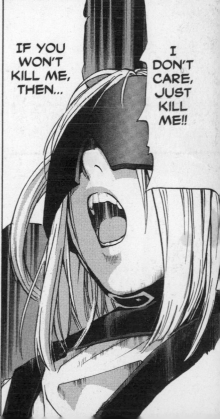

READ THIS WAY

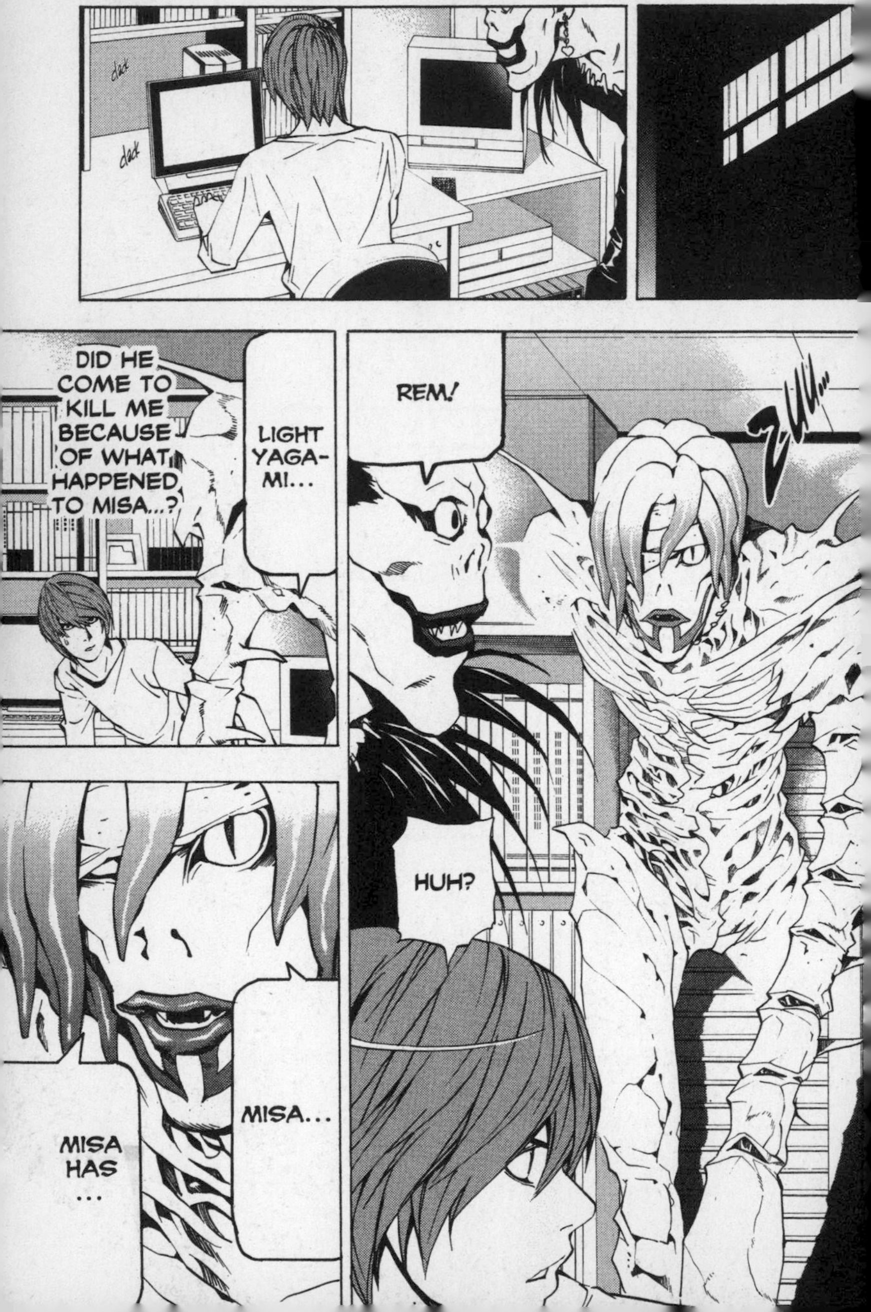
clack
clack
ZUU...
REM!
LIGHT YAGAMI...
DID HE COME TO KILL ME BECAUSE OF WHAT HAPPENED TO MISA...?
MISA...
MISA HAS ...
HUH?

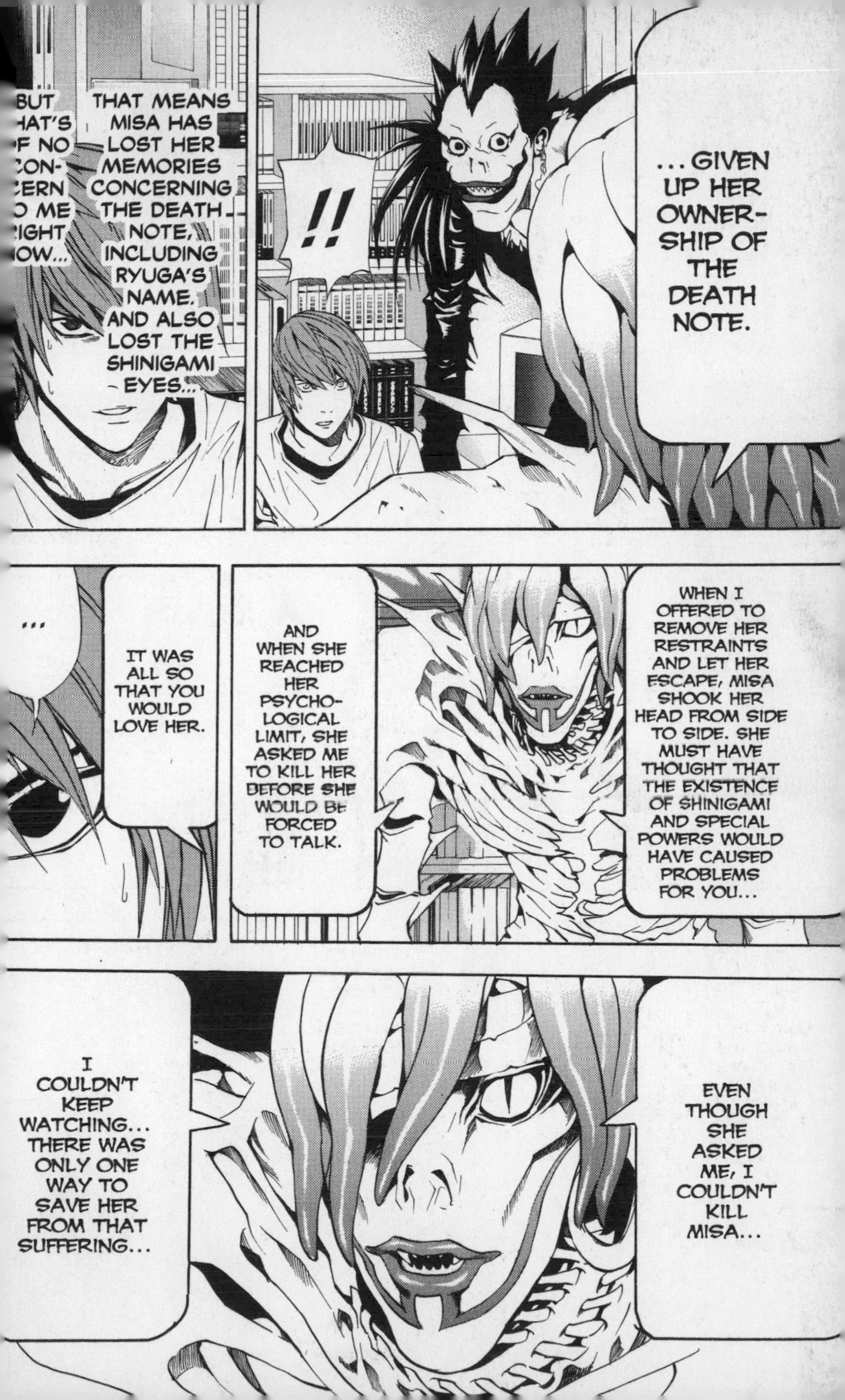
...GIVEN UP HER OWNER-SHIP OF THE DEATH NOTE.
!!
THAT MEANS MISA HAS LOST HER MEMORIES CONCERNING THE DEATH NOTE, INCLUDING RYUGA'S NAME. AND ALSO LOST THE SHINIGAMI EYES...
BUT HAT'S F NO CON- CERN O ME IGHT OW...
WHEN I OFFERED TO REMOVE HER RESTRAINTS AND LET HER ESCAPE, MISA SHOOK HER HEAD FROM SIDE TO SIDE. SHE MUST HAVE THOUGHT THAT THE EXISTENCE OF SHINIGAMI AND SPECIAL POWERS WOULD HAVE CAUSED PROBLEMS FOR YOU...
AND WHEN SHE REACHED HER PSYCHO-LOGICAL LIMIT, SHE ASKED ME TO KILL HER BEFORE SHE WOULD BE FORCED TO TALK.
IT WAS ALL SO THAT YOU WOULD LOVE HER.
...
EVEN THOUGH SHE ASKED ME, I COULDN'T KILL MISA...
I COULDN'T KEEP WATCHING... THERE WAS ONLY ONE WAY TO SAVE HER FROM THAT SUFFERING...

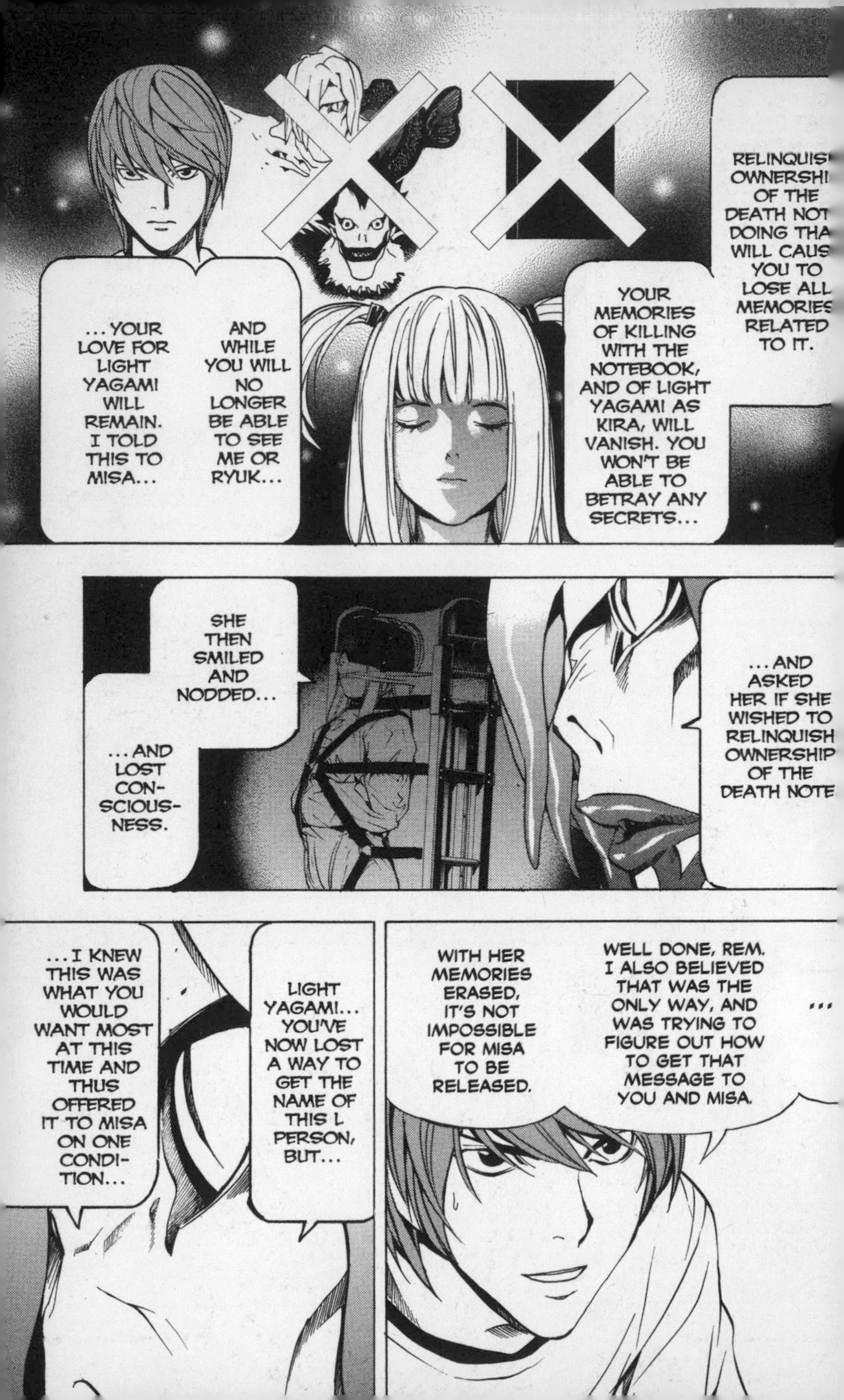
RELINQUIS OWNERSHI OF THE DEATH NOT DOING THA WILL CAUS YOU TO LOSE ALL MEMORIES RELATED TO IT.
YOUR MEMORIES OF KILLING WITH THE NOTEBOOK, AND OF LIGHT YAGAMI AS KIRA, WILL VANISH. YOU WON'T BE ABLE TO BETRAY ANY SECRETS...
AND WHILE YOU WILL NO LONGER BE ABLE TO SEE ME OR RYUK...
...YOUR LOVE FOR LIGHT YAGAMI WILL REMAIN. I TOLD THIS TO MISA...
...AND ASKED HER IF SHE WISHED TO RELINQUISH OWNERSHIP OF THE DEATH NOTE
SHE THEN SMILED AND NODDED...
...AND LOST CON-SCIOUS-NESS.
...
WELL DONE, REM. I ALSO BELIEVED THAT WAS THE ONLY WAY, AND WAS TRYING TO FIGURE OUT HOW TO GET THAT MESSAGE TO YOU AND MISA.
WITH HER MEMORIES ERASED, IT'S NOT IMPOSSIBLE FOR MISA TO BE RELEASED.
LIGHT YAGAMI... YOU'VE NOW LOST A WAY TO GET THE NAME OF THIS L PERSON, BUT...
...I KNEW THIS WAS WHAT YOU WOULD WANT MOST AT THIS TIME AND THUS OFFERED IT TO MISA ON ONE CONDI-TION...

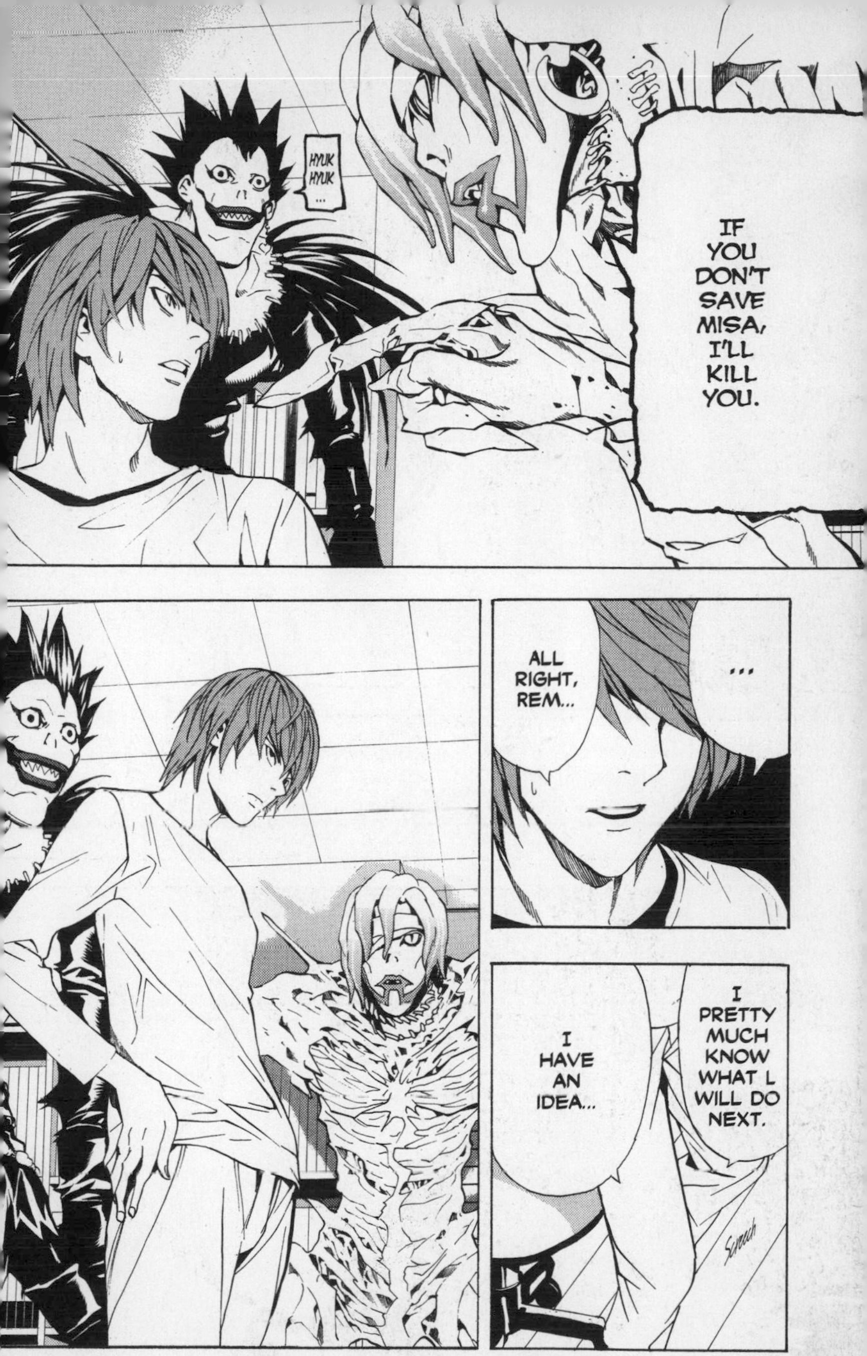
IF YOU DON'T SAVE MISA, I'LL KILL YOU.
HYUK HYUK ...
...
ALL RIGHT, REM...
I PRETTY MUCH KNOW WHAT L WILL DO NEXT.
I HAVE AN IDEA...
Scratch

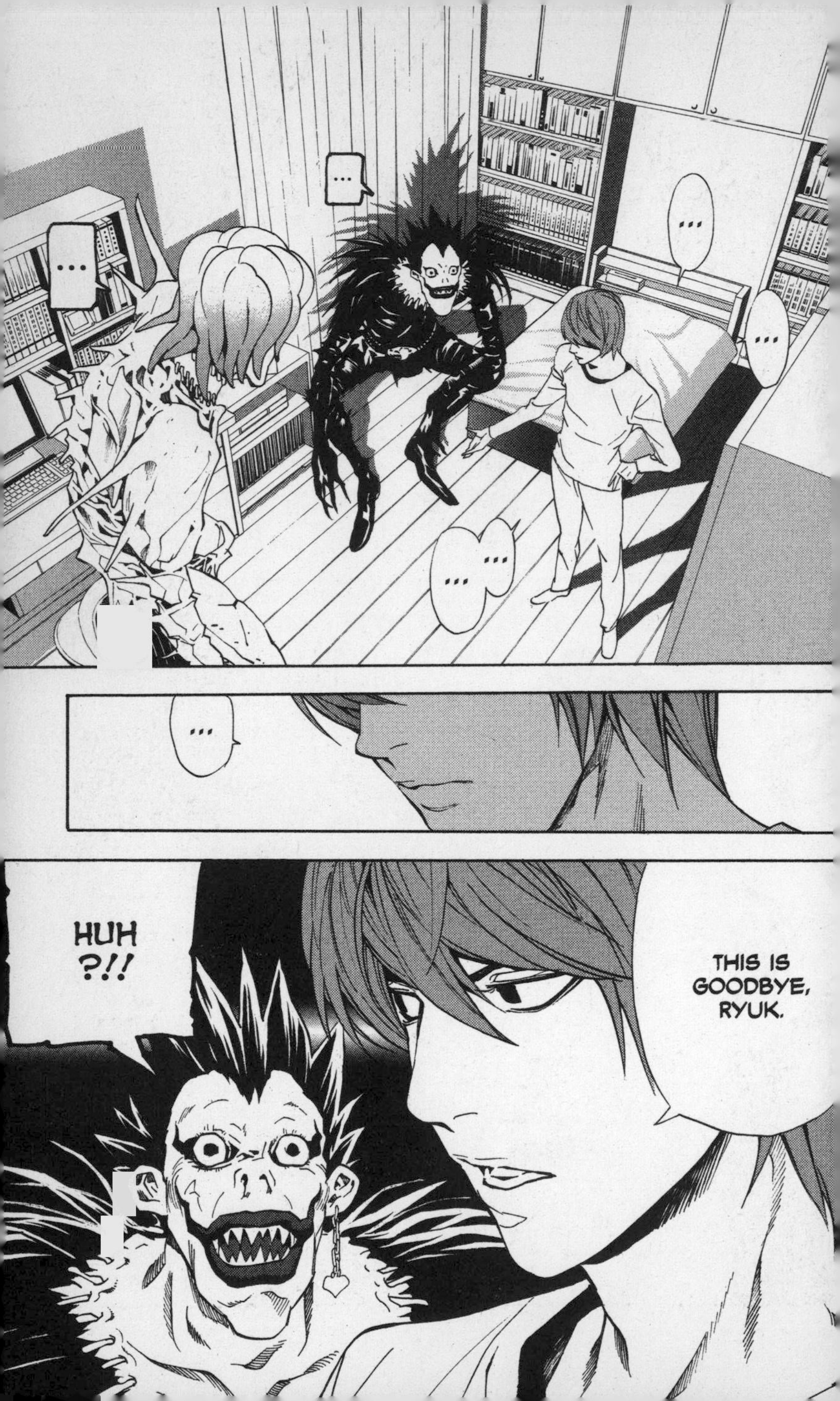
...
...
...
...
... ...
...
THIS IS GOODBYE, RYUK.
HUH ?!!

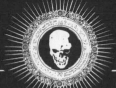

DEATH NOTE
HOW TO USE IT

XXXI

° the individuals who lose the ownership of the DEATH NOTE

will also lose their memory of the usage of the DEATH NOTE.

This does not mean that he will lose all the memory from

the day he owned it to the day he loses possession,

but means he will only lose the memory involving

the DEATH NOTE.

デスノートの所有権を失った人間は自分がデスノートを使用した事等の記憶が一切なくなる。しかし、ノートを持ってから失うまでの全ての記憶を喪失するのではなく、自分のしてきた行動はデスノートの所有者であった事が絡まない形で残る。

chapter 34 Imprisonment

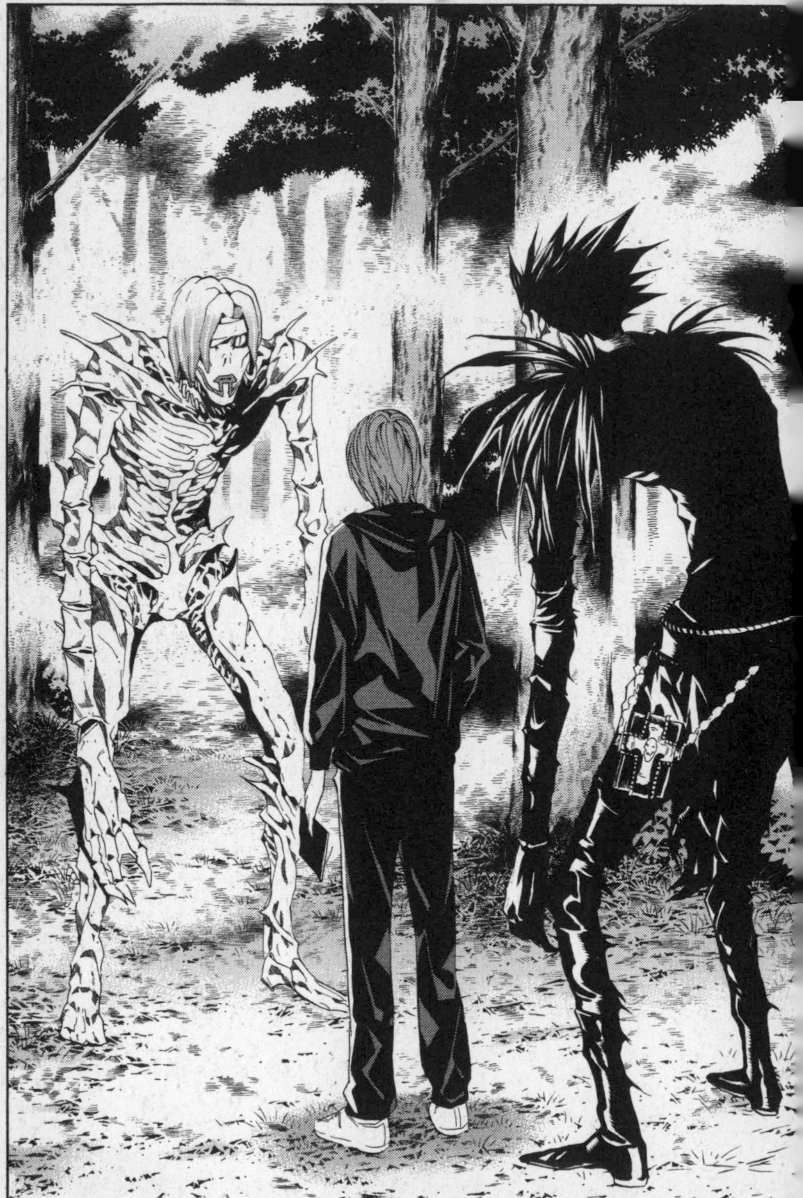

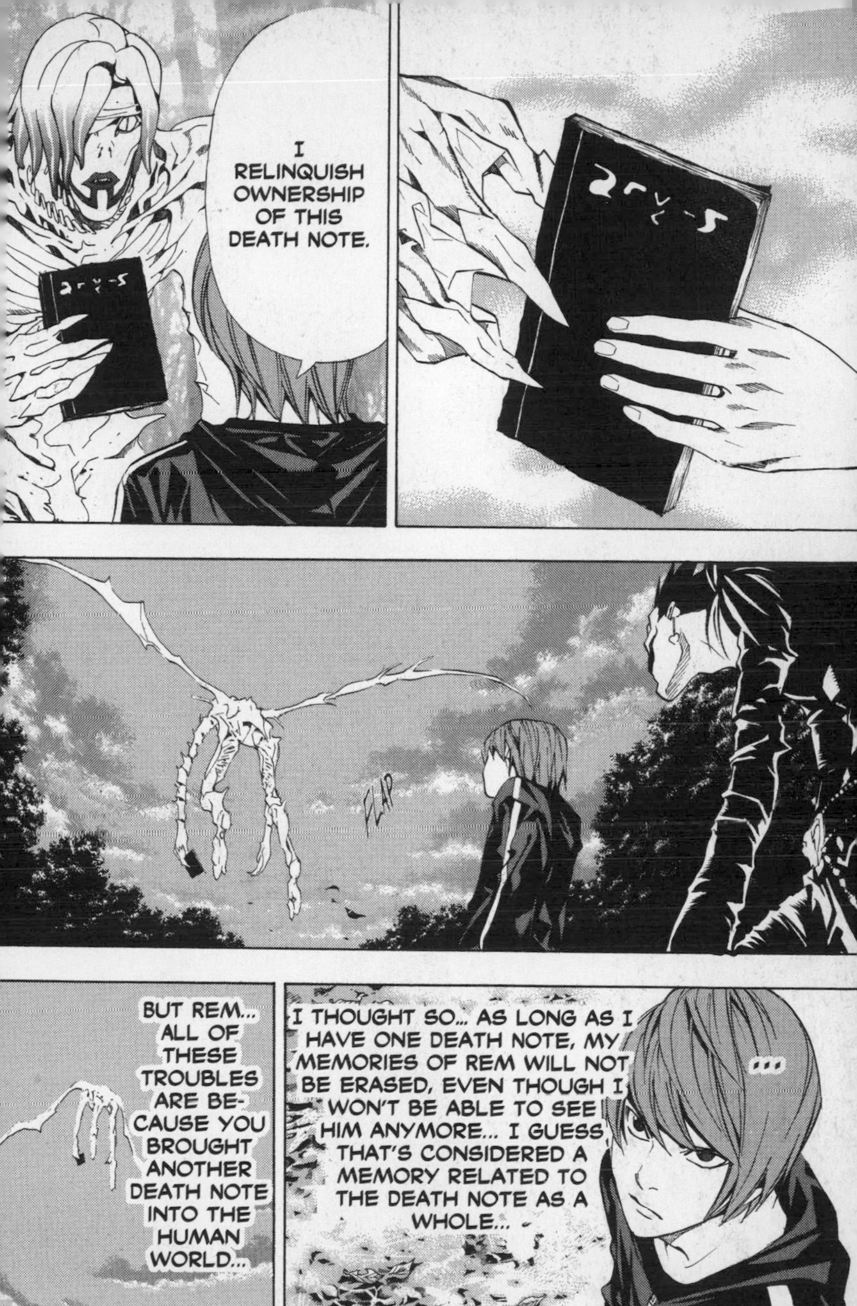
I RELINQUISH OWNERSHIP OF THIS DEATH NOTE.
FLAP
...
I THOUGHT SO... AS LONG AS I HAVE ONE DEATH NOTE, MY MEMORIES OF REM WILL NOT BE ERASED, EVEN THOUGH I WON'T BE ABLE TO SEE HIM ANYMORE... I GUESS THAT'S CONSIDERED A MEMORY RELATED TO THE DEATH NOTE AS A WHOLE...
BUT REM... ALL OF THESE TROUBLES ARE BE-CAUSE YOU BROUGHT ANOTHER DEATH NOTE INTO THE HUMAN WORLD...

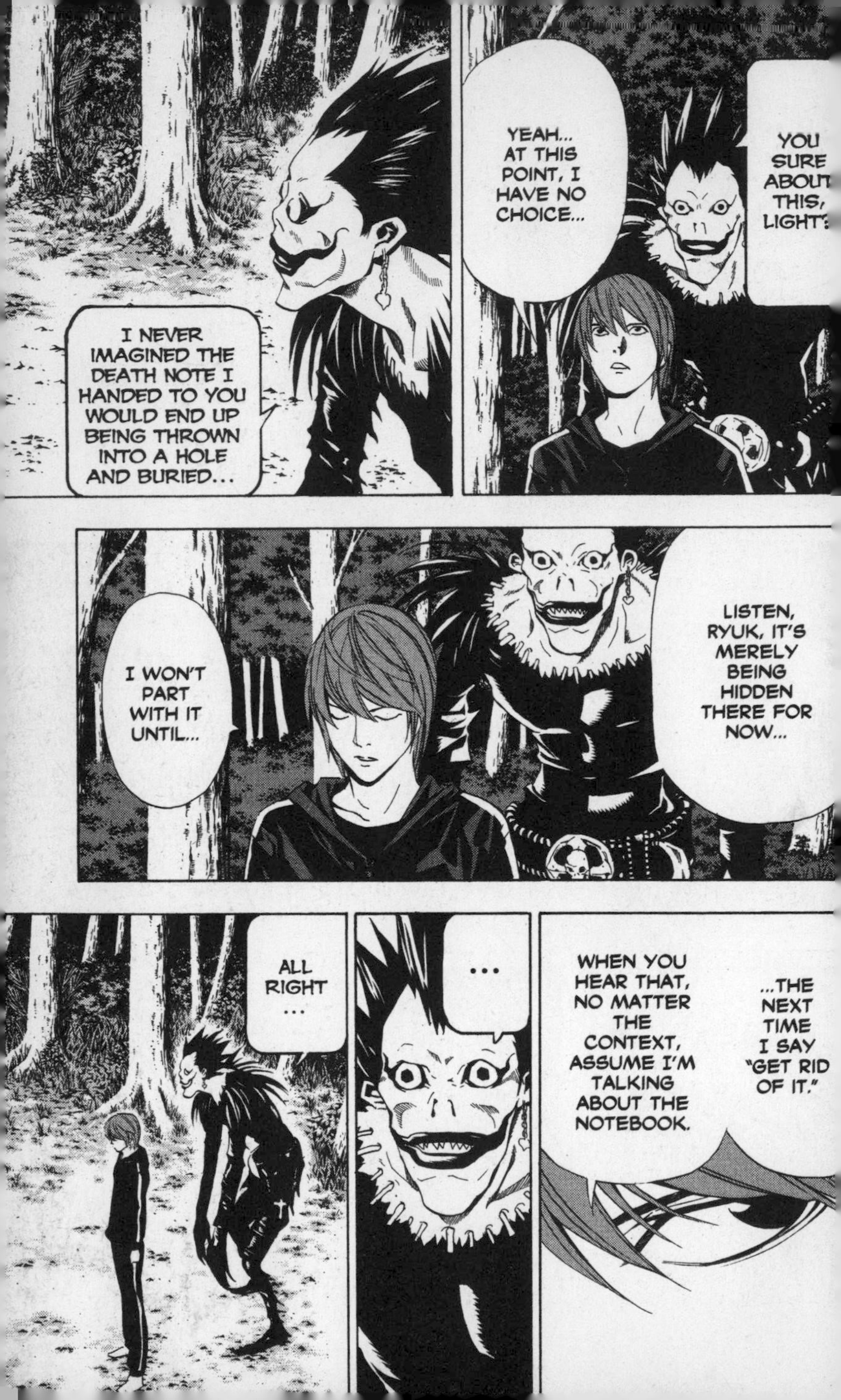
YOU SURE ABOUT THIS, LIGHT?
YEAH... AT THIS POINT, I HAVE NO CHOICE...
I NEVER IMAGINED THE DEATH NOTE I HANDED TO YOU WOULD END UP BEING THROWN INTO A HOLE AND BURIED...
LISTEN, RYUK, IT'S MERELY BEING HIDDEN THERE FOR NOW...
I WON'T PART WITH IT UNTIL...
...THE NEXT TIME I SAY "GET RID OF IT."
WHEN YOU HEAR THAT, NO MATTER THE CONTEXT, ASSUME I'M TALKING ABOUT THE NOTEBOOK.
...
ALL RIGHT ...

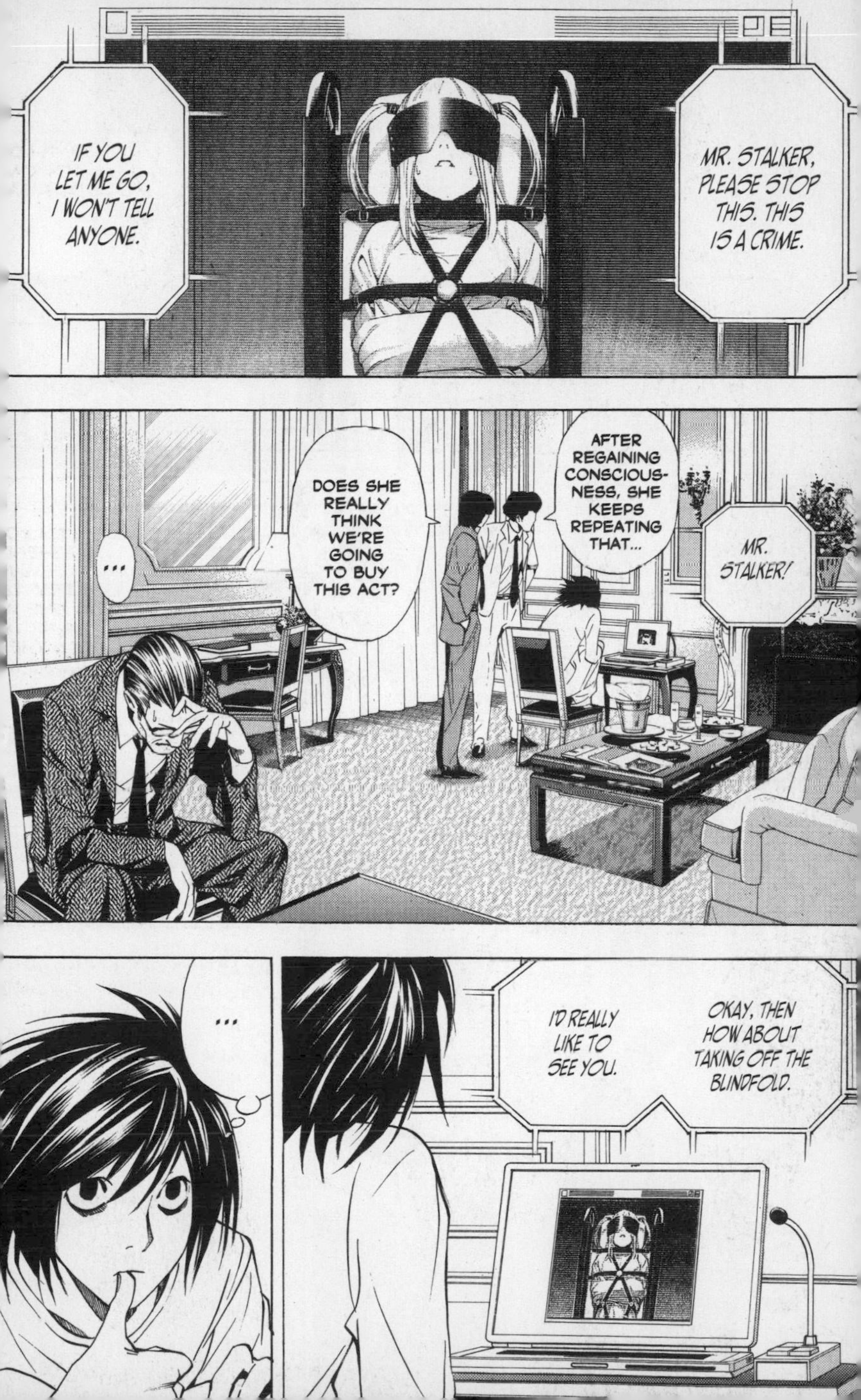
MR. STALKER, PLEASE STOP THIS. THIS IS A CRIME.
IF YOU LET ME GO, I WON'T TELL ANYONE.
MR. STALKER!
AFTER REGAINING CONSCIOUSNESS, SHE KEEPS REPEATING THAT...
DOES SHE REALLY THINK WE'RE GOING TO BUY THIS ACT?
...
OKAY, THEN HOW ABOUT TAKING OFF THE BLINDFOLD.
I'D REALLY LIKE TO SEE YOU.
...

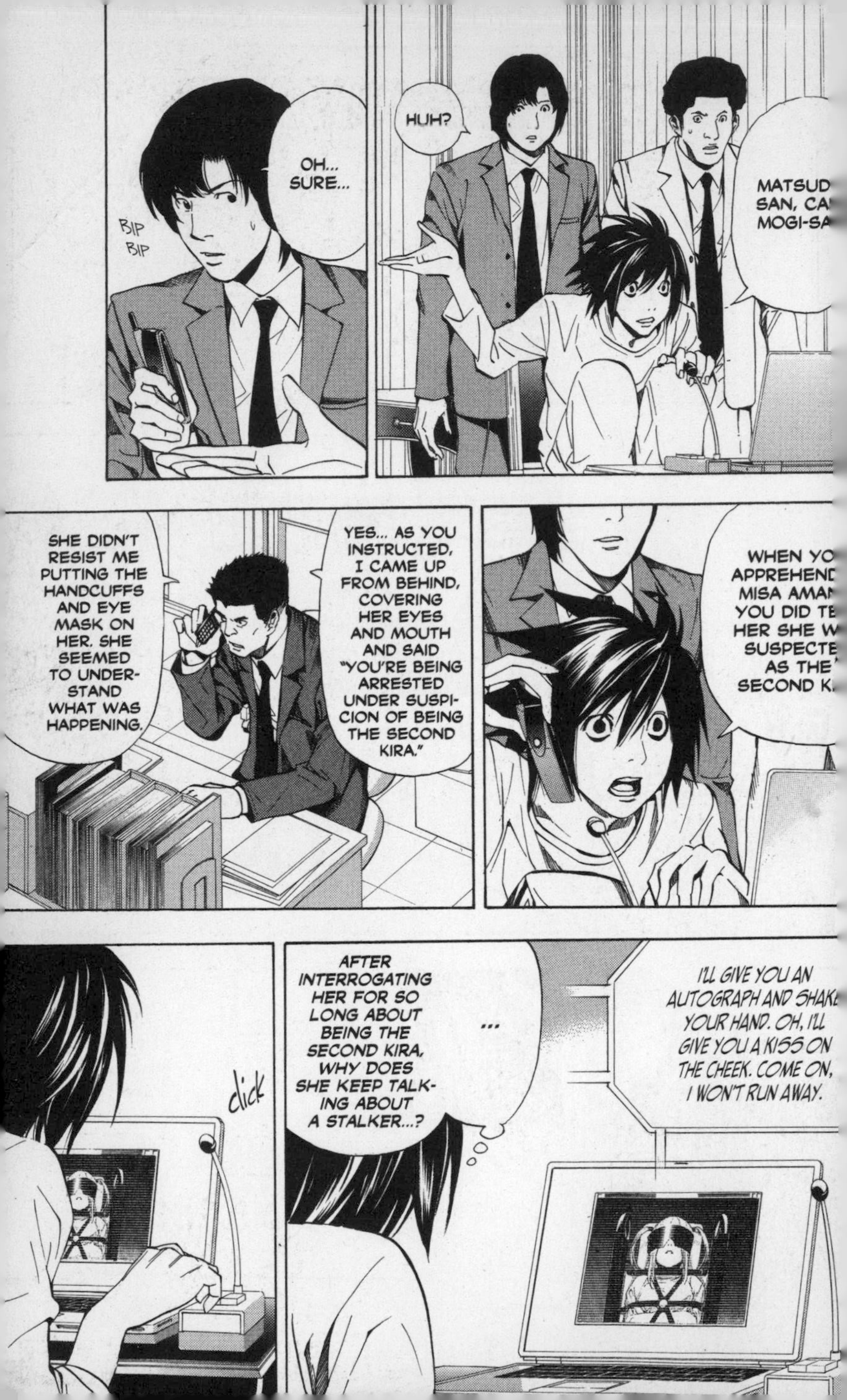
MATSUD SAN, CA MOGI-SA
HUH?
BIP BIP
OH... SURE...
WHEN YO APPREHEND MISA AMAN YOU DID TE HER SHE W SUSPECTE AS THE SECOND K
YES... AS YOU INSTRUCTED, I CAME UP FROM BEHIND, COVERING HER EYES AND MOUTH AND SAID "YOU'RE BEING ARRESTED UNDER SUSPICION OF BEING THE SECOND KIRA."
SHE DIDN'T RESIST ME PUTTING THE HANDCUFFS AND EYE MASK ON HER. SHE SEEMED TO UNDERSTAND WHAT WAS HAPPENING.
I'LL GIVE YOU AN AUTOGRAPH AND SHAKE YOUR HAND. OH, I'LL GIVE YOU A KISS ON THE CHEEK. COME ON, I WON'T RUN AWAY.
...
AFTER INTERROGATING HER FOR SO LONG ABOUT BEING THE SECOND KIRA, WHY DOES SHE KEEP TALKING ABOUT A STALKER...?
click

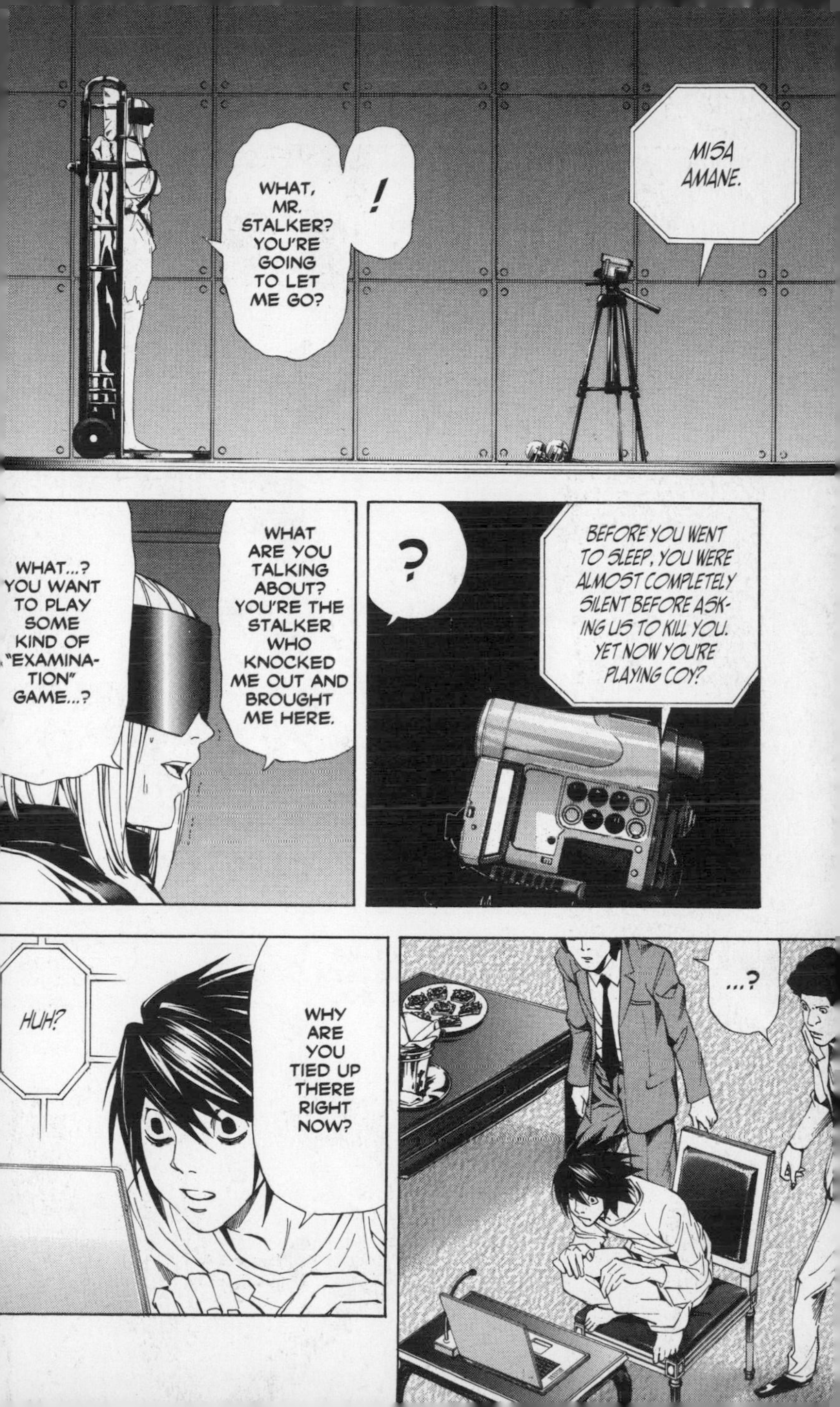
MISA AMANE.
!
WHAT, MR. STALKER? YOU'RE GOING TO LET ME GO?
BEFORE YOU WENT TO SLEEP, YOU WERE ALMOST COMPLETELY SILENT BEFORE ASKING US TO KILL YOU. YET NOW YOU'RE PLAYING COY?
?
WHAT ARE YOU TALKING ABOUT? YOU'RE THE STALKER WHO KNOCKED ME OUT AND BROUGHT ME HERE.
WHAT...? YOU WANT TO PLAY SOME KIND OF "EXAMINATION" GAME...?
...?
WHY ARE YOU TIED UP THERE RIGHT NOW?
HUH?

READ THIS WAY

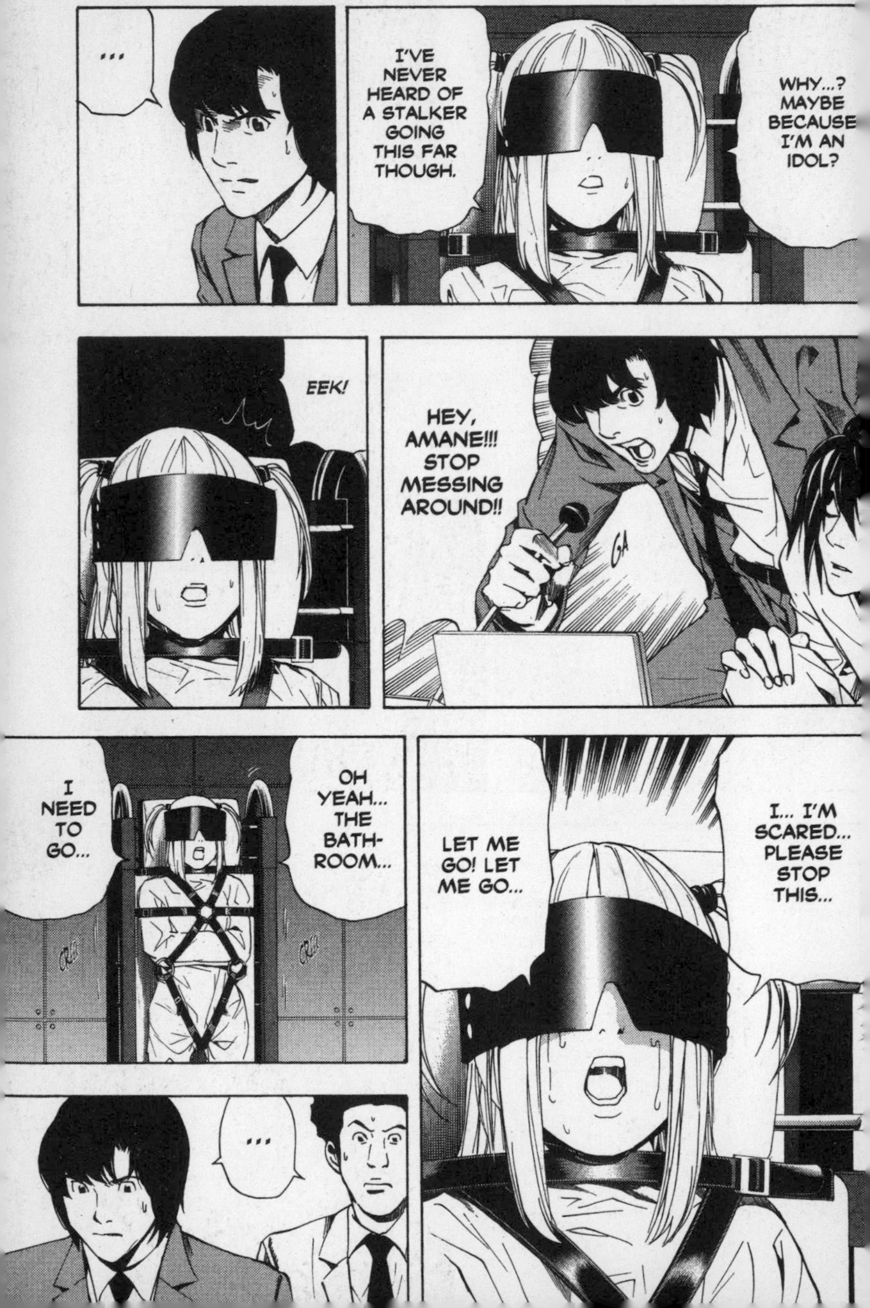
WHY...? MAYBE BECAUSE I'M AN IDOL?
I'VE NEVER HEARD OF A STALKER GOING THIS FAR THOUGH.
...
HEY, AMANE!!! STOP MESSING AROUND!!
GA
EEK!
I... I'M SCARED... PLEASE STOP THIS...
LET ME GO! LET ME GO...
OH YEAH... THE BATH-ROOM...
I NEED TO GO...
...

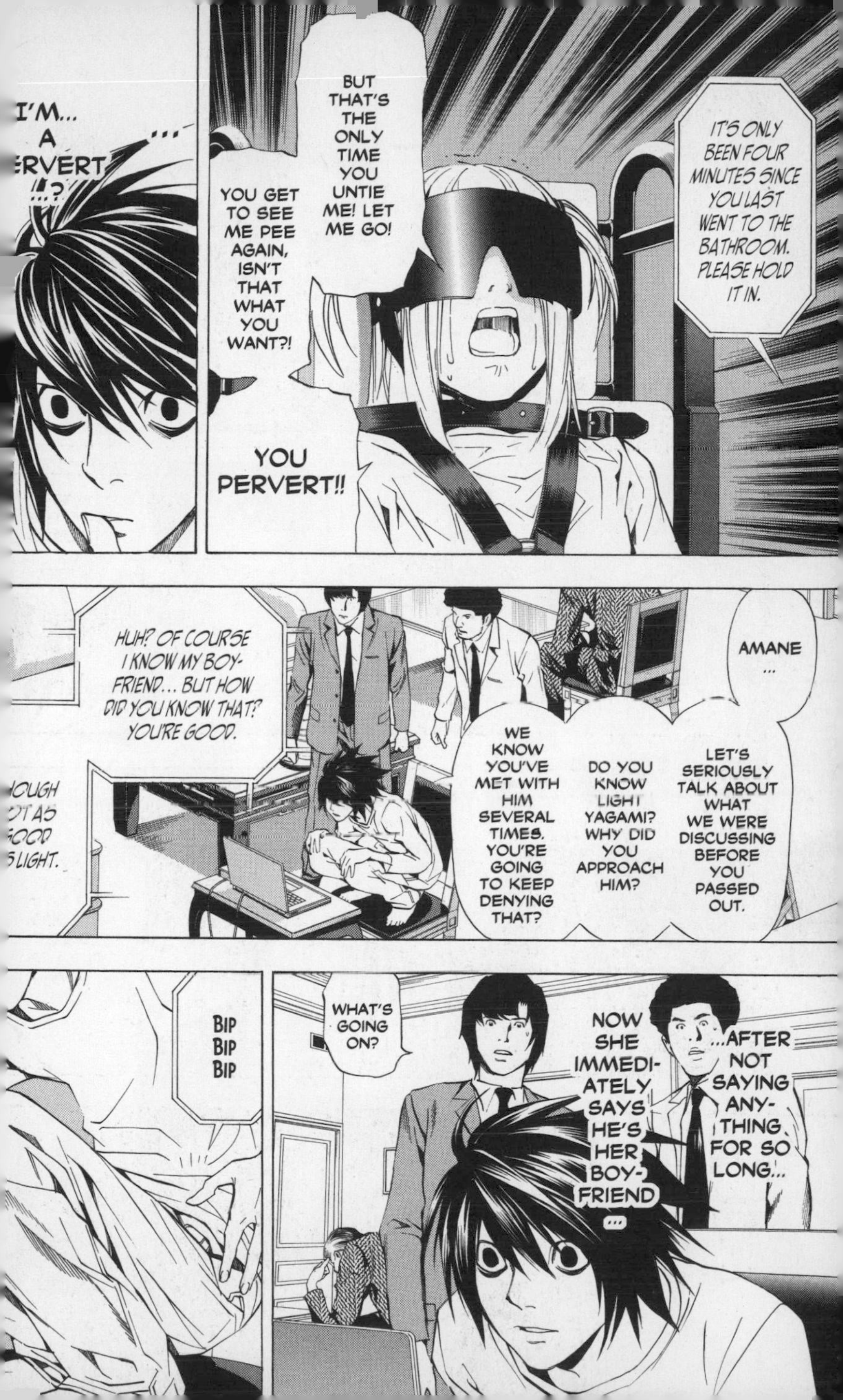
IT'S ONLY BEEN FOUR MINUTES SINCE YOU LAST WENT TO THE BATHROOM. PLEASE HOLD IT IN.
BUT THAT'S THE ONLY TIME YOU UNTIE ME! LET ME GO!
YOU GET TO SEE ME PEE AGAIN, ISN'T THAT WHAT YOU WANT?!
YOU PERVERT!!
...
I'M... A ERVERT !!...?
AMANE...
LET'S SERIOUSLY TALK ABOUT WHAT WE WERE DISCUSSING BEFORE YOU PASSED OUT.
DO YOU KNOW LIGHT YAGAMI? WHY DID YOU APPROACH HIM?
WE KNOW YOU'VE MET WITH HIM SEVERAL TIMES. YOU'RE GOING TO KEEP DENYING THAT?
HUH? OF COURSE I KNOW MY BOY-FRIEND... BUT HOW DID YOU KNOW THAT? YOU'RE GOOD.
HOUGH OT AS GOOD S LIGHT.
...AFTER NOT SAYING ANY-THING FOR SO LONG...
NOW SHE IMMEDI-ATELY SAYS HE'S HER BOY-FRIEND...
WHAT'S GOING ON?
BIP BIP BIP

READ THIS WAY

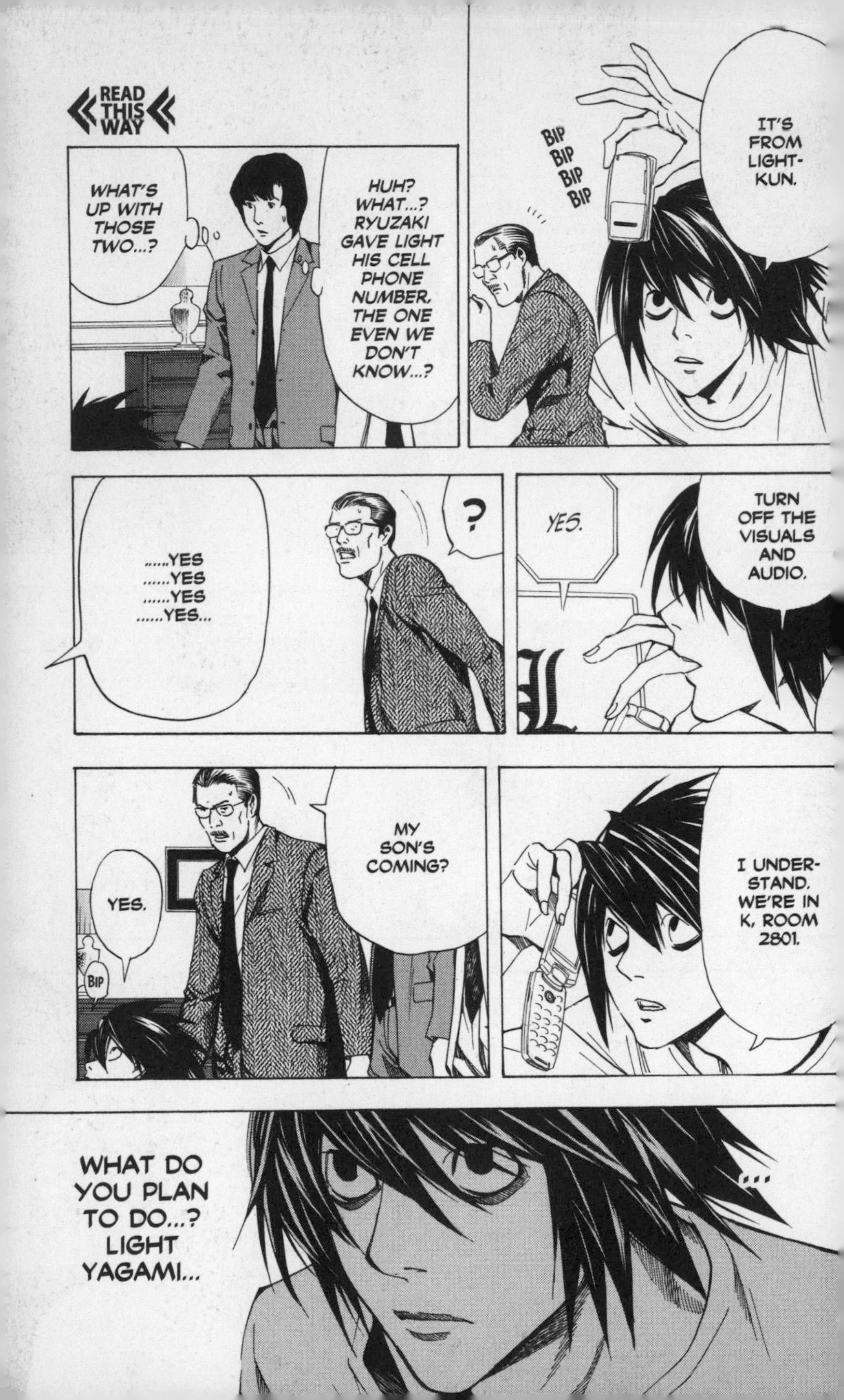
BIP BIP BIP BIP
IT'S FROM LIGHT-KUN.
HUH? WHAT...? RYUZAKI GAVE LIGHT HIS CELL PHONE NUMBER, THE ONE EVEN WE DON'T KNOW...?
WHAT'S UP WITH THOSE TWO...?
TURN OFF THE VISUALS AND AUDIO.
YES.
?
......YES ......YES ......YES ......YES...
I UNDER-STAND. WE'RE IN K, ROOM 2801.
MY SON'S COMING?
YES.
BIP
...
WHAT DO YOU PLAN TO DO...? LIGHT YAGAMI...

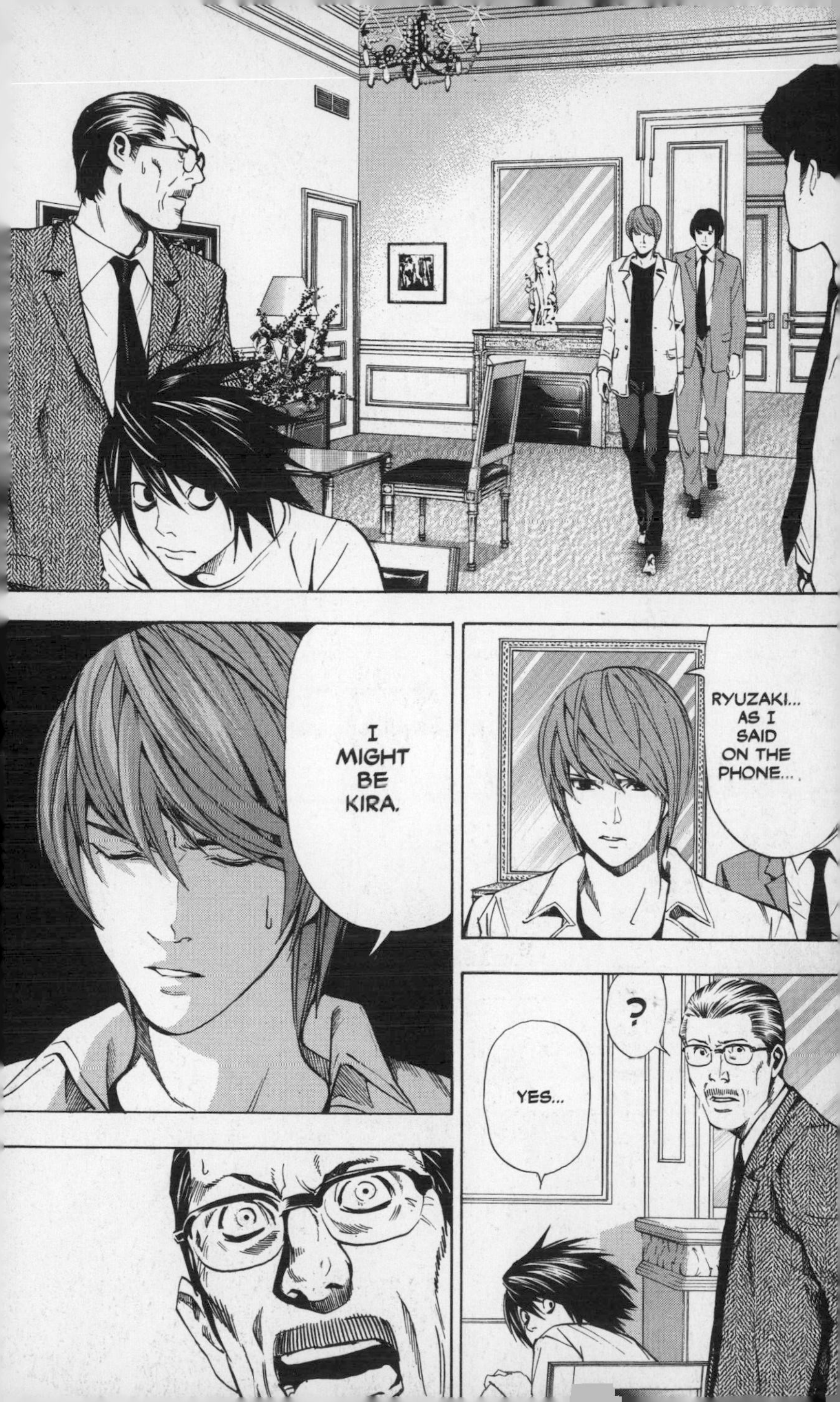
RYUZAKI... AS I SAID ON THE PHONE...
I MIGHT BE KIRA.
?
YES...

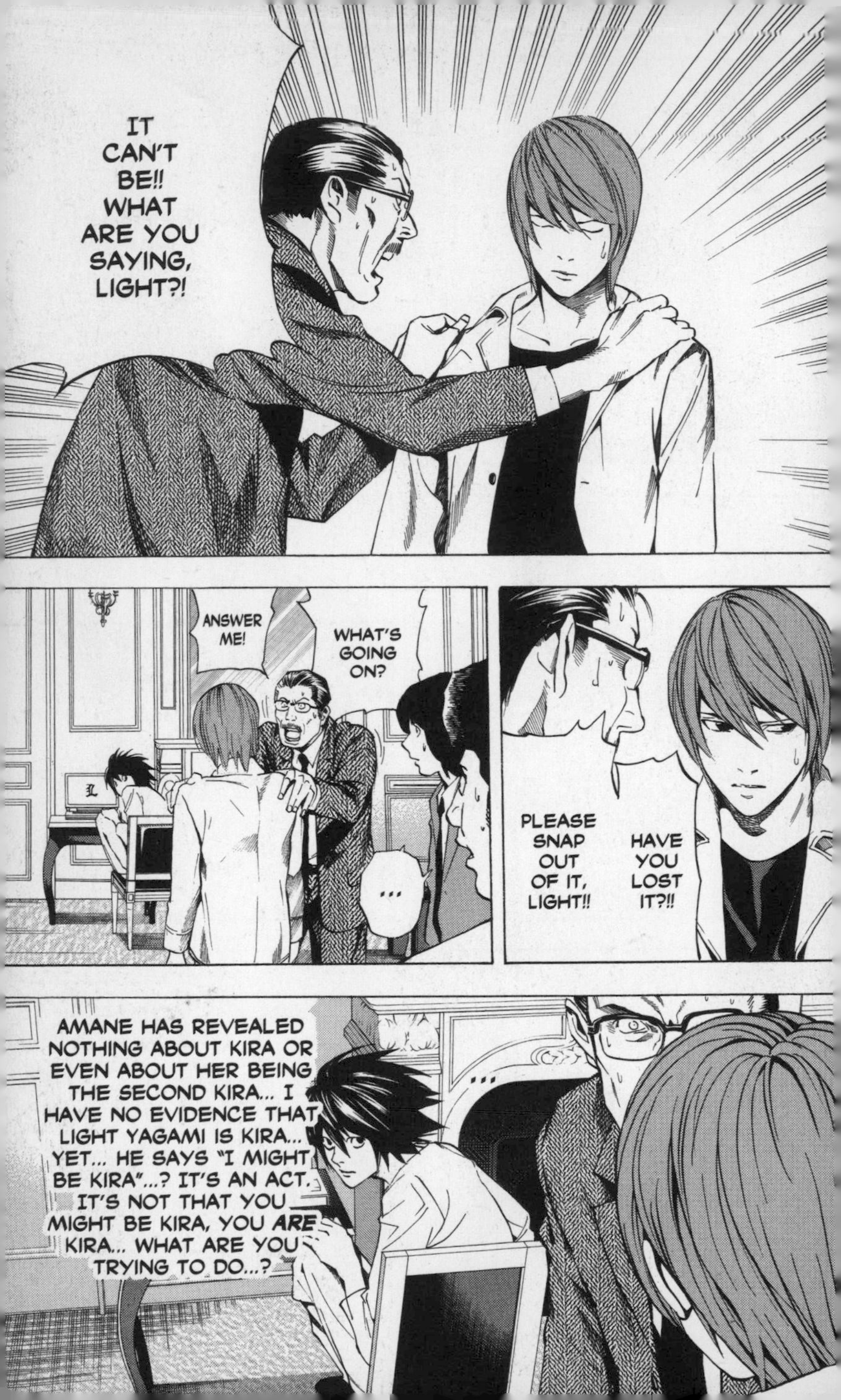
IT CAN'T BE!! WHAT ARE YOU SAYING, LIGHT?!
HAVE YOU LOST IT?!!
PLEASE SNAP OUT OF IT, LIGHT!!
WHAT'S GOING ON?
ANSWER ME!
...
...
AMANE HAS REVEALED NOTHING ABOUT KIRA OR EVEN ABOUT HER BEING THE SECOND KIRA... I HAVE NO EVIDENCE THAT LIGHT YAGAMI IS KIRA... YET... HE SAYS "I MIGHT BE KIRA"...? IT'S AN ACT. IT'S NOT THAT YOU MIGHT BE KIRA, YOU *ARE* KIRA... WHAT ARE YOU TRYING TO DO...?

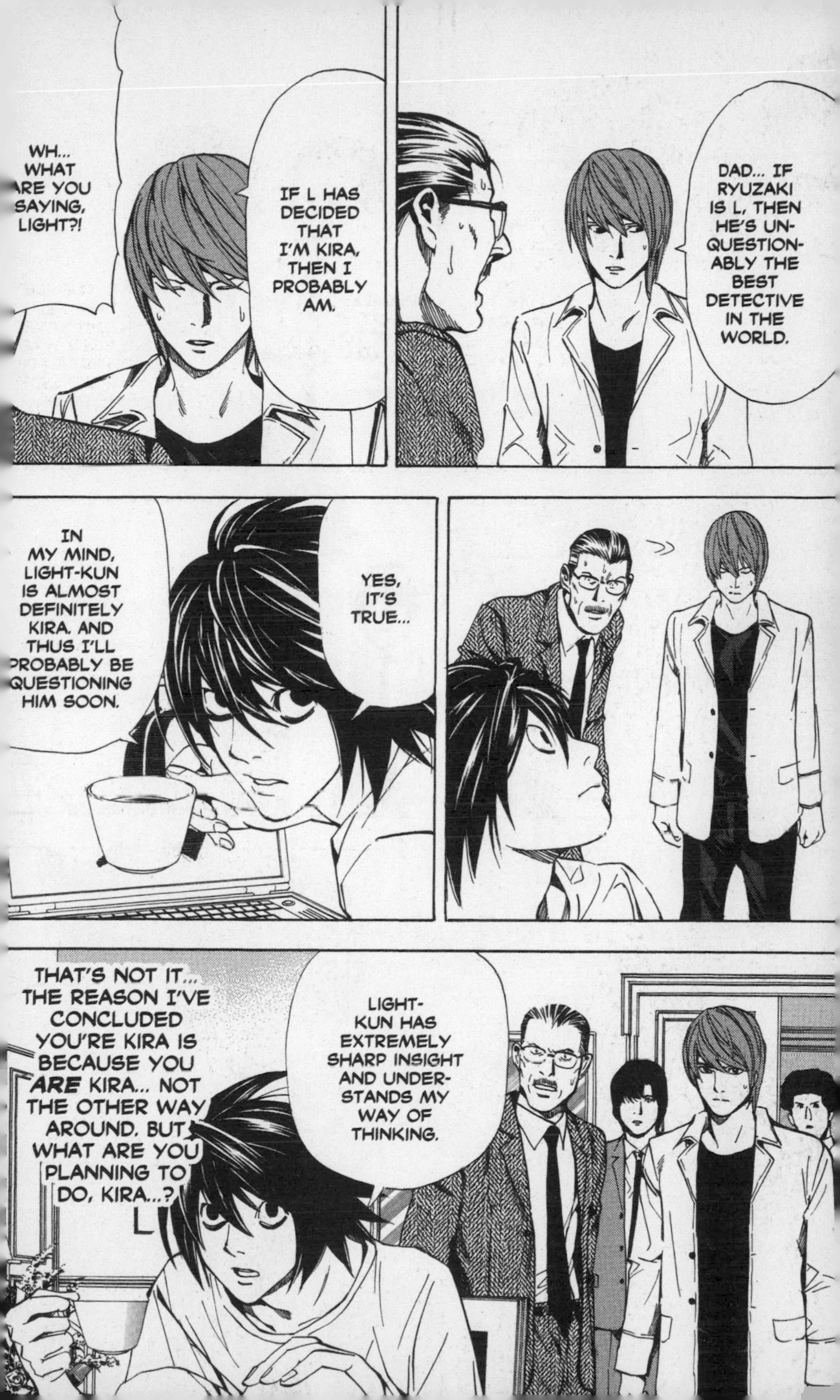
DAD... IF RYUZAKI IS L, THEN HE'S UNQUESTIONABLY THE BEST DETECTIVE IN THE WORLD.
IF L HAS DECIDED THAT I'M KIRA, THEN I PROBABLY AM.
WH... WHAT ARE YOU SAYING, LIGHT?!
YES, IT'S TRUE...
IN MY MIND, LIGHT-KUN IS ALMOST DEFINITELY KIRA. AND THUS I'LL PROBABLY BE QUESTIONING HIM SOON.
LIGHT-KUN HAS EXTREMELY SHARP INSIGHT AND UNDERSTANDS MY WAY OF THINKING.
THAT'S NOT IT... THE REASON I'VE CONCLUDED YOU'RE KIRA IS BECAUSE YOU *ARE* KIRA... NOT THE OTHER WAY AROUND. BUT WHAT ARE YOU PLANNING TO DO, KIRA...?
L

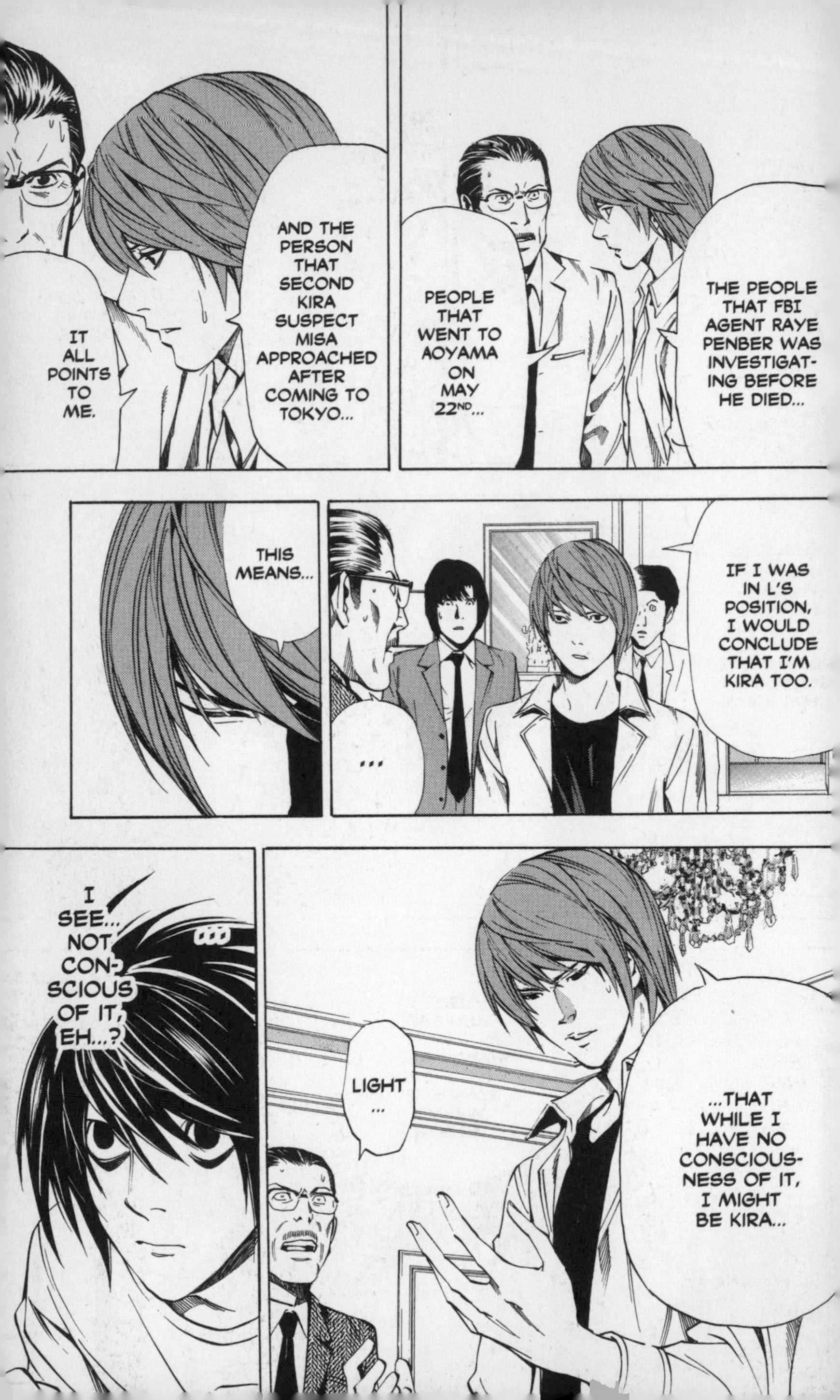
THE PEOPLE THAT FBI AGENT RAYE PENBER WAS INVESTIGATING BEFORE HE DIED...
PEOPLE THAT WENT TO AOYAMA ON MAY 22ND...
AND THE PERSON THAT SECOND KIRA SUSPECT MISA APPROACHED AFTER COMING TO TOKYO...
IT ALL POINTS TO ME.
IF I WAS IN L'S POSITION, I WOULD CONCLUDE THAT I'M KIRA TOO.
...
THIS MEANS...
...THAT WHILE I HAVE NO CONSCIOUSNESS OF IT, I MIGHT BE KIRA...
LIGHT...
I SEE... NOT CONSCIOUS OF IT, EH...?

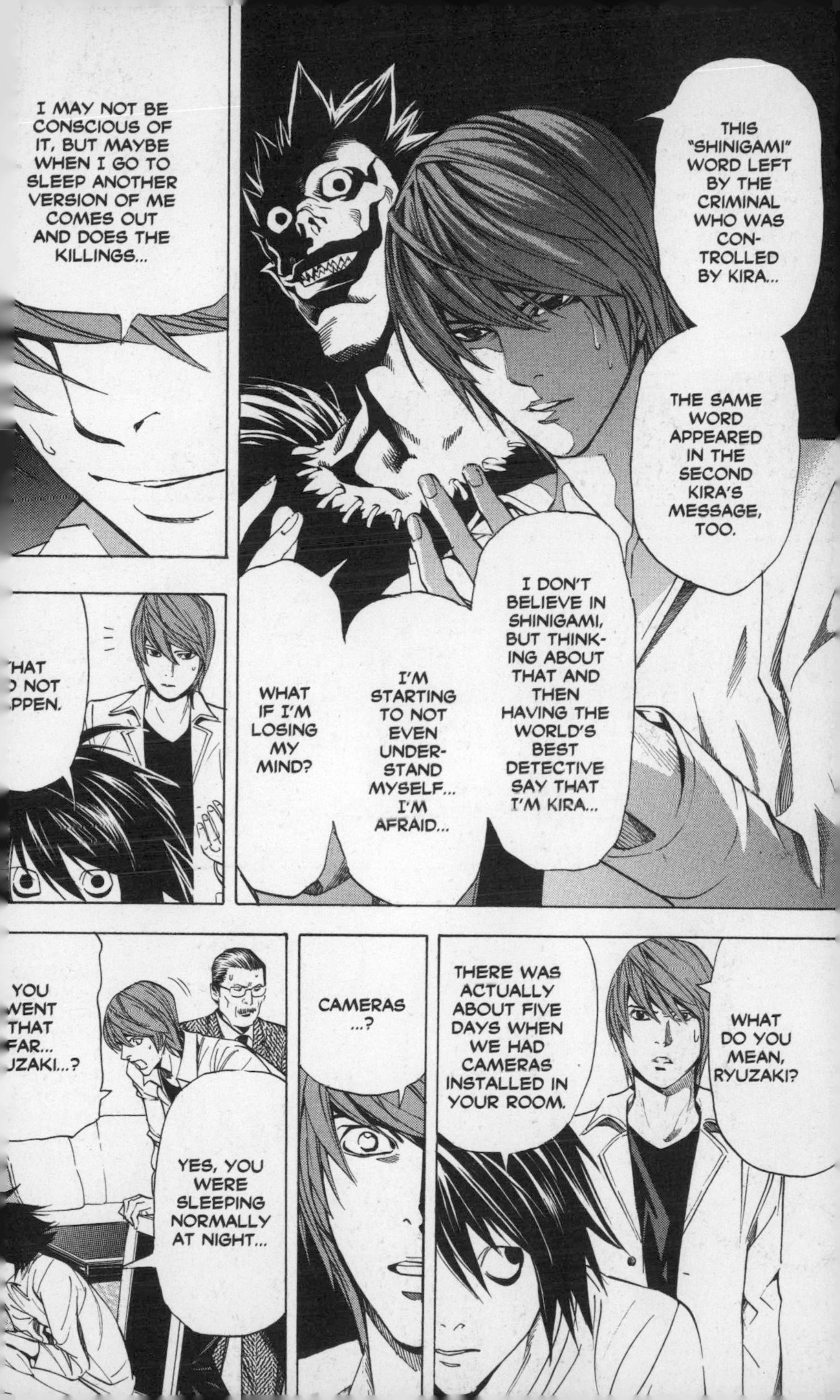
THIS "SHINIGAMI" WORD LEFT BY THE CRIMINAL WHO WAS CON-TROLLED BY KIRA...
THE SAME WORD APPEARED IN THE SECOND KIRA'S MESSAGE, TOO.
I DON'T BELIEVE IN SHINIGAMI, BUT THINK-ING ABOUT THAT AND THEN HAVING THE WORLD'S BEST DETECTIVE SAY THAT I'M KIRA...
I'M STARTING TO NOT EVEN UNDER-STAND MYSELF... I'M AFRAID...
WHAT IF I'M LOSING MY MIND?
I MAY NOT BE CONSCIOUS OF IT, BUT MAYBE WHEN I GO TO SLEEP ANOTHER VERSION OF ME COMES OUT AND DOES THE KILLINGS...
HAT NOT PPEN.
WHAT DO YOU MEAN, RYUZAKI?
THERE WAS ACTUALLY ABOUT FIVE DAYS WHEN WE HAD CAMERAS INSTALLED IN YOUR ROOM.
CAMERAS ...?
YES, YOU WERE SLEEPING NORMALLY AT NIGHT...
YOU WENT THAT FAR... UZAKI...?

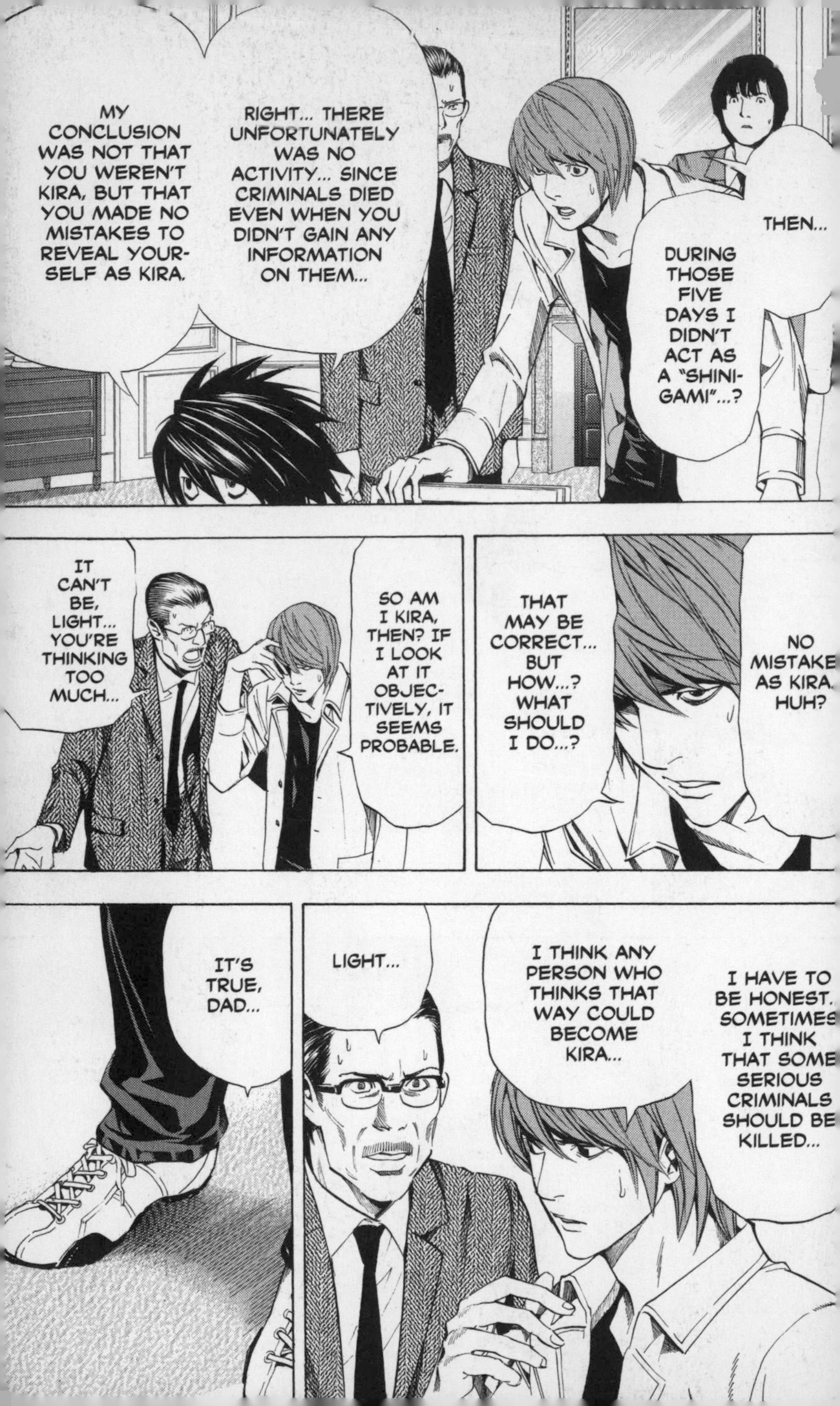
THEN...
DURING THOSE FIVE DAYS I DIDN'T ACT AS A "SHINIGAMI"...?
RIGHT... THERE UNFORTUNATELY WAS NO ACTIVITY... SINCE CRIMINALS DIED EVEN WHEN YOU DIDN'T GAIN ANY INFORMATION ON THEM...
MY CONCLUSION WAS NOT THAT YOU WEREN'T KIRA, BUT THAT YOU MADE NO MISTAKES TO REVEAL YOURSELF AS KIRA.
NO MISTAKE AS KIRA, HUH?
THAT MAY BE CORRECT... BUT HOW...? WHAT SHOULD I DO...?
SO AM I KIRA, THEN? IF I LOOK AT IT OBJECTIVELY, IT SEEMS PROBABLE.
IT CAN'T BE, LIGHT... YOU'RE THINKING TOO MUCH...
I HAVE TO BE HONEST. SOMETIMES I THINK THAT SOME SERIOUS CRIMINALS SHOULD BE KILLED...
I THINK ANY PERSON WHO THINKS THAT WAY COULD BECOME KIRA...
LIGHT...
IT'S TRUE, DAD...

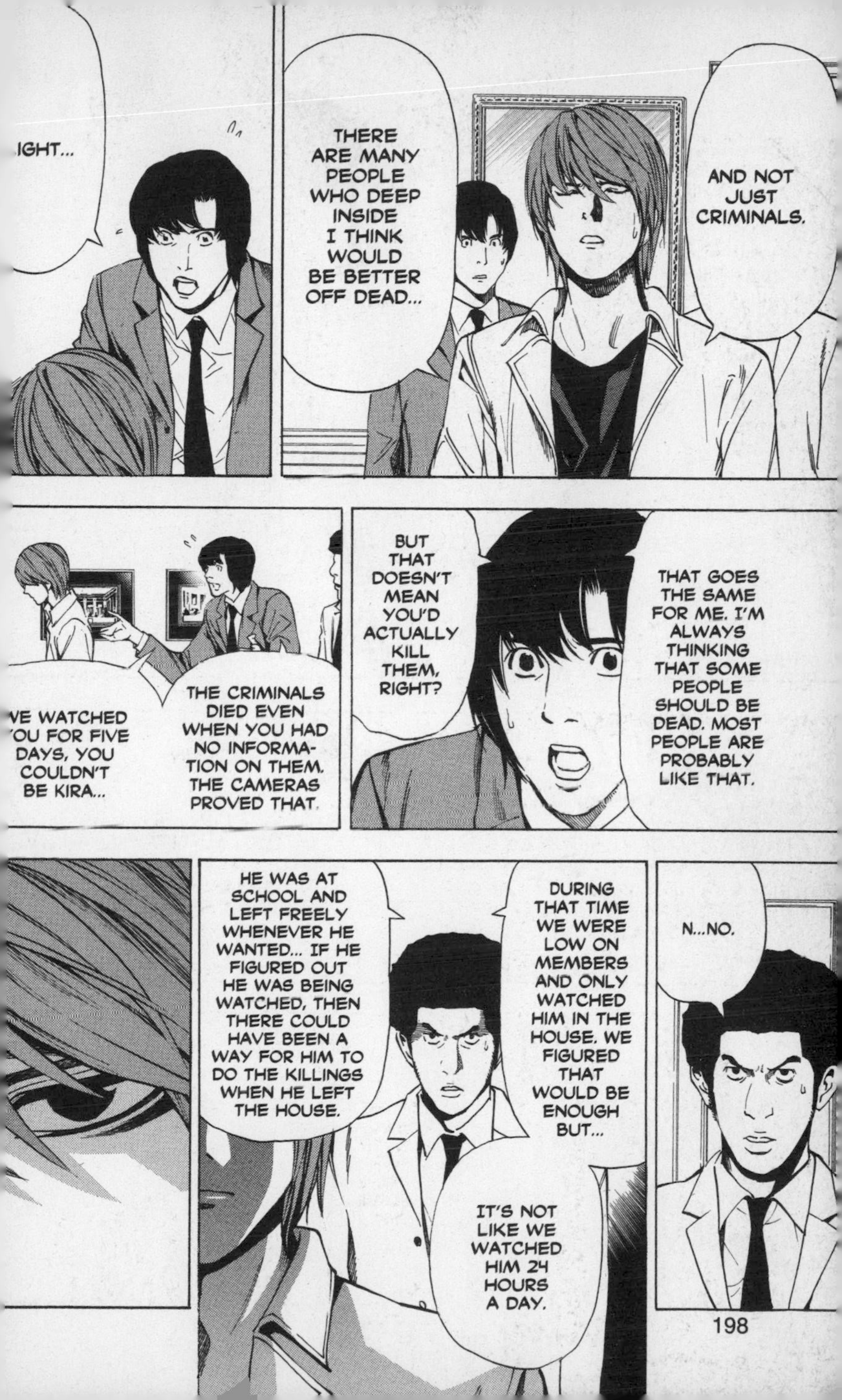
AND NOT JUST CRIMINALS.
THERE ARE MANY PEOPLE WHO DEEP INSIDE I THINK WOULD BE BETTER OFF DEAD...
IGHT...
THAT GOES THE SAME FOR ME. I'M ALWAYS THINKING THAT SOME PEOPLE SHOULD BE DEAD. MOST PEOPLE ARE PROBABLY LIKE THAT.
BUT THAT DOESN'T MEAN YOU'D ACTUALLY KILL THEM, RIGHT?
THE CRIMINALS DIED EVEN WHEN YOU HAD NO INFORMATION ON THEM. THE CAMERAS PROVED THAT.
VE WATCHED 'OU FOR FIVE DAYS, YOU COULDN'T BE KIRA...
N...NO.
DURING THAT TIME WE WERE LOW ON MEMBERS AND ONLY WATCHED HIM IN THE HOUSE. WE FIGURED THAT WOULD BE ENOUGH BUT...
HE WAS AT SCHOOL AND LEFT FREELY WHENEVER HE WANTED... IF HE FIGURED OUT HE WAS BEING WATCHED, THEN THERE COULD HAVE BEEN A WAY FOR HIM TO DO THE KILLINGS WHEN HE LEFT THE HOUSE.
IT'S NOT LIKE WE WATCHED HIM 24 HOURS A DAY.

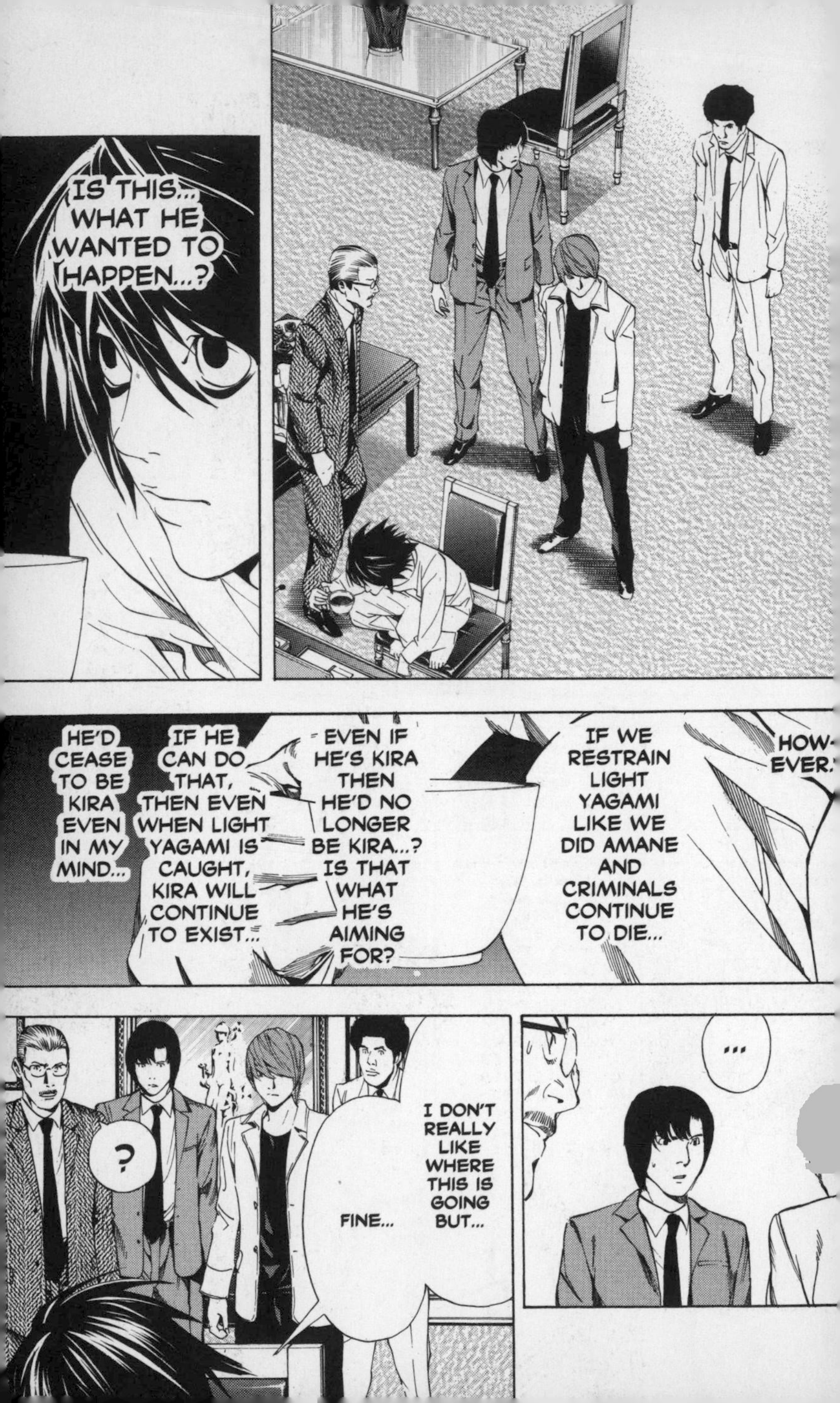
IS THIS... WHAT HE WANTED TO HAPPEN...?
HOW-EVER.
IF WE RESTRAIN LIGHT YAGAMI LIKE WE DID AMANE AND CRIMINALS CONTINUE TO DIE...
EVEN IF HE'S KIRA THEN HE'D NO LONGER BE KIRA...? IS THAT WHAT HE'S AIMING FOR?
IF HE CAN DO THAT, THEN EVEN WHEN LIGHT YAGAMI IS CAUGHT, KIRA WILL CONTINUE TO EXIST...
HE'D CEASE TO BE KIRA EVEN IN MY MIND...
...
I DON'T REALLY LIKE WHERE THIS IS GOING BUT...
FINE...
?

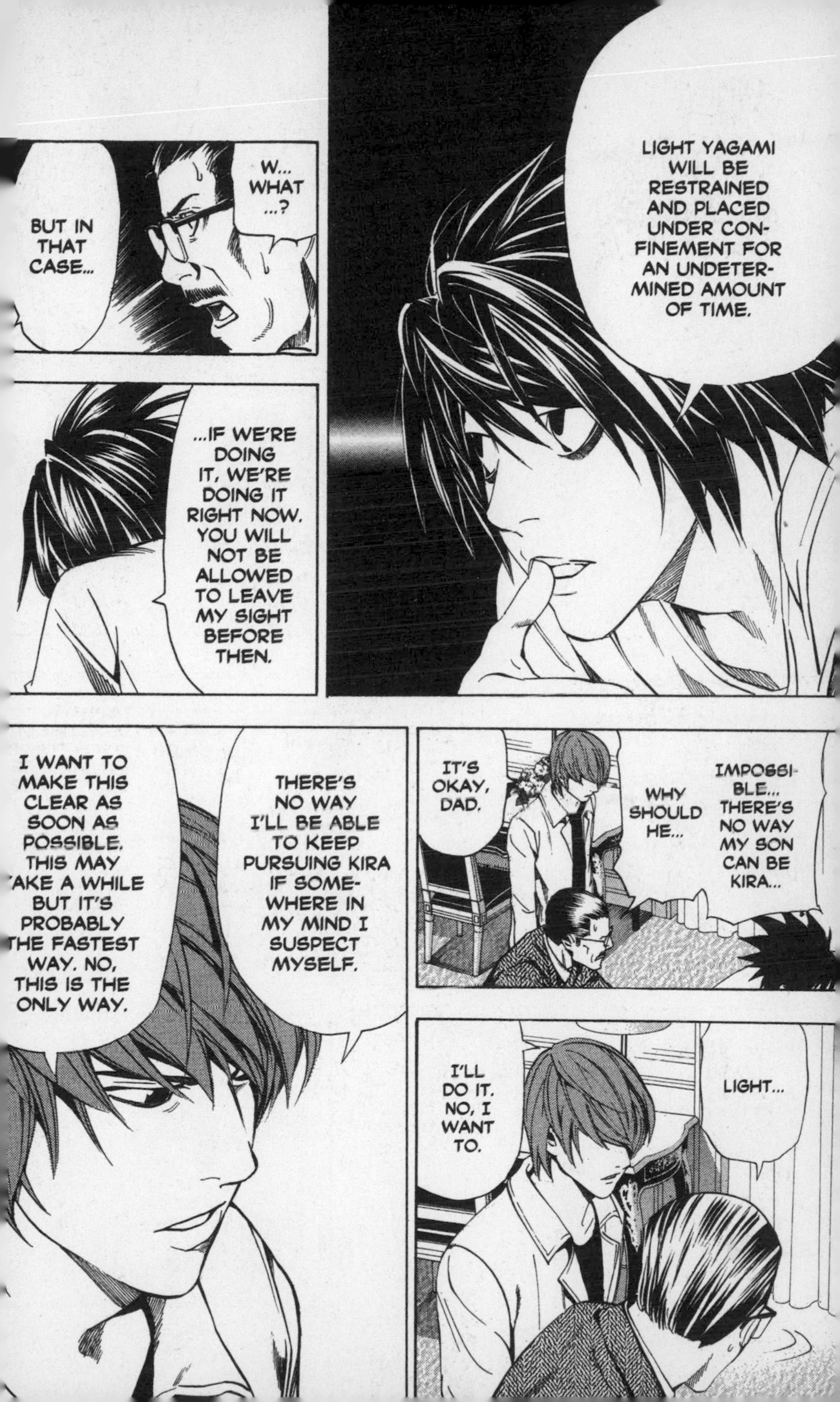
LIGHT YAGAMI WILL BE RESTRAINED AND PLACED UNDER CON-FINEMENT FOR AN UNDETER-MINED AMOUNT OF TIME.
W... WHAT ...?
BUT IN THAT CASE...
...IF WE'RE DOING IT, WE'RE DOING IT RIGHT NOW. YOU WILL NOT BE ALLOWED TO LEAVE MY SIGHT BEFORE THEN.
IMPOSSI-BLE... THERE'S NO WAY MY SON CAN BE KIRA...
WHY SHOULD HE...
IT'S OKAY, DAD.
LIGHT...
I'LL DO IT. NO, I WANT TO.
THERE'S NO WAY I'LL BE ABLE TO KEEP PURSUING KIRA IF SOME-WHERE IN MY MIND I SUSPECT MYSELF.
I WANT TO MAKE THIS CLEAR AS SOON AS POSSIBLE. THIS MAY TAKE A WHILE BUT IT'S PROBABLY THE FASTEST WAY. NO, THIS IS THE ONLY WAY.

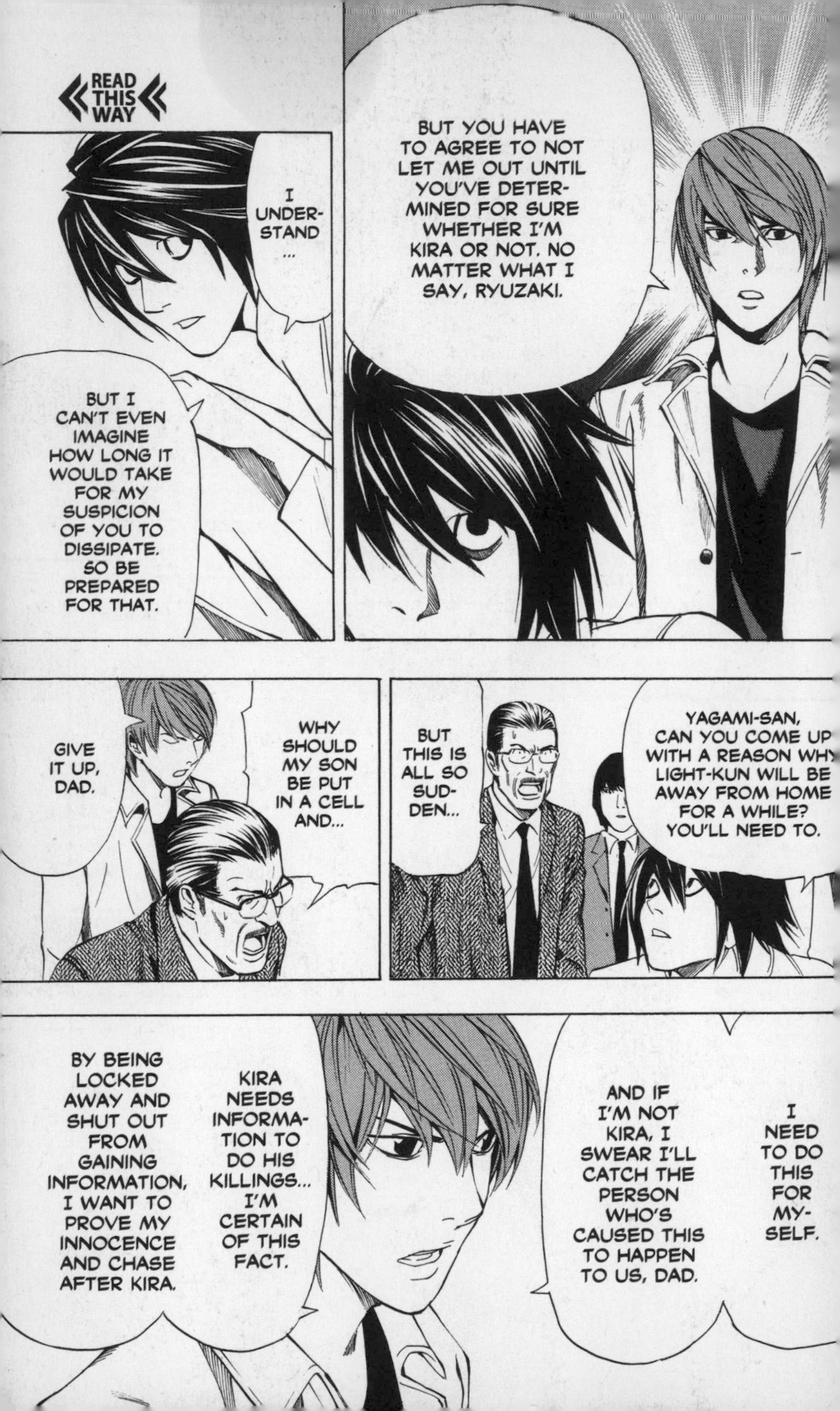
READ THIS WAY
BUT YOU HAVE TO AGREE TO NOT LET ME OUT UNTIL YOU'VE DETERMINED FOR SURE WHETHER I'M KIRA OR NOT. NO MATTER WHAT I SAY, RYUZAKI.
I UNDERSTAND...
BUT I CAN'T EVEN IMAGINE HOW LONG IT WOULD TAKE FOR MY SUSPICION OF YOU TO DISSIPATE. SO BE PREPARED FOR THAT.
YAGAMI-SAN, CAN YOU COME UP WITH A REASON WHY LIGHT-KUN WILL BE AWAY FROM HOME FOR A WHILE? YOU'LL NEED TO.
BUT THIS IS ALL SO SUDDEN...
WHY SHOULD MY SON BE PUT IN A CELL AND...
GIVE IT UP, DAD.
I NEED TO DO THIS FOR MYSELF.
AND IF I'M NOT KIRA, I SWEAR I'LL CATCH THE PERSON WHO'S CAUSED THIS TO HAPPEN TO US, DAD.
KIRA NEEDS INFORMATION TO DO HIS KILLINGS... I'M CERTAIN OF THIS FACT.
BY BEING LOCKED AWAY AND SHUT OUT FROM GAINING INFORMATION, I WANT TO PROVE MY INNOCENCE AND CHASE AFTER KIRA.

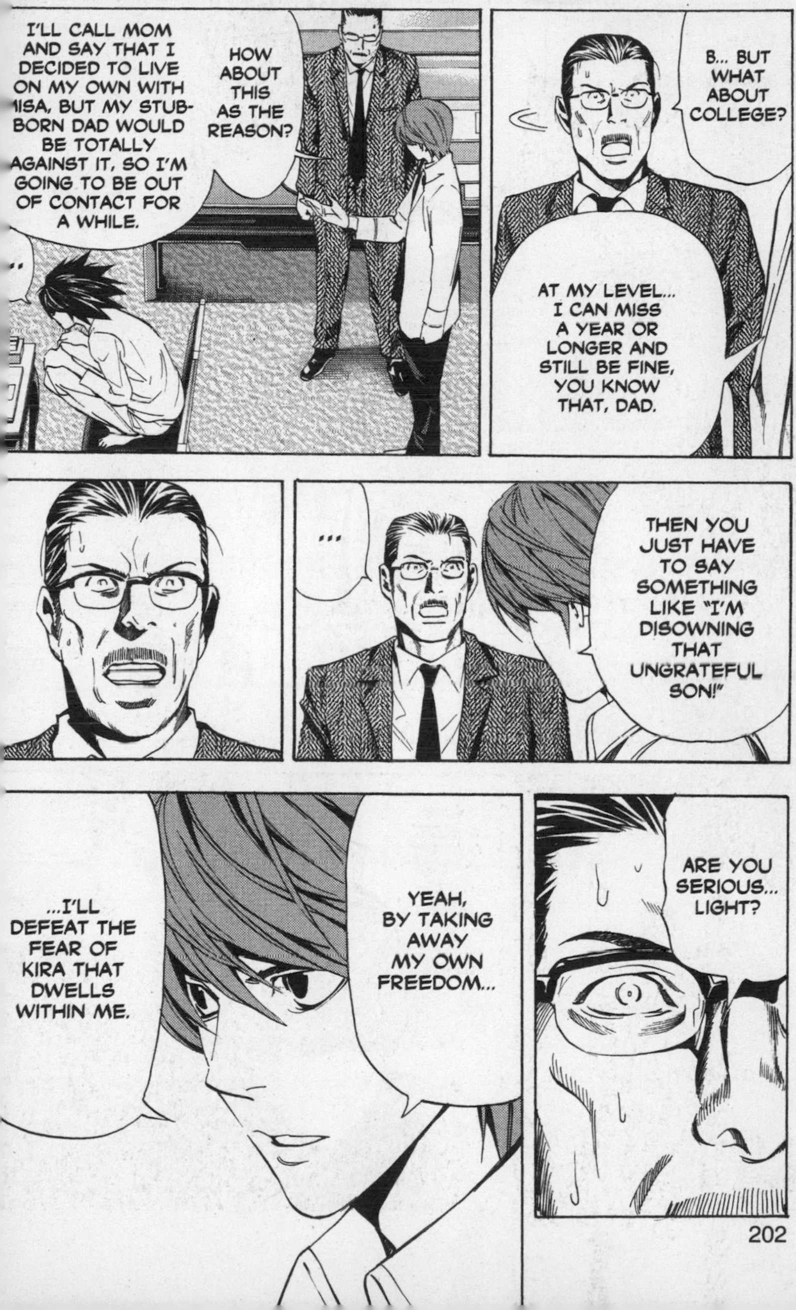
B... BUT WHAT ABOUT COLLEGE?
AT MY LEVEL... I CAN MISS A YEAR OR LONGER AND STILL BE FINE, YOU KNOW THAT, DAD.
HOW ABOUT THIS AS THE REASON?
I'LL CALL MOM AND SAY THAT I DECIDED TO LIVE ON MY OWN WITH MISA, BUT MY STUBBORN DAD WOULD BE TOTALLY AGAINST IT, SO I'M GOING TO BE OUT OF CONTACT FOR A WHILE.
..
THEN YOU JUST HAVE TO SAY SOMETHING LIKE "I'M DISOWNING THAT UNGRATEFUL SON!"
...
ARE YOU SERIOUS... LIGHT?
YEAH, BY TAKING AWAY MY OWN FREEDOM...
...I'LL DEFEAT THE FEAR OF KIRA THAT DWELLS WITHIN ME.

READ THIS WAY

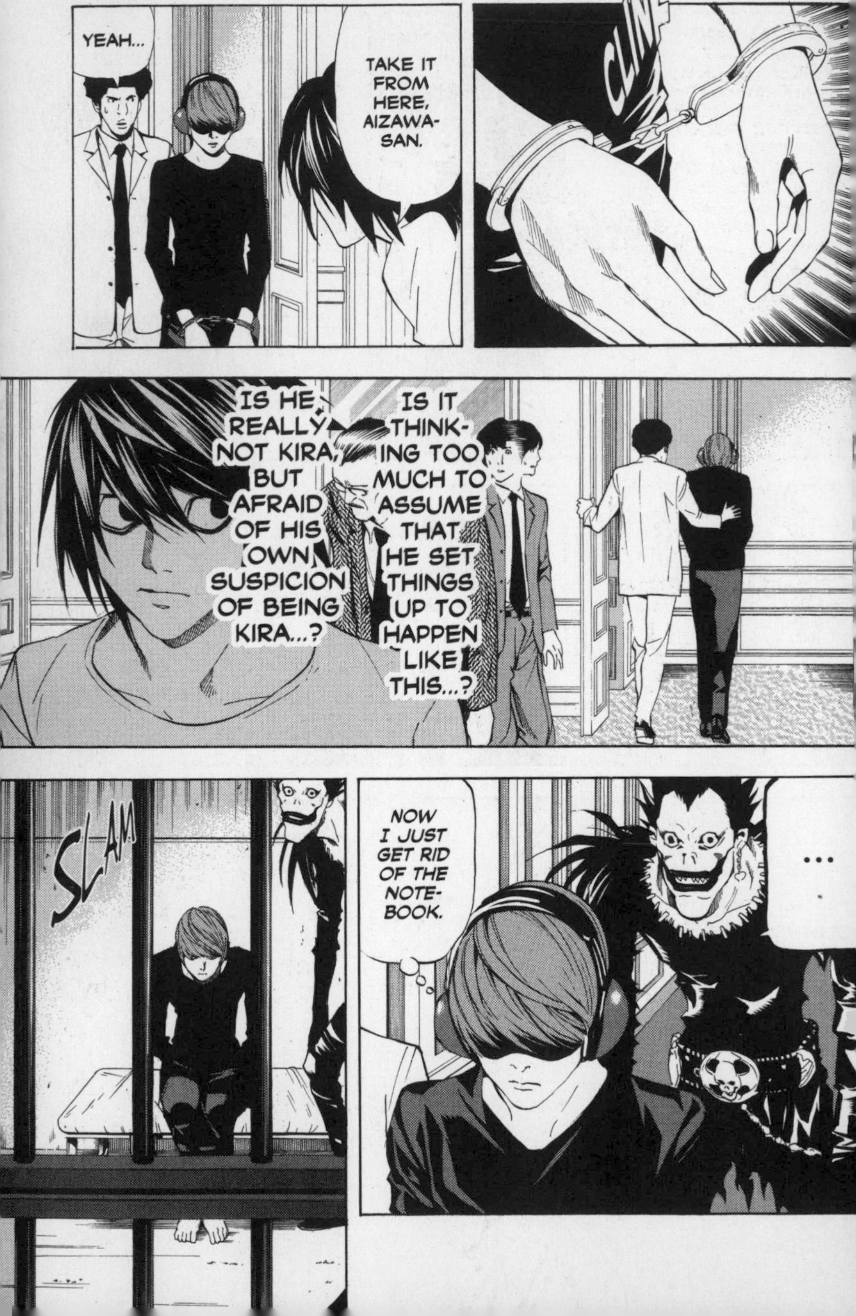
CLINK
TAKE IT FROM HERE, AIZAWA-SAN.
YEAH...
IS IT THINKING TOO MUCH TO ASSUME THAT HE SET THINGS UP TO HAPPEN LIKE THIS...?
IS HE REALLY NOT KIRA, BUT AFRAID OF HIS OWN SUSPICION OF BEING KIRA...?
...
NOW I JUST GET RID OF THE NOTEBOOK.
SLAM

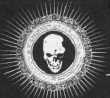

DEATH NOTE
How to use it
XXIII

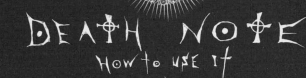

- Whenever an individual with ownership of more than

two DEATH NOTES loses possession to one of the DEATH NOTES,

he will not be able to recognize that DEATH NOTE's god of

death's appearance or voice anymore.

The god of death himself will leave, but all the memory

involving that DEATH NOTE will remain as long as he

maintains ownership of at least one other DEATH NOTE.

二冊以上のデスノートの所有権を得た人間は、一冊の所有権を失うと
その失ったノートに憑いていた死神の姿や声を認知できなくなり死神も
離れるが、一冊でも所有している限り、
関わった全てのデスノートの記憶は消えない。

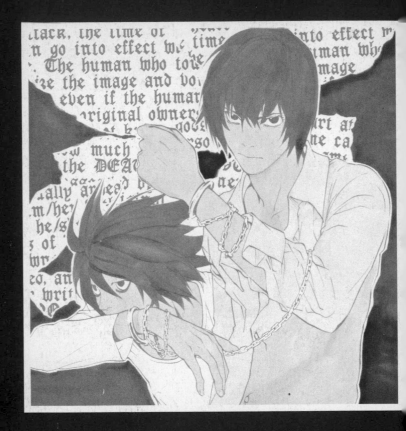

In the Next Volume

Light has given up the Death Note and with it all memories of Ryuk and Kira. But despite Light's own belief in his innocence, L still has grave doubts—especially since Kira stopped killing as soon as Light was incarcerated. But when a *third* Kira joins the game, Light is desperate to help track him down. L agrees, but with the condition that Light further prove his innocence. But just how far will L take the tests?

Available Now!

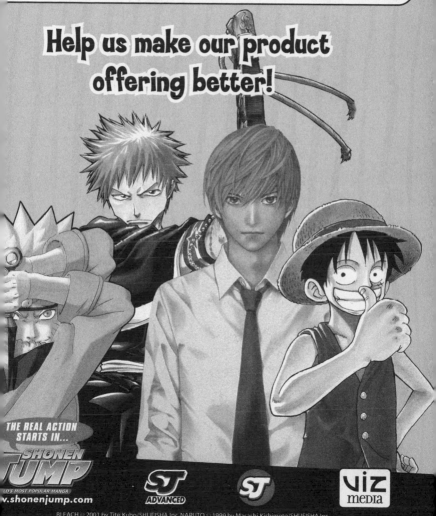

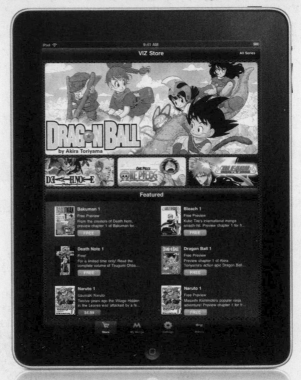
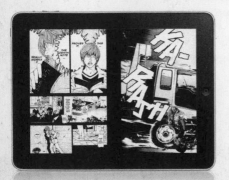

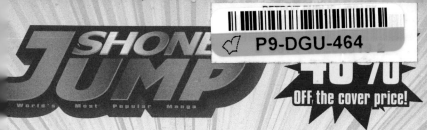